Ao Haru Ride

The scent of air after rain...
In the light around us, I felt your heartbeat.

13

IO SAKISAKA

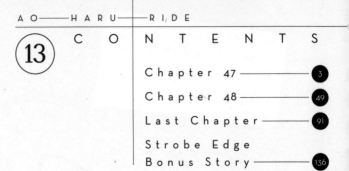

STORY THUS FAR

Futaba Yoshioka was quiet and awkward around boys in junior high, but she's taken on a tomboy persona in high school. It's there that she once again meets her first love, Tanaka (now Kou Mabuchi), and falls for him again. But a series of missed connections and problems with timing have kept the two apart...

Kou says goodbye to Yui. After admitting who she truly wants, Futaba breaks up with Toma. On Christmas Eve, Futaba and Kou confess their feelings for each other. Having taken the long road to get together, and having hurt others along the way, they recognize the importance of cherishing the love they share.

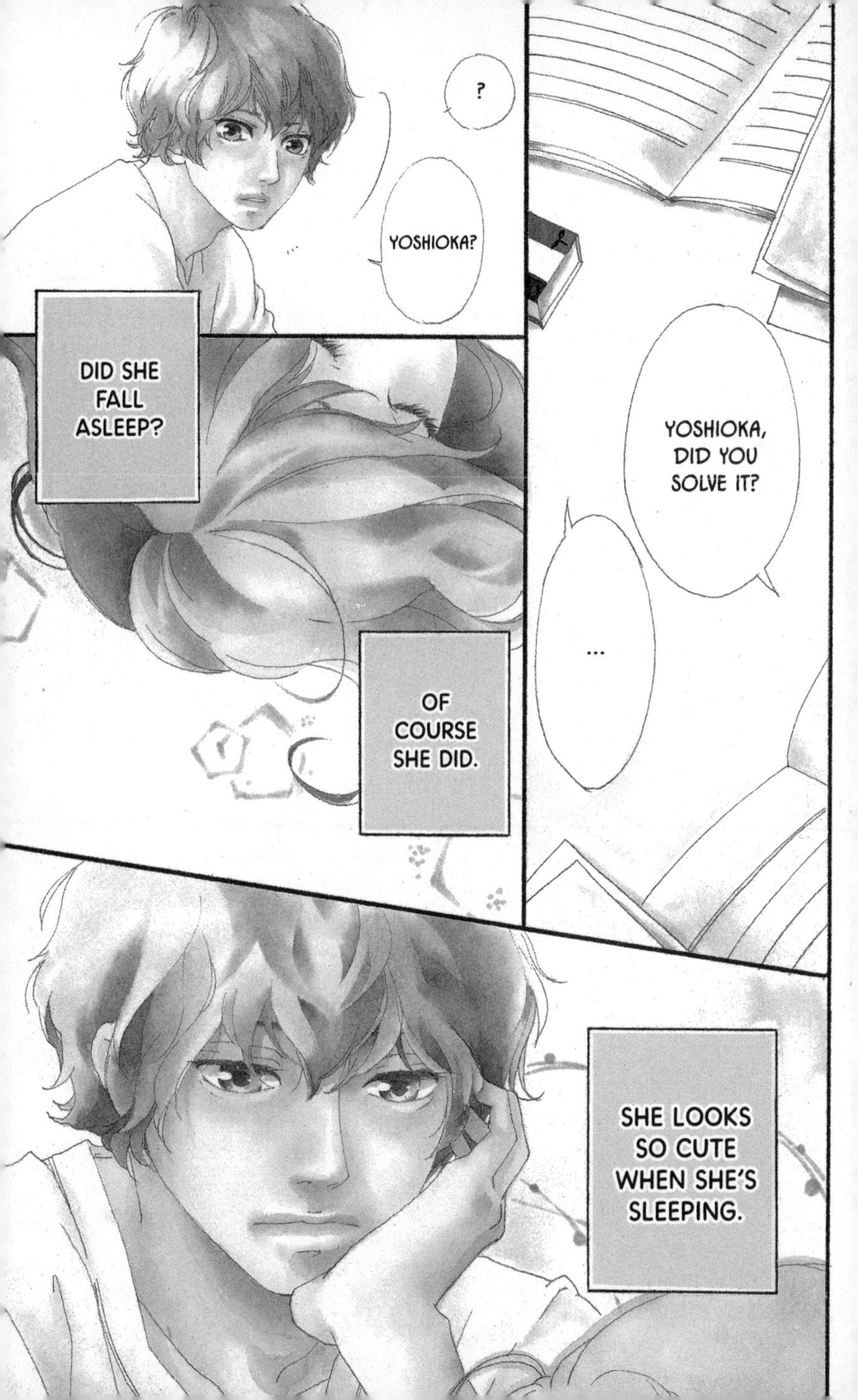
YOSHIOKA, DID YOU SOLVE IT?
...
?
YOSHIOKA?
DID SHE FALL ASLEEP?
OF COURSE SHE DID.
SHE LOOKS SO CUTE WHEN SHE'S SLEEPING.

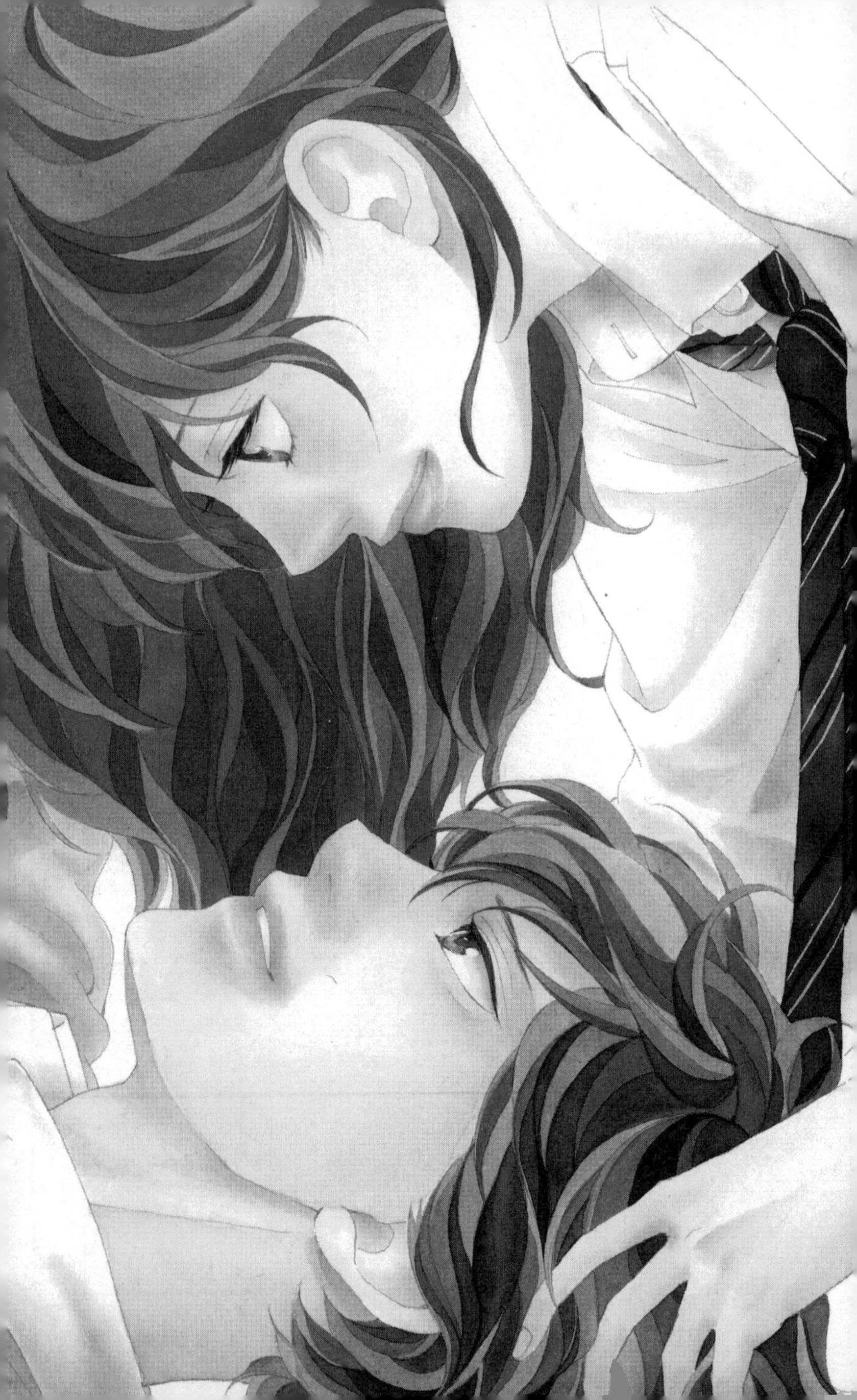

Ao Haru Ride

The scent of air after rain...
In the light around us, I felt your heartbeat.

CHAPTER 47

IO SAKISAKA

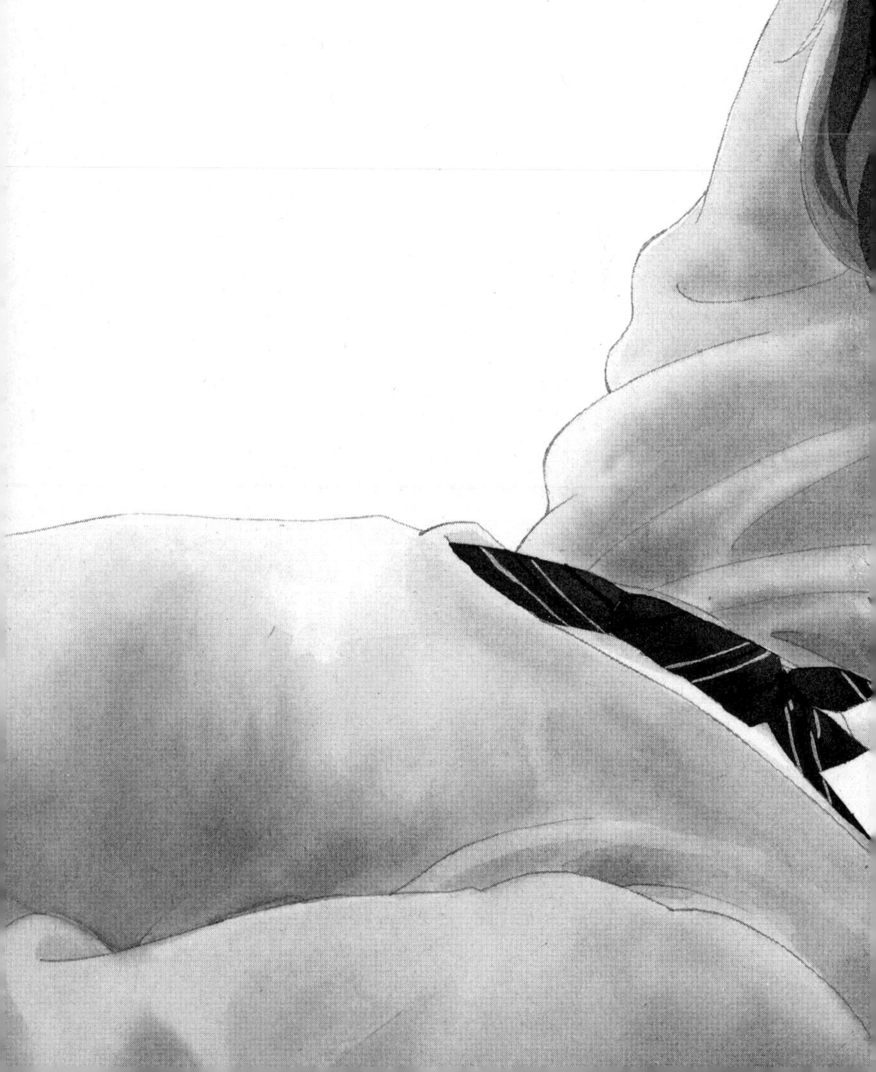

Greetings

Hi! I'm Io Sakisaka. Thank you for picking up a copy of
Ao Haru Ride volume 13!

We've reached the final volume of *Ao Haru Ride*...

I truly enjoyed telling the story of Futaba, Kou and their friends.
What I took the most care with in this series was ensuring the
characters felt realistic. Because this story is fiction, there's a
need to exaggerate some events, scenes or lines. Within those
parameters, I believe that planting realistic actions, choices and
dialogue can help a reader transition between the 2D and 3D
worlds. I was careful not to make the story too neat and tidy.
Of course, actions that are too realistic can take away from the
fantasy (ha ha), so it's a constant struggle to find the right level
of reality within fiction. Sometimes things came together well, and
sometimes they didn't. But thanks to the effort I put in, I once
again realized the joy of developing characters and their story. I
am truly grateful to *Ao Haru Ride* for that.

And now, I hope that you enjoy the final volume of *Ao Haru Ride*
through to the end!

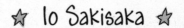

☆ Io Sakisaka ☆

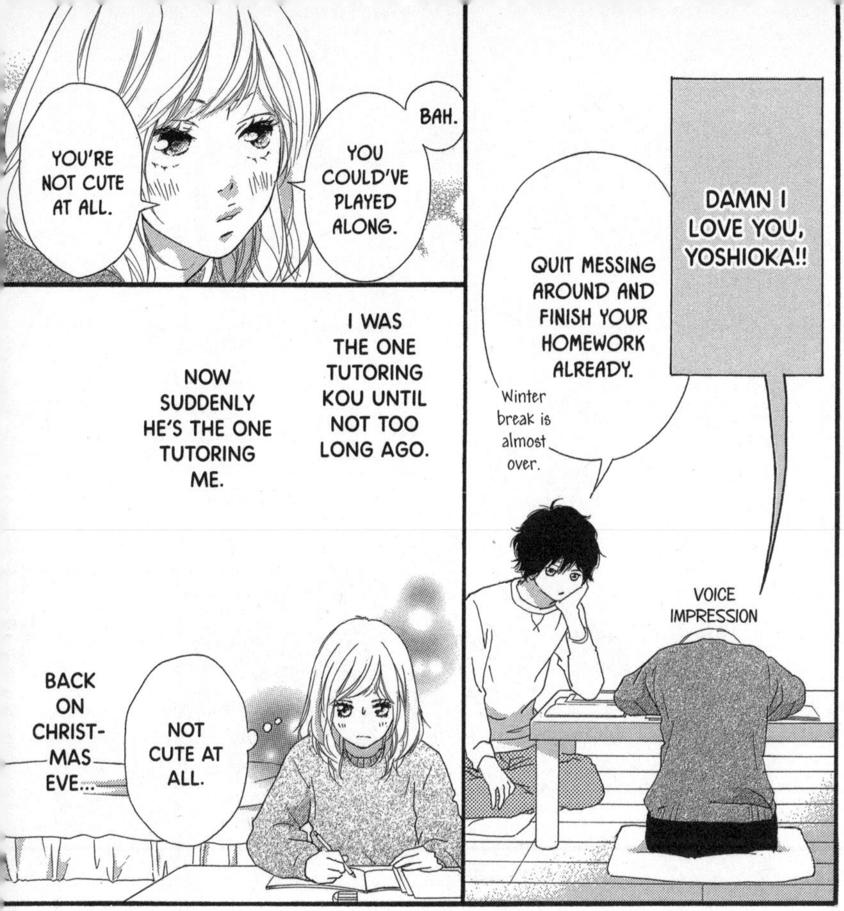
DAMN I LOVE YOU, YOSHIOKA!!
QUIT MESSING AROUND AND FINISH YOUR HOMEWORK ALREADY.
Winter break is almost over.
VOICE IMPRESSION
BAH.
YOU COULD'VE PLAYED ALONG.
YOU'RE NOT CUTE AT ALL.
I WAS THE ONE TUTORING KOU UNTIL NOT TOO LONG AGO.
NOW SUDDENLY HE'S THE ONE TUTORING ME.
NOT CUTE AT ALL.
BACK ON CHRIST-MAS EVE...

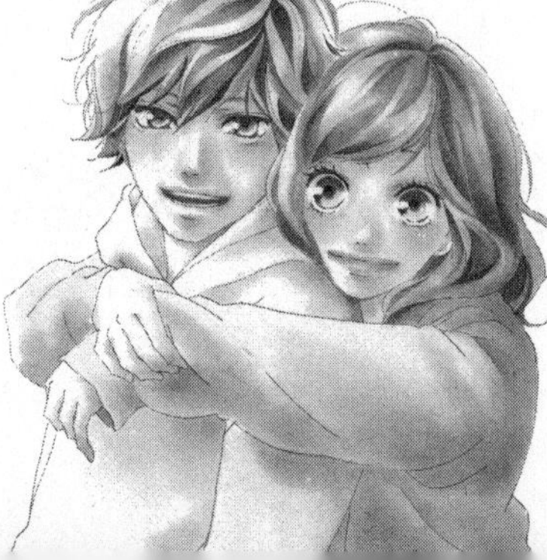

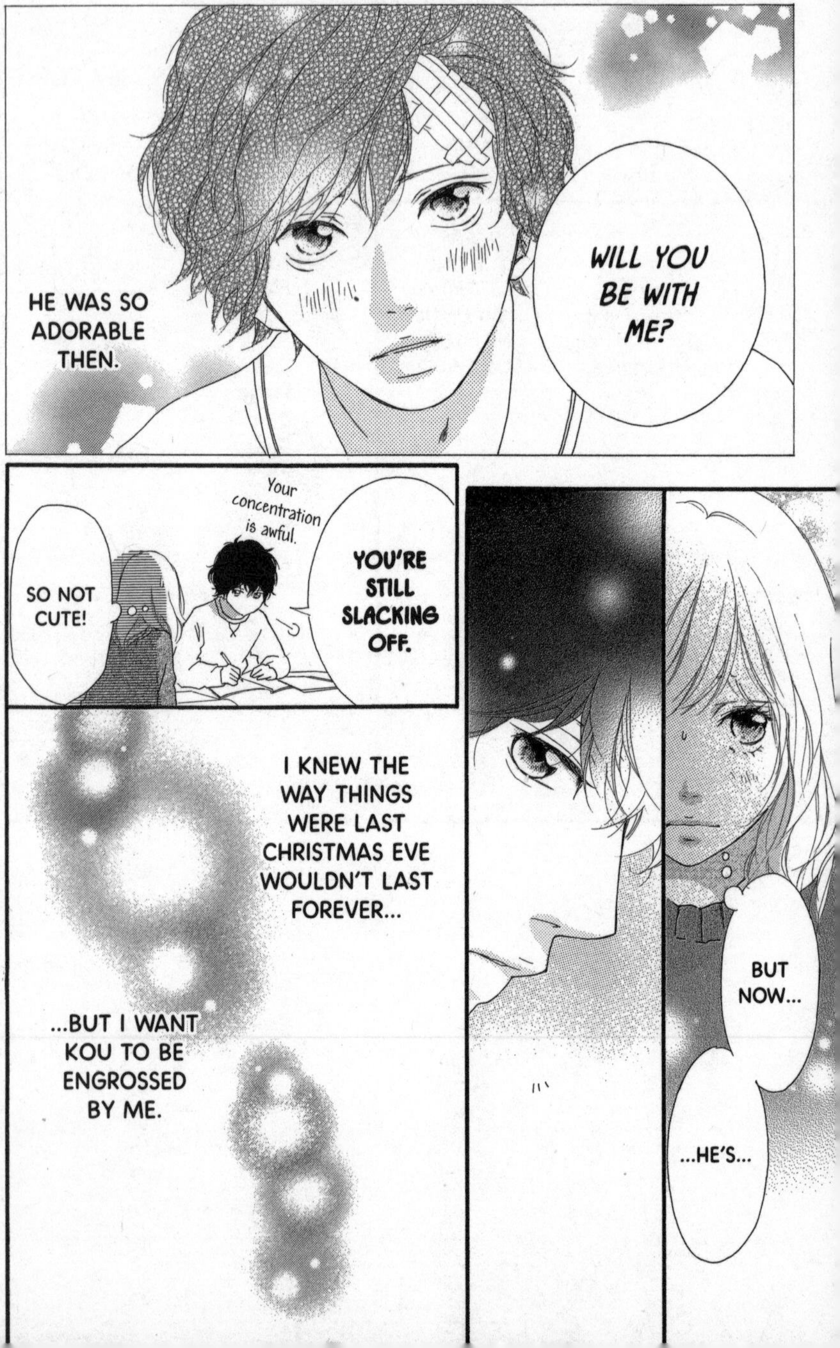
WILL YOU BE WITH ME?
HE WAS SO ADORABLE THEN.
BUT NOW...
...HE'S...
Your concentration is awful.
YOU'RE STILL SLACKING OFF.
SO NOT CUTE!
I KNEW THE WAY THINGS WERE LAST CHRISTMAS EVE WOULDN'T LAST FOREVER...
...BUT I WANT KOU TO BE ENGROSSED BY ME.

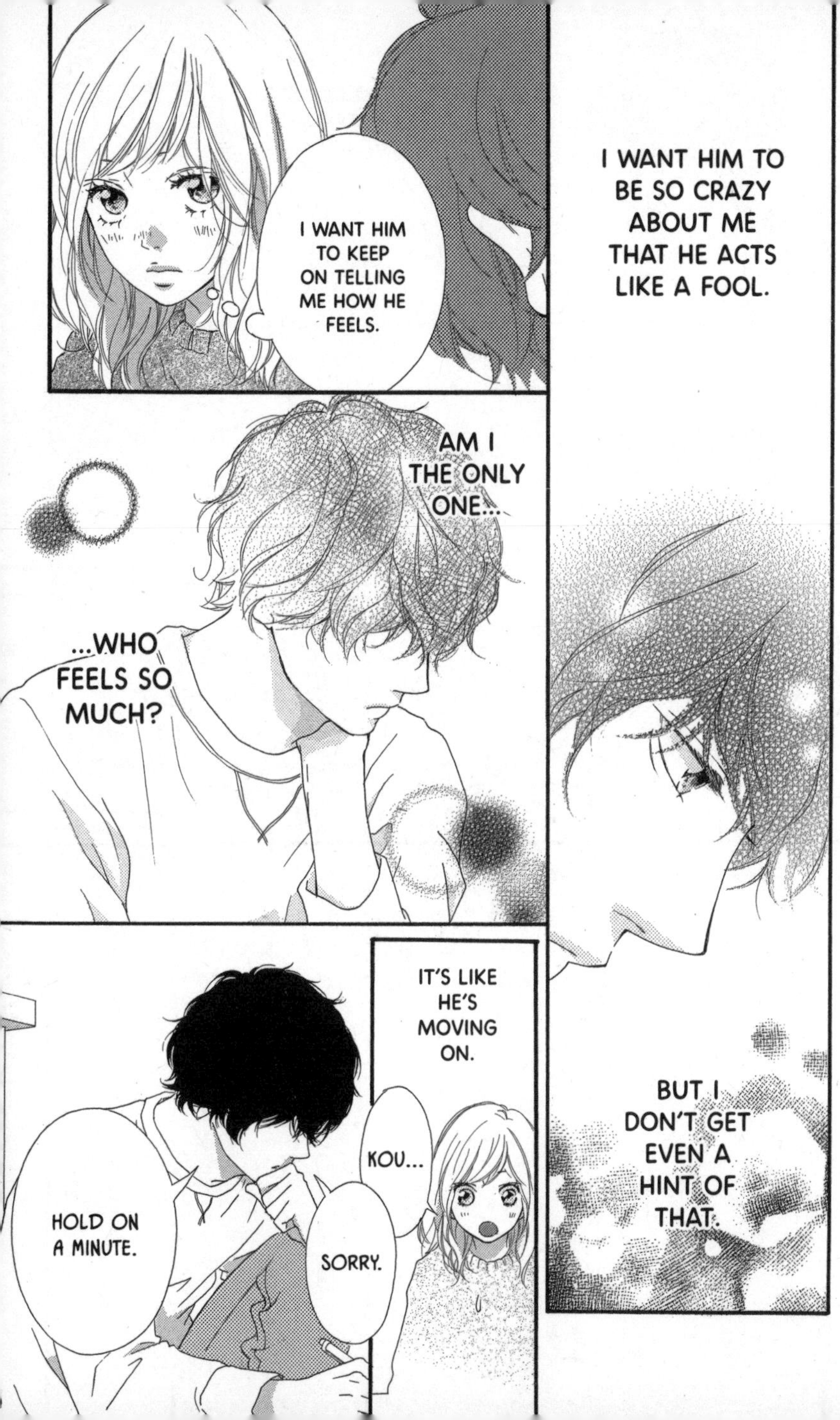
I WANT HIM TO BE SO CRAZY ABOUT ME THAT HE ACTS LIKE A FOOL.
BUT I DON'T GET EVEN A HINT OF THAT.
I WANT HIM TO KEEP ON TELLING ME HOW HE FEELS.
AM I THE ONLY ONE...
...WHO FEELS SO MUCH?
IT'S LIKE HE'S MOVING ON.
KOU...
SORRY.
HOLD ON A MINUTE.

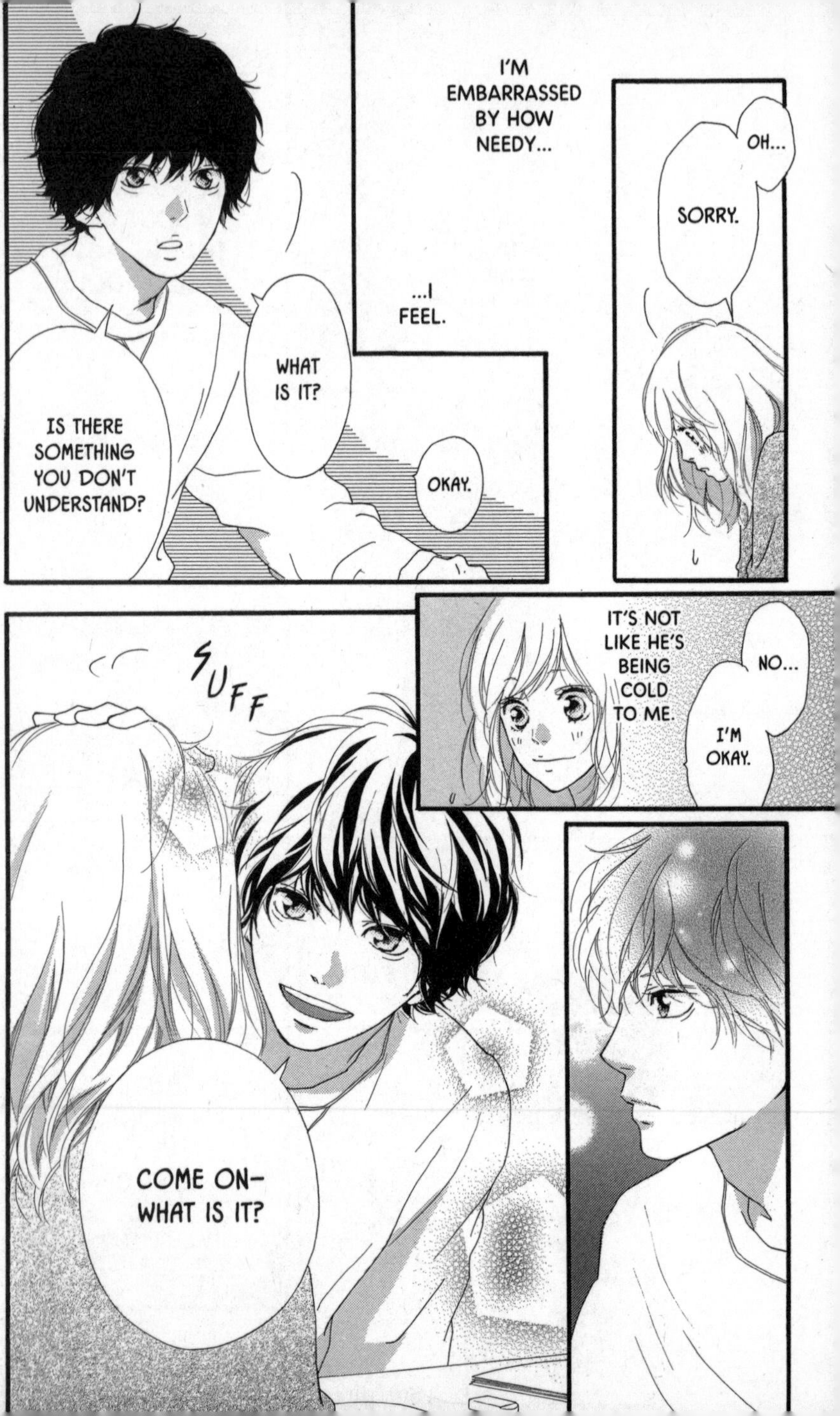
OH...
SORRY.
I'M EMBARRASSED BY HOW NEEDY...
...I FEEL.
OKAY.
WHAT IS IT?
IS THERE SOMETHING YOU DON'T UNDERSTAND?
NO...
I'M OKAY.
IT'S NOT LIKE HE'S BEING COLD TO ME.
SUFF
COME ON— WHAT IS IT?

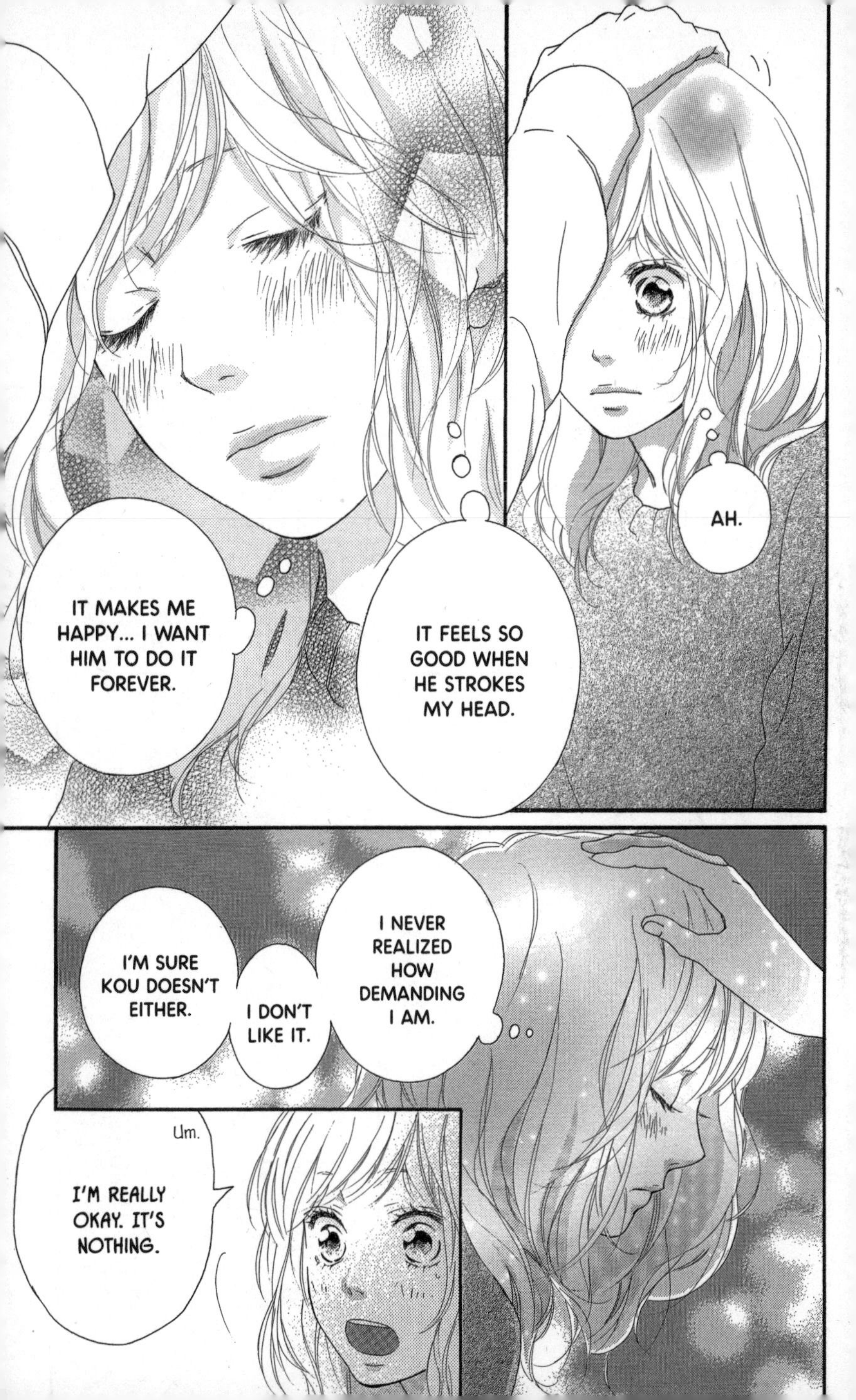
AH.
IT FEELS SO GOOD WHEN HE STROKES MY HEAD.
IT MAKES ME HAPPY... I WANT HIM TO DO IT FOREVER.
I NEVER REALIZED HOW DEMANDING I AM.
I DON'T LIKE IT.
I'M SURE KOU DOESN'T EITHER.
Um.
I'M REALLY OKAY. IT'S NOTHING.

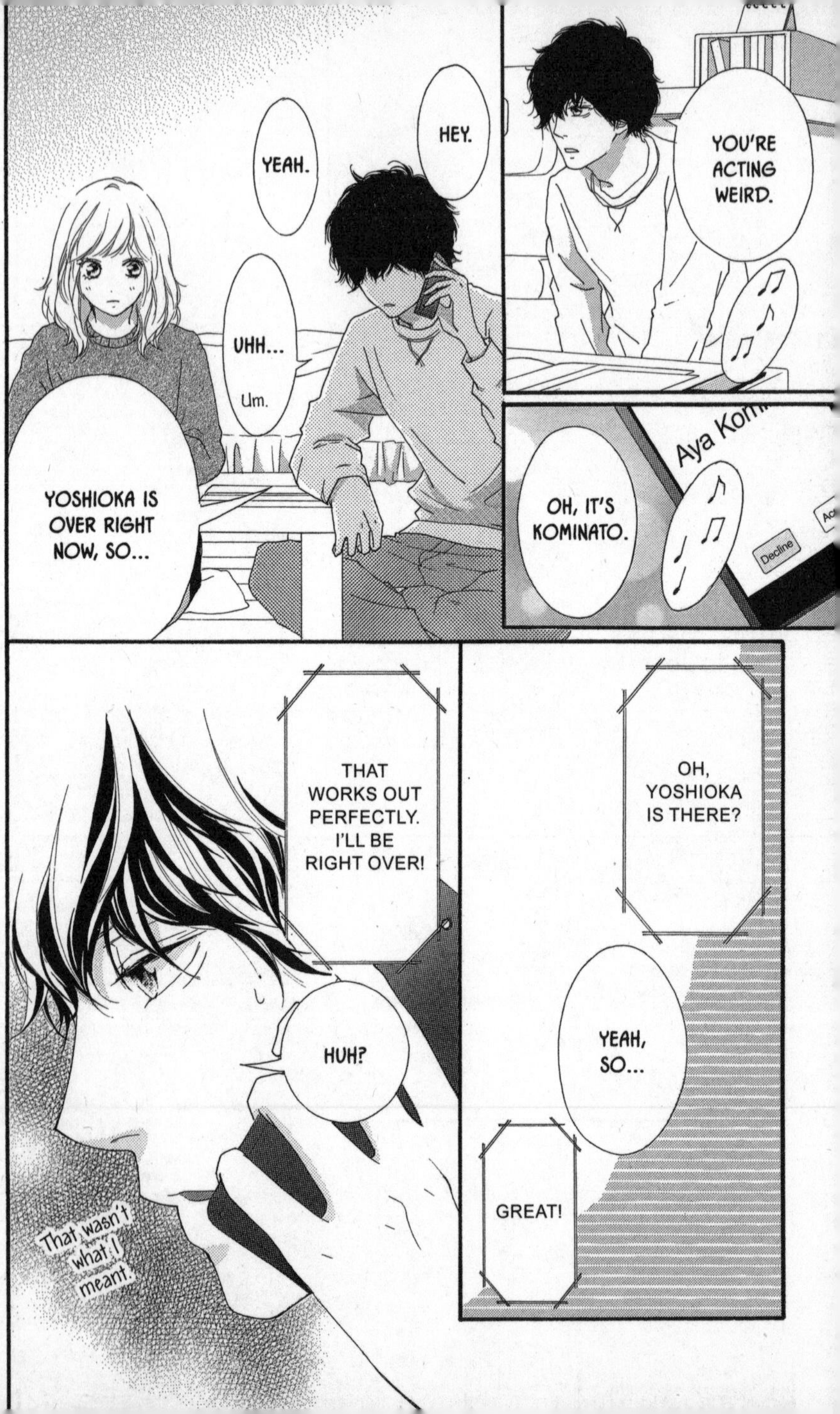
YOU'RE ACTING WEIRD.
OH, IT'S KOMINATO.
Decline
HEY.
YEAH.
UHH...
Um.
YOSHIOKA IS OVER RIGHT NOW, SO...
OH, YOSHIOKA IS THERE?
YEAH, SO...
GREAT!
THAT WORKS OUT PERFECTLY. I'LL BE RIGHT OVER!
HUH?
That wasn't what I meant.

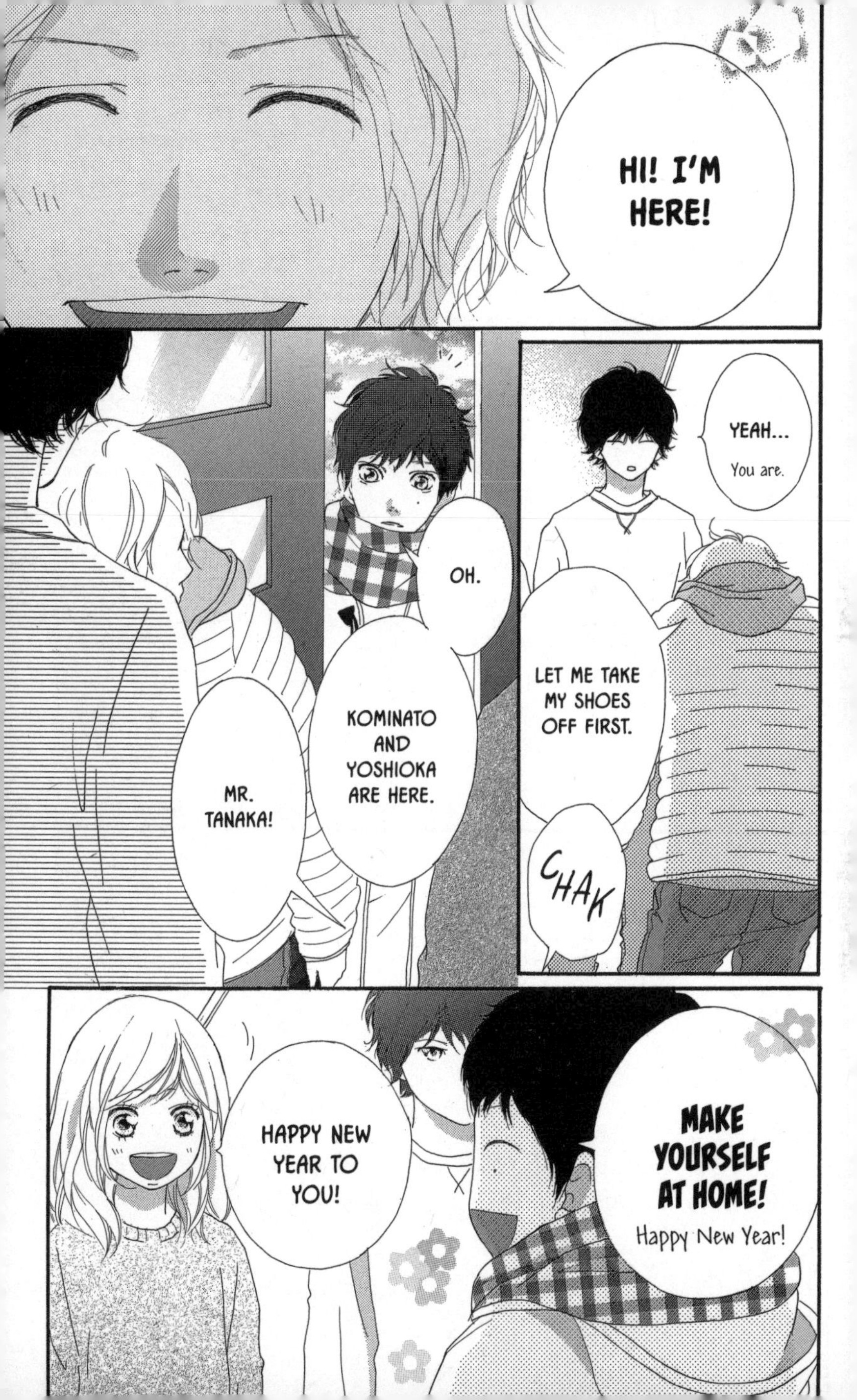
HI! I'M HERE!
YEAH... You are.
LET ME TAKE MY SHOES OFF FIRST.
CHAK
OH.
KOMINATO AND YOSHIOKA ARE HERE.
MR. TANAKA!
MAKE YOURSELF AT HOME! Happy New Year!
HAPPY NEW YEAR TO YOU!

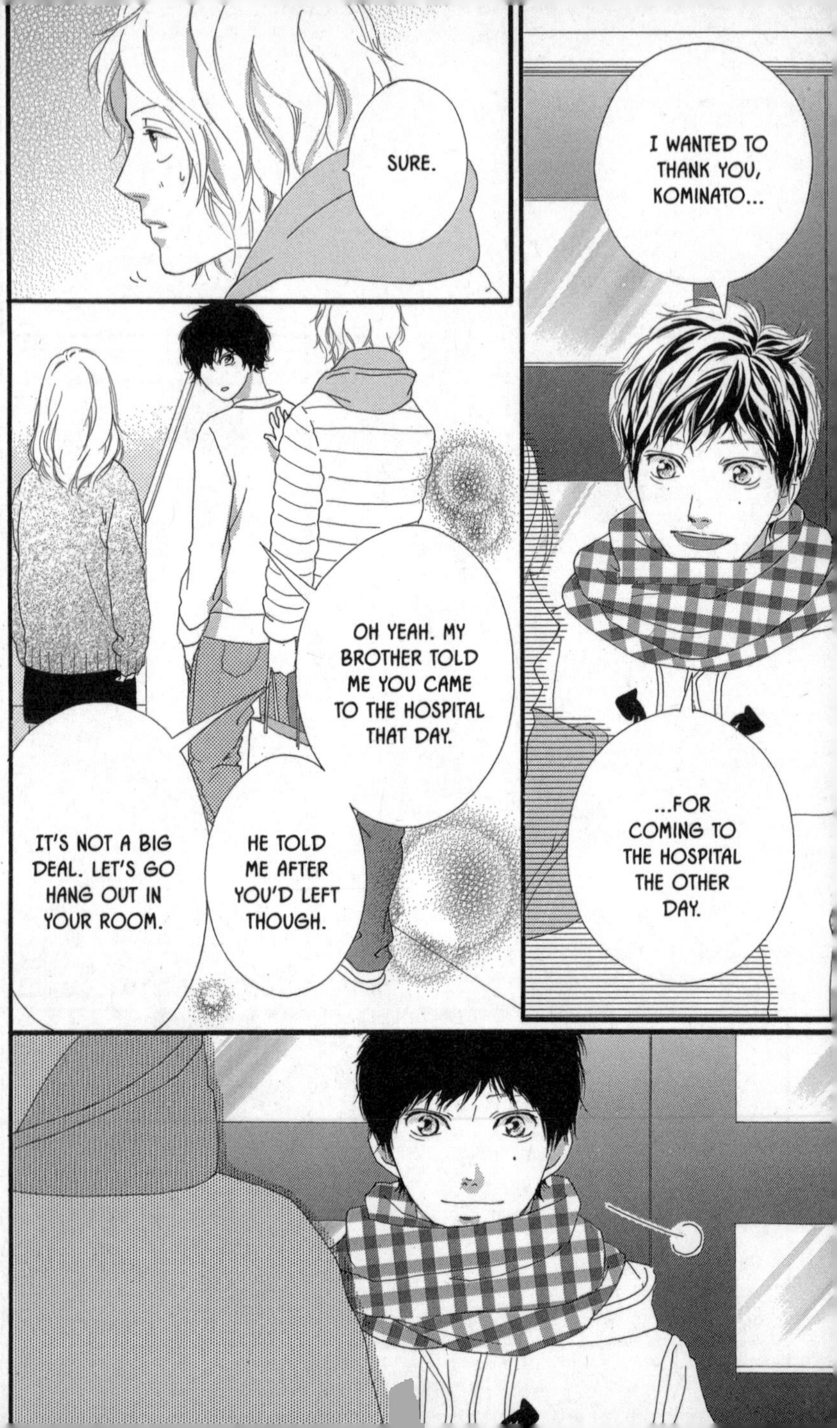
I WANTED TO THANK YOU, KOMINATO...
...FOR COMING TO THE HOSPITAL THE OTHER DAY.
SURE.
OH YEAH. MY BROTHER TOLD ME YOU CAME TO THE HOSPITAL THAT DAY.
HE TOLD ME AFTER YOU'D LEFT THOUGH.
IT'S NOT A BIG DEAL. LET'S GO HANG OUT IN YOUR ROOM.

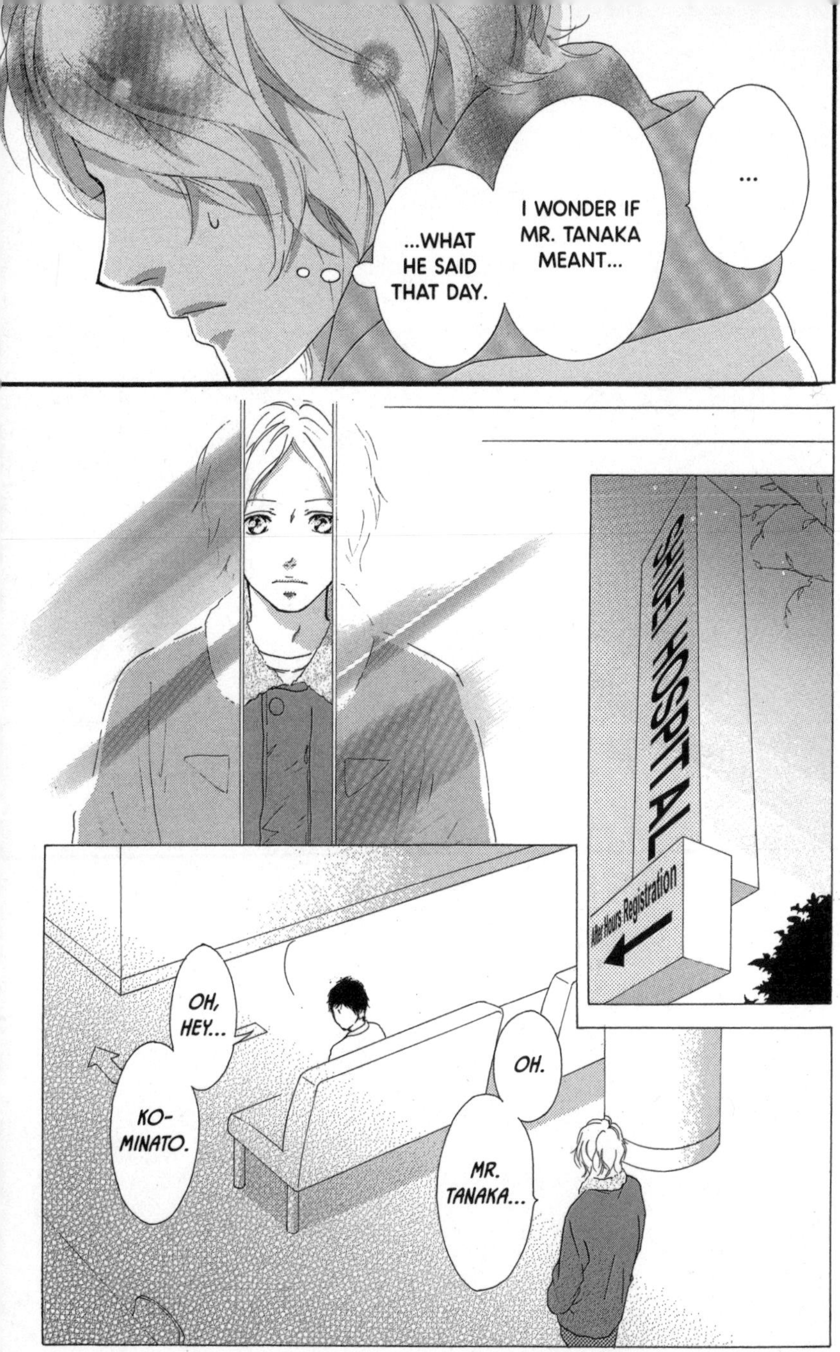
...
I WONDER IF MR. TANAKA MEANT...
...WHAT HE SAID THAT DAY.
SHUEI HOSPITAL
After Hours Registration
OH.
MR. TANAKA...
OH, HEY...
KO-MINATO.

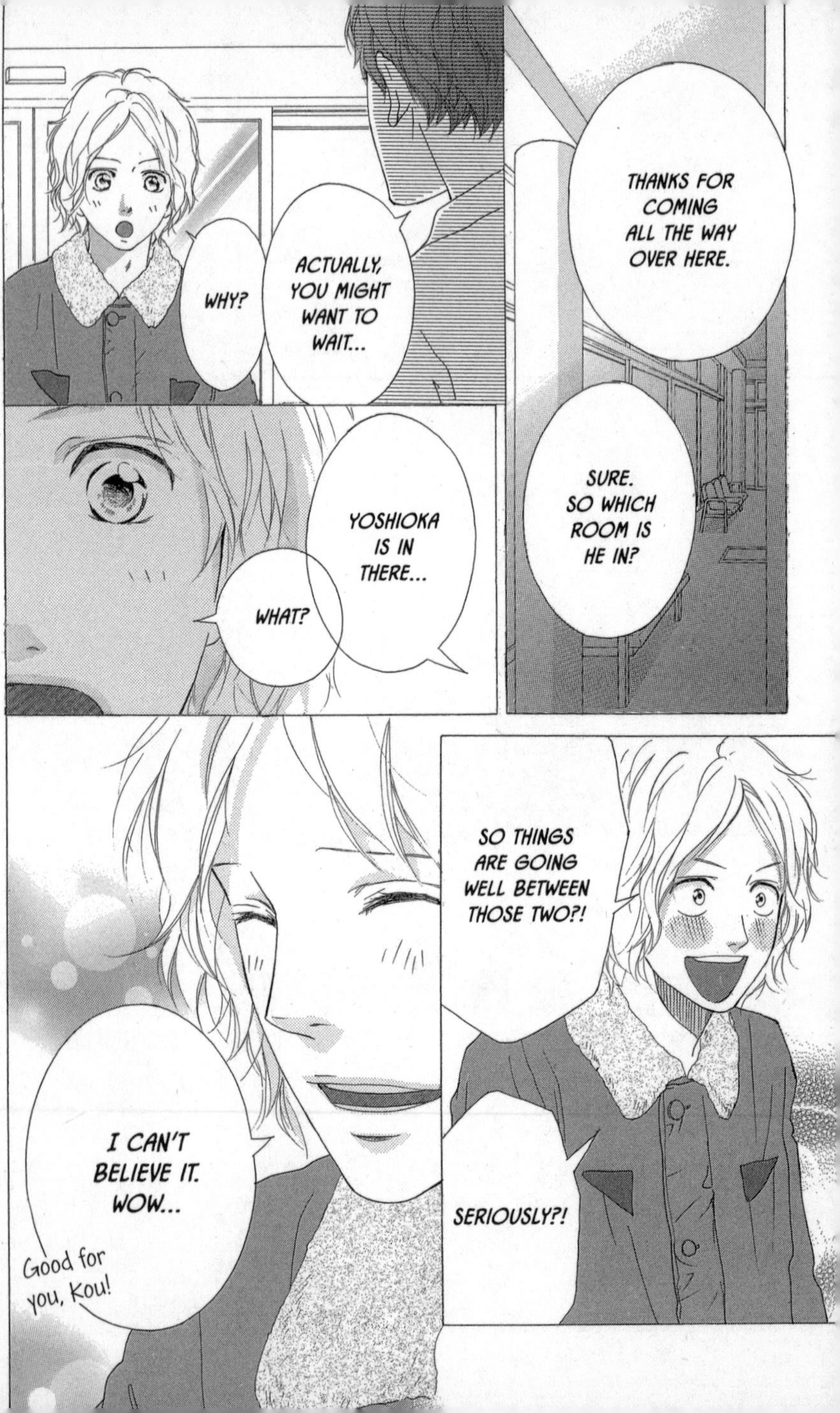
THANKS FOR COMING ALL THE WAY OVER HERE.
SURE. SO WHICH ROOM IS HE IN?
ACTUALLY, YOU MIGHT WANT TO WAIT...
WHY?
YOSHIOKA IS IN THERE...
WHAT?
SO THINGS ARE GOING WELL BETWEEN THOSE TWO?!
SERIOUSLY?!
I CAN'T BELIEVE IT. WOW...
Good for you, Kou!

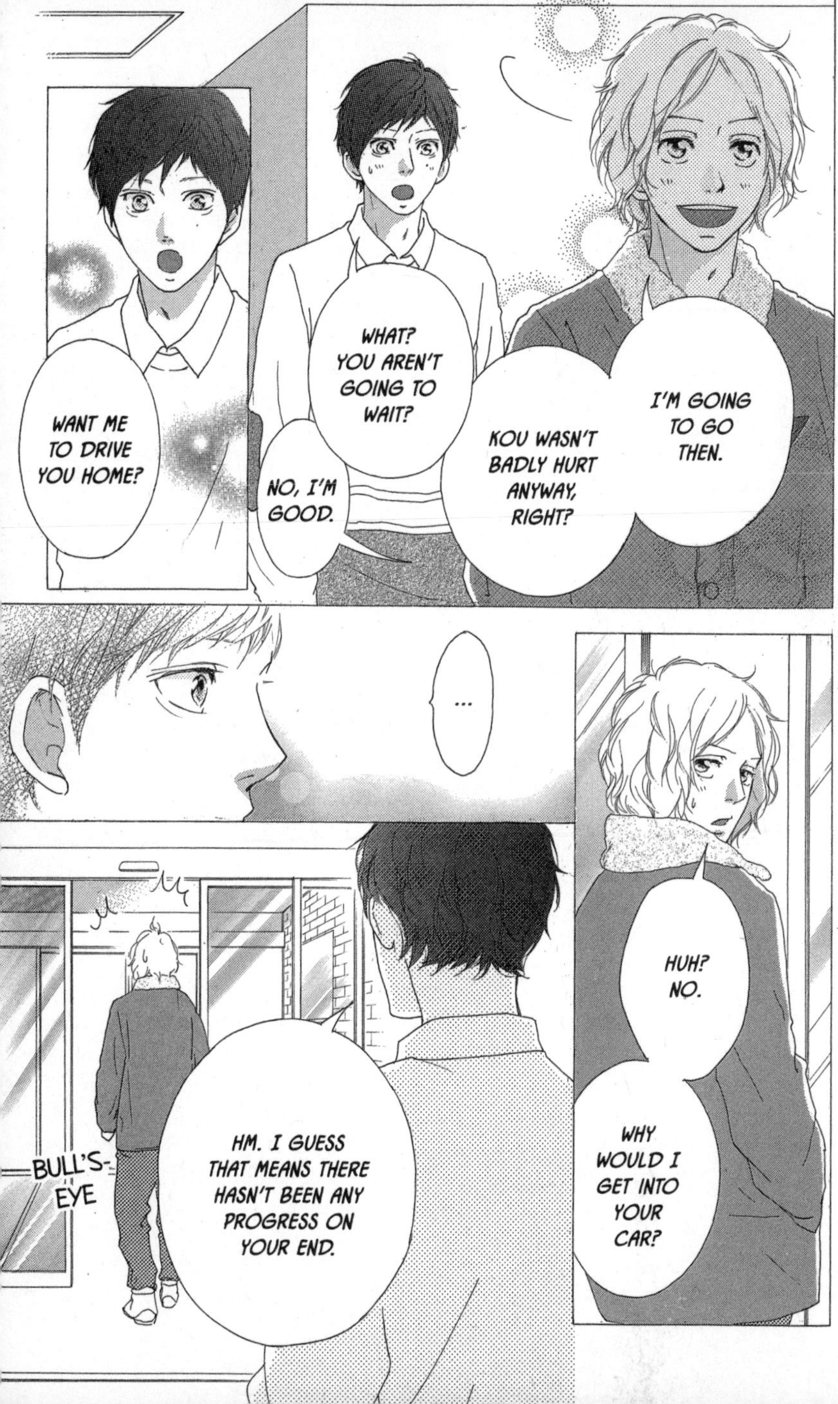
I'M GOING TO GO THEN.
KOU WASN'T BADLY HURT ANYWAY, RIGHT?
WHAT? YOU AREN'T GOING TO WAIT?
NO, I'M GOOD.
WANT ME TO DRIVE YOU HOME?
HUH? NO.
WHY WOULD I GET INTO YOUR CAR?
...
HM. I GUESS THAT MEANS THERE HASN'T BEEN ANY PROGRESS ON YOUR END.
BULL'S-EYE

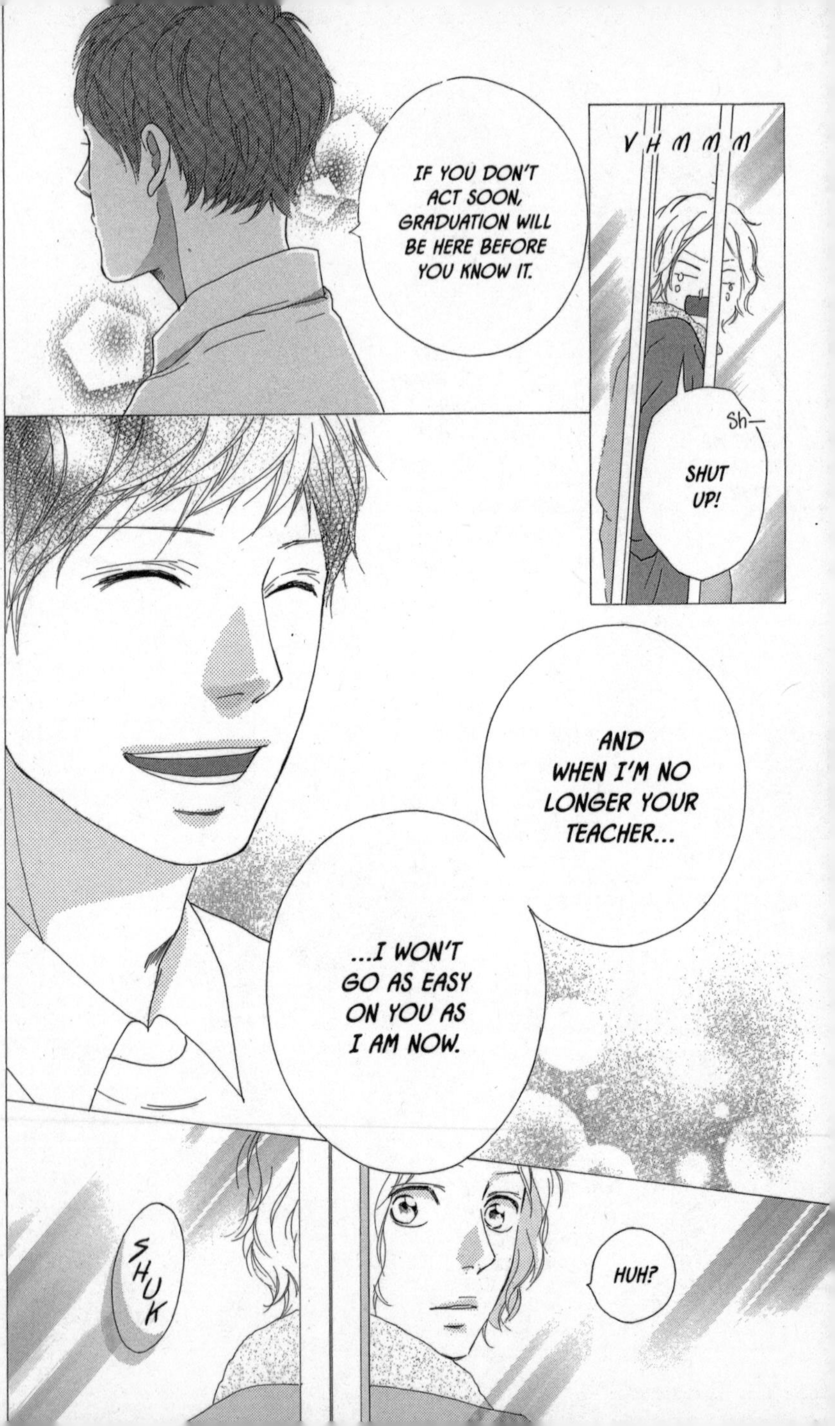
VHMMM
Sh—
SHUT UP!
IF YOU DON'T ACT SOON, GRADUATION WILL BE HERE BEFORE YOU KNOW IT.
AND WHEN I'M NO LONGER YOUR TEACHER...
...I WON'T GO AS EASY ON YOU AS I AM NOW.
HUH?
SHUK

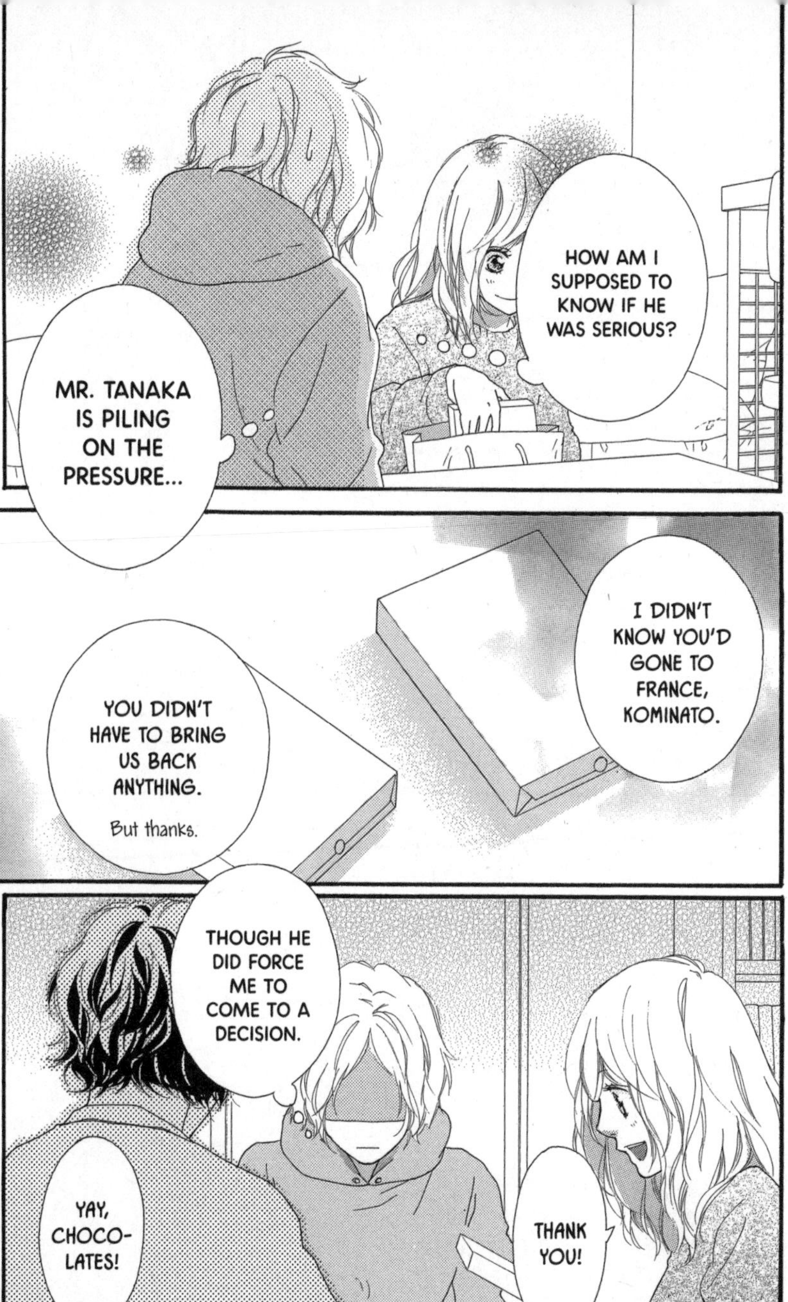
HOW AM I SUPPOSED TO KNOW IF HE WAS SERIOUS?
MR. TANAKA IS PILING ON THE PRESSURE...
I DIDN'T KNOW YOU'D GONE TO FRANCE, KOMINATO.
YOU DIDN'T HAVE TO BRING US BACK ANYTHING.
But thanks.
THOUGH HE DID FORCE ME TO COME TO A DECISION.
THANK YOU!
YAY, CHOCO- LATES!

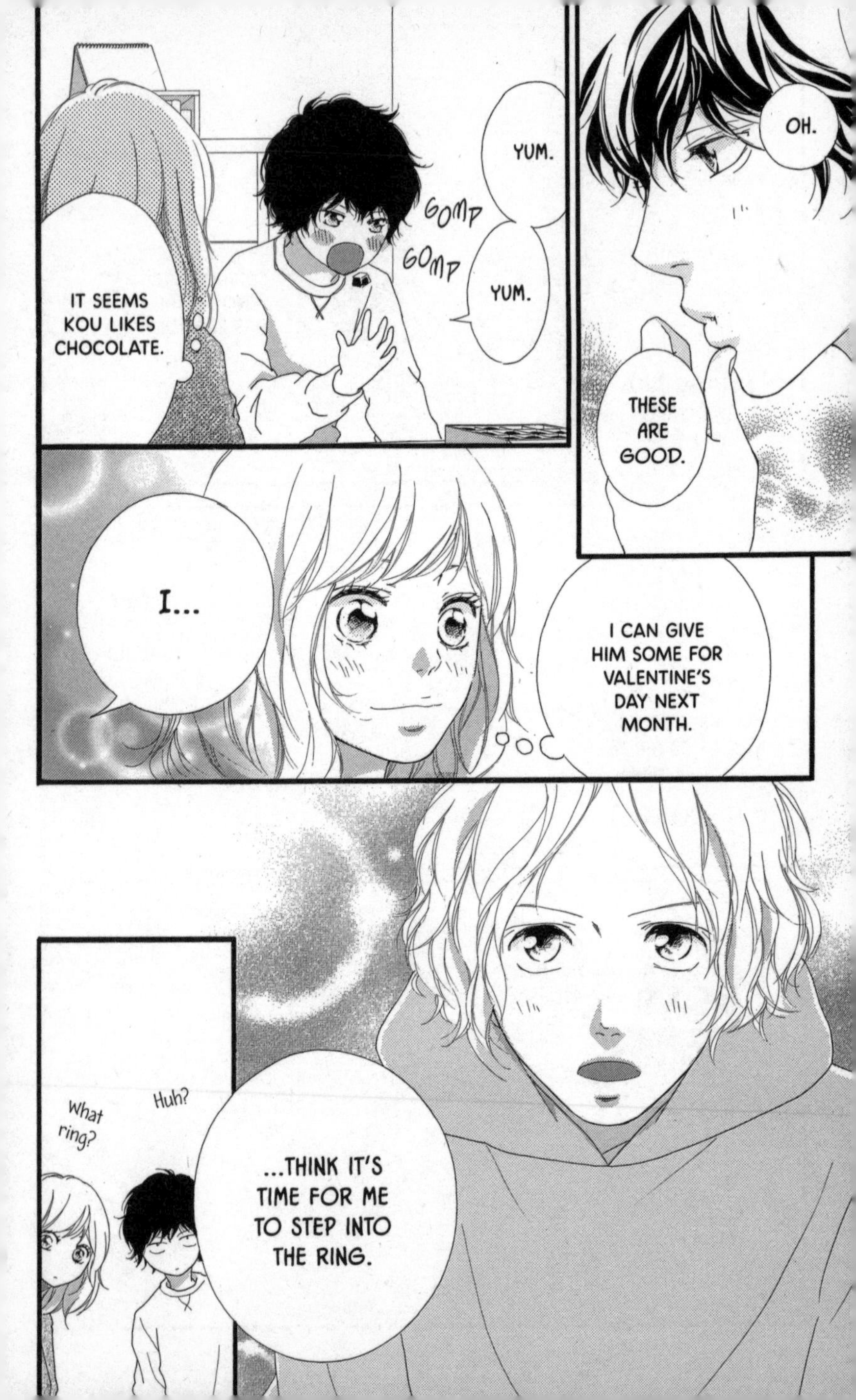
OH.
THESE ARE GOOD.
YUM.
GOMP
GOMP
YUM.
IT SEEMS KOU LIKES CHOCOLATE.
I CAN GIVE HIM SOME FOR VALENTINE'S DAY NEXT MONTH.
I...
...THINK IT'S TIME FOR ME TO STEP INTO THE RING.
Huh?
What ring?

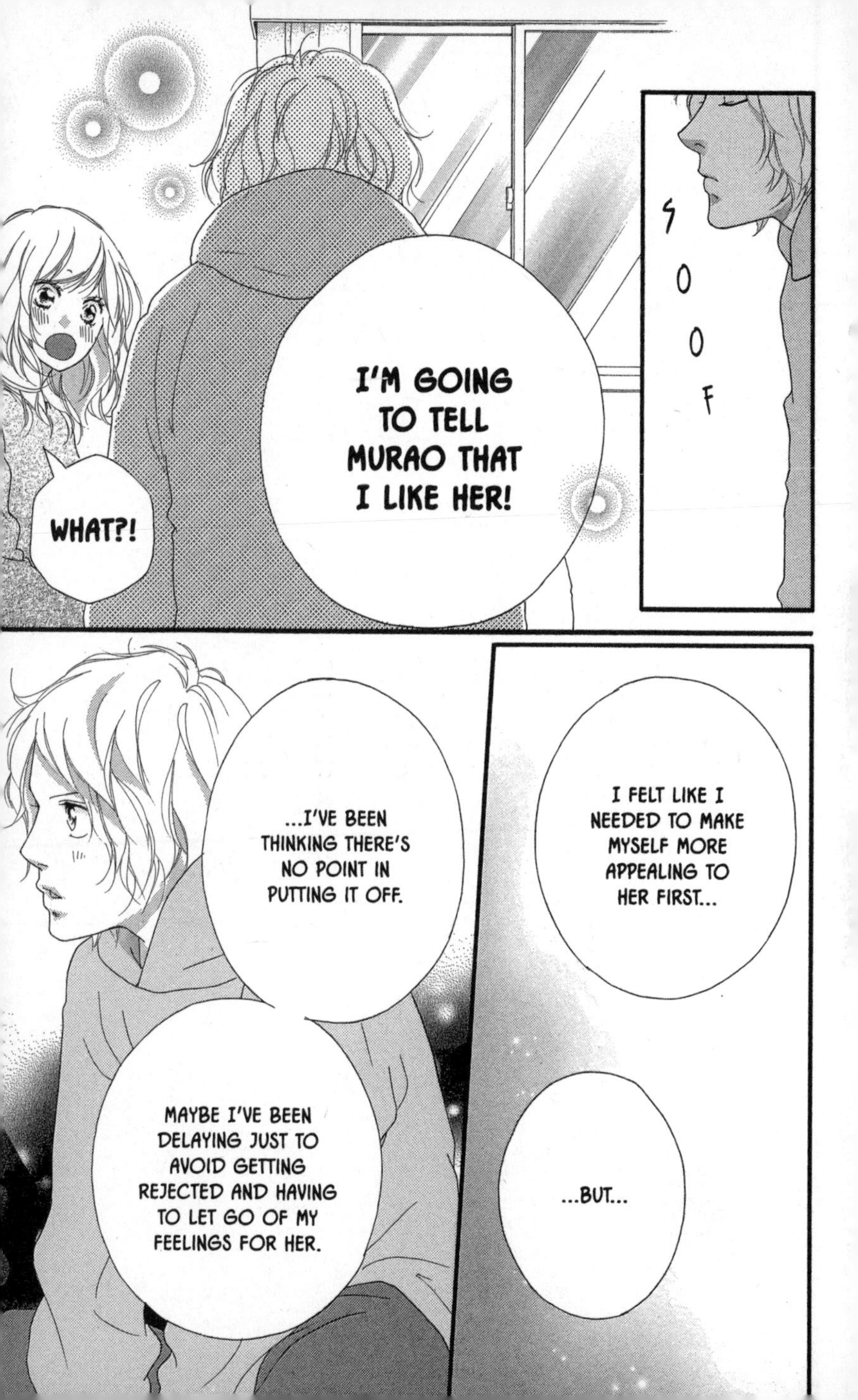
SOOF
I'M GOING TO TELL MURAO THAT I LIKE HER!
WHAT?!
I FELT LIKE I NEEDED TO MAKE MYSELF MORE APPEALING TO HER FIRST...
...BUT...
...I'VE BEEN THINKING THERE'S NO POINT IN PUTTING IT OFF.
MAYBE I'VE BEEN DELAYING JUST TO AVOID GETTING REJECTED AND HAVING TO LET GO OF MY FEELINGS FOR HER.

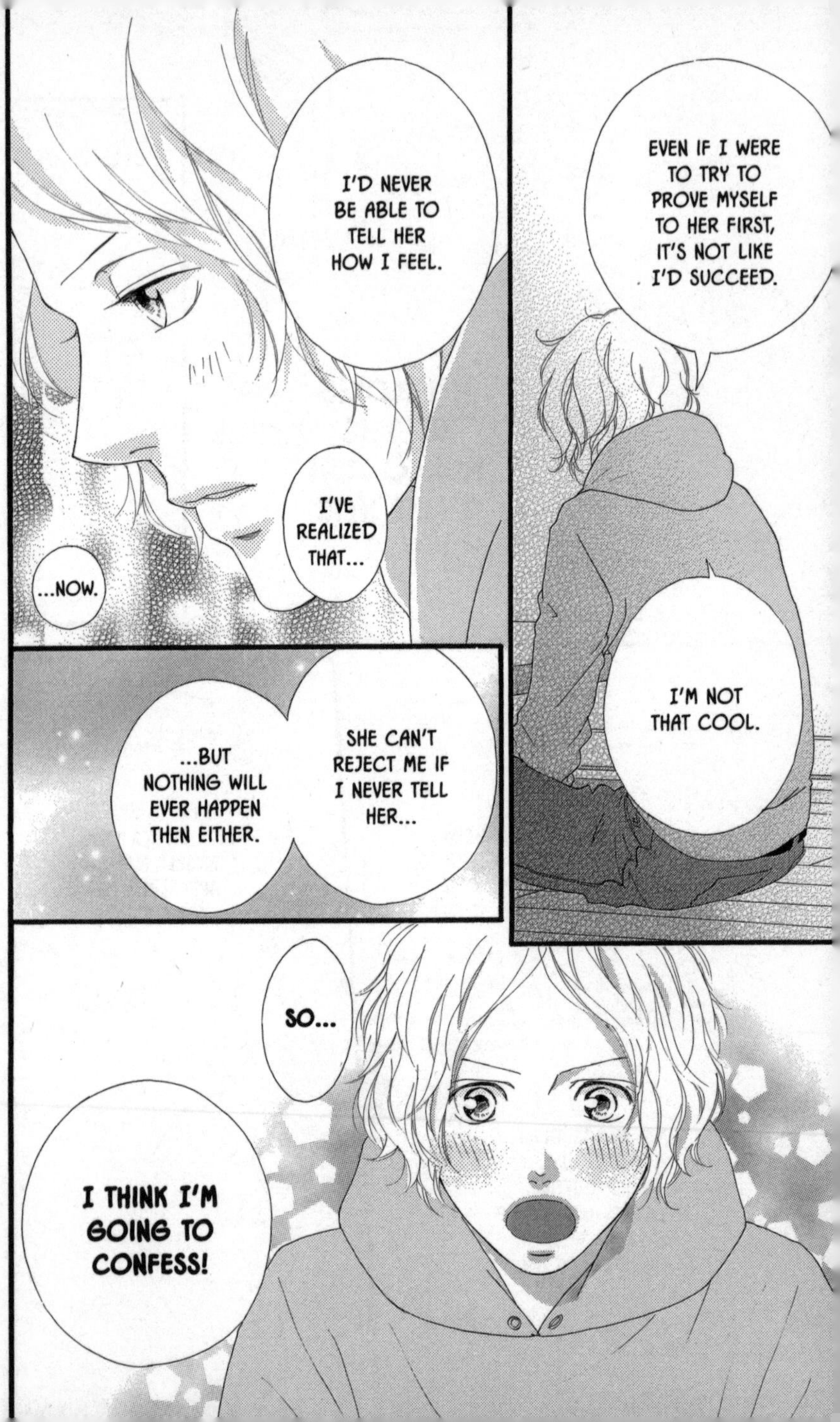
EVEN IF I WERE TO TRY TO PROVE MYSELF TO HER FIRST, IT'S NOT LIKE I'D SUCCEED.
I'M NOT THAT COOL.
I'D NEVER BE ABLE TO TELL HER HOW I FEEL.
I'VE REALIZED THAT...
...NOW.
SHE CAN'T REJECT ME IF I NEVER TELL HER...
...BUT NOTHING WILL EVER HAPPEN THEN EITHER.
SO...
I THINK I'M GOING TO CONFESS!

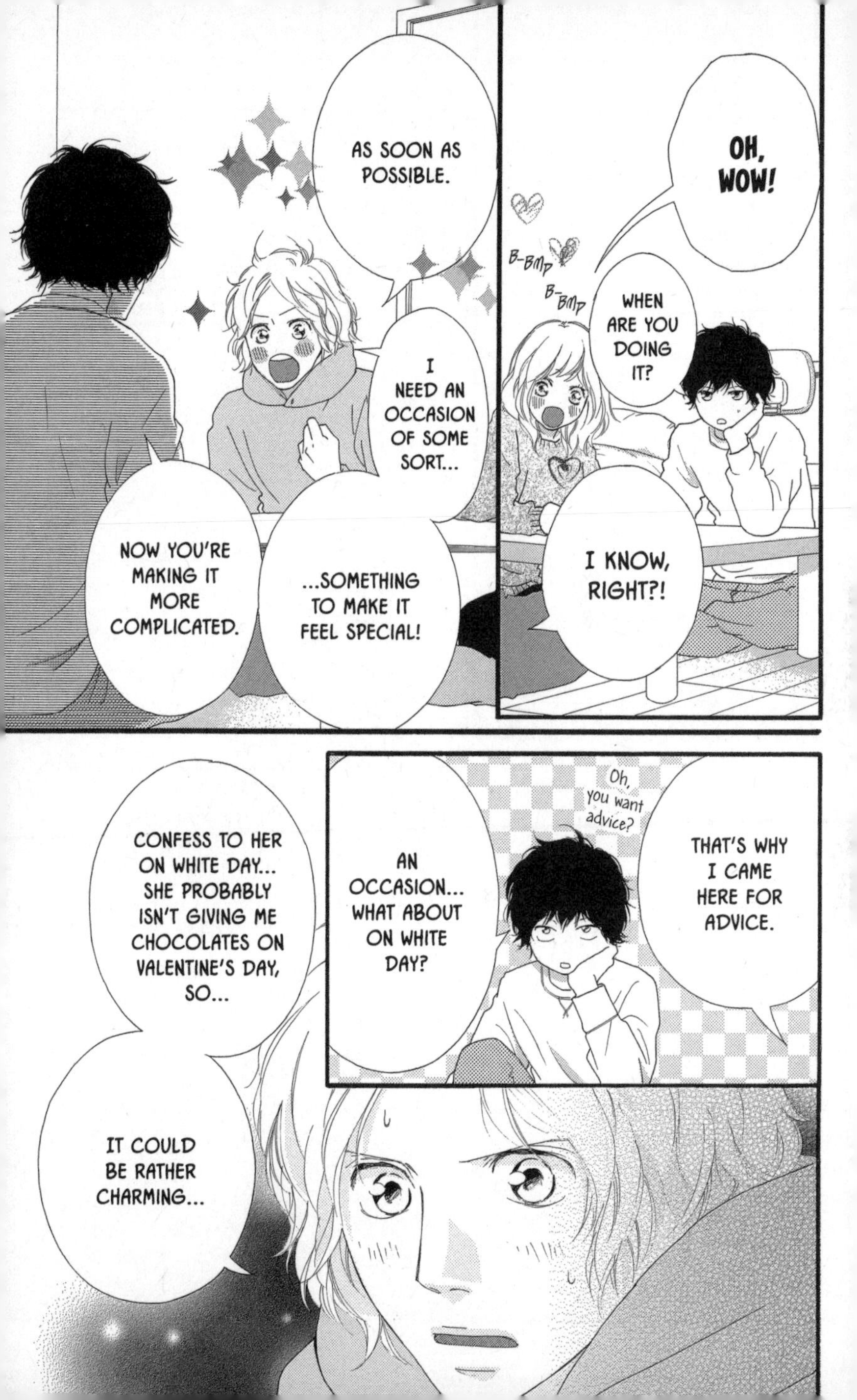
OH, WOW!
B-BMP
B-BMP
WHEN ARE YOU DOING IT?
I KNOW, RIGHT?!
AS SOON AS POSSIBLE.
I NEED AN OCCASION OF SOME SORT...
...SOMETHING TO MAKE IT FEEL SPECIAL!
NOW YOU'RE MAKING IT MORE COMPLICATED.
THAT'S WHY I CAME HERE FOR ADVICE.
Oh, you want advice?
AN OCCASION... WHAT ABOUT ON WHITE DAY?
CONFESS TO HER ON WHITE DAY... SHE PROBABLY ISN'T GIVING ME CHOCOLATES ON VALENTINE'S DAY, SO...
IT COULD BE RATHER CHARMING...

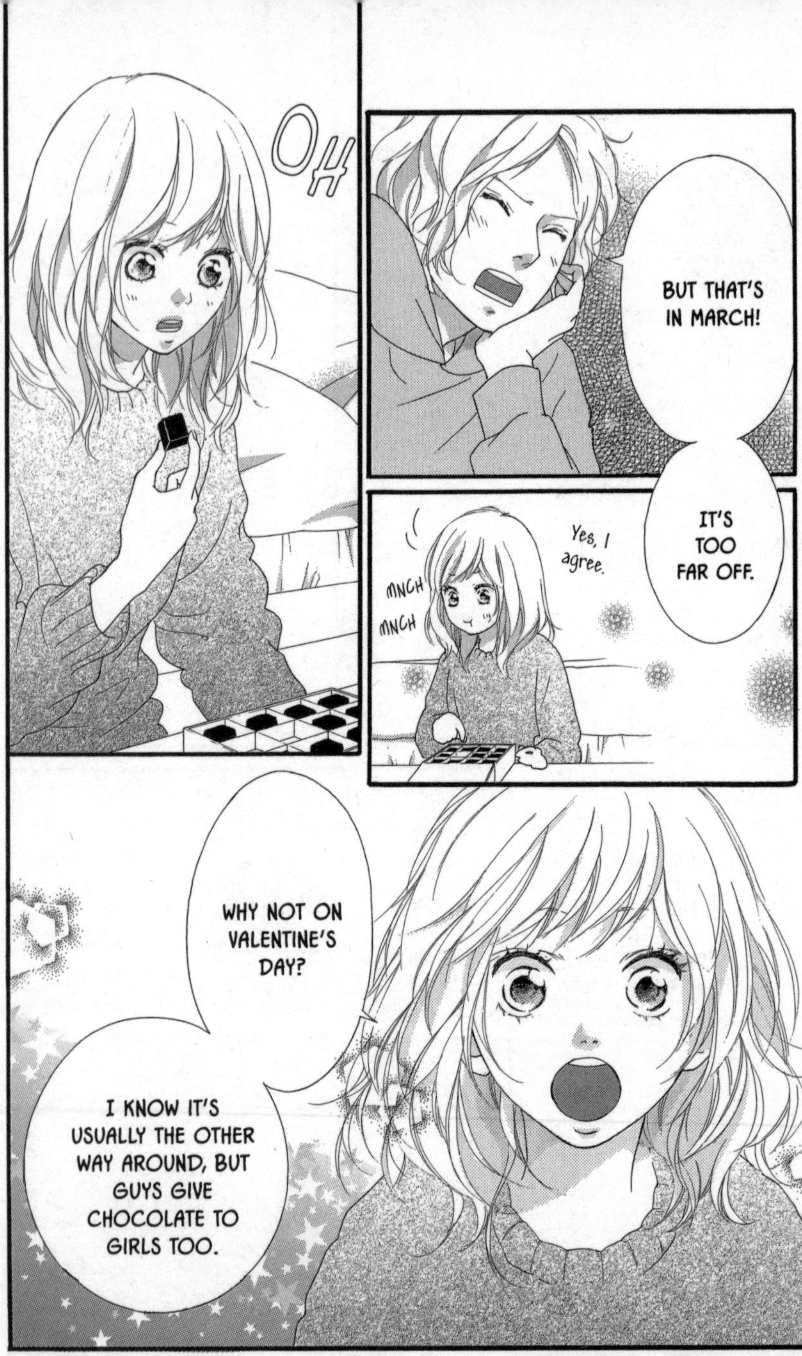
BUT THAT'S IN MARCH!
IT'S TOO FAR OFF.
Yes, I agree.
MNCH MNCH
OH
WHY NOT ON VALENTINE'S DAY?
I KNOW IT'S USUALLY THE OTHER WAY AROUND, BUT GUYS GIVE CHOCOLATE TO GIRLS TOO.

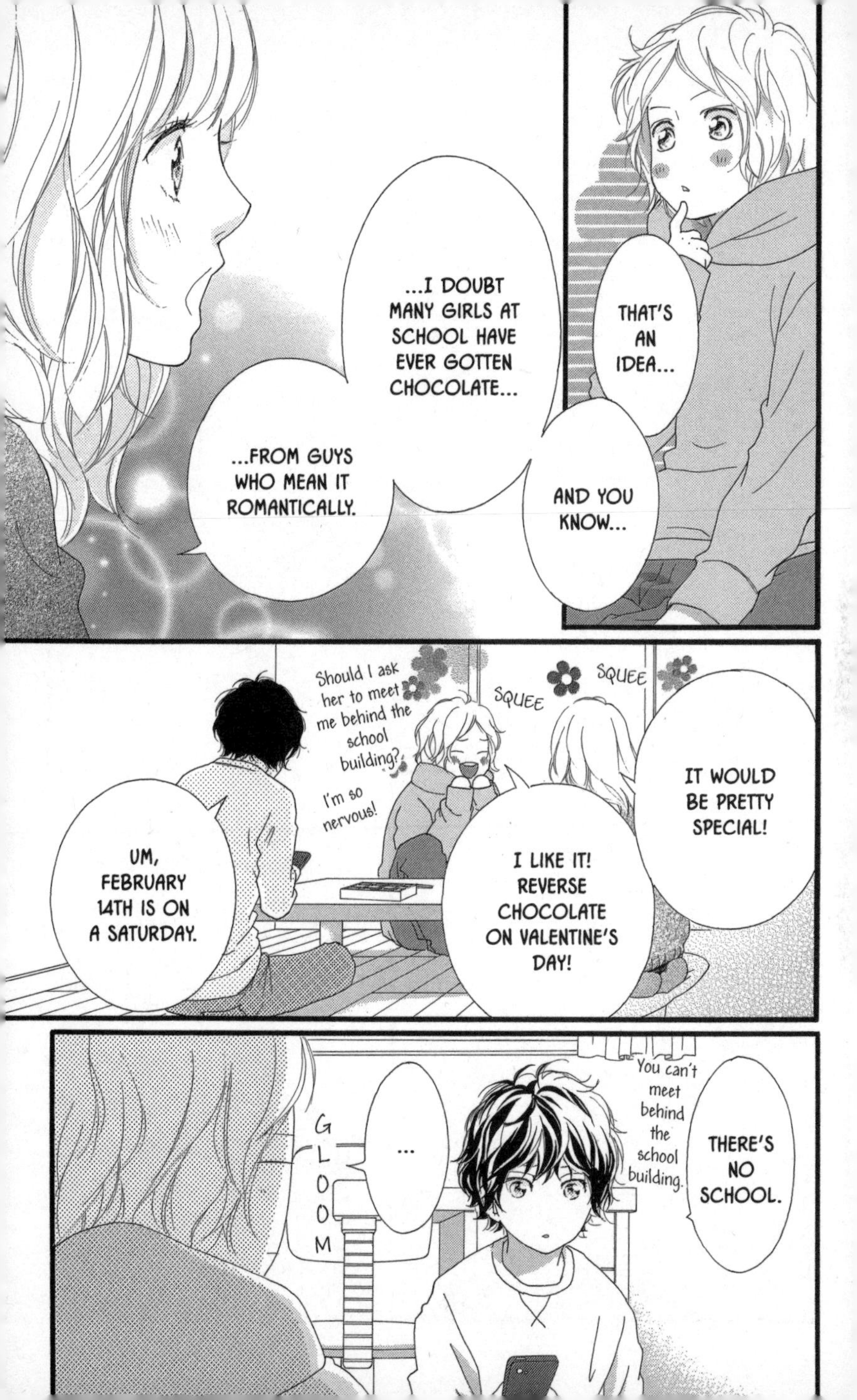
THAT'S AN IDEA...
AND YOU KNOW...
...I DOUBT MANY GIRLS AT SCHOOL HAVE EVER GOTTEN CHOCOLATE...
...FROM GUYS WHO MEAN IT ROMANTICALLY.
IT WOULD BE PRETTY SPECIAL!
SQUEE
SQUEE
I LIKE IT! REVERSE CHOCOLATE ON VALENTINE'S DAY!
Should I ask her to meet me behind the school building?
I'm so nervous!
UM, FEBRUARY 14TH IS ON A SATURDAY.
THERE'S NO SCHOOL.
You can't meet behind the school building.
...
GLOOM

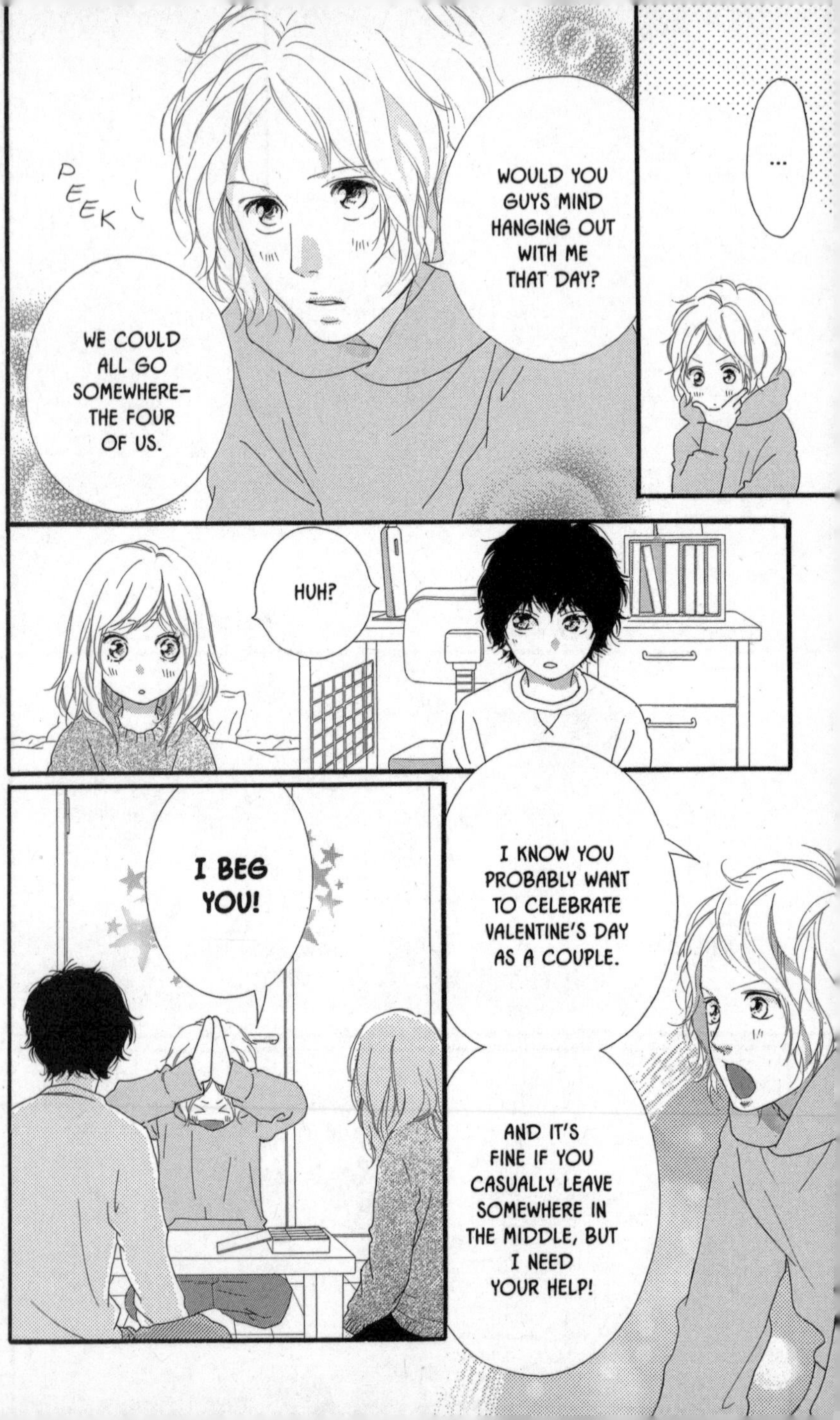
...
WOULD YOU GUYS MIND HANGING OUT WITH ME THAT DAY?
PEEK
WE COULD ALL GO SOMEWHERE—THE FOUR OF US.
HUH?
I KNOW YOU PROBABLY WANT TO CELEBRATE VALENTINE'S DAY AS A COUPLE.
AND IT'S FINE IF YOU CASUALLY LEAVE SOMEWHERE IN THE MIDDLE, BUT I NEED YOUR HELP!
I BEG YOU!

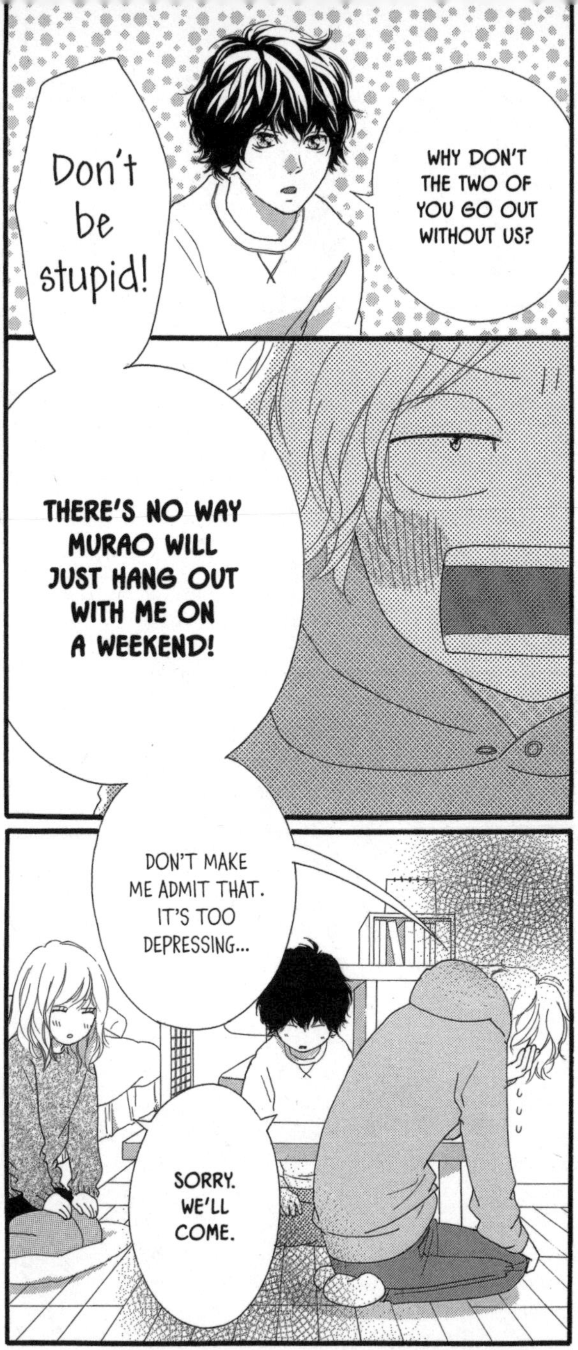
WHY DON'T THE TWO OF YOU GO OUT WITHOUT US?
Don't be stupid!
THERE'S NO WAY MURAO WILL JUST HANG OUT WITH ME ON A WEEKEND!
DON'T MAKE ME ADMIT THAT. IT'S TOO DEPRESSING...
SORRY. WE'LL COME.

Sankaku Park came up in this story over and over. Its visual inspiration came from a reference book, so I believe that a park with that clock tower exists somewhere in Japan, though I doubt it's called Sankaku Park. I chose that name to add a realistic feel to the story. I imagined a park that has another official name, but is known by locals by its nickname, or rather, popular name. I hoped that readers would be somewhat intrigued by this setting that could exist in any town. Years ago, I used to live near what people called "Hachinoji Park" [*Hachinoji* means "in the shape of an eight"], but its true name was "003 Park." It's supposed to be like that. What I always found odd was that the park didn't have any structures in the shape of an eight, and it didn't look like an eight when viewed from above either.

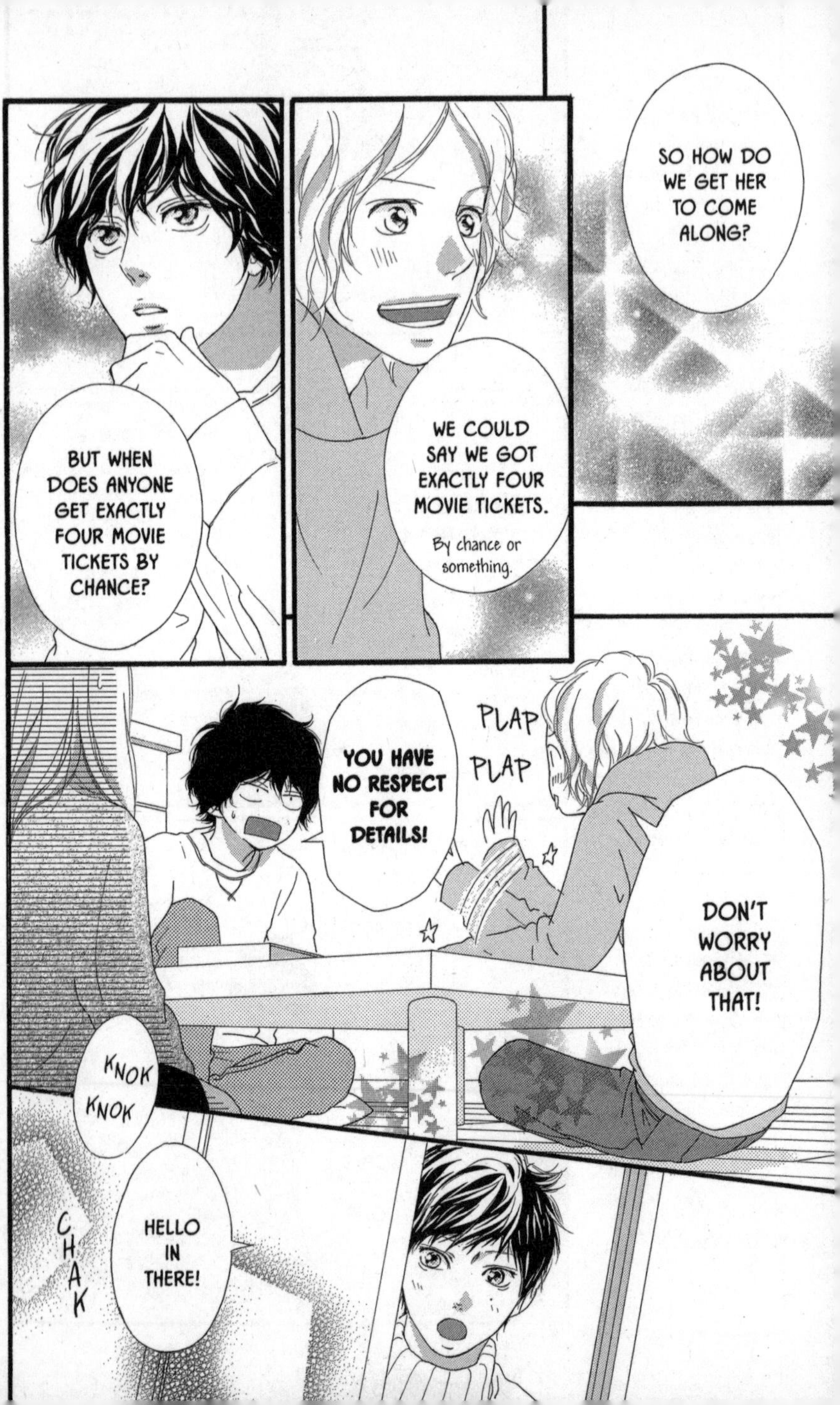
SO HOW DO WE GET HER TO COME ALONG?
WE COULD SAY WE GOT EXACTLY FOUR MOVIE TICKETS.
By chance or something.
BUT WHEN DOES ANYONE GET EXACTLY FOUR MOVIE TICKETS BY CHANCE?
DON'T WORRY ABOUT THAT!
PLAP PLAP
YOU HAVE NO RESPECT FOR DETAILS!
KNOK KNOK
CHAK
HELLO IN THERE!

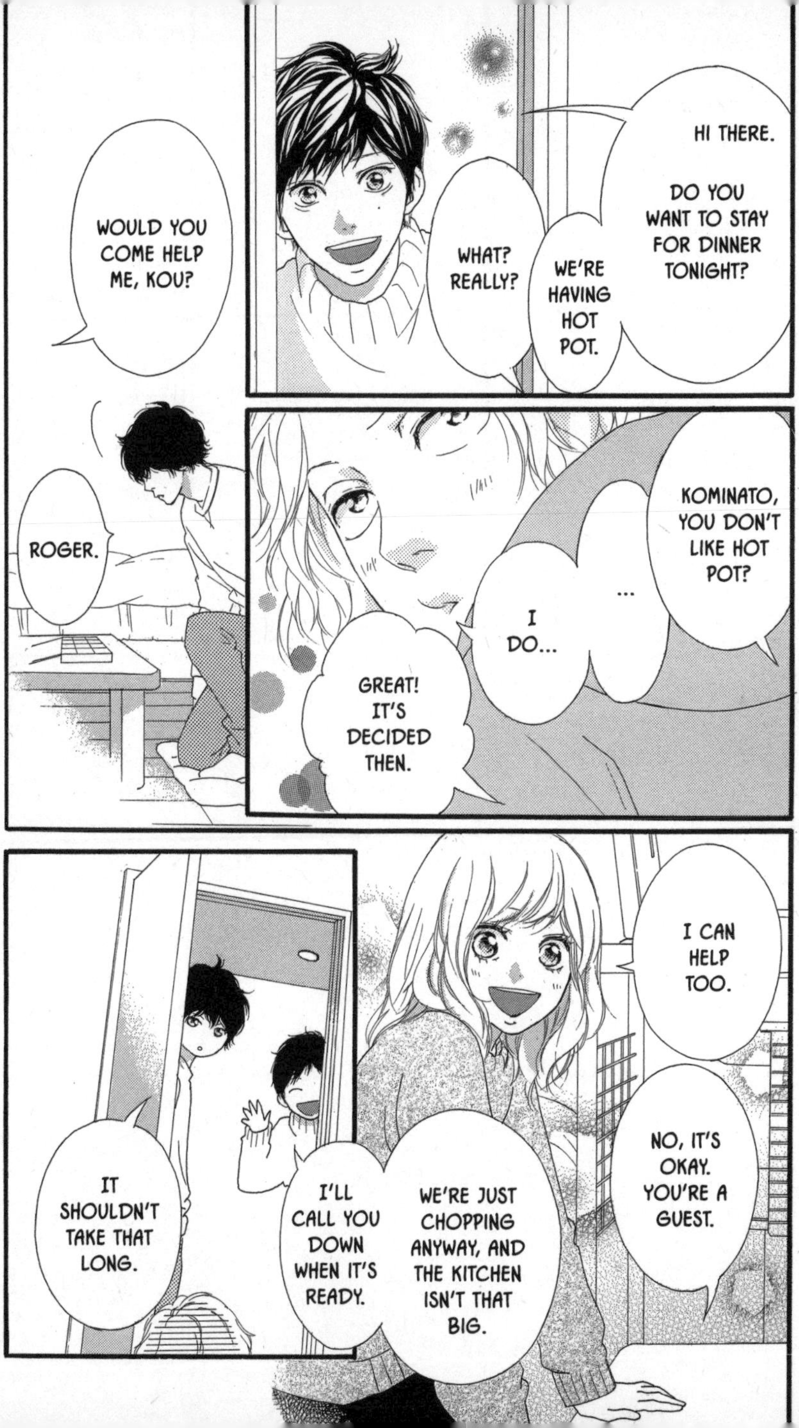
HI THERE.
DO YOU WANT TO STAY FOR DINNER TONIGHT?
WE'RE HAVING HOT POT.
WHAT? REALLY?
KOMINATO, YOU DON'T LIKE HOT POT?
...
I DO...
GREAT! IT'S DECIDED THEN.
WOULD YOU COME HELP ME, KOU?
ROGER.
I CAN HELP TOO.
NO, IT'S OKAY. YOU'RE A GUEST.
WE'RE JUST CHOPPING ANYWAY, AND THE KITCHEN ISN'T THAT BIG.
I'LL CALL YOU DOWN WHEN IT'S READY.
IT SHOULDN'T TAKE THAT LONG.

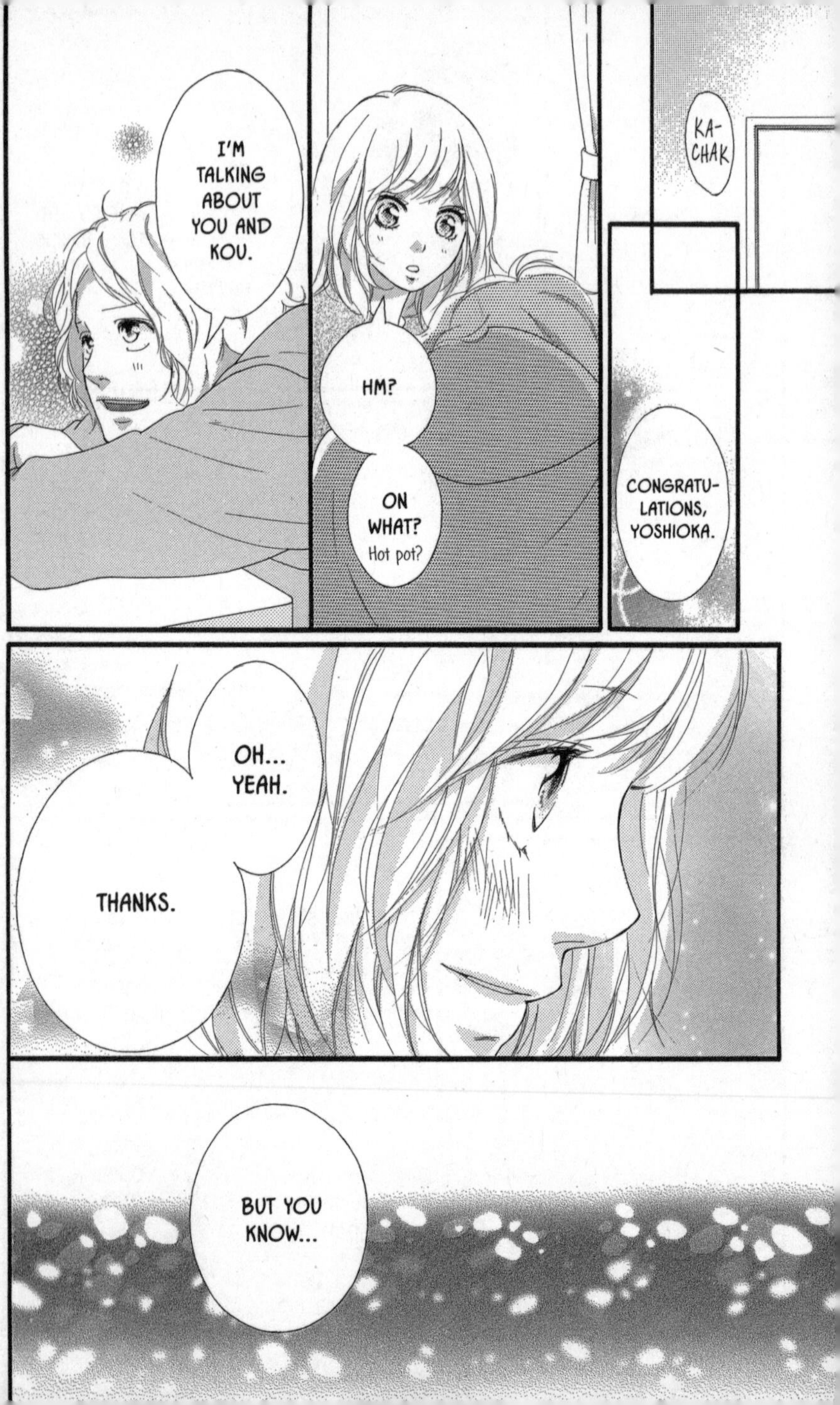
KA-CHAK
CONGRATU-LATIONS, YOSHIOKA.
HM?
ON WHAT? Hot pot?
I'M TALKING ABOUT YOU AND KOU.
OH... YEAH.
THANKS.
BUT YOU KNOW...

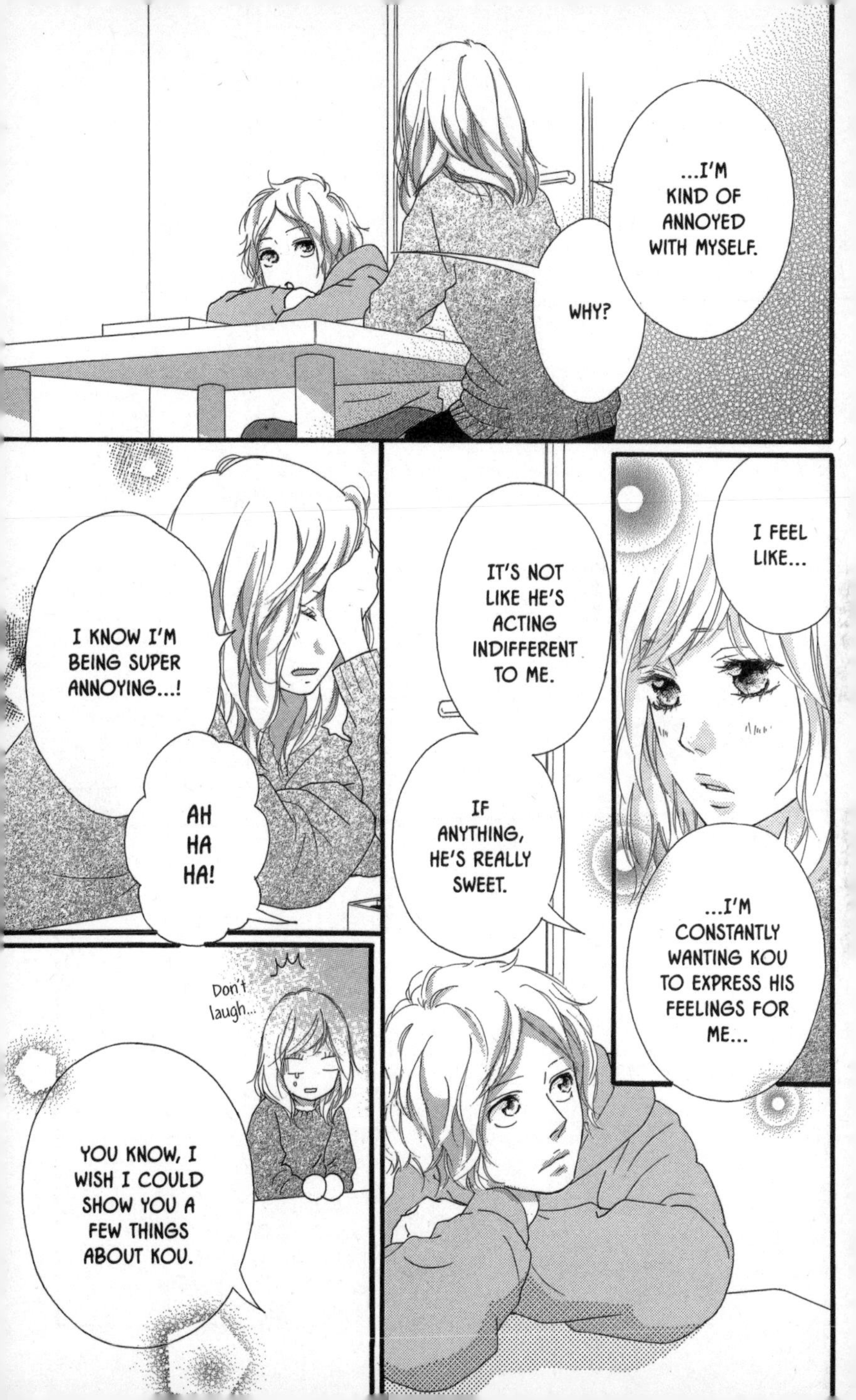
...I'M KIND OF ANNOYED WITH MYSELF.
WHY?
I FEEL LIKE...
...I'M CONSTANTLY WANTING KOU TO EXPRESS HIS FEELINGS FOR ME...
IT'S NOT LIKE HE'S ACTING INDIFFERENT TO ME.
IF ANYTHING, HE'S REALLY SWEET.
I KNOW I'M BEING SUPER ANNOYING...!
AH HA HA!
Don't laugh...
YOU KNOW, I WISH I COULD SHOW YOU A FEW THINGS ABOUT KOU.

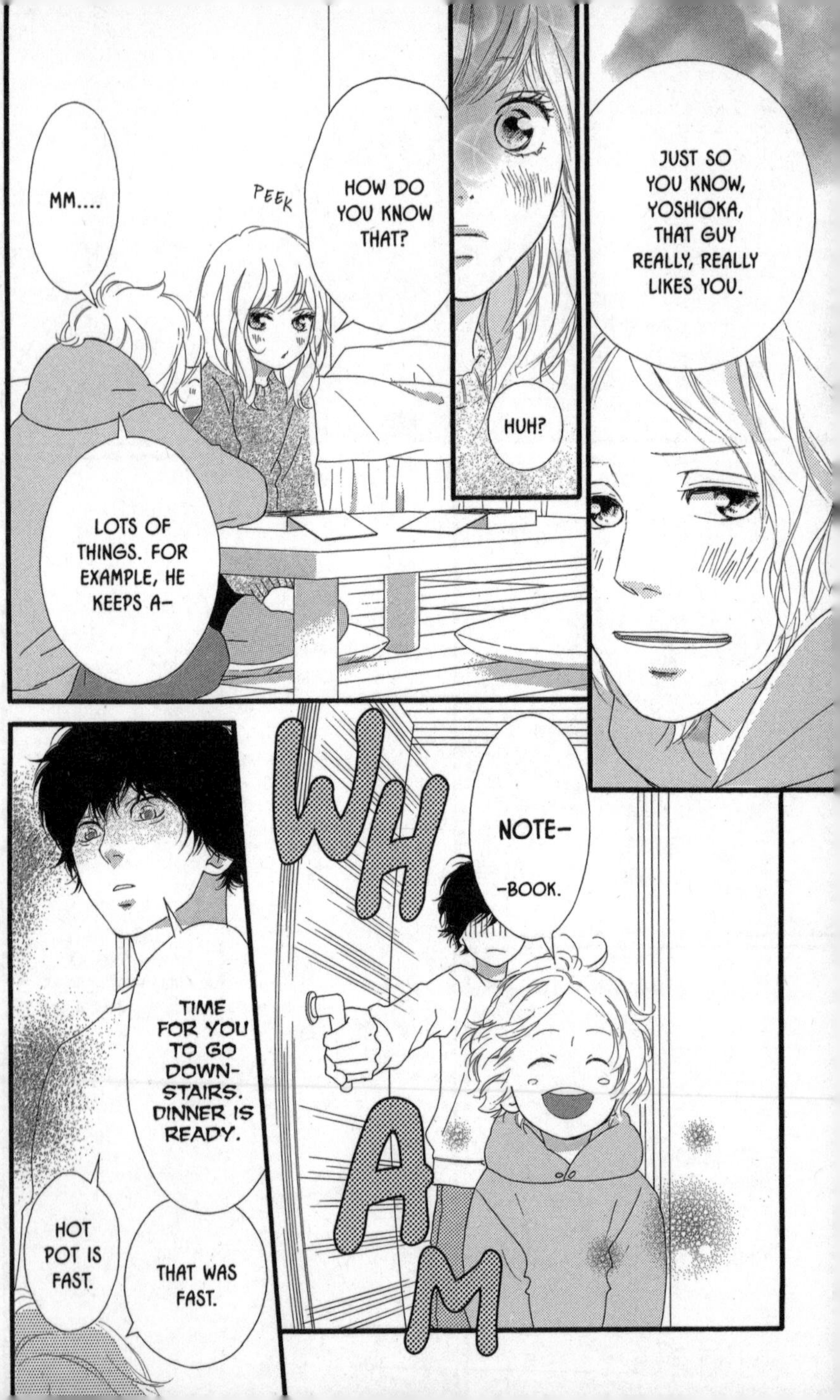
JUST SO YOU KNOW, YOSHIOKA, THAT GUY REALLY, REALLY LIKES YOU.
HUH?
HOW DO YOU KNOW THAT?
PEEK
MM....
LOTS OF THINGS. FOR EXAMPLE, HE KEEPS A–
NOTE–
-BOOK.
WHAM
TIME FOR YOU TO GO DOWN-STAIRS. DINNER IS READY.
THAT WAS FAST.
HOT POT IS FAST.

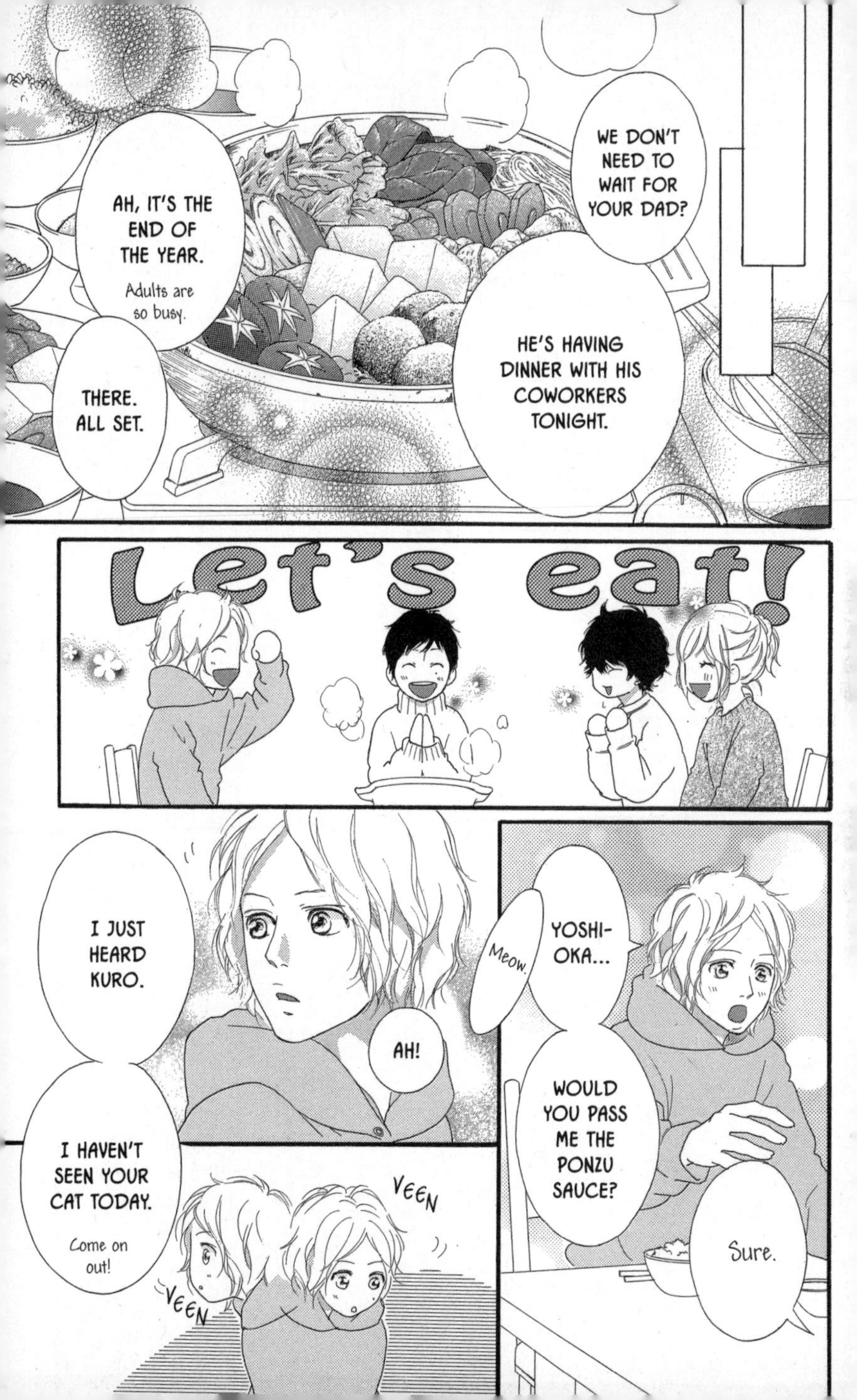
WE DON'T NEED TO WAIT FOR YOUR DAD?
HE'S HAVING DINNER WITH HIS COWORKERS TONIGHT.
AH, IT'S THE END OF THE YEAR.
Adults are so busy.
THERE. ALL SET.
Let's eat!
YOSHI-OKA...
Meow.
WOULD YOU PASS ME THE PONZU SAUCE?
Sure.
I JUST HEARD KURO.
AH!
I HAVEN'T SEEN YOUR CAT TODAY.
Come on out!
VEEN
VEEN

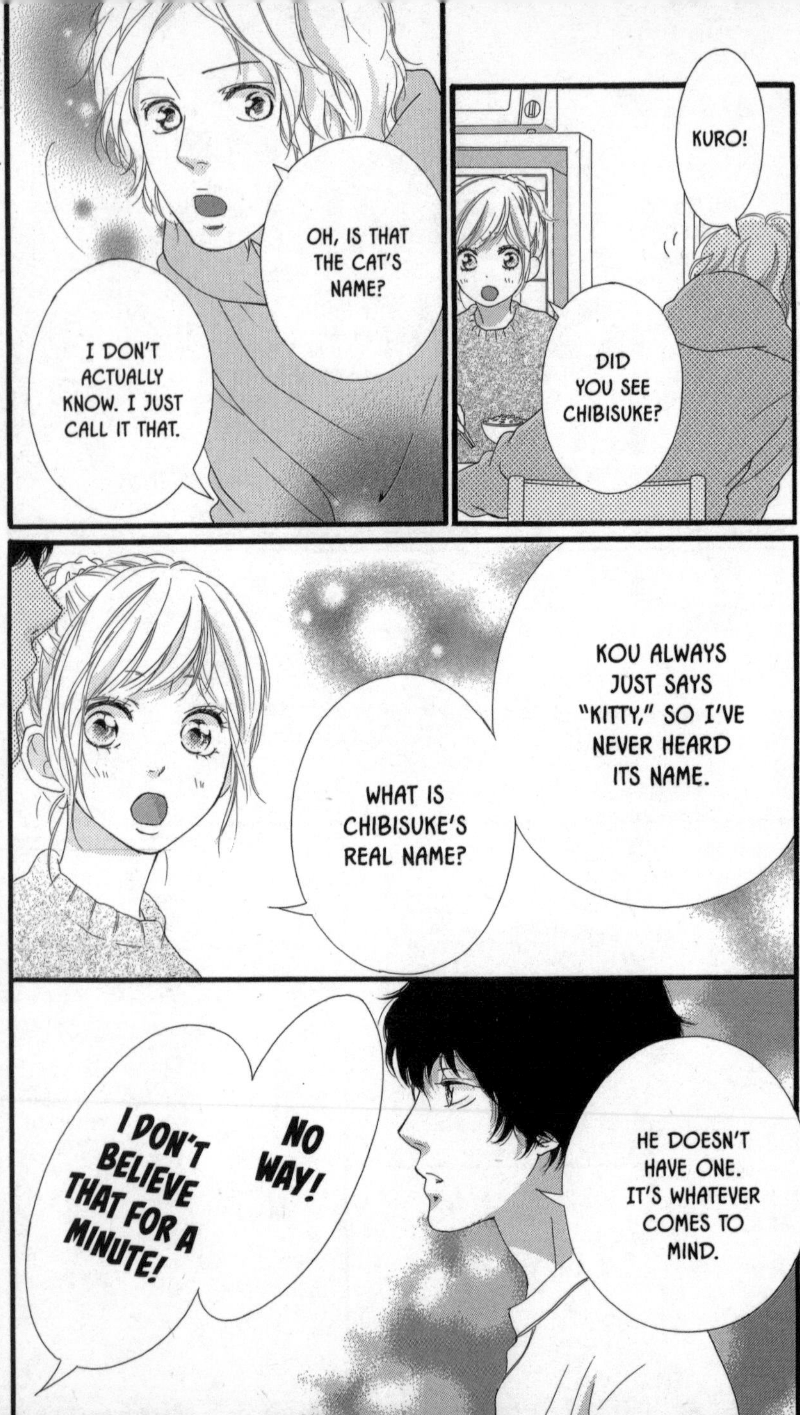
KURO!
DID YOU SEE CHIBISUKE?
OH, IS THAT THE CAT'S NAME?
I DON'T ACTUALLY KNOW. I JUST CALL IT THAT.
KOU ALWAYS JUST SAYS "KITTY," SO I'VE NEVER HEARD ITS NAME.
WHAT IS CHIBISUKE'S REAL NAME?
HE DOESN'T HAVE ONE. IT'S WHATEVER COMES TO MIND.
NO WAY!
I DON'T BELIEVE THAT FOR A MINUTE!

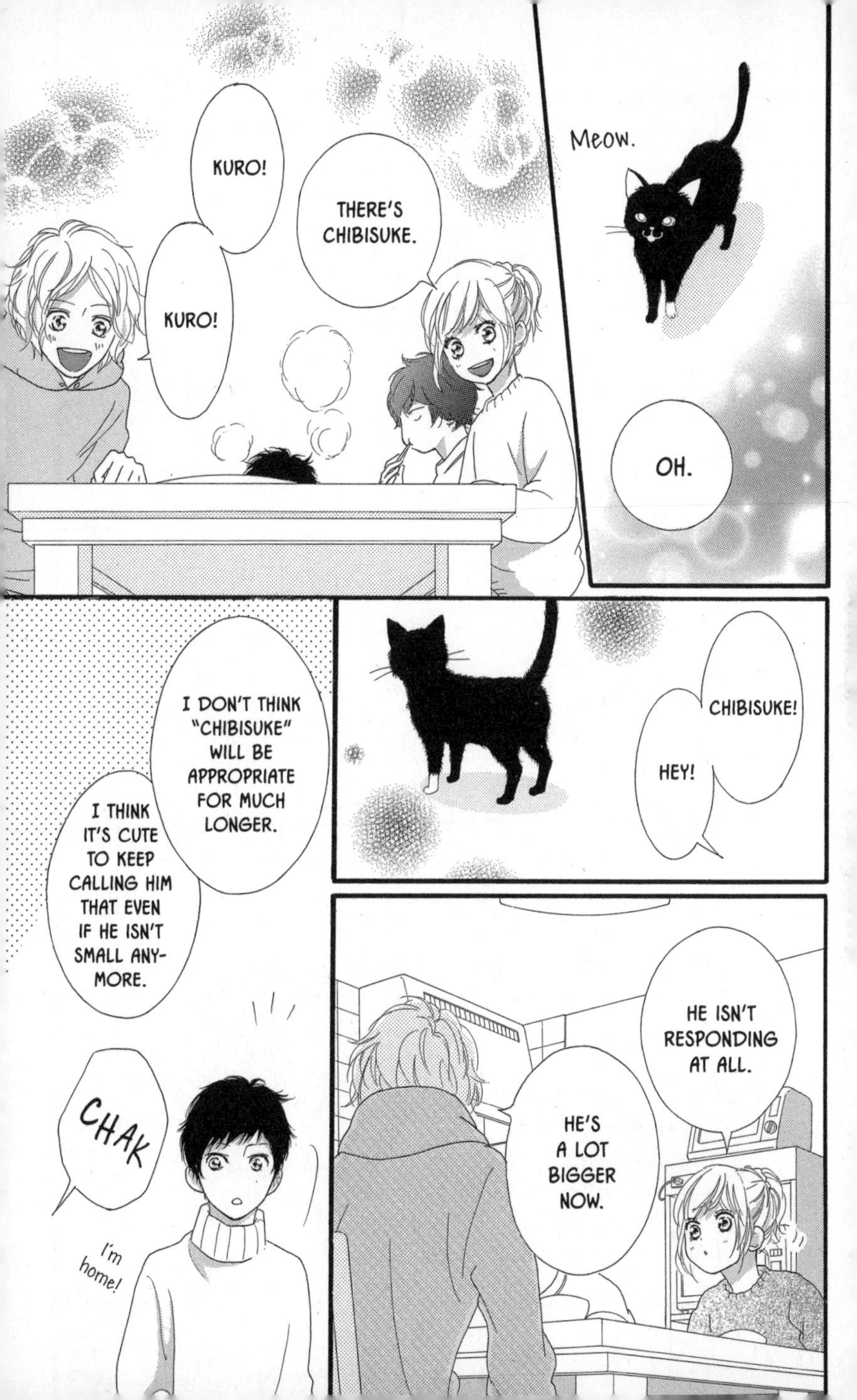
Meow.
OH.
THERE'S CHIBISUKE.
KURO!
KURO!
CHIBISUKE!
HEY!
HE ISN'T RESPONDING AT ALL.
HE'S A LOT BIGGER NOW.
I DON'T THINK "CHIBISUKE" WILL BE APPROPRIATE FOR MUCH LONGER.
I THINK IT'S CUTE TO KEEP CALLING HIM THAT EVEN IF HE ISN'T SMALL ANY-MORE.
CHAK
I'm home!

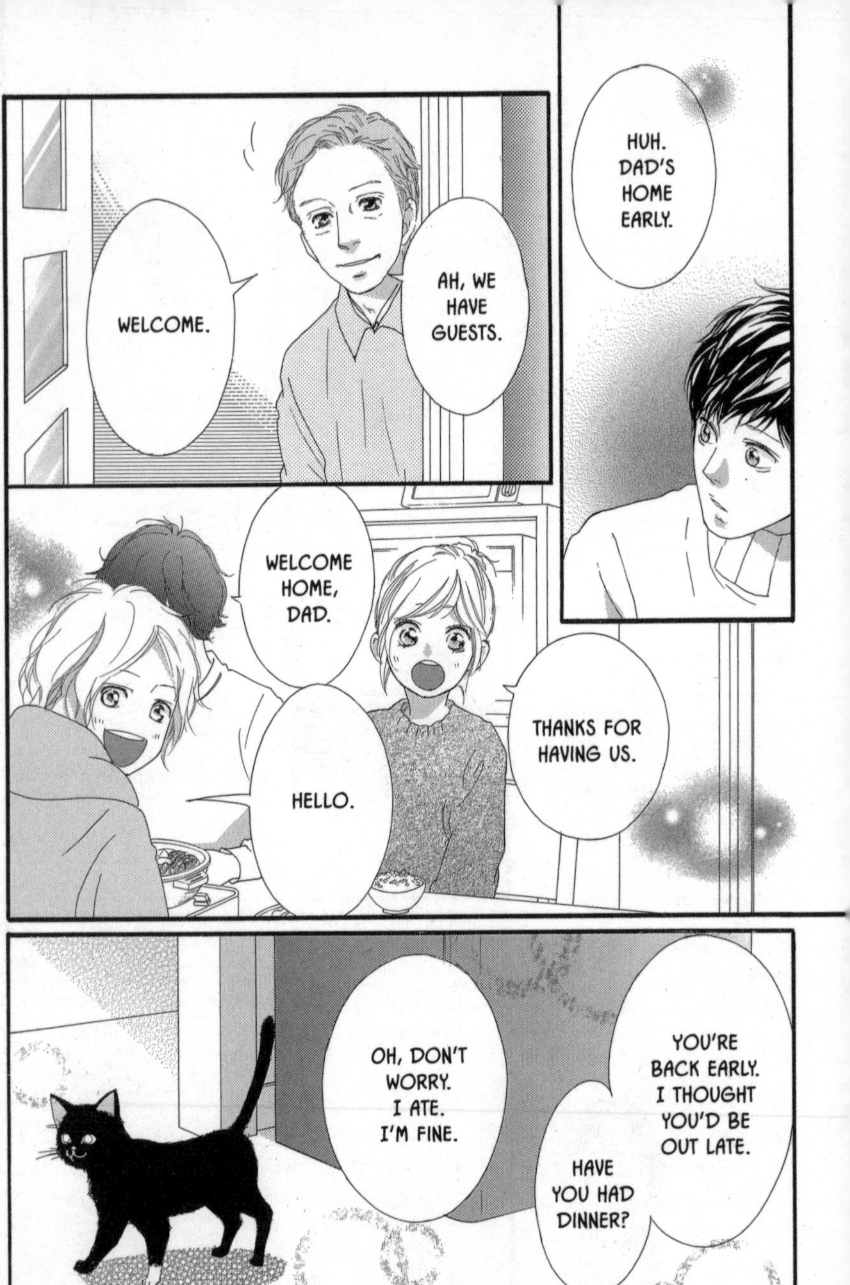
HUH. DAD'S HOME EARLY.
AH, WE HAVE GUESTS.
WELCOME.
THANKS FOR HAVING US.
WELCOME HOME, DAD.
HELLO.
YOU'RE BACK EARLY. I THOUGHT YOU'D BE OUT LATE.
HAVE YOU HAD DINNER?
OH, DON'T WORRY. I ATE. I'M FINE.

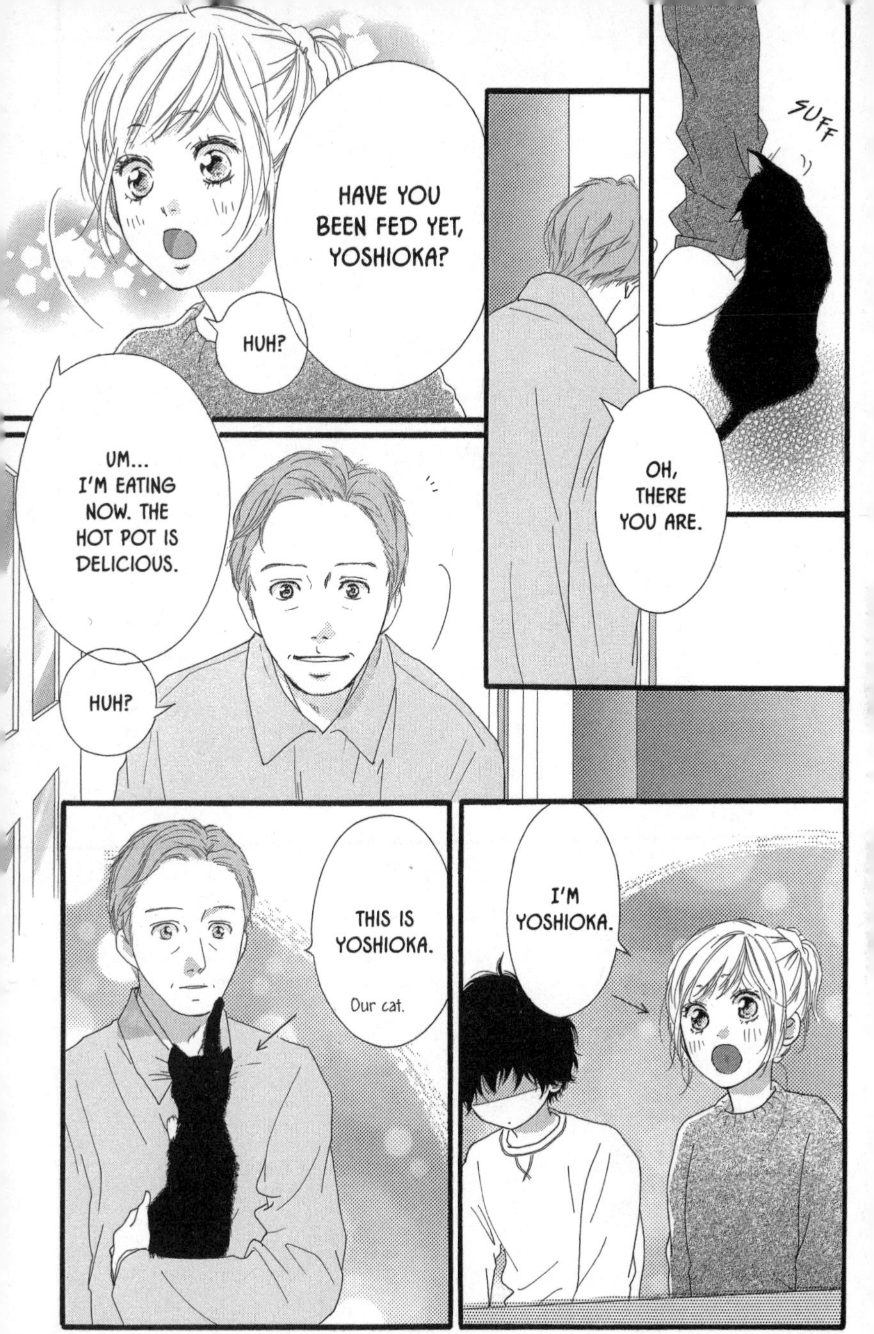
SUFF
OH, THERE YOU ARE.
HAVE YOU BEEN FED YET, YOSHIOKA?
HUH?
UM... I'M EATING NOW. THE HOT POT IS DELICIOUS.
HUH?
I'M YOSHIOKA.
THIS IS YOSHIOKA.
Our cat.

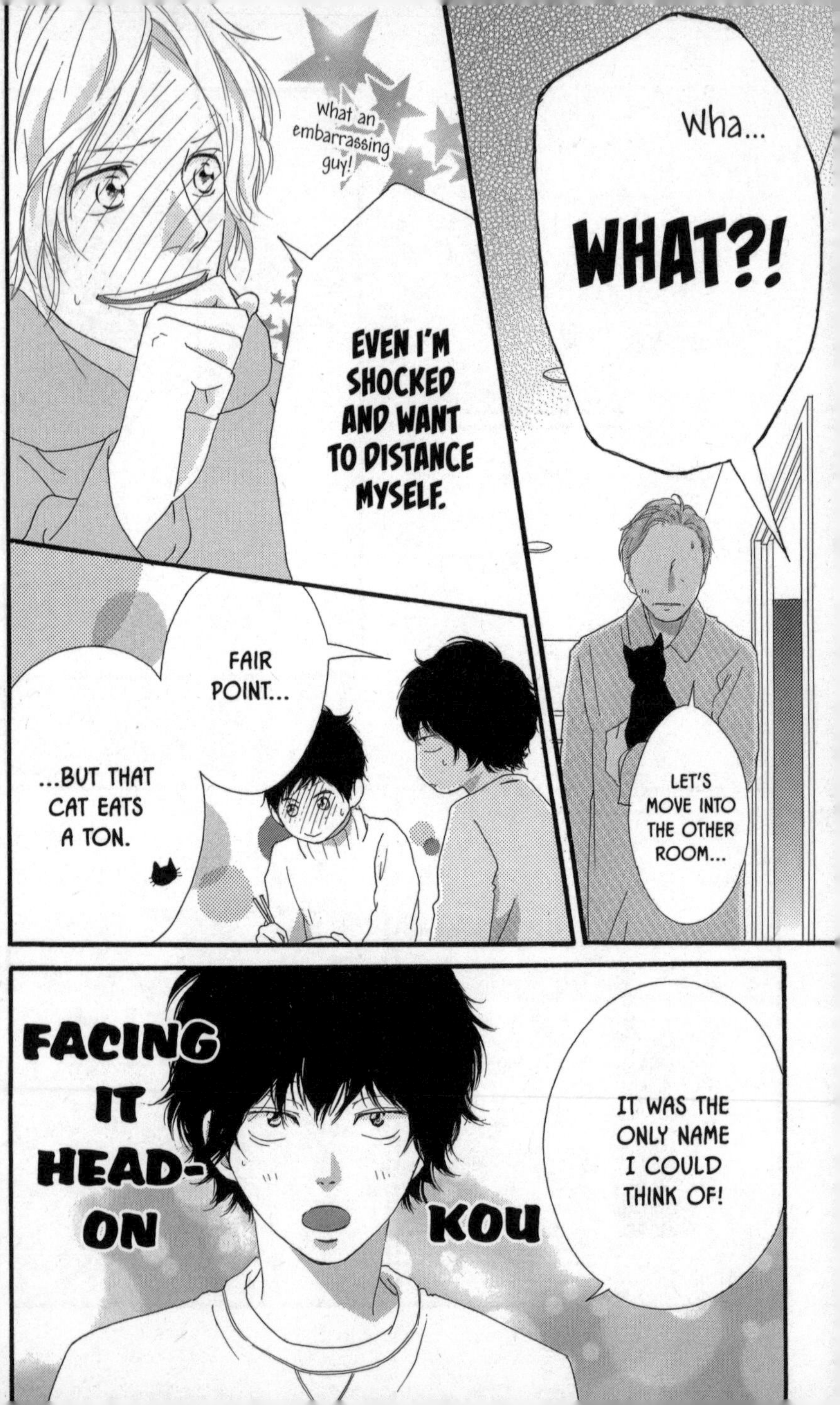
Wha...
WHAT?!
LET'S MOVE INTO THE OTHER ROOM...
What an embarrassing guy!
EVEN I'M SHOCKED AND WANT TO DISTANCE MYSELF.
FAIR POINT...
...BUT THAT CAT EATS A TON.
IT WAS THE ONLY NAME I COULD THINK OF!
FACING IT HEAD-ON KOU

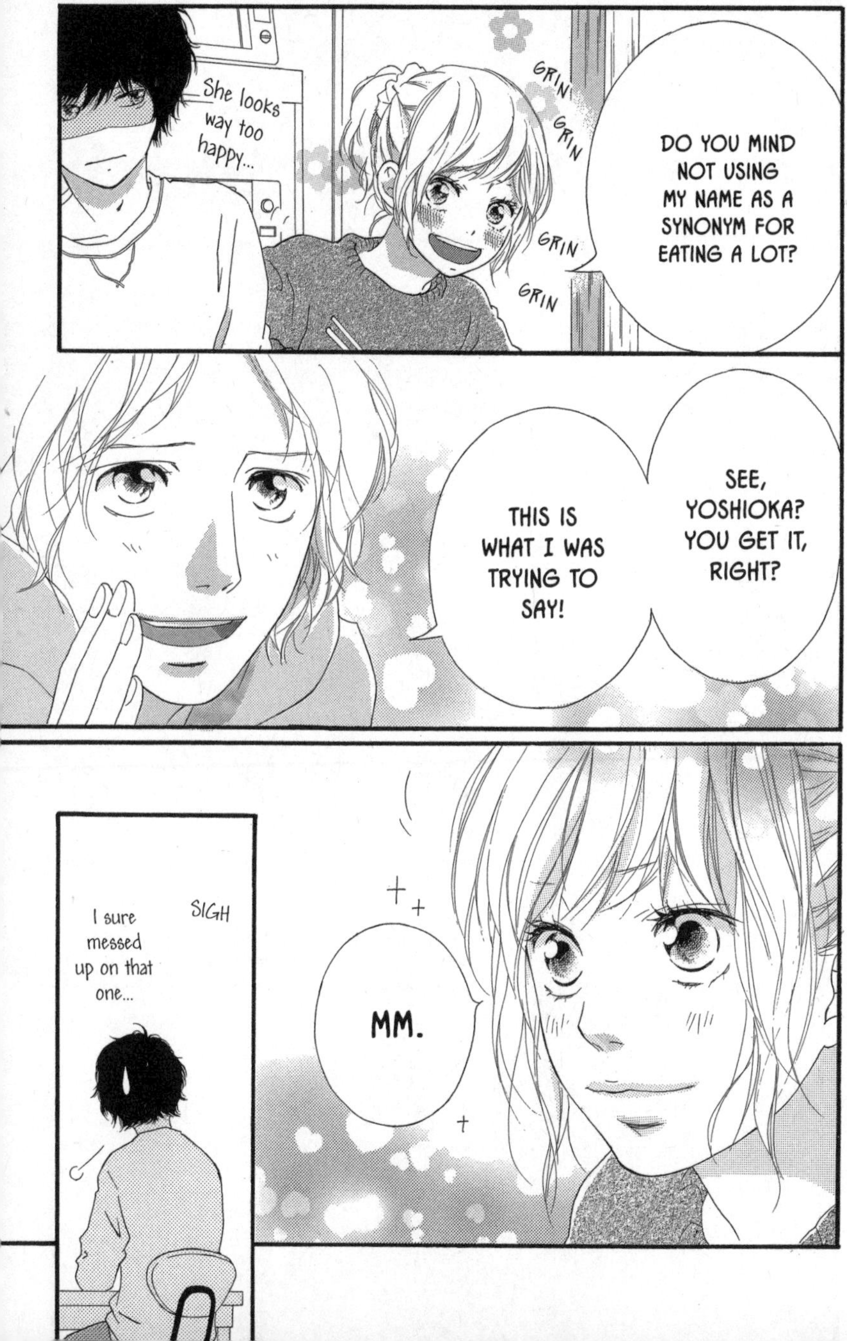
DO YOU MIND NOT USING MY NAME AS A SYNONYM FOR EATING A LOT?
GRIN GRIN GRIN GRIN
She looks way too happy...
SEE, YOSHIOKA? YOU GET IT, RIGHT?
THIS IS WHAT I WAS TRYING TO SAY!
MM.
SIGH
I sure messed up on that one...

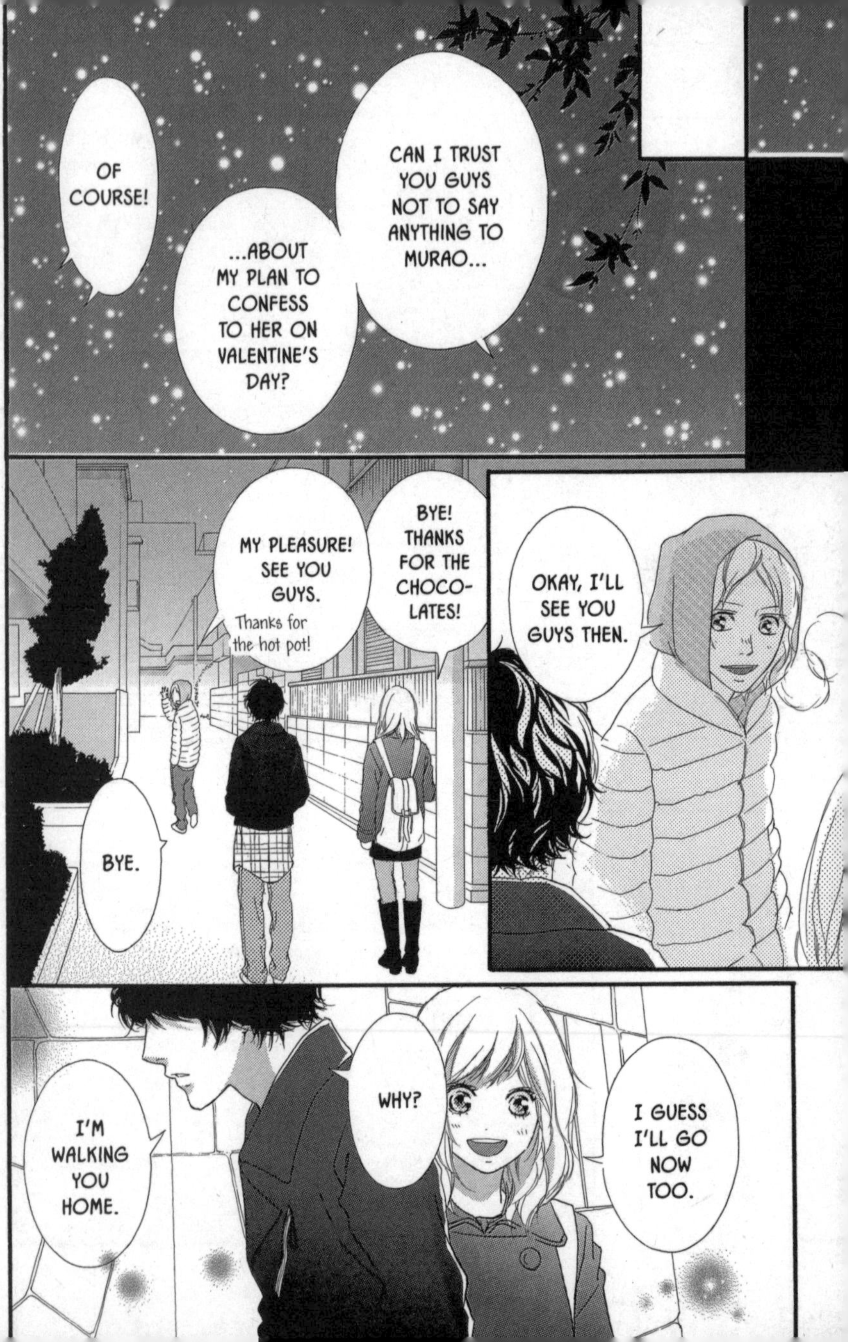
CAN I TRUST YOU GUYS NOT TO SAY ANYTHING TO MURAO...
...ABOUT MY PLAN TO CONFESS TO HER ON VALENTINE'S DAY?
OF COURSE!
OKAY, I'LL SEE YOU GUYS THEN.
BYE! THANKS FOR THE CHOCO-LATES!
MY PLEASURE! SEE YOU GUYS.
Thanks for the hot pot!
BYE.
I GUESS I'LL GO NOW TOO.
WHY?
I'M WALKING YOU HOME.

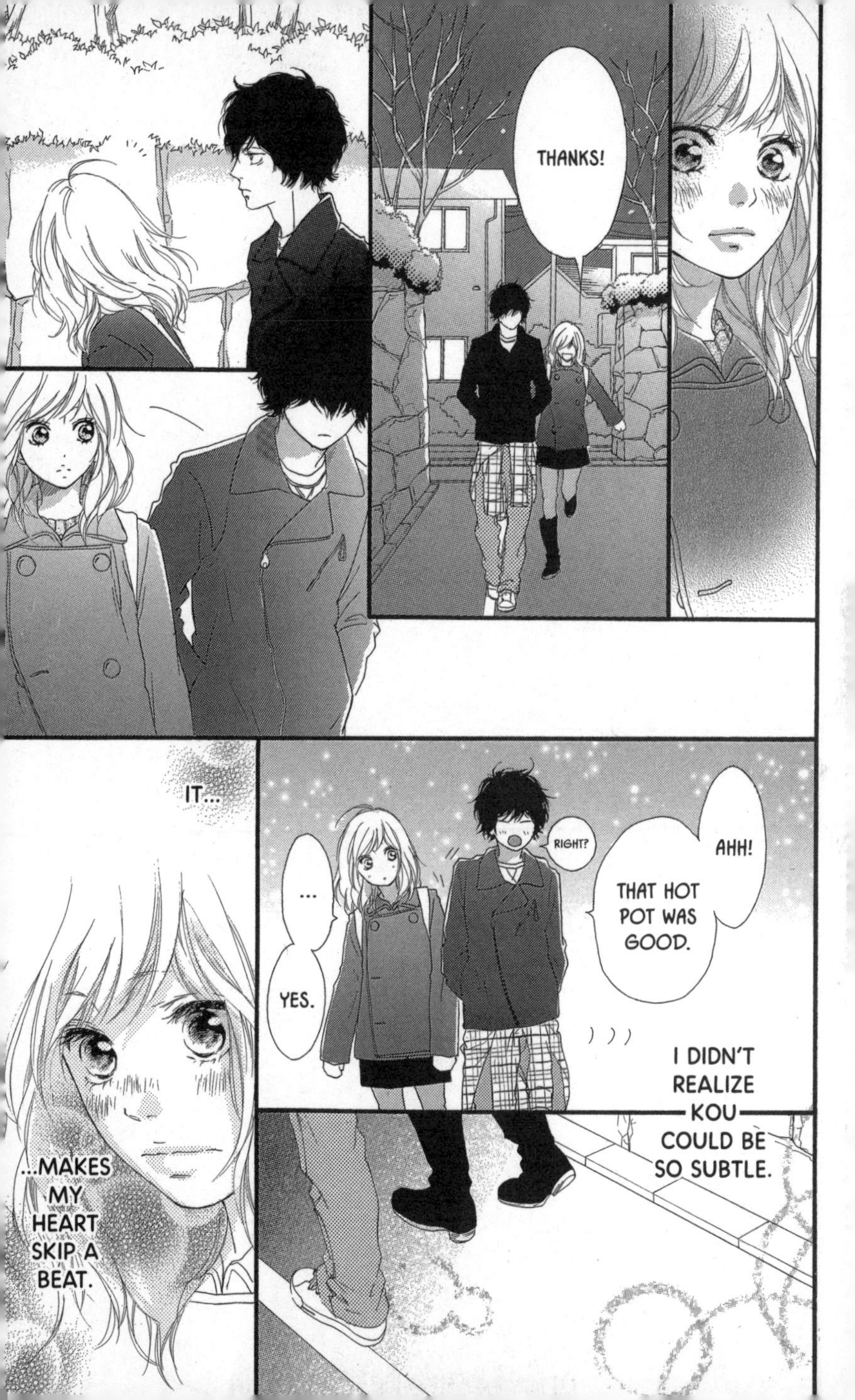
THANKS!
AHH!
THAT HOT POT WAS GOOD.
RIGHT?
...
YES.
I DIDN'T REALIZE KOU COULD BE SO SUBTLE.
IT...
...MAKES MY HEART SKIP A BEAT.

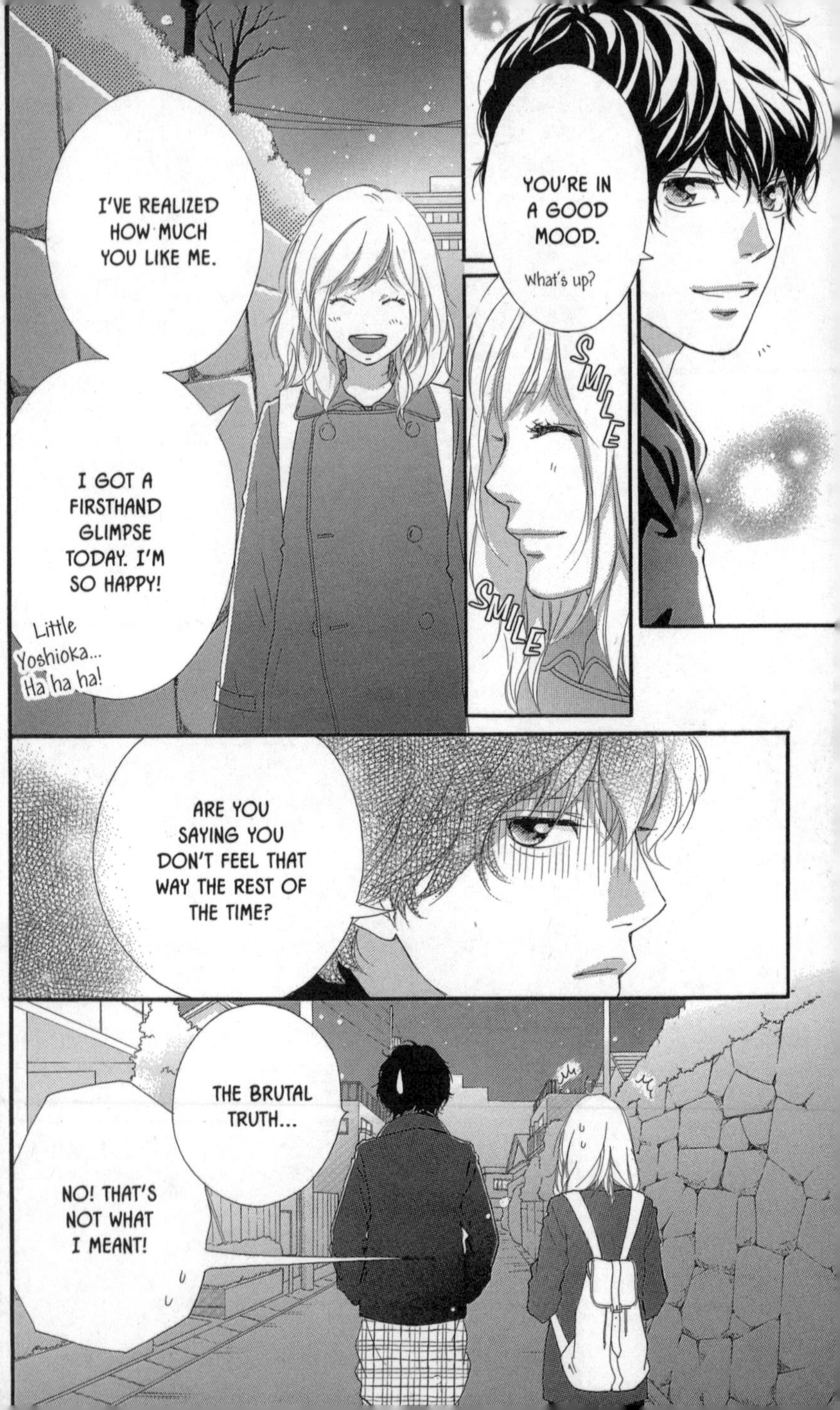
YOU'RE IN A GOOD MOOD.
What's up?
SMILE
SMILE
I'VE REALIZED HOW MUCH YOU LIKE ME.
I GOT A FIRSTHAND GLIMPSE TODAY. I'M SO HAPPY!
Little Yoshioka... Ha ha ha!
ARE YOU SAYING YOU DON'T FEEL THAT WAY THE REST OF THE TIME?
THE BRUTAL TRUTH...
NO! THAT'S NOT WHAT I MEANT!

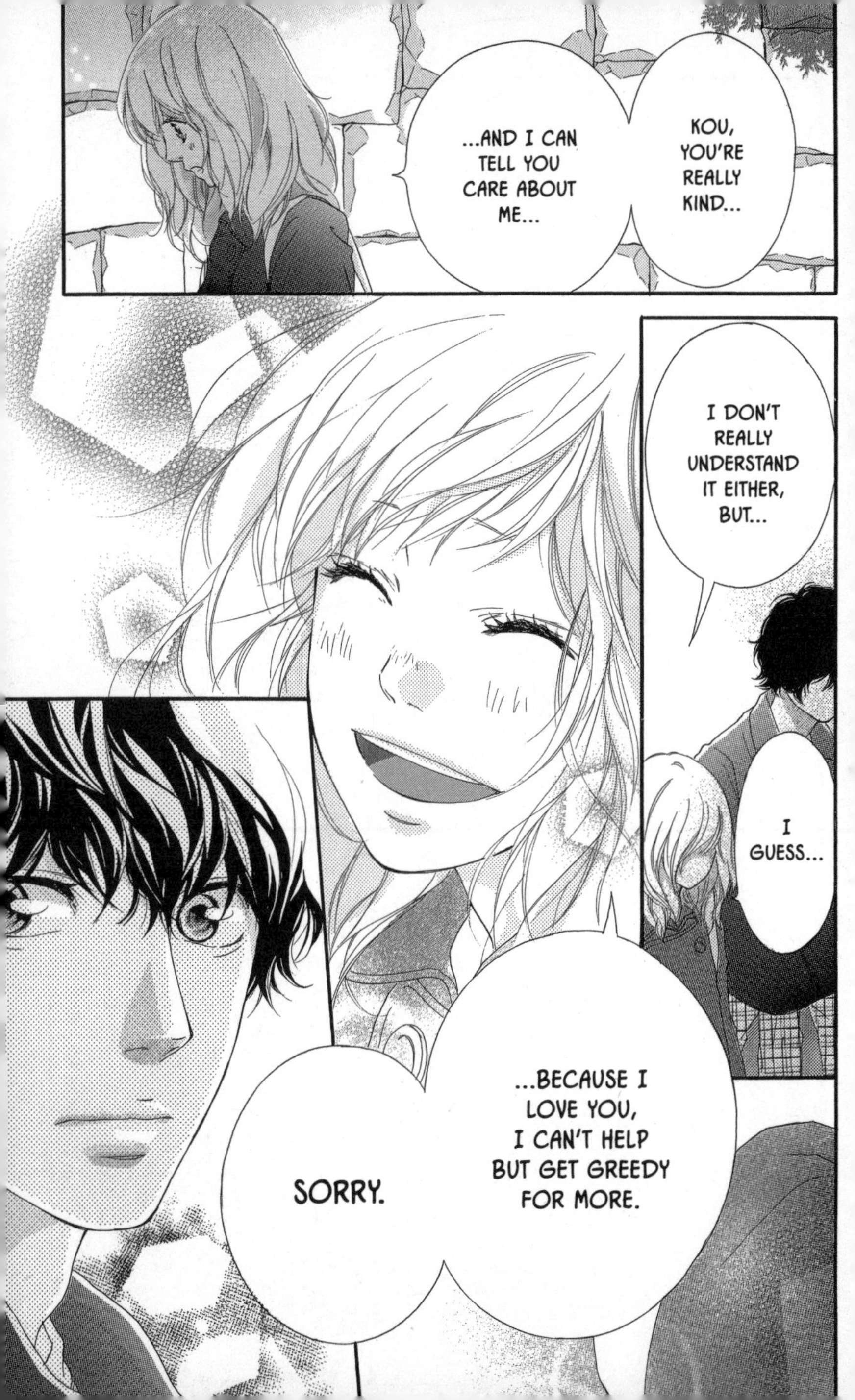
KOU, YOU'RE REALLY KIND...
...AND I CAN TELL YOU CARE ABOUT ME...
I DON'T REALLY UNDERSTAND IT EITHER, BUT...
I GUESS...
...BECAUSE I LOVE YOU, I CAN'T HELP BUT GET GREEDY FOR MORE.
SORRY.

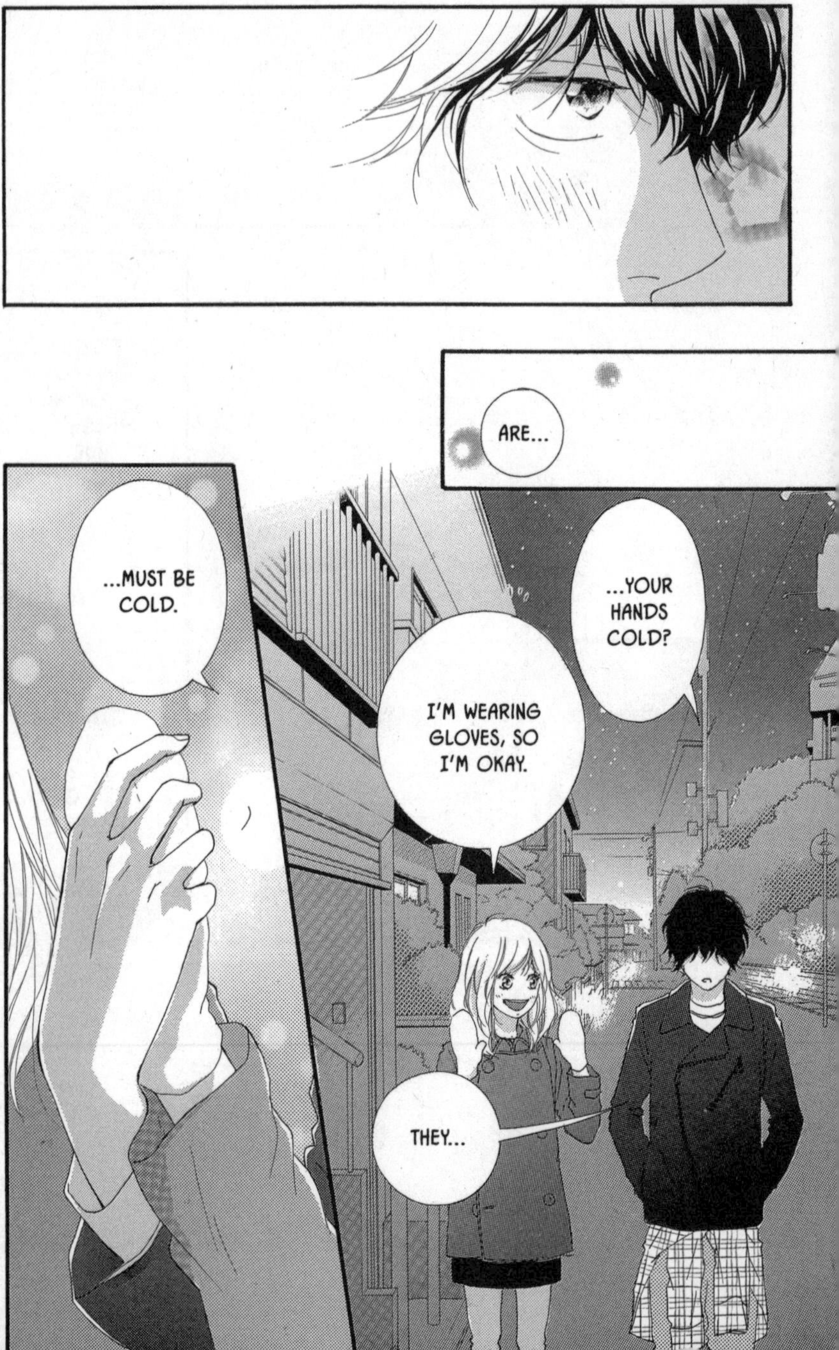
ARE...
...YOUR HANDS COLD?
I'M WEARING GLOVES, SO I'M OKAY.
THEY...
...MUST BE COLD.

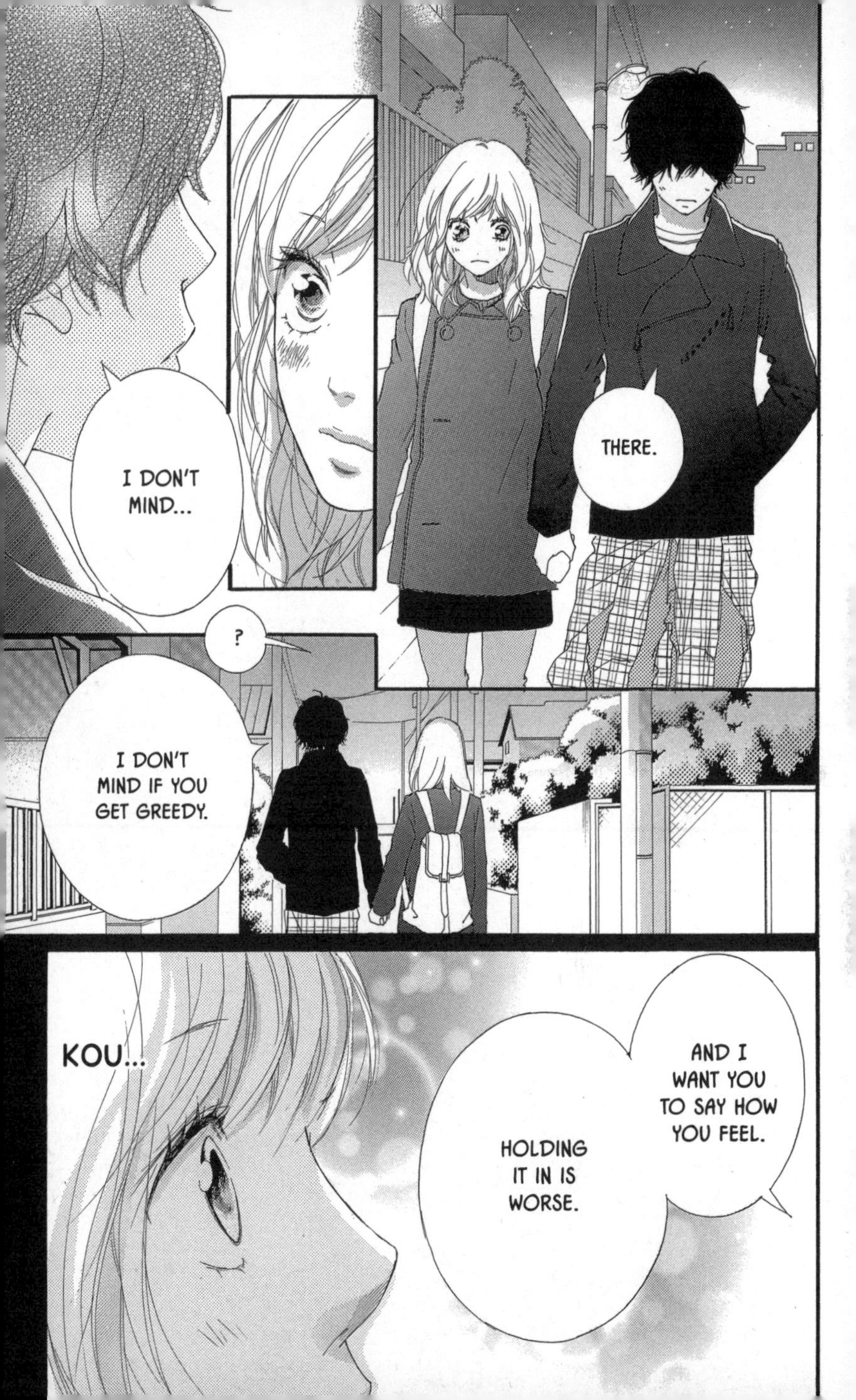
THERE.
I DON'T MIND...
?
I DON'T MIND IF YOU GET GREEDY.
AND I WANT YOU TO SAY HOW YOU FEEL.
HOLDING IT IN IS WORSE.
KOU...

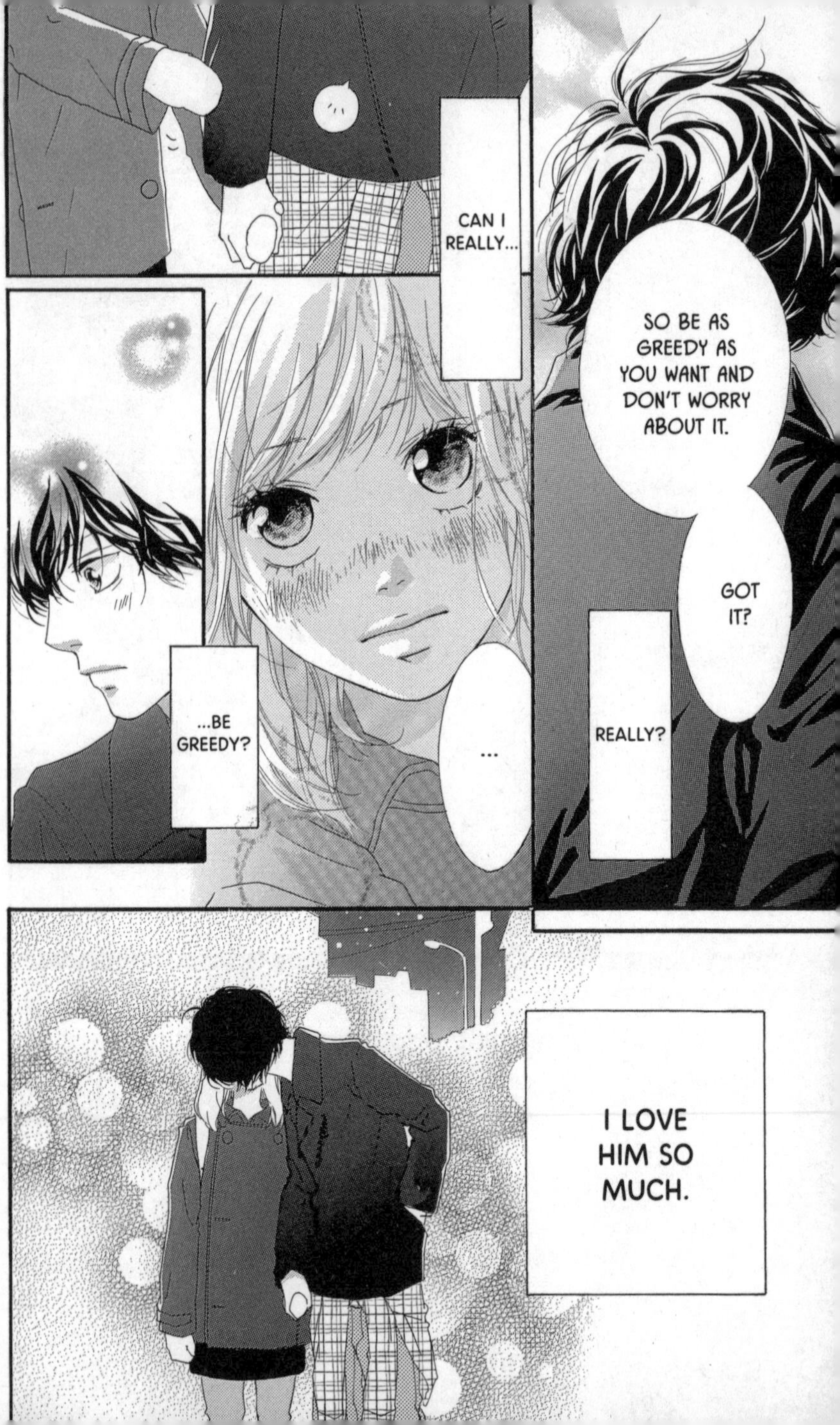
SO BE AS GREEDY AS YOU WANT AND DON'T WORRY ABOUT IT.
GOT IT?
REALLY?
CAN I REALLY...
...
...BE GREEDY?
I LOVE HIM SO MUCH.

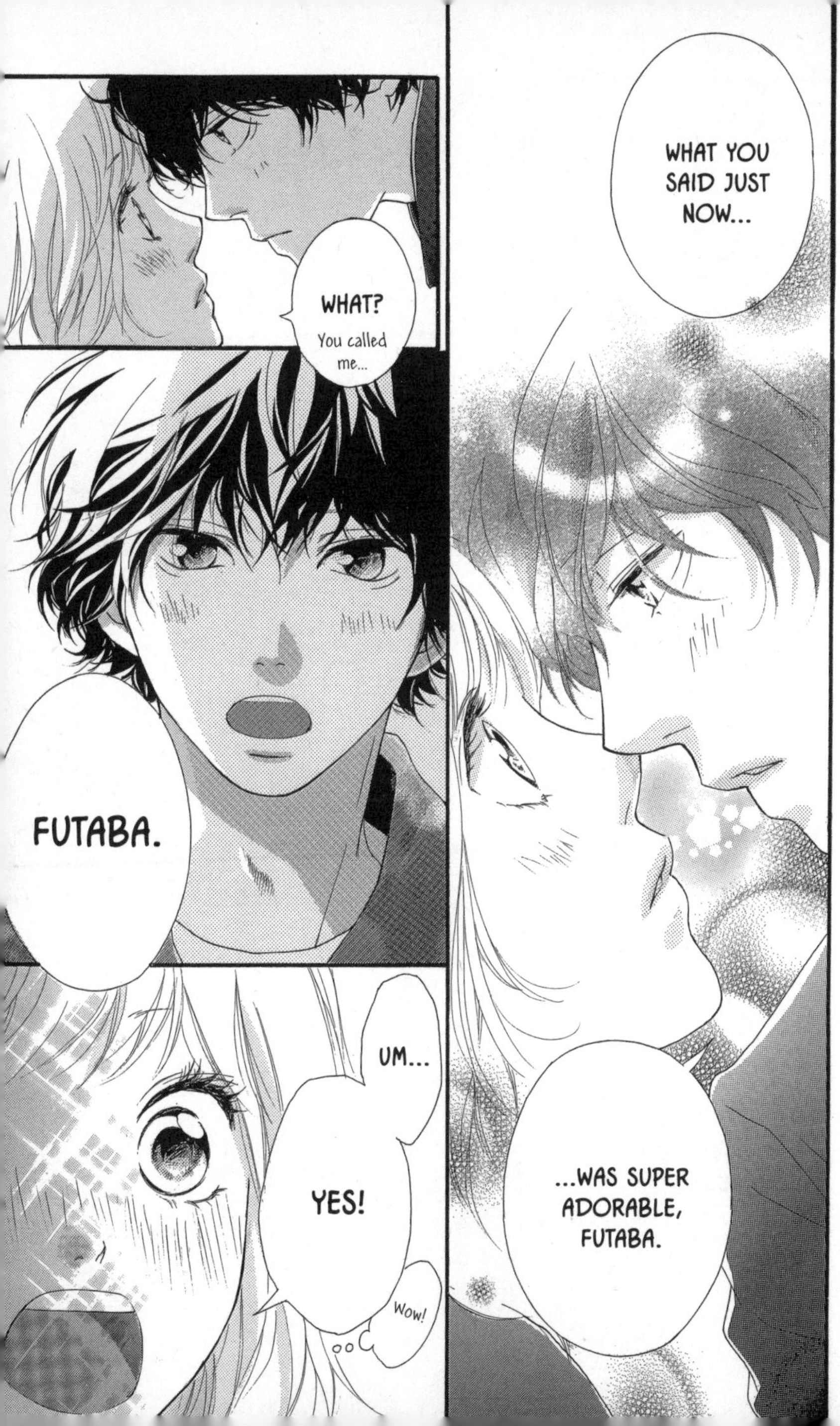
WHAT YOU SAID JUST NOW...
...WAS SUPER ADORABLE, FUTABA.
WHAT?
You called me...
FUTABA.
UM...
YES!
Wow!

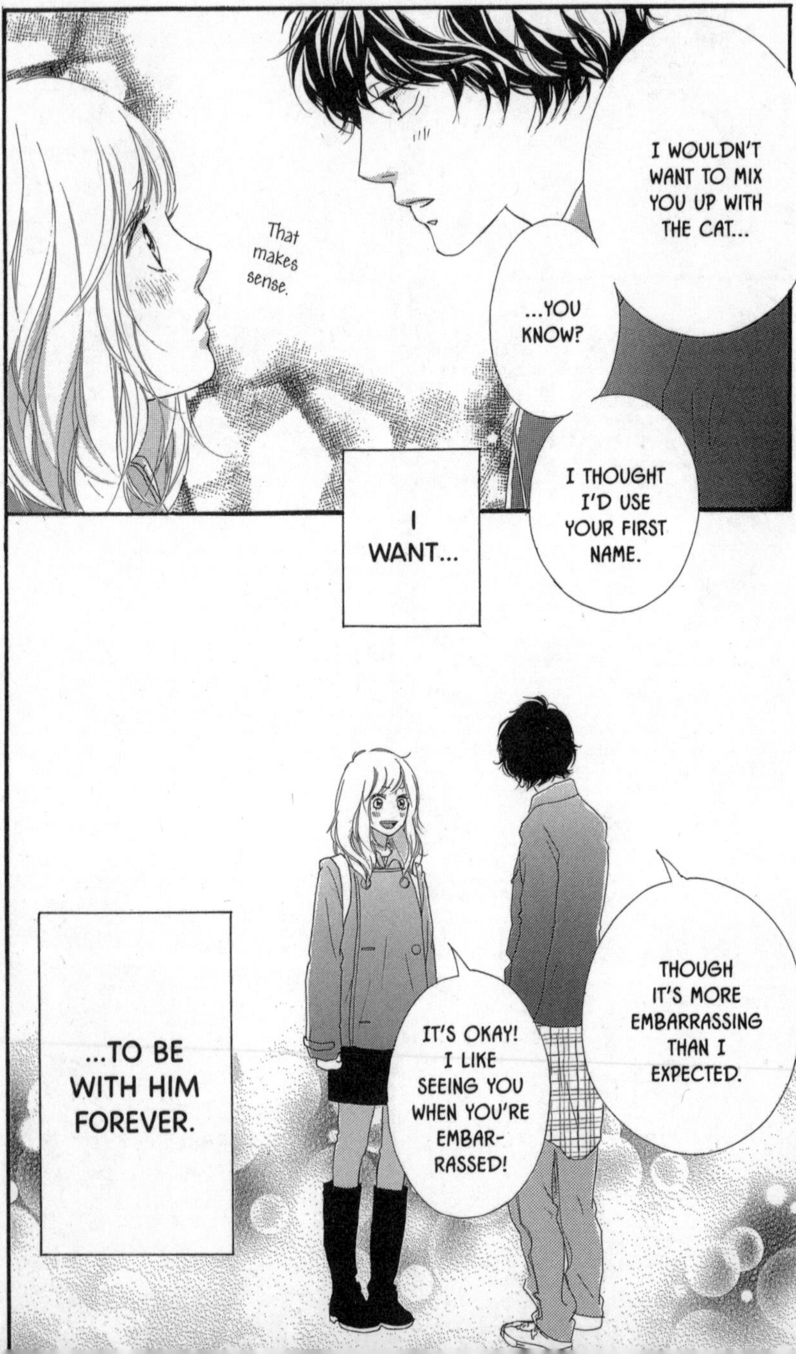

I WOULDN'T WANT TO MIX YOU UP WITH THE CAT...
...YOU KNOW?
That makes sense.
I THOUGHT I'D USE YOUR FIRST NAME.
I WANT...
THOUGH IT'S MORE EMBARRASSING THAN I EXPECTED.
IT'S OKAY! I LIKE SEEING YOU WHEN YOU'RE EMBAR-RASSED!
...TO BE WITH HIM FOREVER.

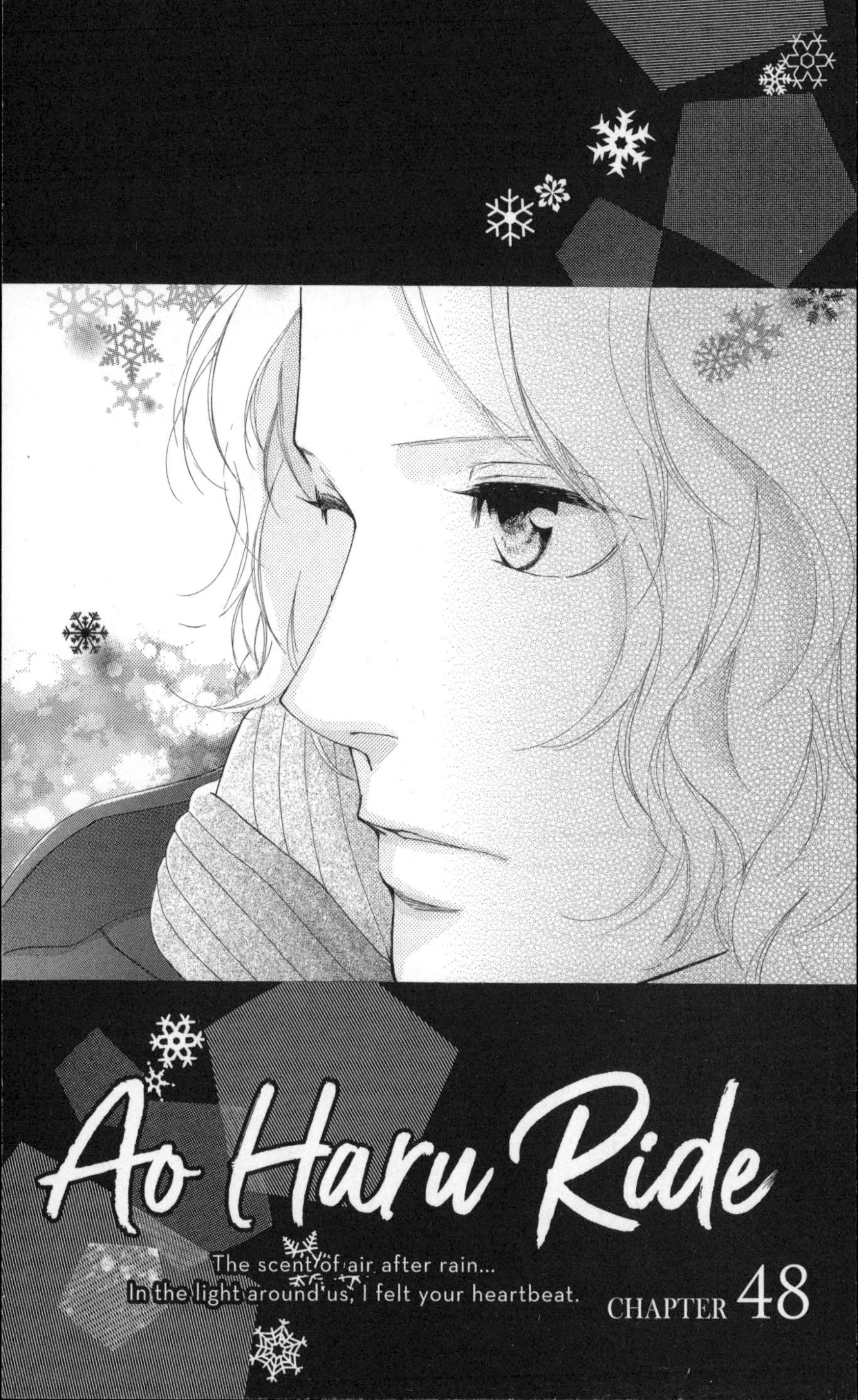
Ao Haru Ride
The scent of air after rain...
In the light around us, I felt your heartbeat.
CHAPTER 48

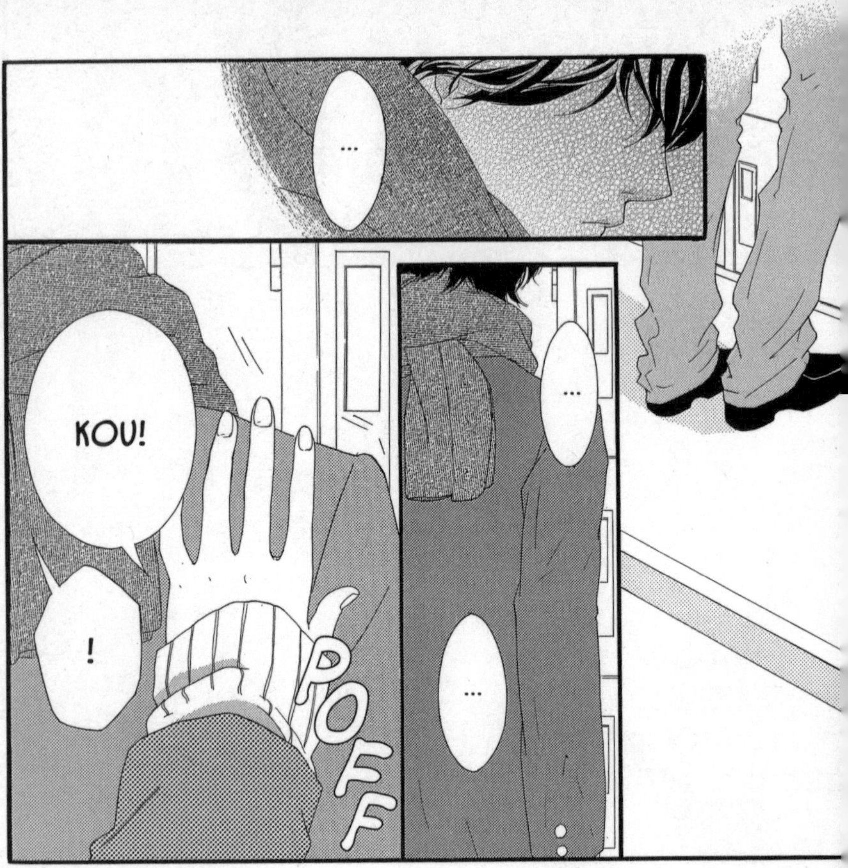
...
...
...
KOU!
!
POFF

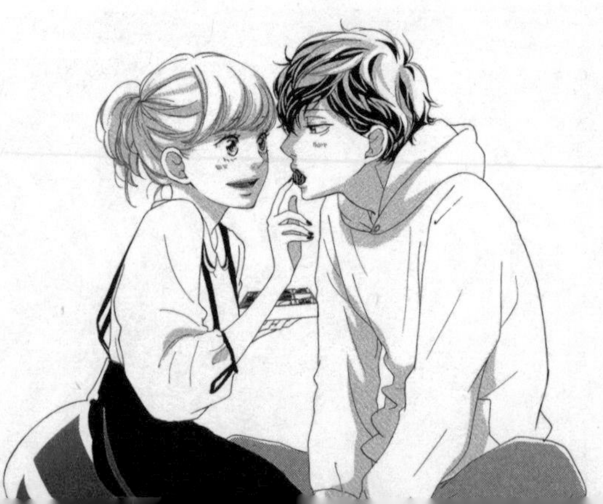

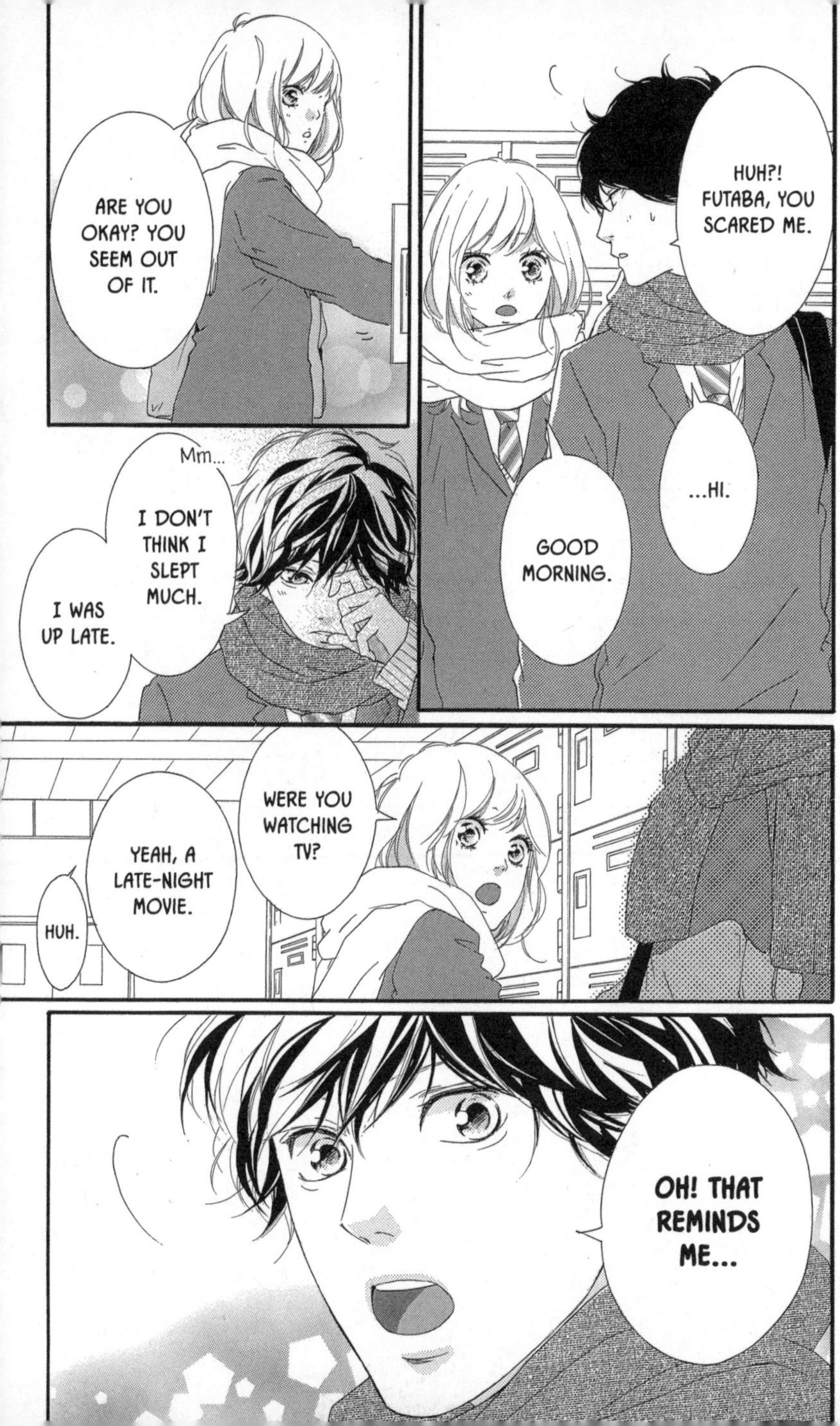
HUH?! FUTABA, YOU SCARED ME.
...HI.
GOOD MORNING.
ARE YOU OKAY? YOU SEEM OUT OF IT.
Mm...
I DON'T THINK I SLEPT MUCH.
I WAS UP LATE.
WERE YOU WATCHING TV?
YEAH, A LATE-NIGHT MOVIE.
HUH.
OH! THAT REMINDS ME...

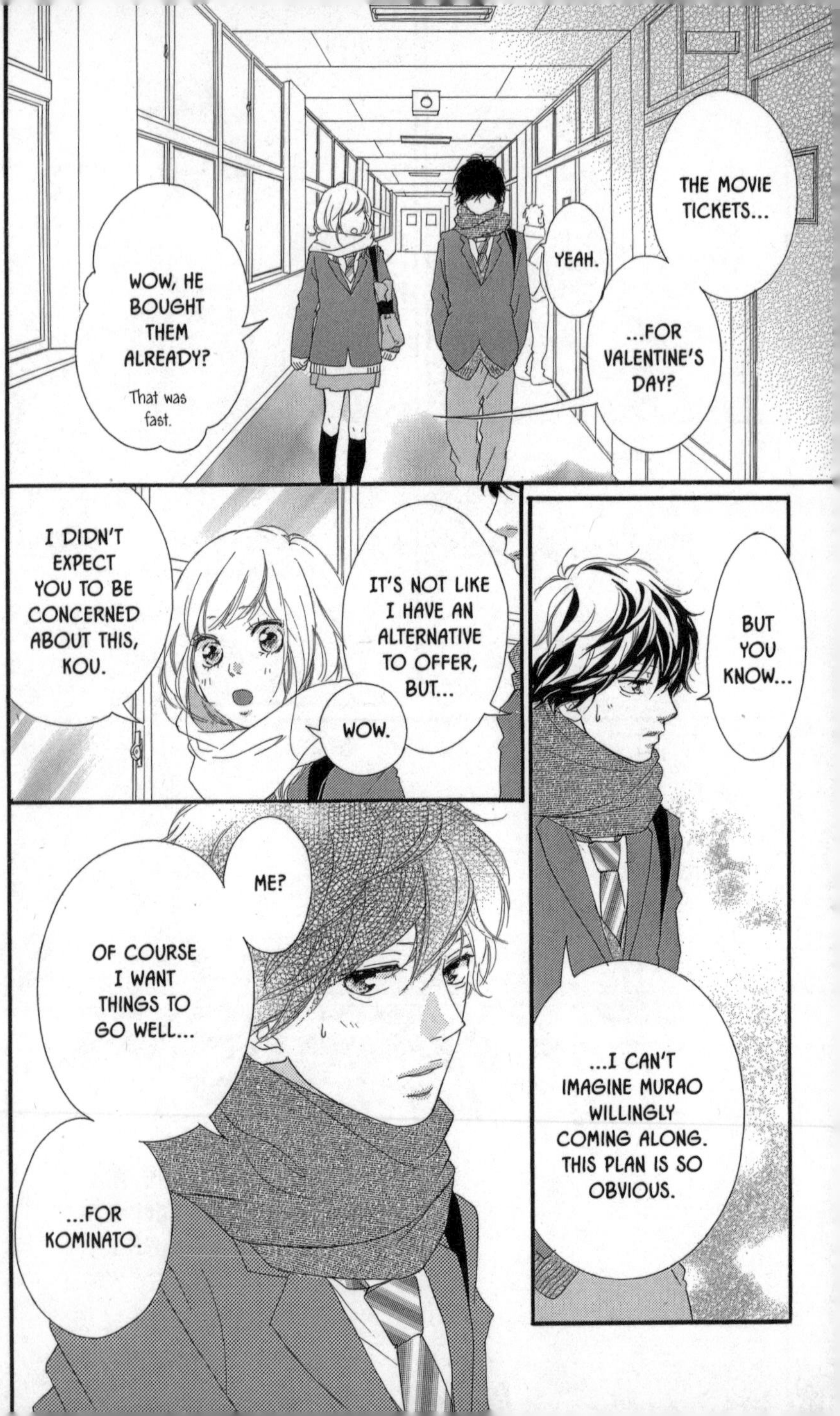
THE MOVIE TICKETS...
YEAH.
...FOR VALENTINE'S DAY?
WOW, HE BOUGHT THEM ALREADY?
That was fast.
BUT YOU KNOW...
...I CAN'T IMAGINE MURAO WILLINGLY COMING ALONG. THIS PLAN IS SO OBVIOUS.
IT'S NOT LIKE I HAVE AN ALTERNATIVE TO OFFER, BUT...
WOW.
I DIDN'T EXPECT YOU TO BE CONCERNED ABOUT THIS, KOU.
ME?
OF COURSE I WANT THINGS TO GO WELL...
...FOR KOMINATO.

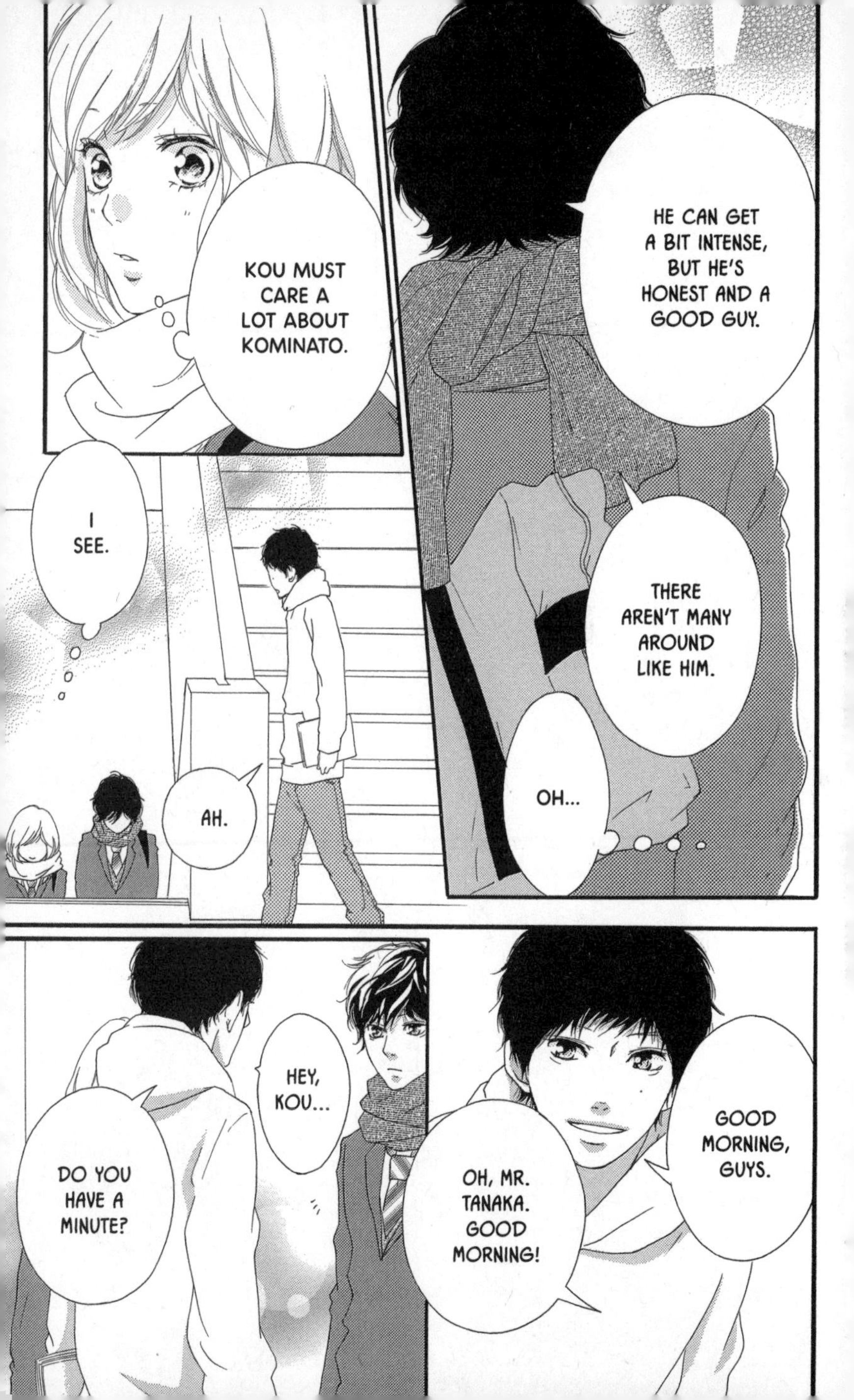
HE CAN GET A BIT INTENSE, BUT HE'S HONEST AND A GOOD GUY.
THERE AREN'T MANY AROUND LIKE HIM.
OH...
KOU MUST CARE A LOT ABOUT KOMINATO.
I SEE.
AH.
GOOD MORNING, GUYS.
OH, MR. TANAKA. GOOD MORNING!
HEY, KOU...
DO YOU HAVE A MINUTE?

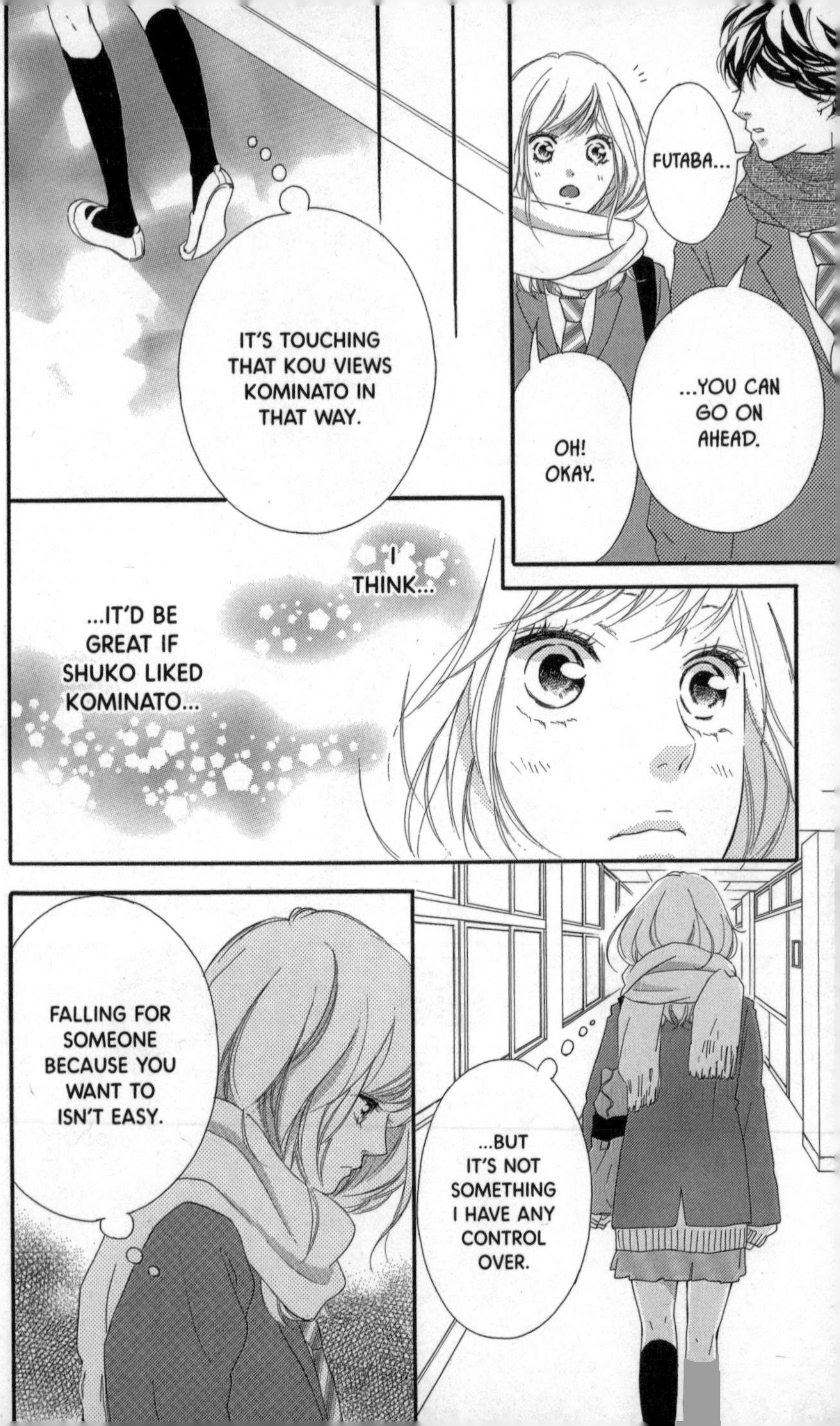
FUTABA...
...YOU CAN GO ON AHEAD.
OH! OKAY.
IT'S TOUCHING THAT KOU VIEWS KOMINATO IN THAT WAY.
I THINK...
...IT'D BE GREAT IF SHUKO LIKED KOMINATO...
...BUT IT'S NOT SOMETHING I HAVE ANY CONTROL OVER.
FALLING FOR SOMEONE BECAUSE YOU WANT TO ISN'T EASY.

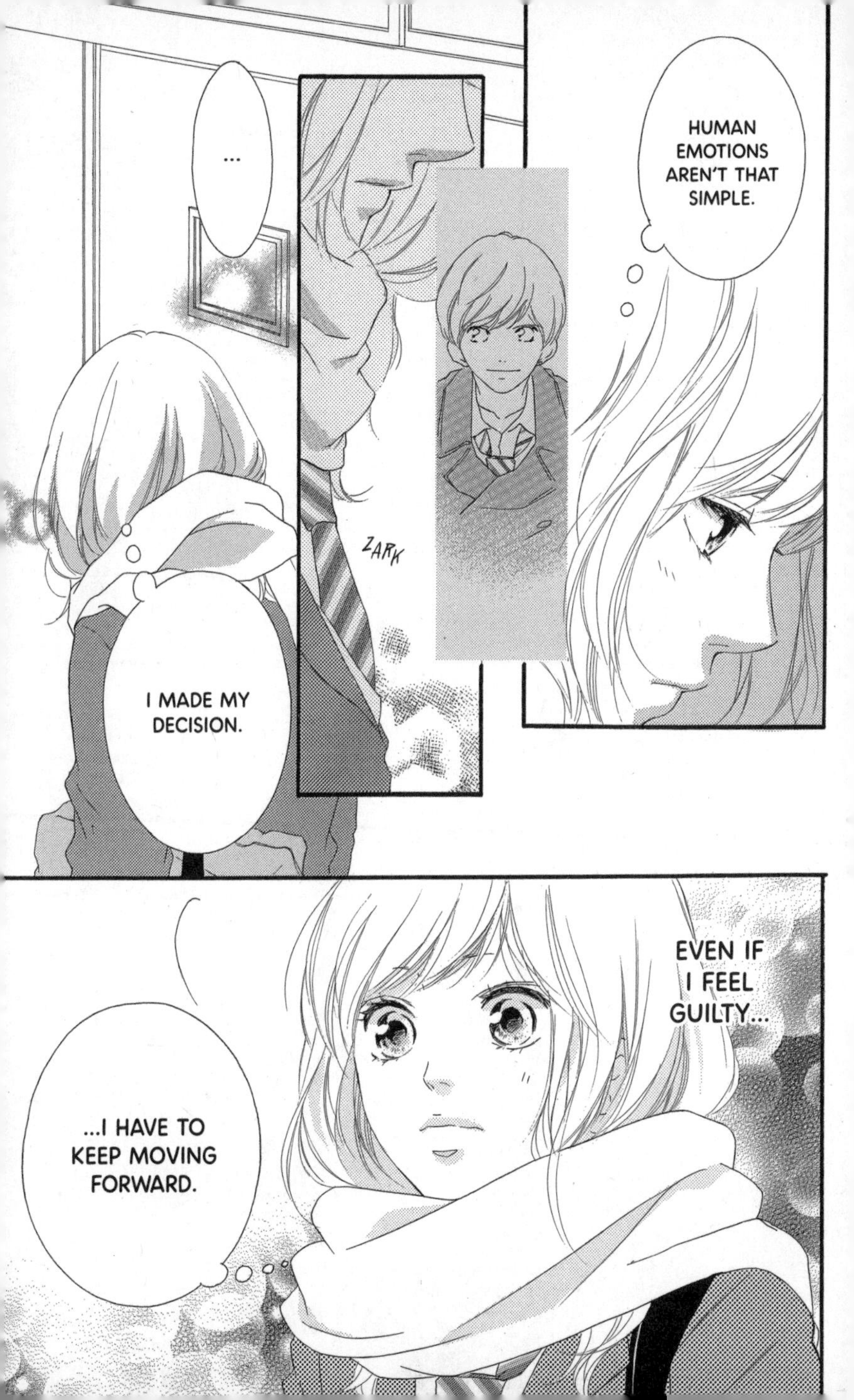
HUMAN EMOTIONS AREN'T THAT SIMPLE.
ZARK
...
I MADE MY DECISION.
EVEN IF I FEEL GUILTY...
...I HAVE TO KEEP MOVING FORWARD.

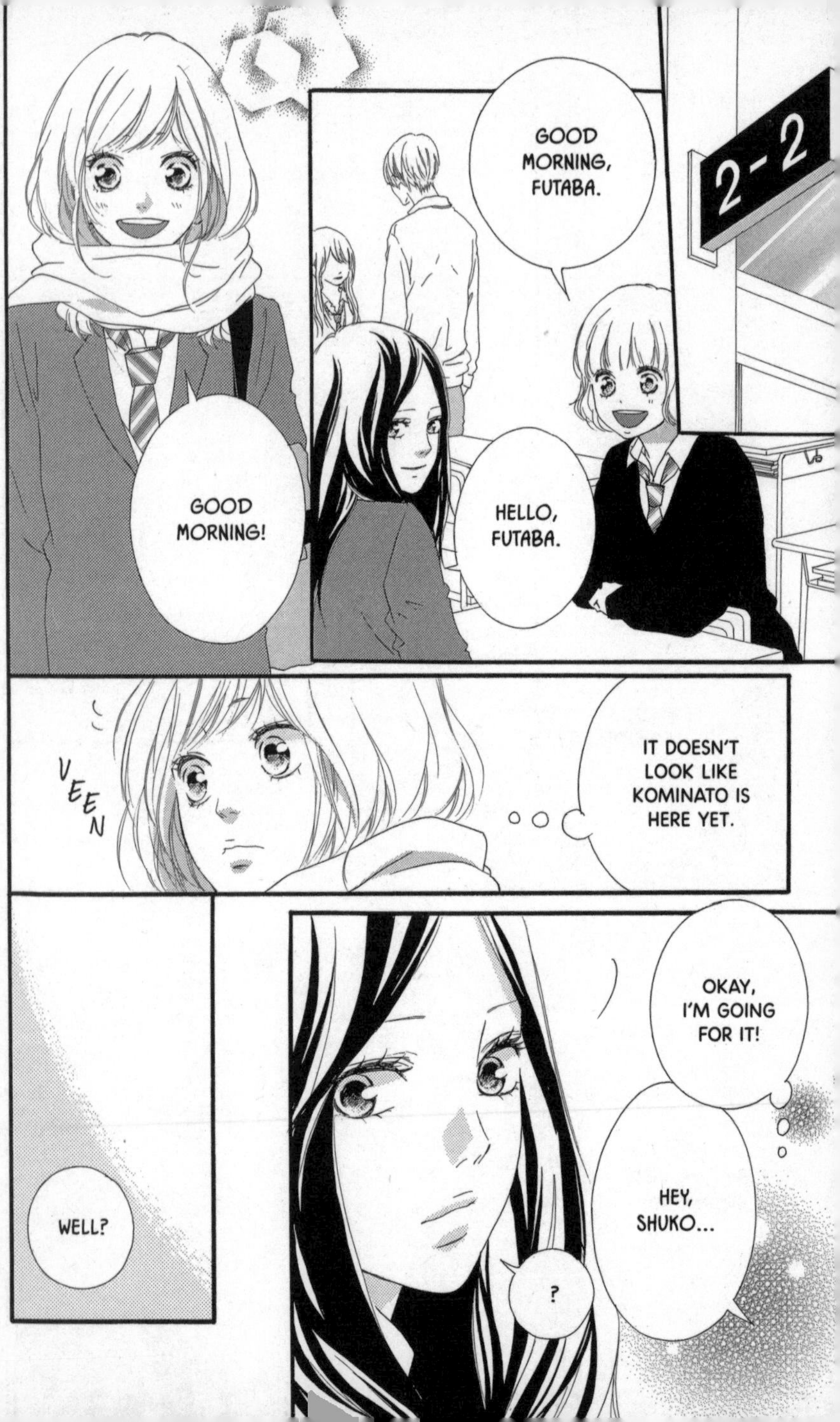
GOOD MORNING, FUTABA.
HELLO, FUTABA.
GOOD MORNING!
IT DOESN'T LOOK LIKE KOMINATO IS HERE YET.
VEEN
OKAY, I'M GOING FOR IT!
HEY, SHUKO...
?
WELL?

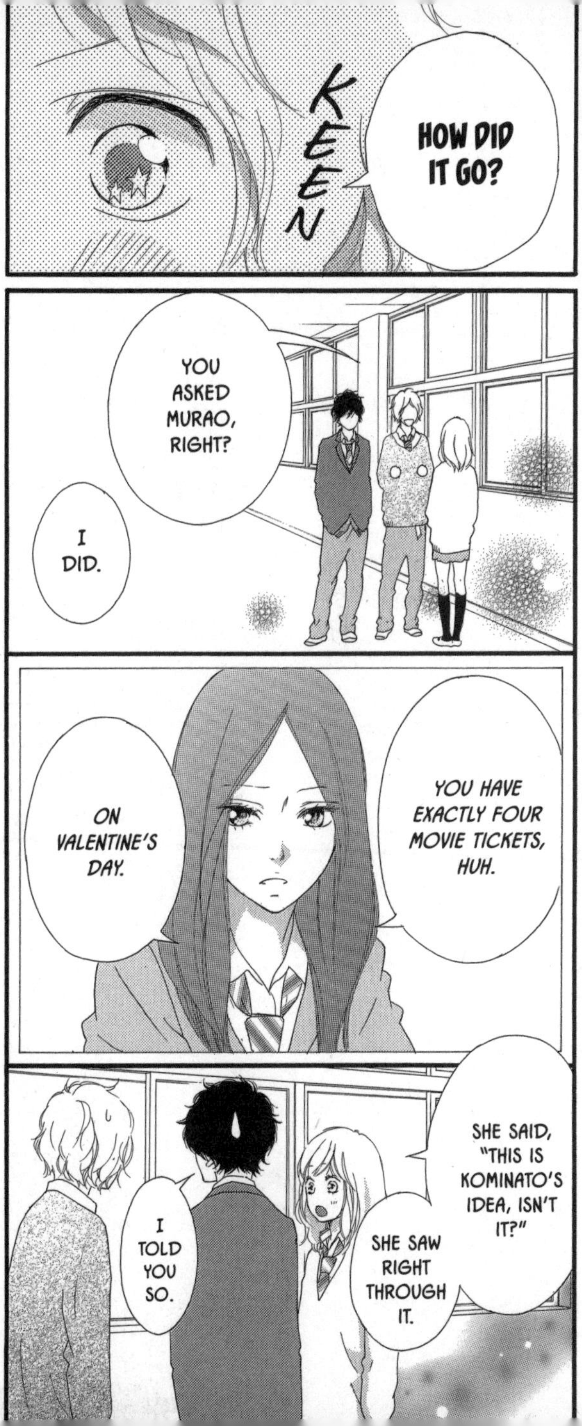
HOW DID IT GO?
KEEN
YOU ASKED MURAO, RIGHT?
I DID.
YOU HAVE EXACTLY FOUR MOVIE TICKETS, HUH.
ON VALENTINE'S DAY.
SHE SAID, "THIS IS KOMINATO'S IDEA, ISN'T IT?"
SHE SAW RIGHT THROUGH IT.
I TOLD YOU SO.

When I can't think of a story idea, it's absolutely agonizing. If I panic, nothing comes out. When I get to the point where I don't know what I'm supposed to be thinking anymore, I become sleepy from using up my energy in vain. (This is also known as escaping reality.) When I'm feeling cornered, but then an inkling of an idea starts to emerge—WAHOO! It's the best feeling. When that happens, I get up and make myself some more coffee, or I start aimlessly roaming around my house. This is how I express my joy. I get so excited that I can't sit still. I do these things to let out some of my pent-up energy before heading back to my desk. But the times when I start working again only to realize the idea won't cut it... Well, that's when I know I'm going to go sulk in bed.

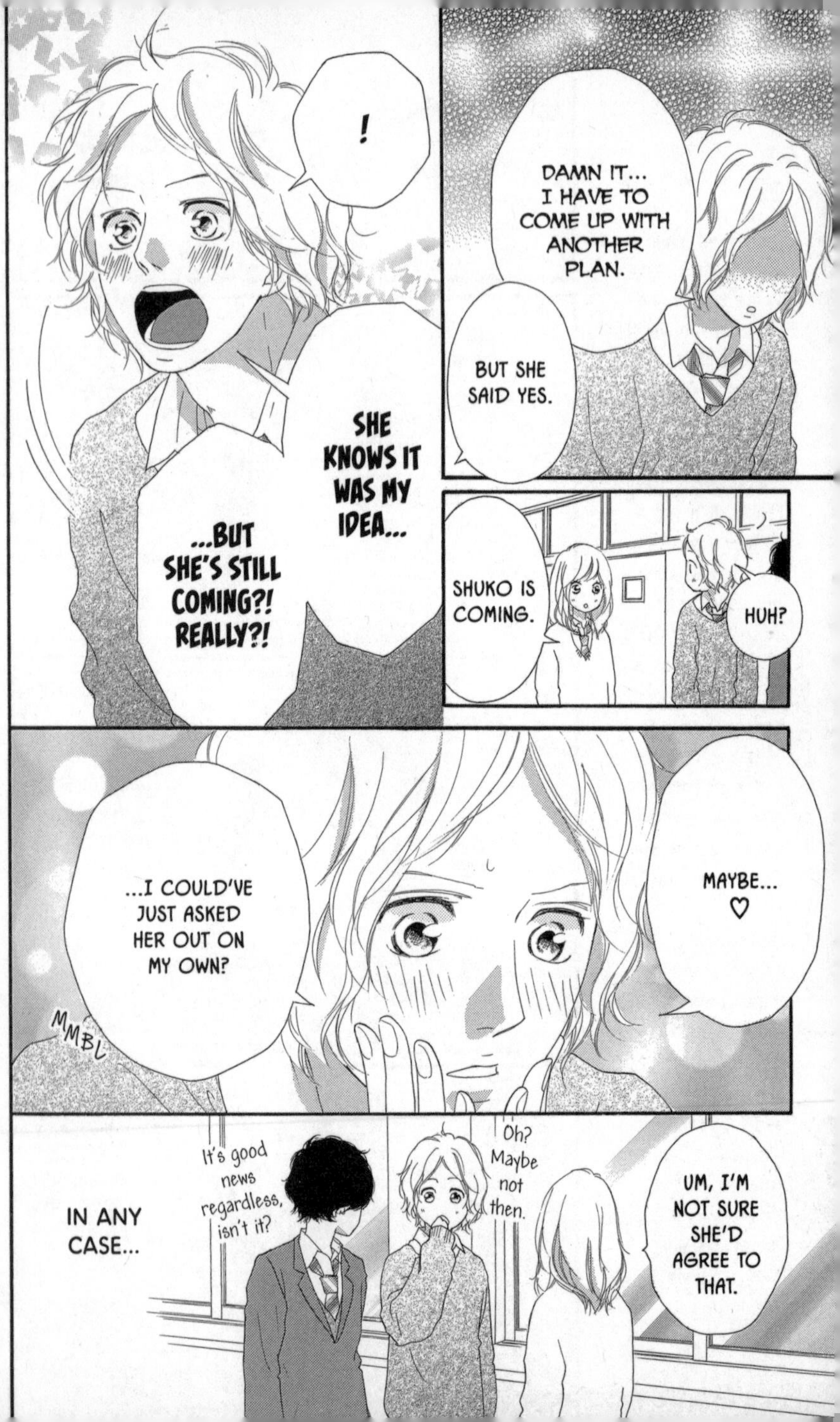
DAMN IT... I HAVE TO COME UP WITH ANOTHER PLAN.
BUT SHE SAID YES.
SHUKO IS COMING.
HUH?
!
SHE KNOWS IT WAS MY IDEA...
...BUT SHE'S STILL COMING?! REALLY?!
MAYBE... ♡
...I COULD'VE JUST ASKED HER OUT ON MY OWN?
MMBL
UM, I'M NOT SURE SHE'D AGREE TO THAT.
Oh? Maybe not then.
It's good news regardless, isn't it?
IN ANY CASE...

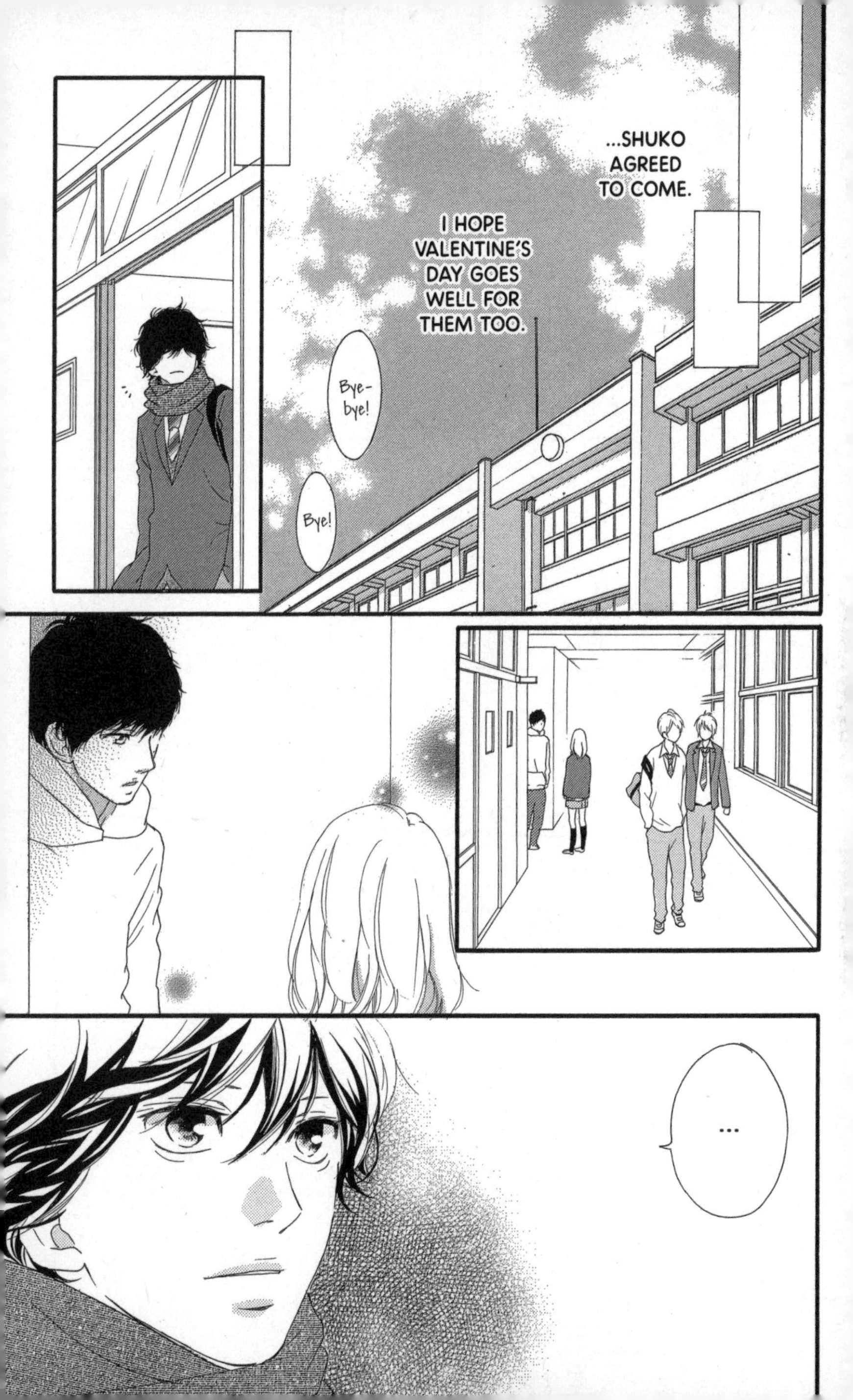
...SHUKO AGREED TO COME.
I HOPE VALENTINE'S DAY GOES WELL FOR THEM TOO.
Bye-bye!
Bye!
...

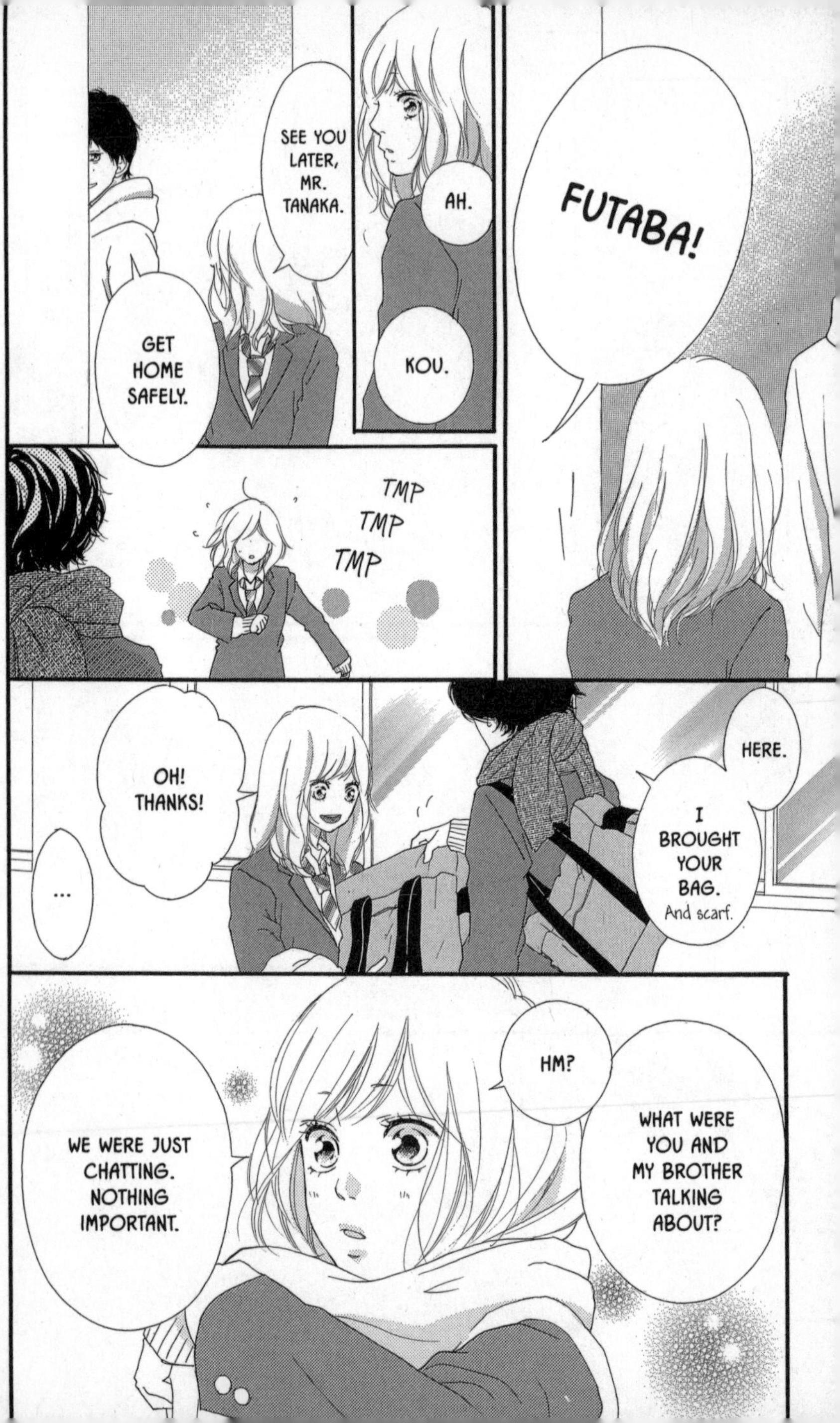
FUTABA!
AH.
KOU.
SEE YOU LATER, MR. TANAKA.
GET HOME SAFELY.
TMP TMP TMP
HERE.
I BROUGHT YOUR BAG. And scarf.
OH! THANKS!
...
HM?
WHAT WERE YOU AND MY BROTHER TALKING ABOUT?
WE WERE JUST CHATTING. NOTHING IMPORTANT.

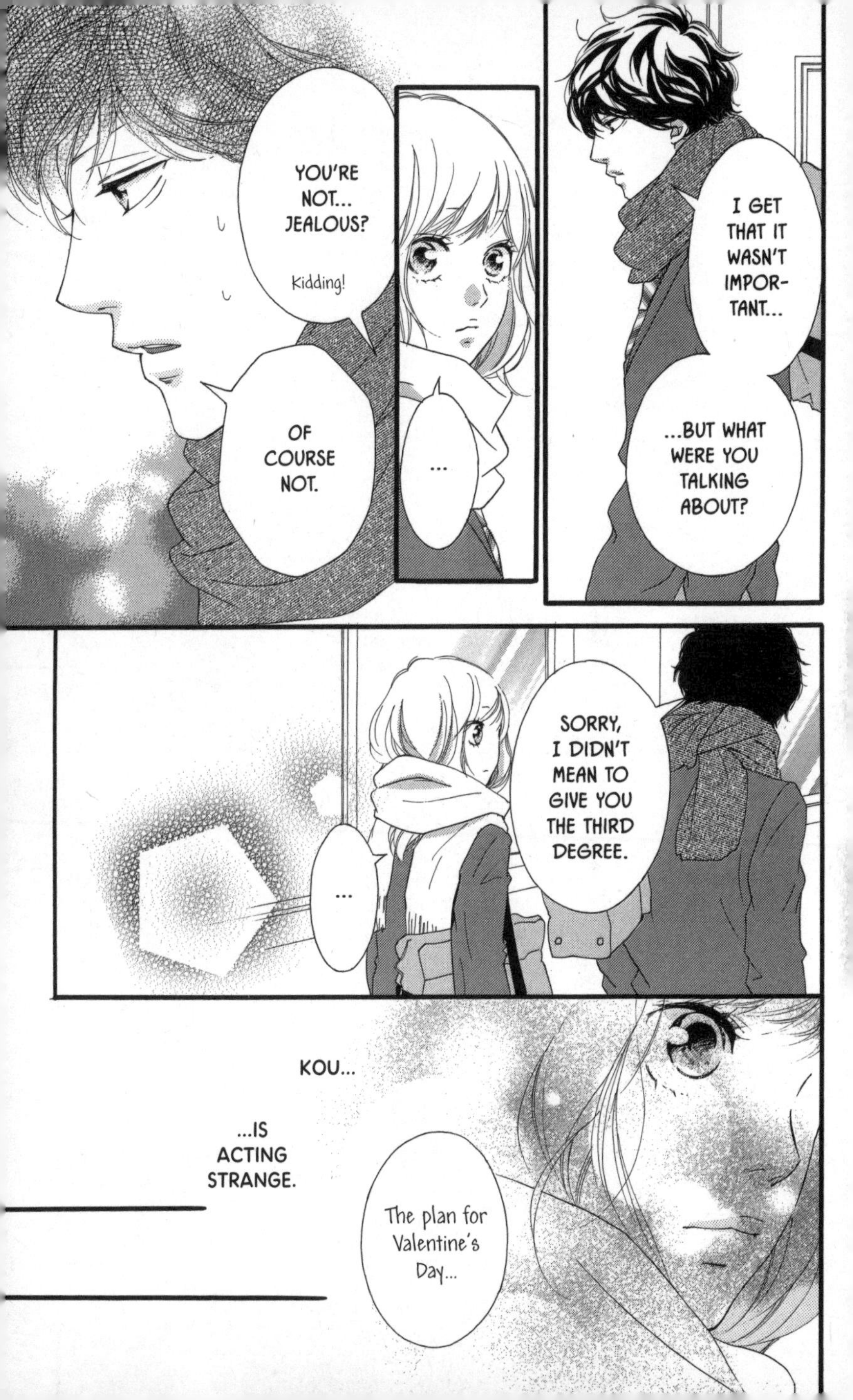

I GET THAT IT WASN'T IMPORTANT...
...BUT WHAT WERE YOU TALKING ABOUT?
...
YOU'RE NOT... JEALOUS?
Kidding!
OF COURSE NOT.
SORRY, I DIDN'T MEAN TO GIVE YOU THE THIRD DEGREE.
...
KOU...
...IS ACTING STRANGE.
The plan for Valentine's Day...

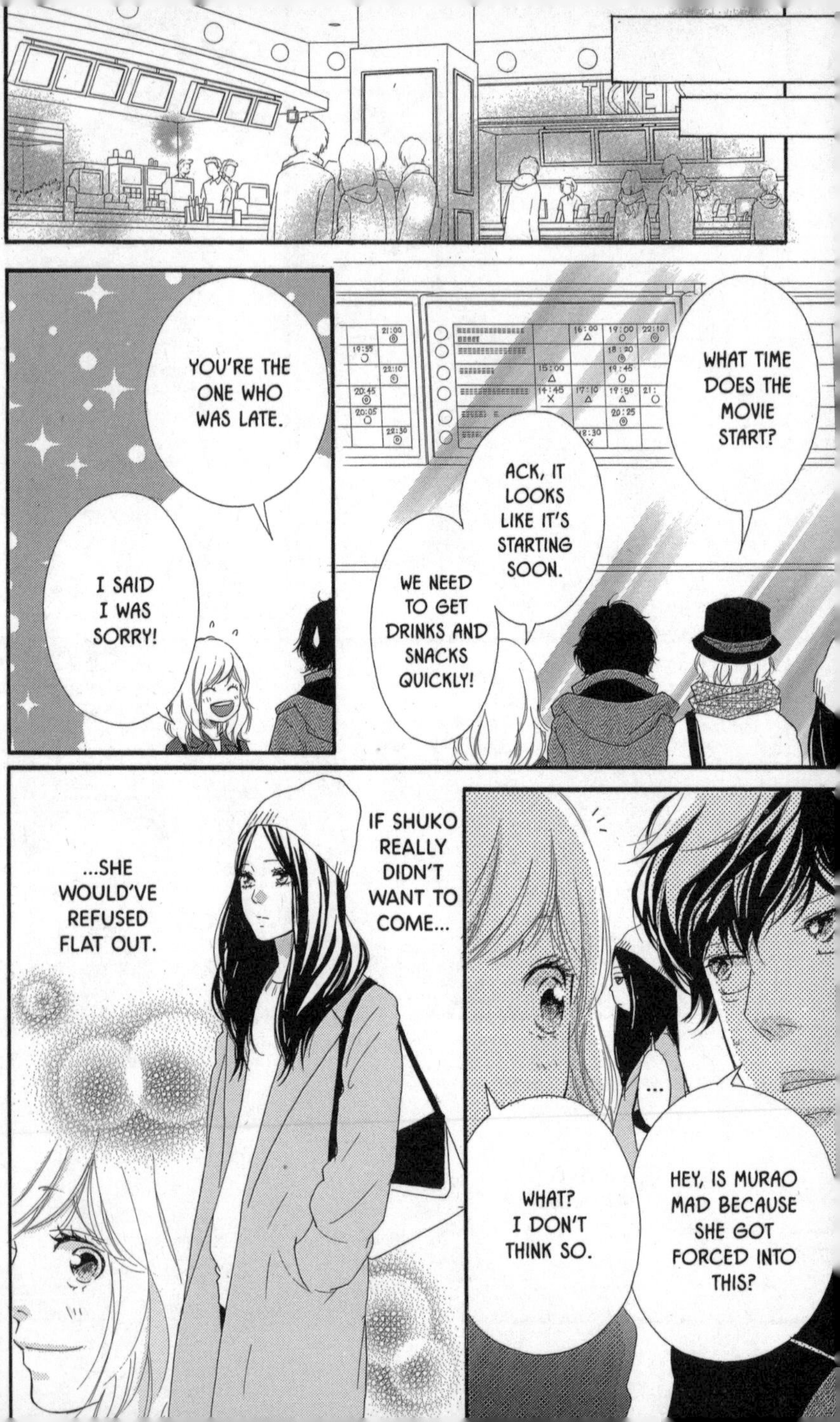
WHAT TIME DOES THE MOVIE START?
ACK, IT LOOKS LIKE IT'S STARTING SOON.
WE NEED TO GET DRINKS AND SNACKS QUICKLY!
YOU'RE THE ONE WHO WAS LATE.
I SAID I WAS SORRY!
...
HEY, IS MURAO MAD BECAUSE SHE GOT FORCED INTO THIS?
WHAT? I DON'T THINK SO.
IF SHUKO REALLY DIDN'T WANT TO COME...
...SHE WOULD'VE REFUSED FLAT OUT.

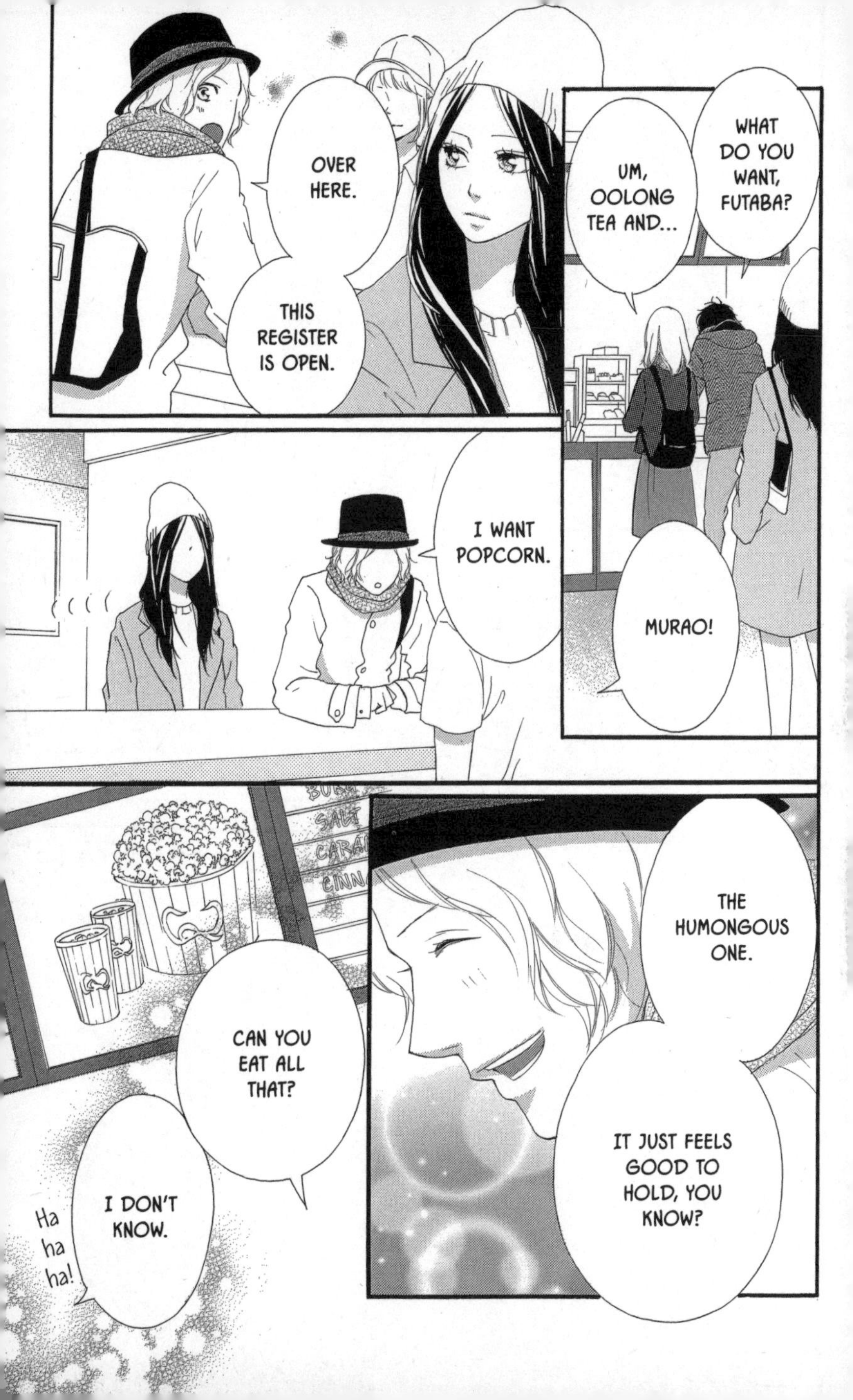
WHAT DO YOU WANT, FUTABA?
UM, OOLONG TEA AND...
MURAO!
OVER HERE.
THIS REGISTER IS OPEN.
I WANT POPCORN.
THE HUMONGOUS ONE.
IT JUST FEELS GOOD TO HOLD, YOU KNOW?
CAN YOU EAT ALL THAT?
I DON'T KNOW.
Ha ha ha!

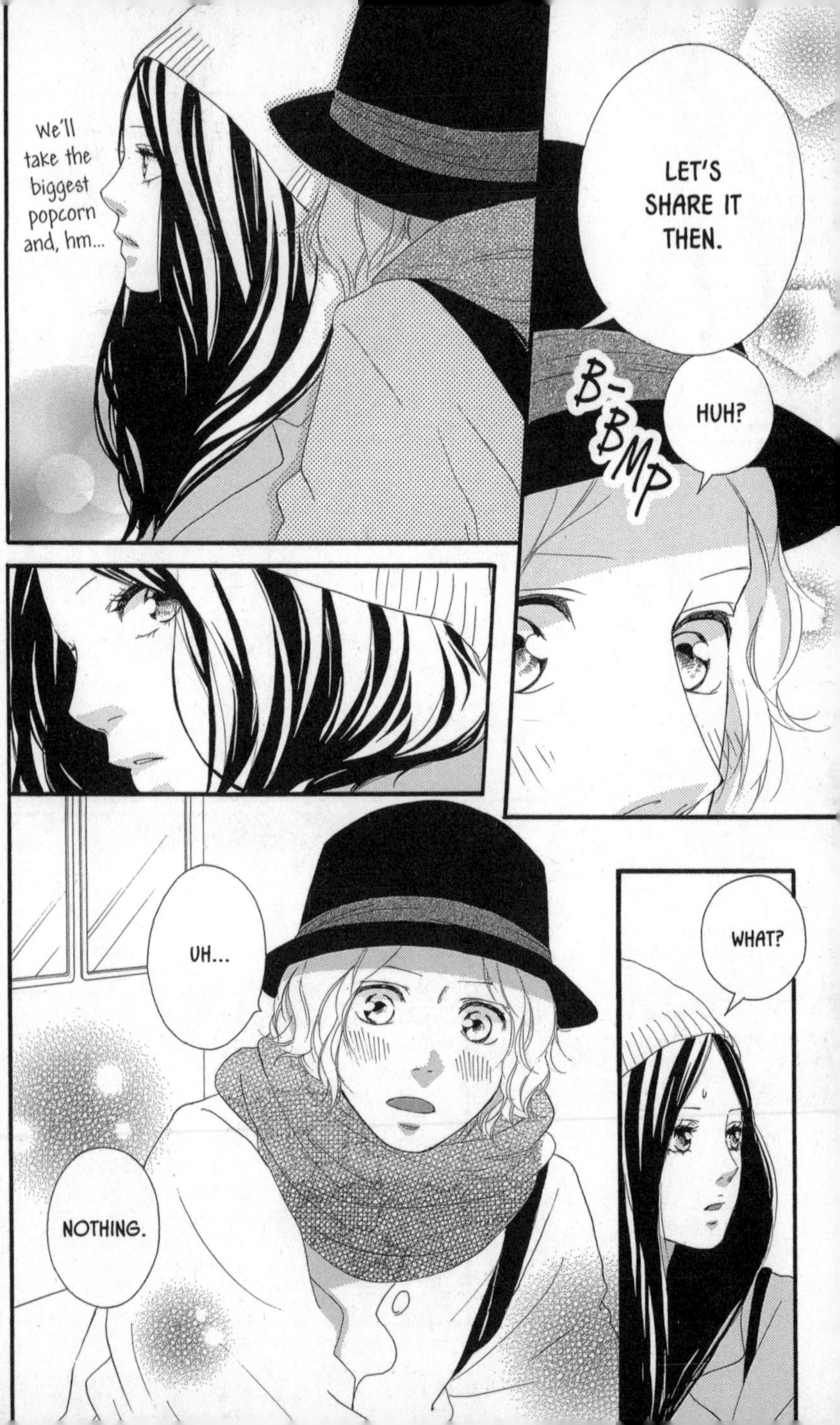
LET'S SHARE IT THEN.
B-BMP
HUH?
We'll take the biggest popcorn and, hm...
WHAT?
UH...
NOTHING.

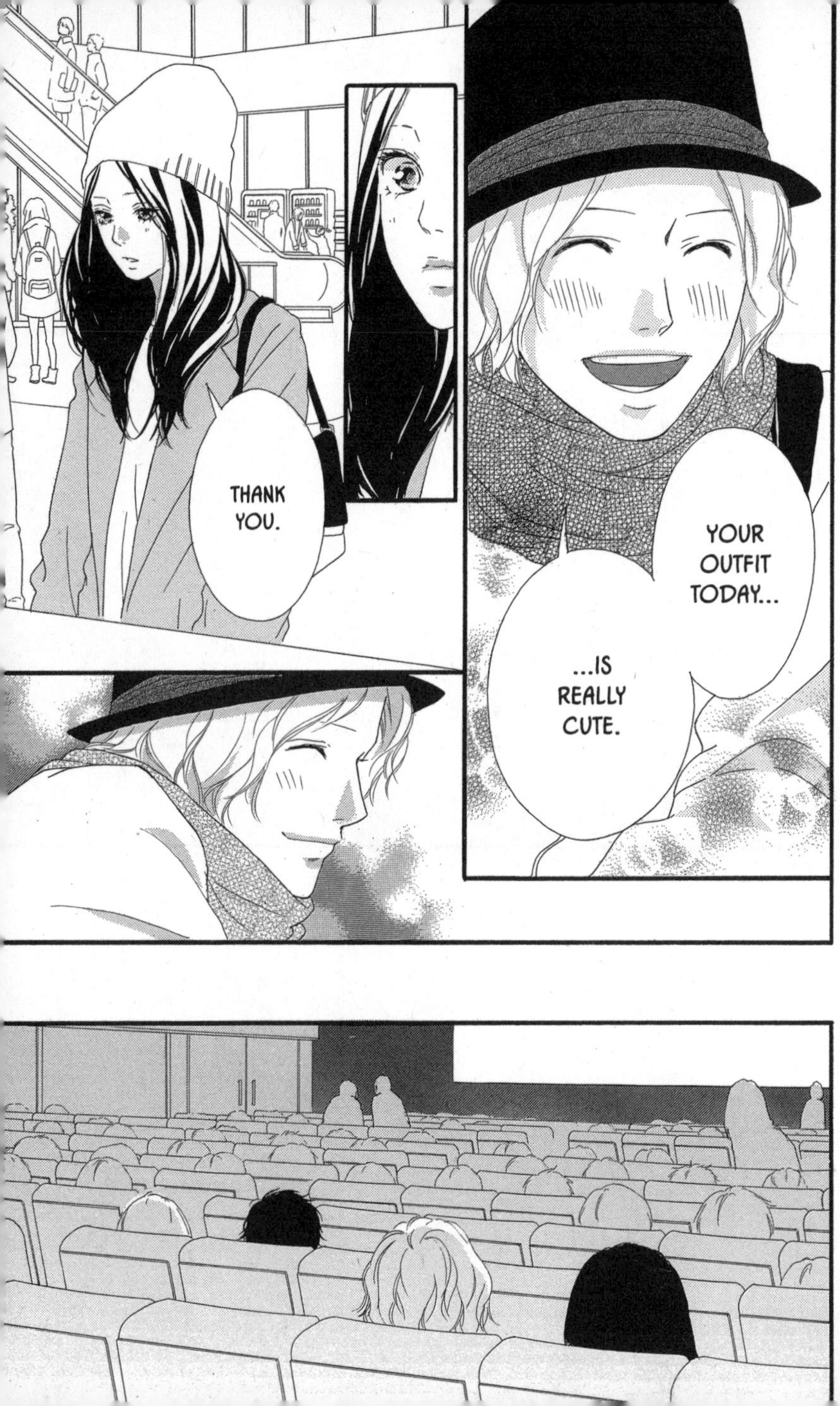
YOUR OUTFIT TODAY...
...IS REALLY CUTE.
THANK YOU.

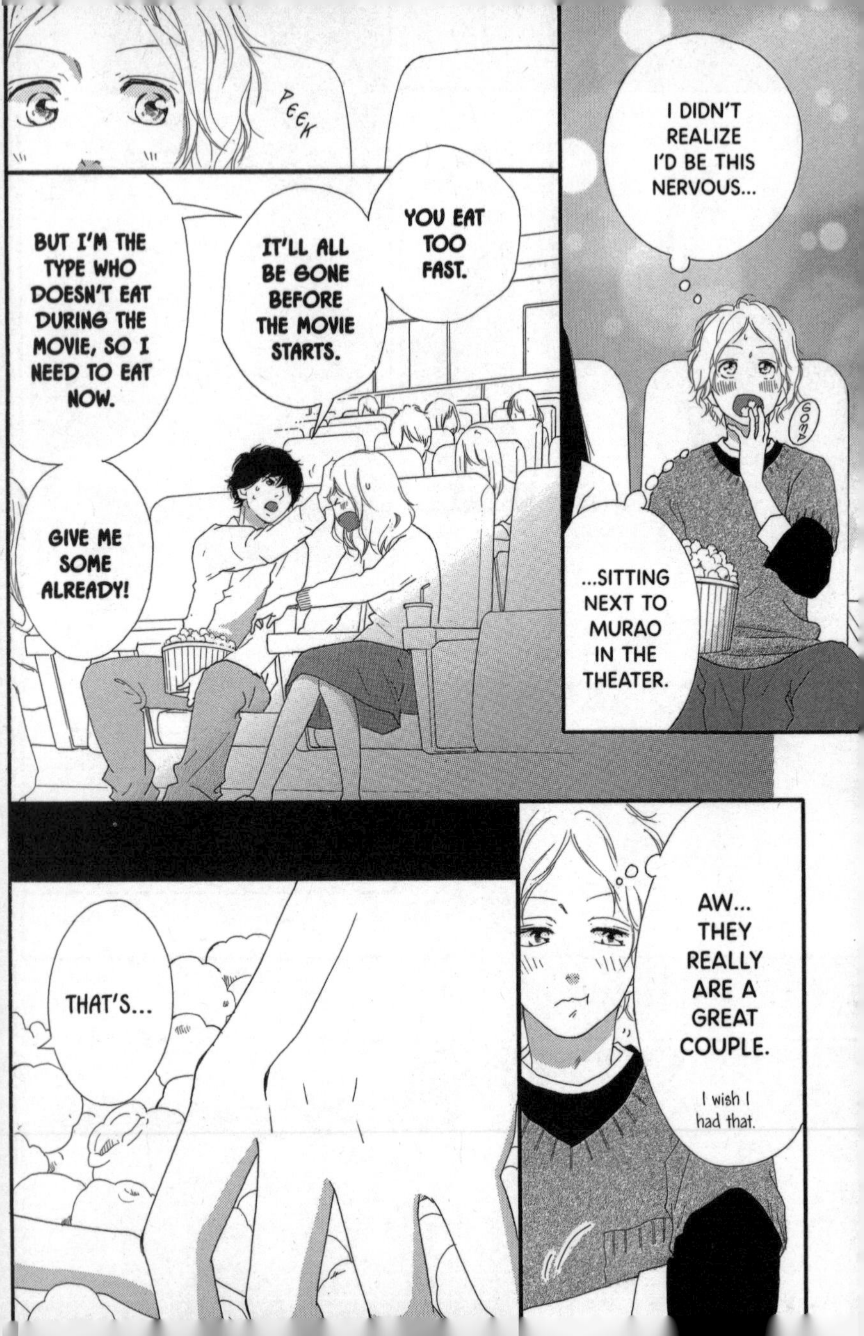
I DIDN'T REALIZE I'D BE THIS NERVOUS...
GOMA
...SITTING NEXT TO MURAO IN THE THEATER.
PEEK
YOU EAT TOO FAST.
IT'LL ALL BE GONE BEFORE THE MOVIE STARTS.
BUT I'M THE TYPE WHO DOESN'T EAT DURING THE MOVIE, SO I NEED TO EAT NOW.
GIVE ME SOME ALREADY!
AW... THEY REALLY ARE A GREAT COUPLE.
I wish I had that.
THAT'S...

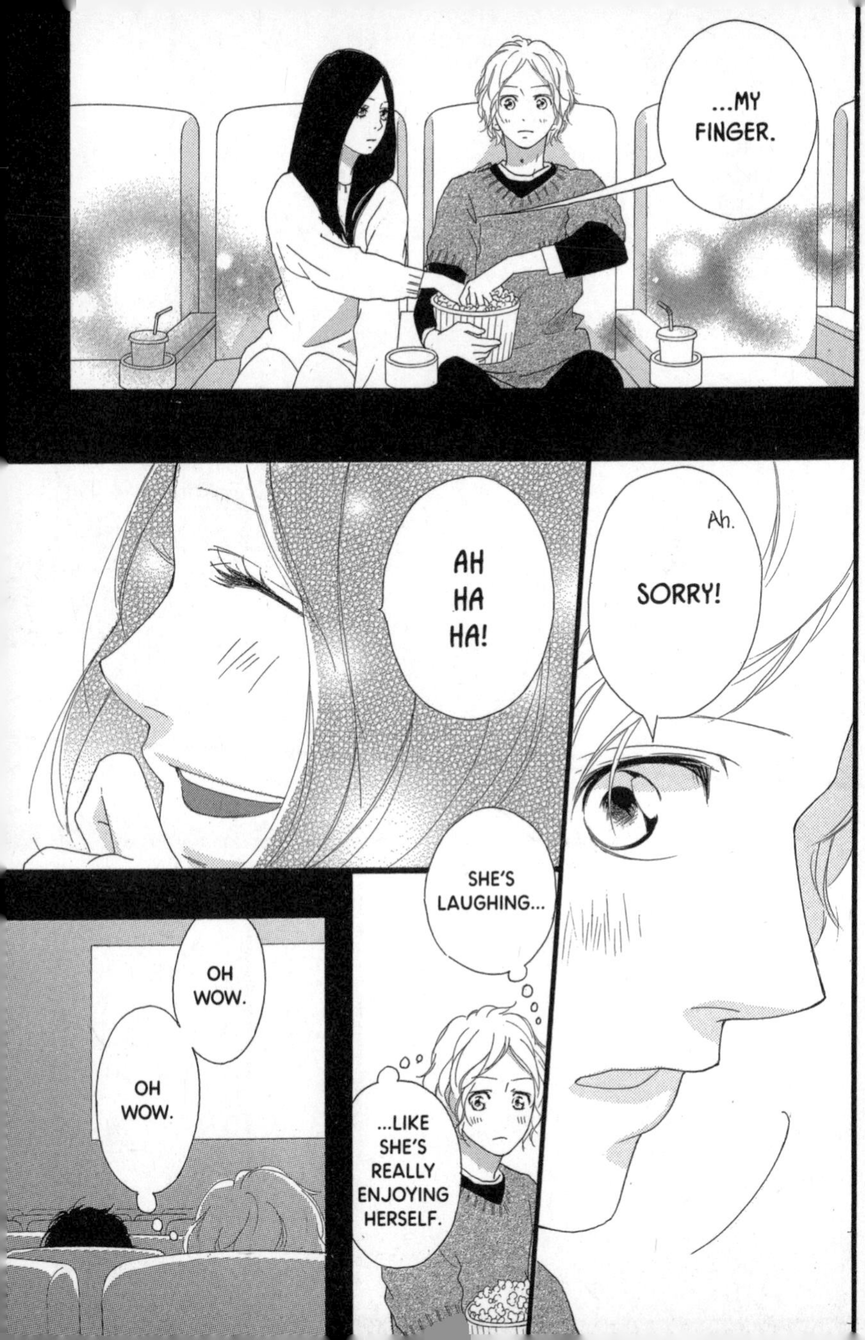
...MY FINGER.
Ah.
SORRY!
AH HA HA!
SHE'S LAUGHING...
...LIKE SHE'S REALLY ENJOYING HERSELF.
OH WOW.
OH WOW.

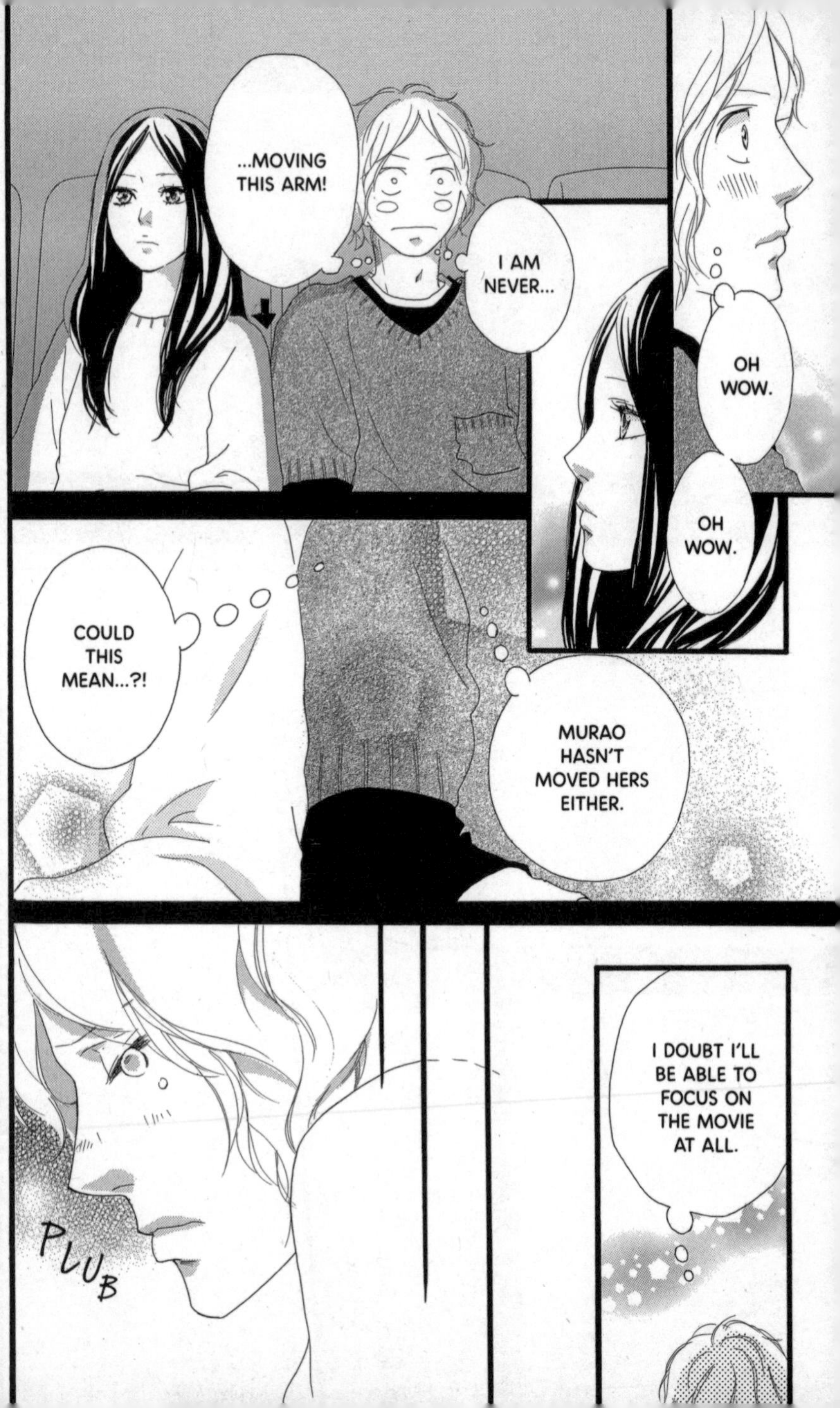
OH WOW.
I AM NEVER...
...MOVING THIS ARM!
OH WOW.
MURAO HASN'T MOVED HERS EITHER.
COULD THIS MEAN...?!
I DOUBT I'LL BE ABLE TO FOCUS ON THE MOVIE AT ALL.
PLUB

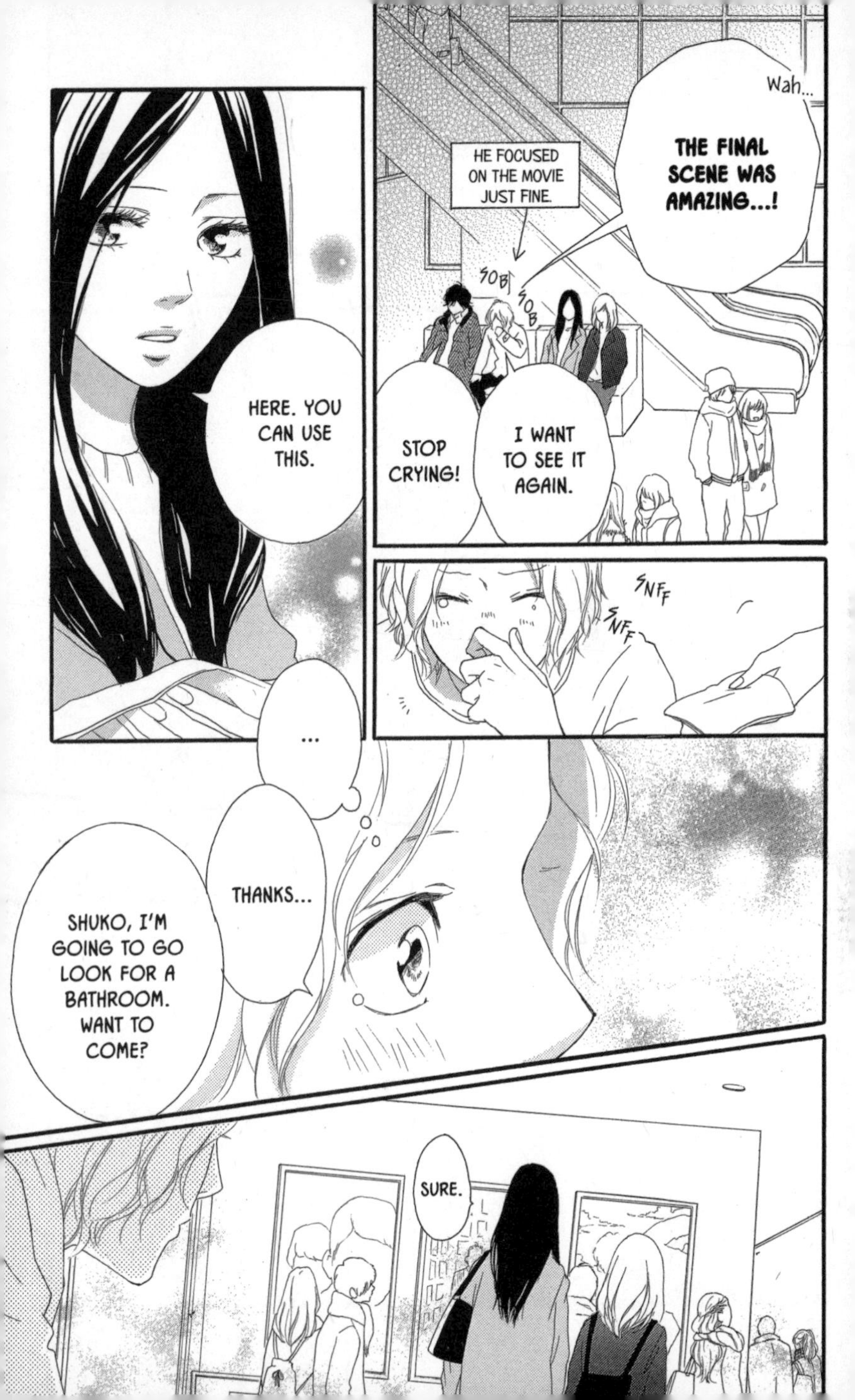
Wah...
THE FINAL SCENE WAS AMAZING...!
HE FOCUSED ON THE MOVIE JUST FINE.
SOB SOB
I WANT TO SEE IT AGAIN.
STOP CRYING!
SNFF SNFF
HERE. YOU CAN USE THIS.
...
THANKS...
SHUKO, I'M GOING TO GO LOOK FOR A BATHROOM. WANT TO COME?
SURE.

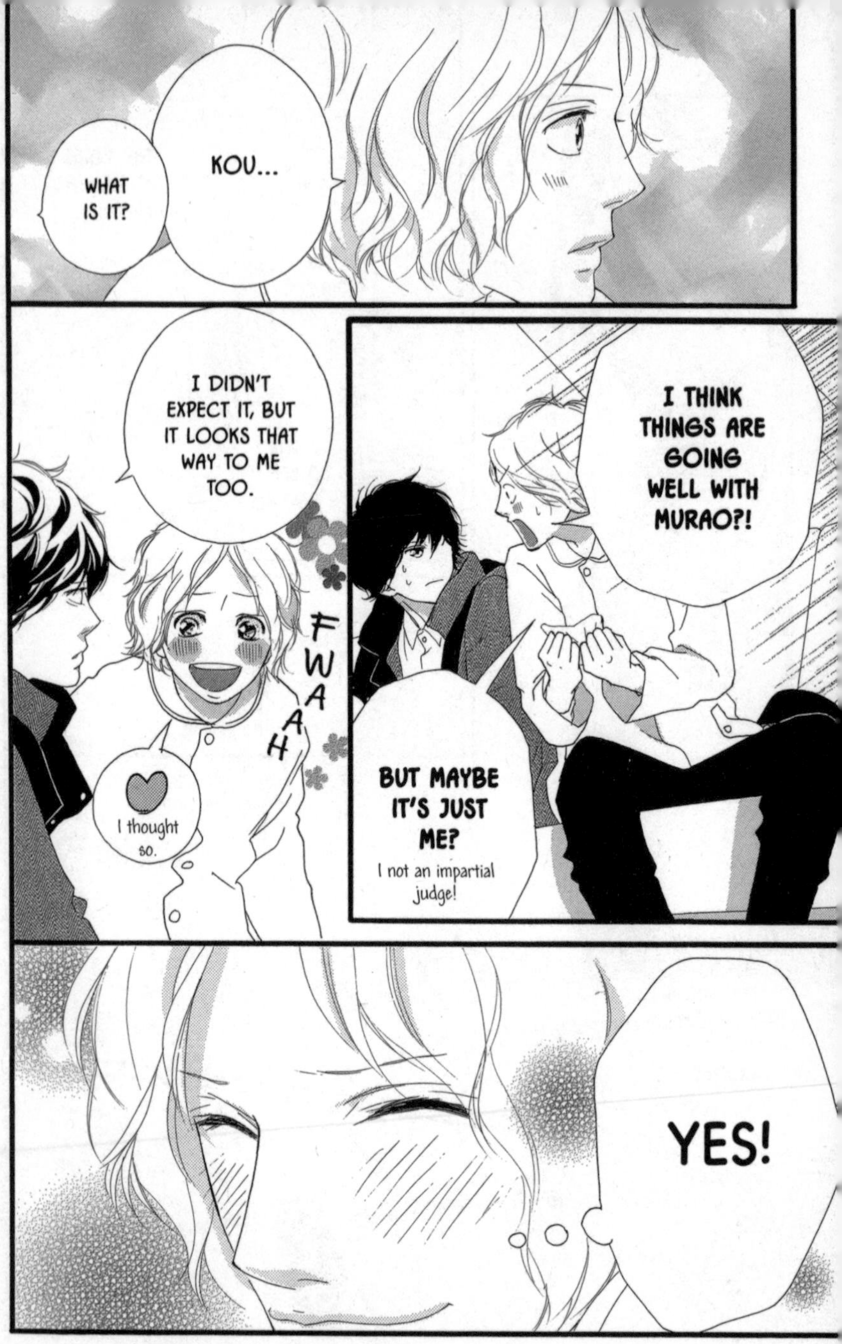
KOU...
WHAT IS IT?
I THINK THINGS ARE GOING WELL WITH MURAO?!
BUT MAYBE IT'S JUST ME?
I not an impartial judge!
I DIDN'T EXPECT IT, BUT IT LOOKS THAT WAY TO ME TOO.
FWAAH
I thought so.
YES!

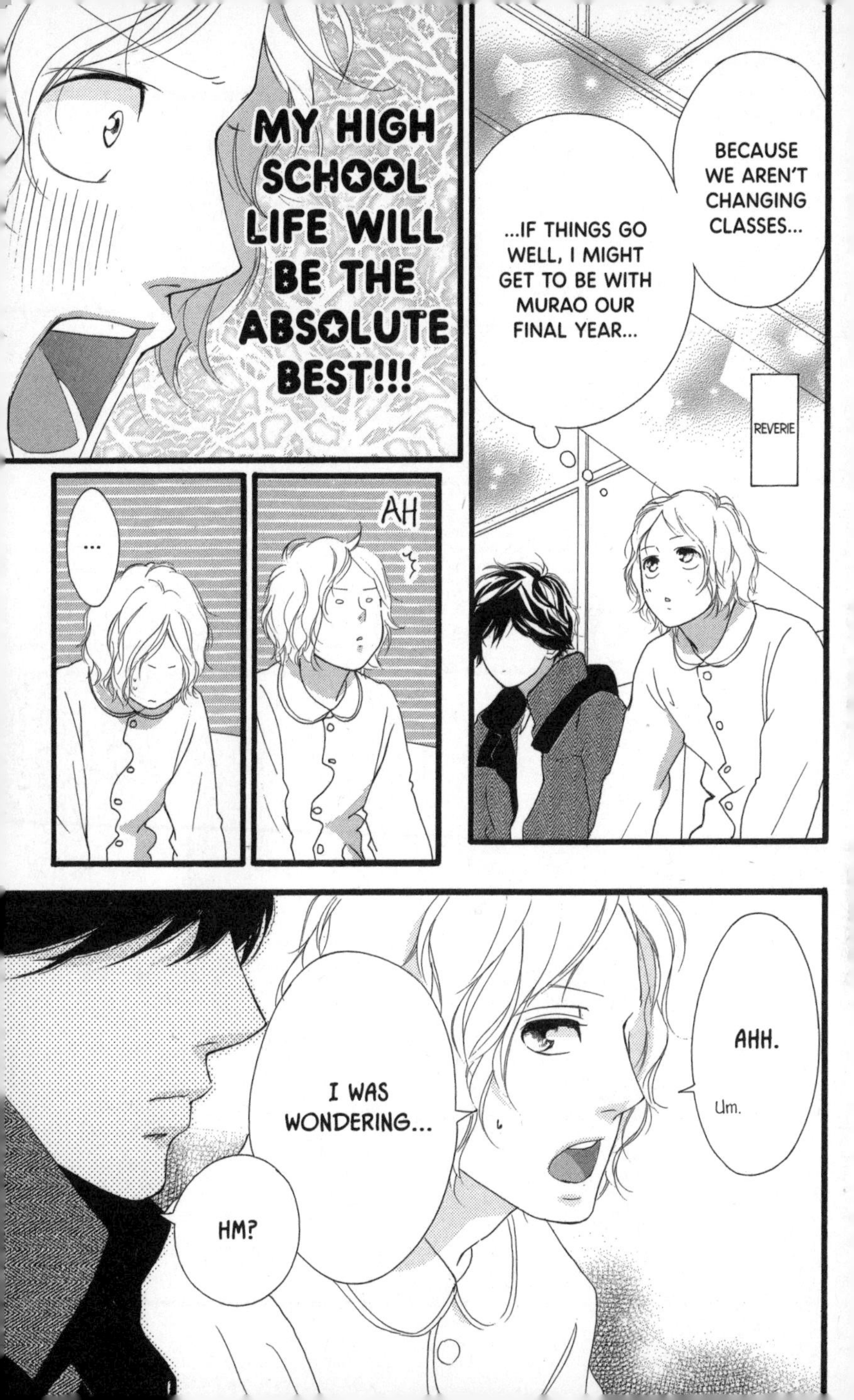

BECAUSE WE AREN'T CHANGING CLASSES...
...IF THINGS GO WELL, I MIGHT GET TO BE WITH MURAO OUR FINAL YEAR...
REVERIE
MY HIGH SCHOOL LIFE WILL BE THE ABSOLUTE BEST!!!
AH
...
AHH.
Um.
I WAS WONDERING...
HM?

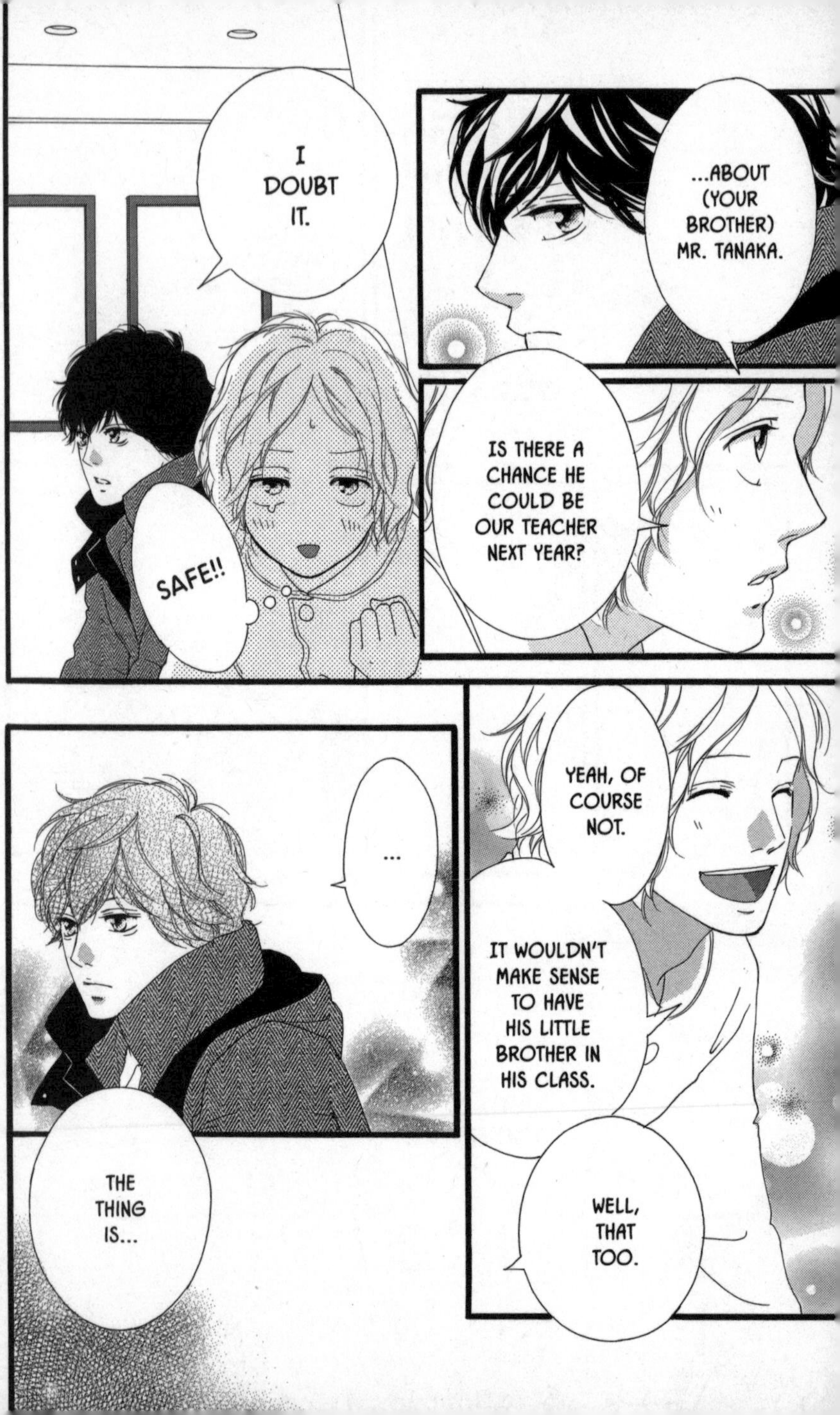
...ABOUT (YOUR BROTHER) MR. TANAKA.
IS THERE A CHANCE HE COULD BE OUR TEACHER NEXT YEAR?
I DOUBT IT.
SAFE!!
YEAH, OF COURSE NOT.
IT WOULDN'T MAKE SENSE TO HAVE HIS LITTLE BROTHER IN HIS CLASS.
WELL, THAT TOO.
...
THE THING IS...

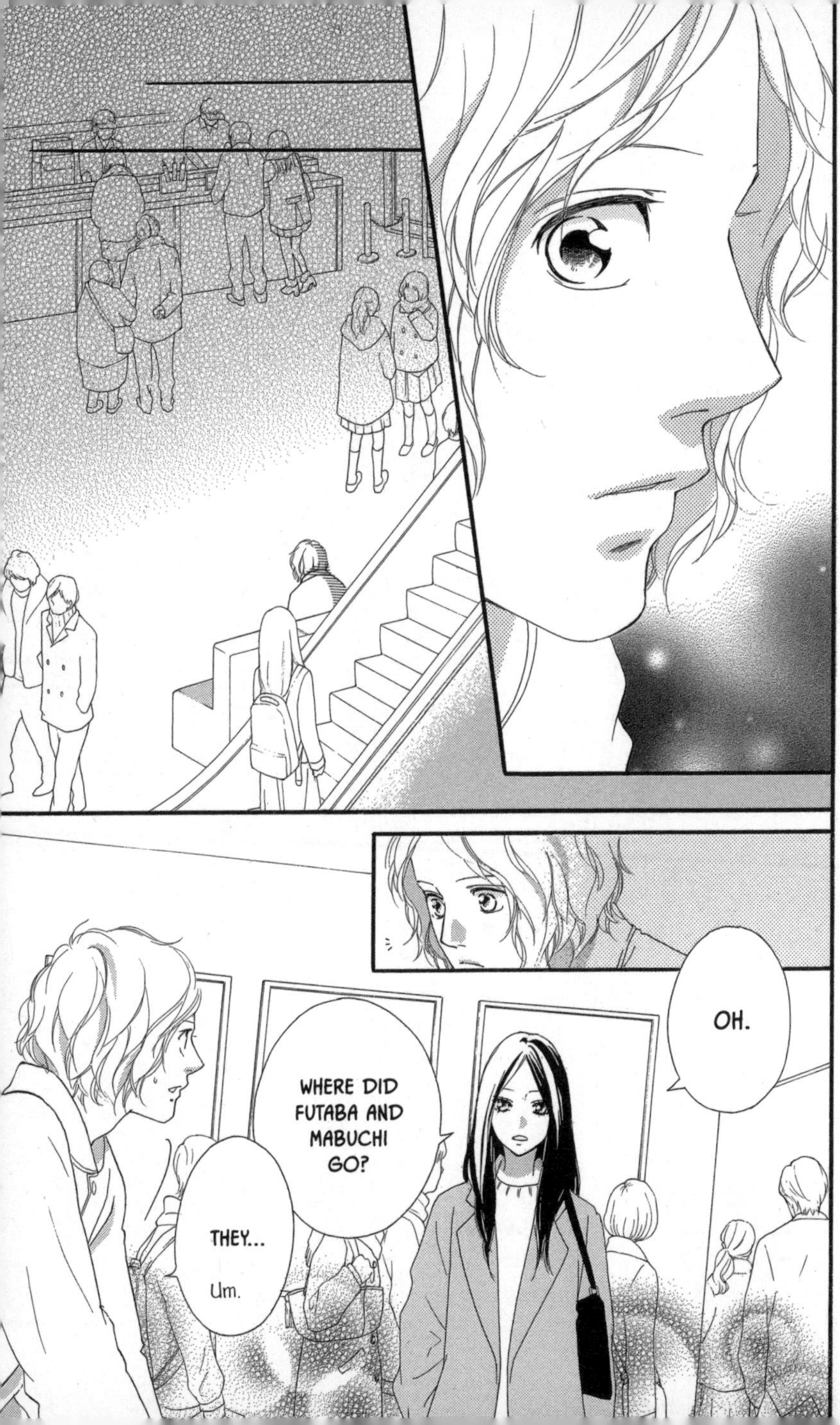
OH.
WHERE DID FUTABA AND MABUCHI GO?
THEY...
Um.

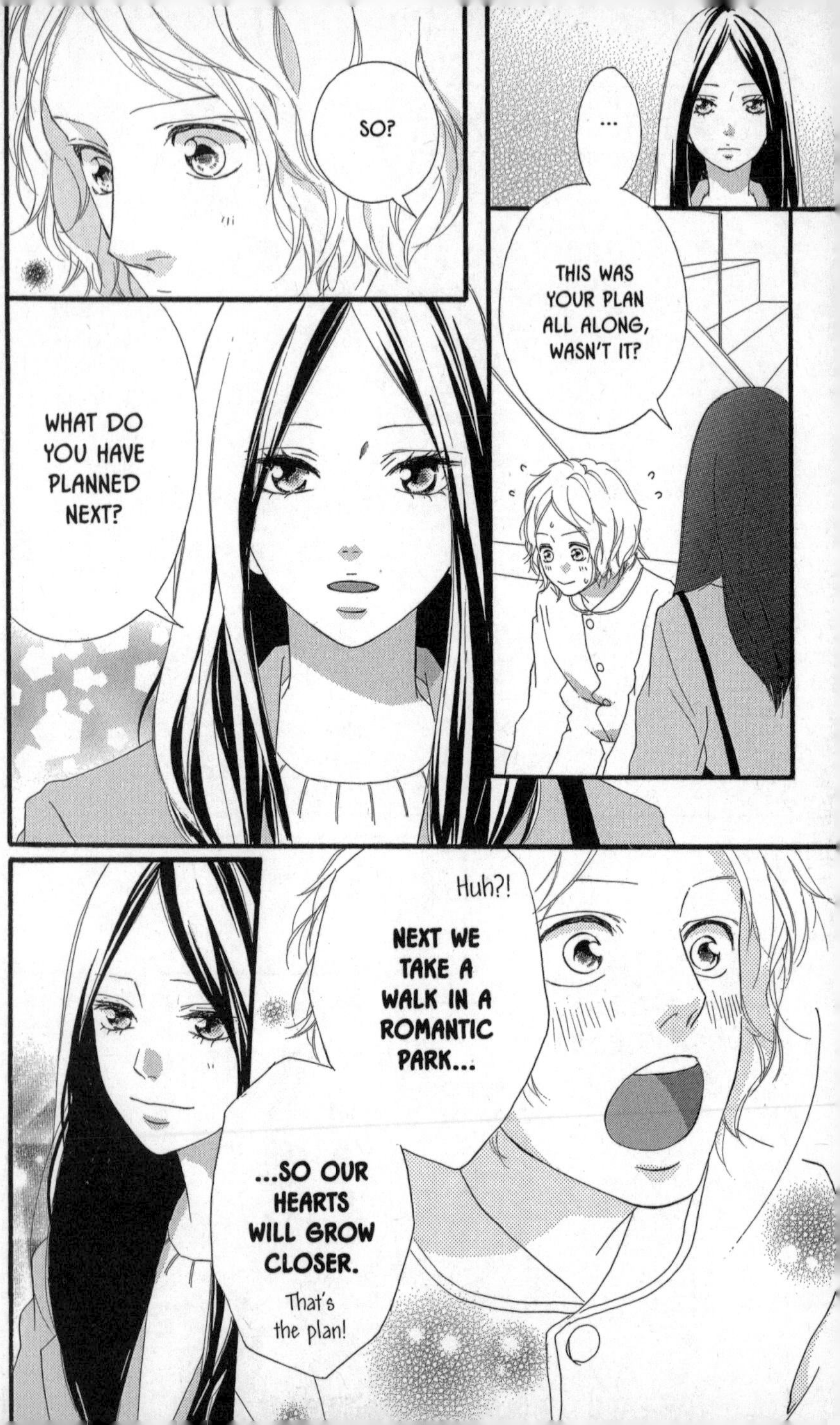
...
SO?
THIS WAS YOUR PLAN ALL ALONG, WASN'T IT?
WHAT DO YOU HAVE PLANNED NEXT?
Huh?!
NEXT WE TAKE A WALK IN A ROMANTIC PARK...
...SO OUR HEARTS WILL GROW CLOSER.
That's the plan!

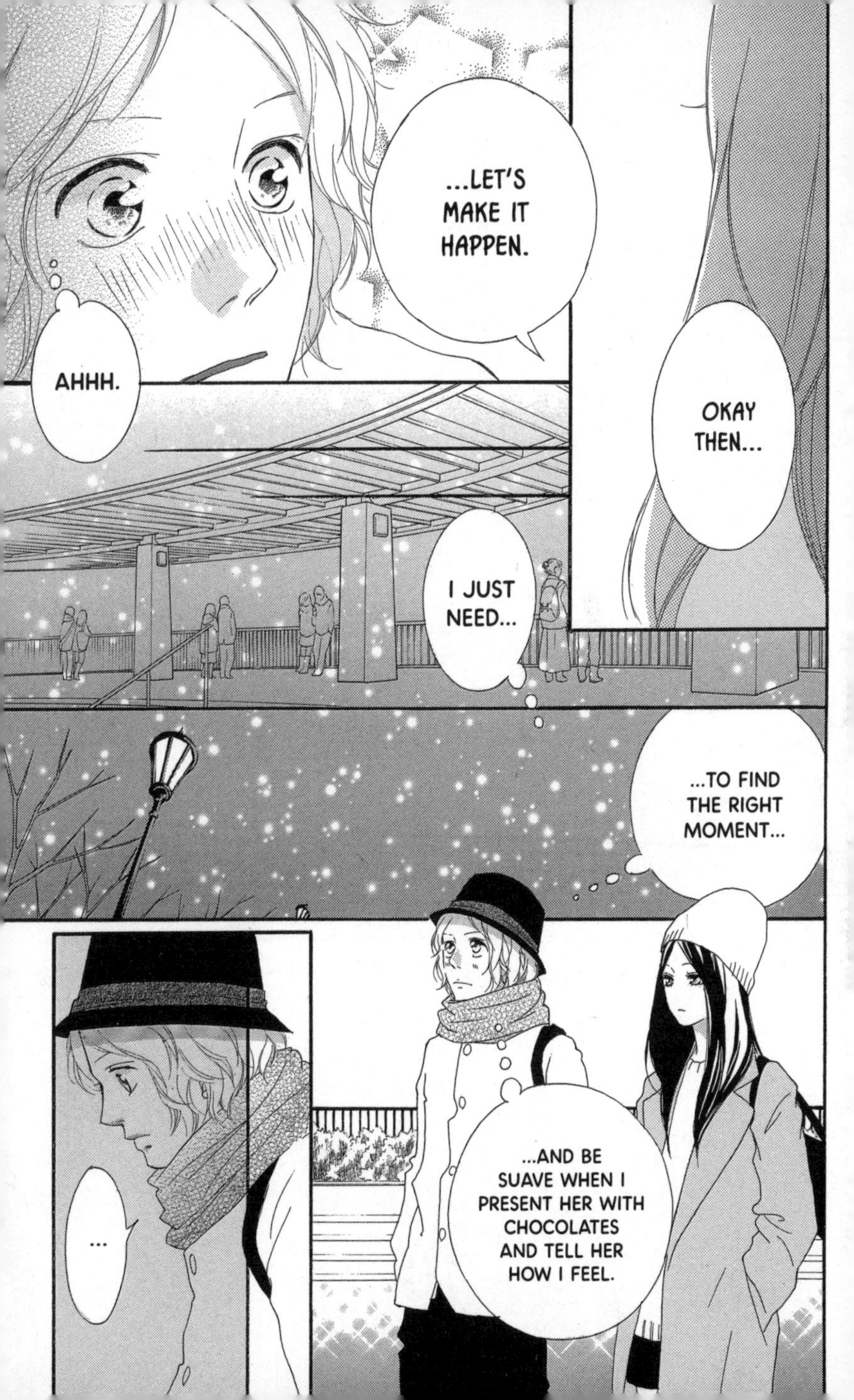
...LET'S MAKE IT HAPPEN.
AHHH.
OKAY THEN...
I JUST NEED...
...TO FIND THE RIGHT MOMENT...
...AND BE SUAVE WHEN I PRESENT HER WITH CHOCOLATES AND TELL HER HOW I FEEL.
...

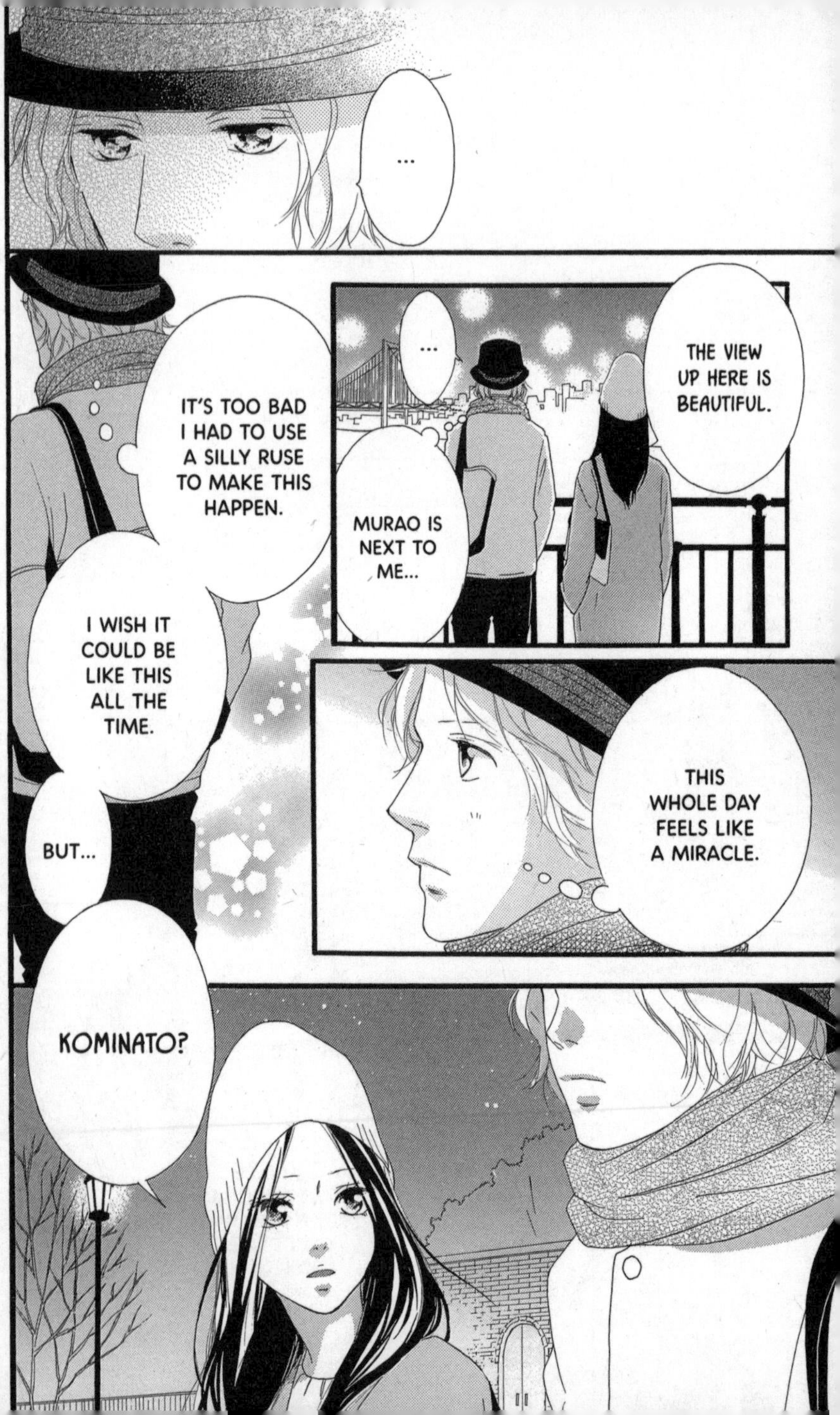
...
THE VIEW UP HERE IS BEAUTIFUL.
...
MURAO IS NEXT TO ME...
THIS WHOLE DAY FEELS LIKE A MIRACLE.
IT'S TOO BAD I HAD TO USE A SILLY RUSE TO MAKE THIS HAPPEN.
I WISH IT COULD BE LIKE THIS ALL THE TIME.
BUT...
KOMINATO?

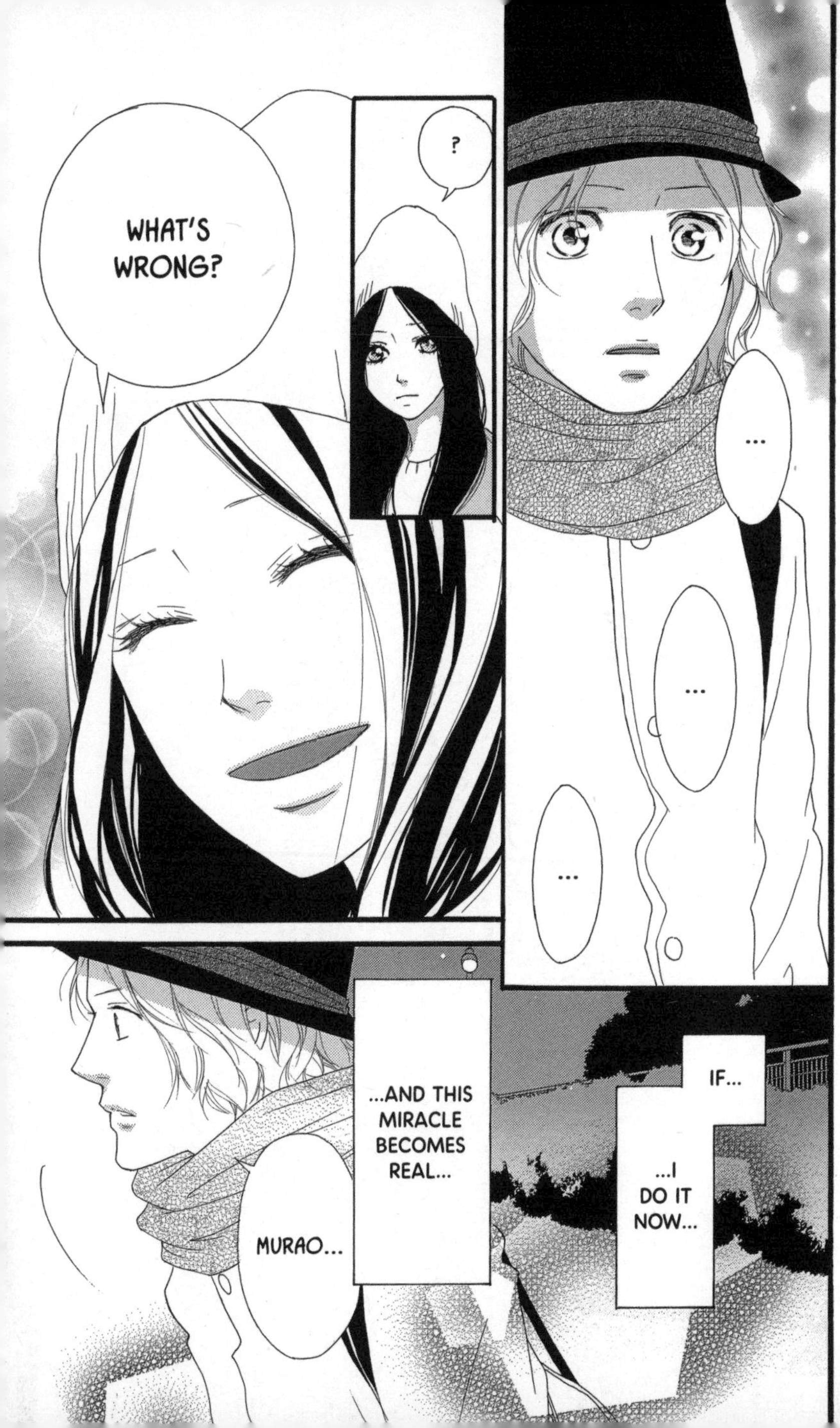
...
...
...
?
WHAT'S WRONG?
IF...
...I DO IT NOW...
...AND THIS MIRACLE BECOMES REAL...
MURAO...

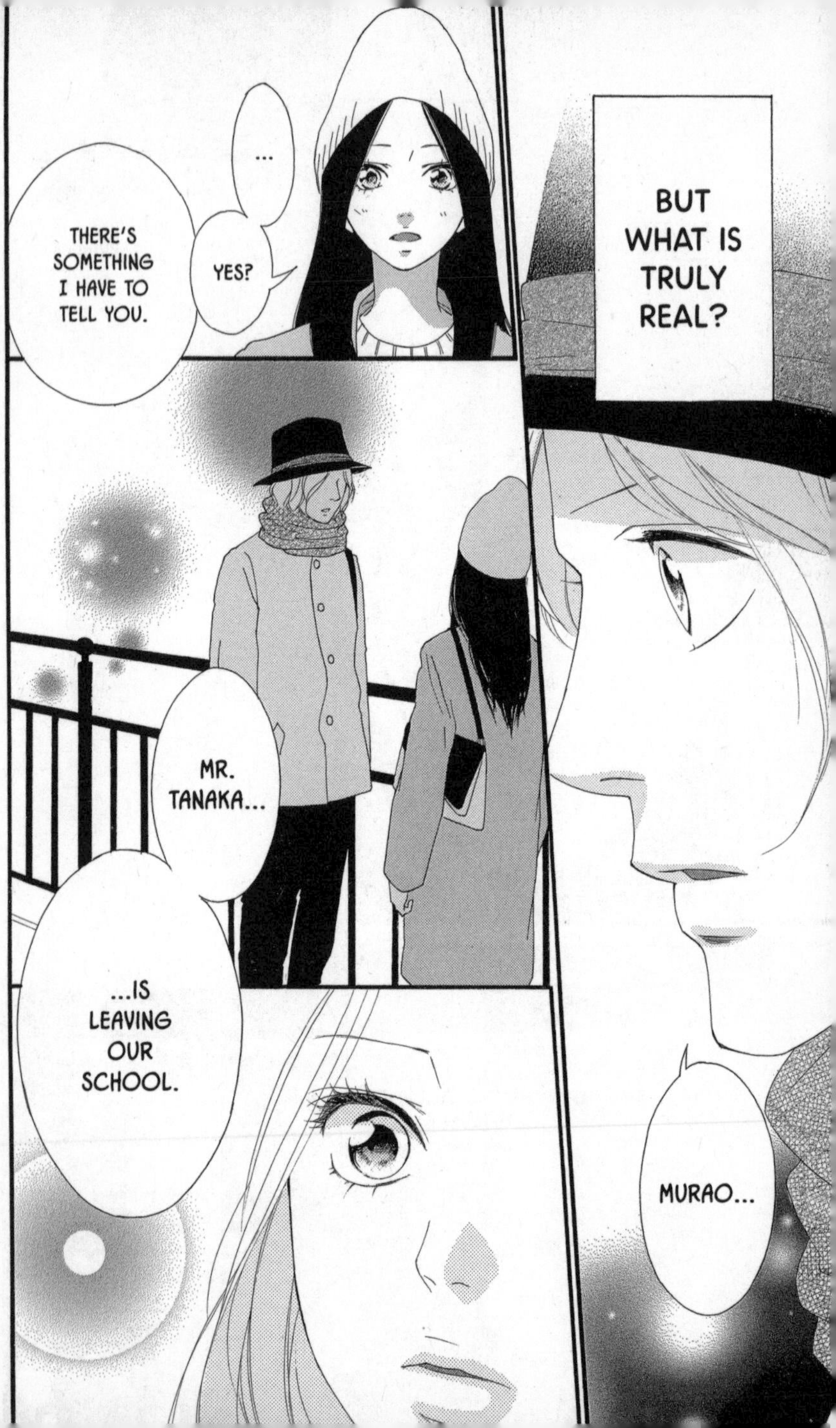
BUT WHAT IS TRULY REAL?
MURAO...
...
YES?
THERE'S SOMETHING I HAVE TO TELL YOU.
MR. TANAKA...
...IS LEAVING OUR SCHOOL.

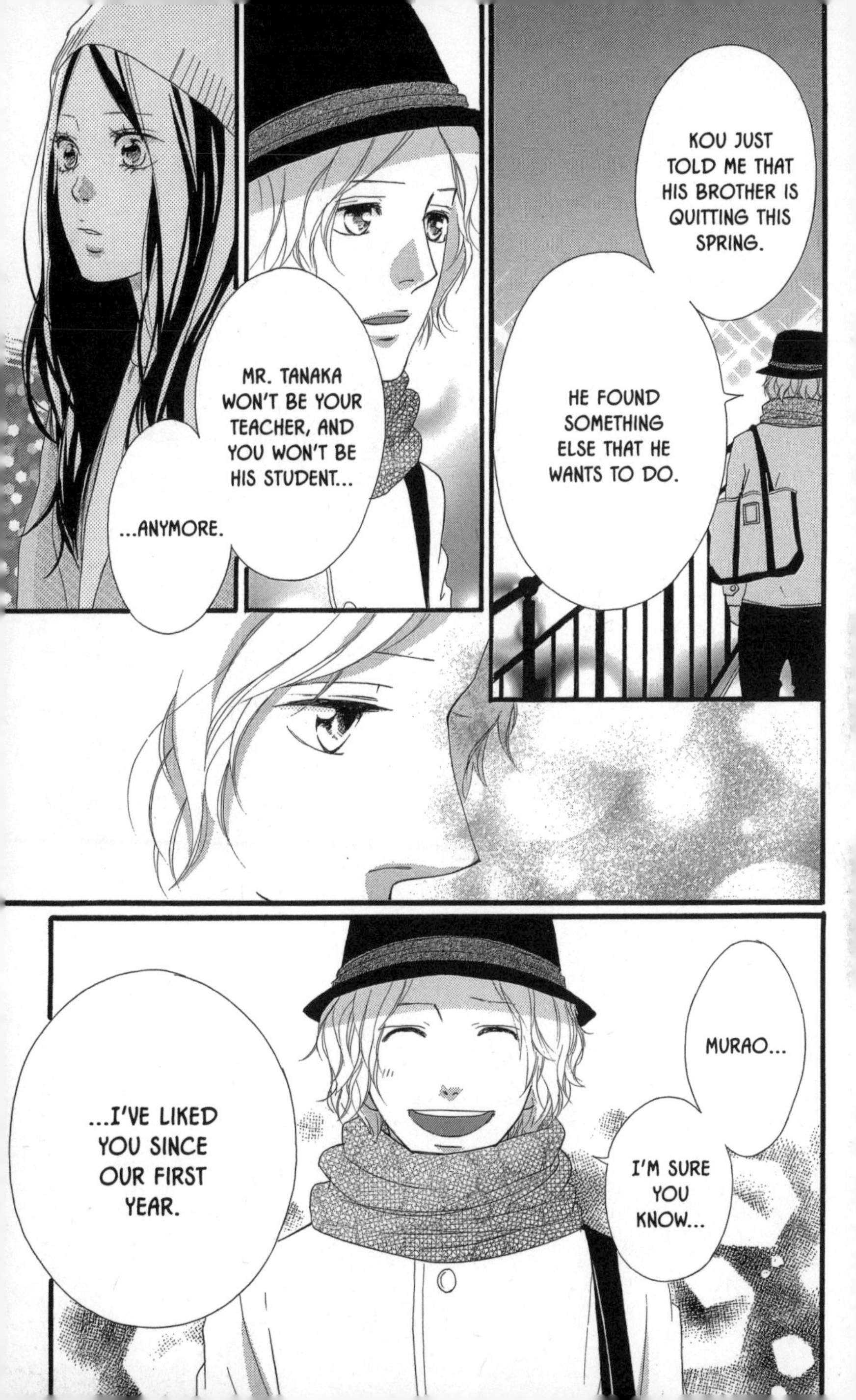
KOU JUST TOLD ME THAT HIS BROTHER IS QUITTING THIS SPRING.
HE FOUND SOMETHING ELSE THAT HE WANTS TO DO.
MR. TANAKA WON'T BE YOUR TEACHER, AND YOU WON'T BE HIS STUDENT...
...ANYMORE.
MURAO...
I'M SURE YOU KNOW...
...I'VE LIKED YOU SINCE OUR FIRST YEAR.

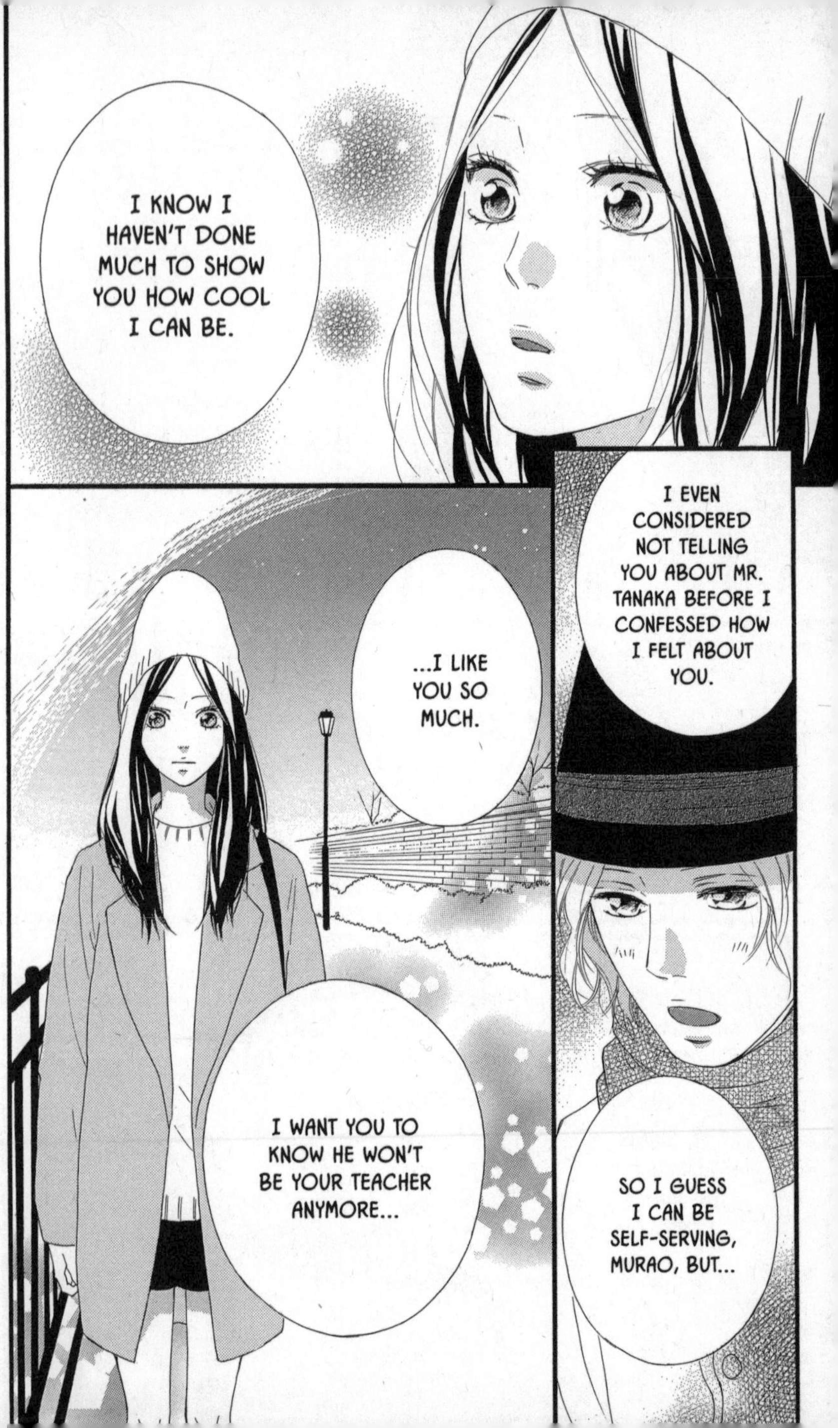
I KNOW I HAVEN'T DONE MUCH TO SHOW YOU HOW COOL I CAN BE.
I EVEN CONSIDERED NOT TELLING YOU ABOUT MR. TANAKA BEFORE I CONFESSED HOW I FELT ABOUT YOU.
SO I GUESS I CAN BE SELF-SERVING, MURAO, BUT...
...I LIKE YOU SO MUCH.
I WANT YOU TO KNOW HE WON'T BE YOUR TEACHER ANYMORE...

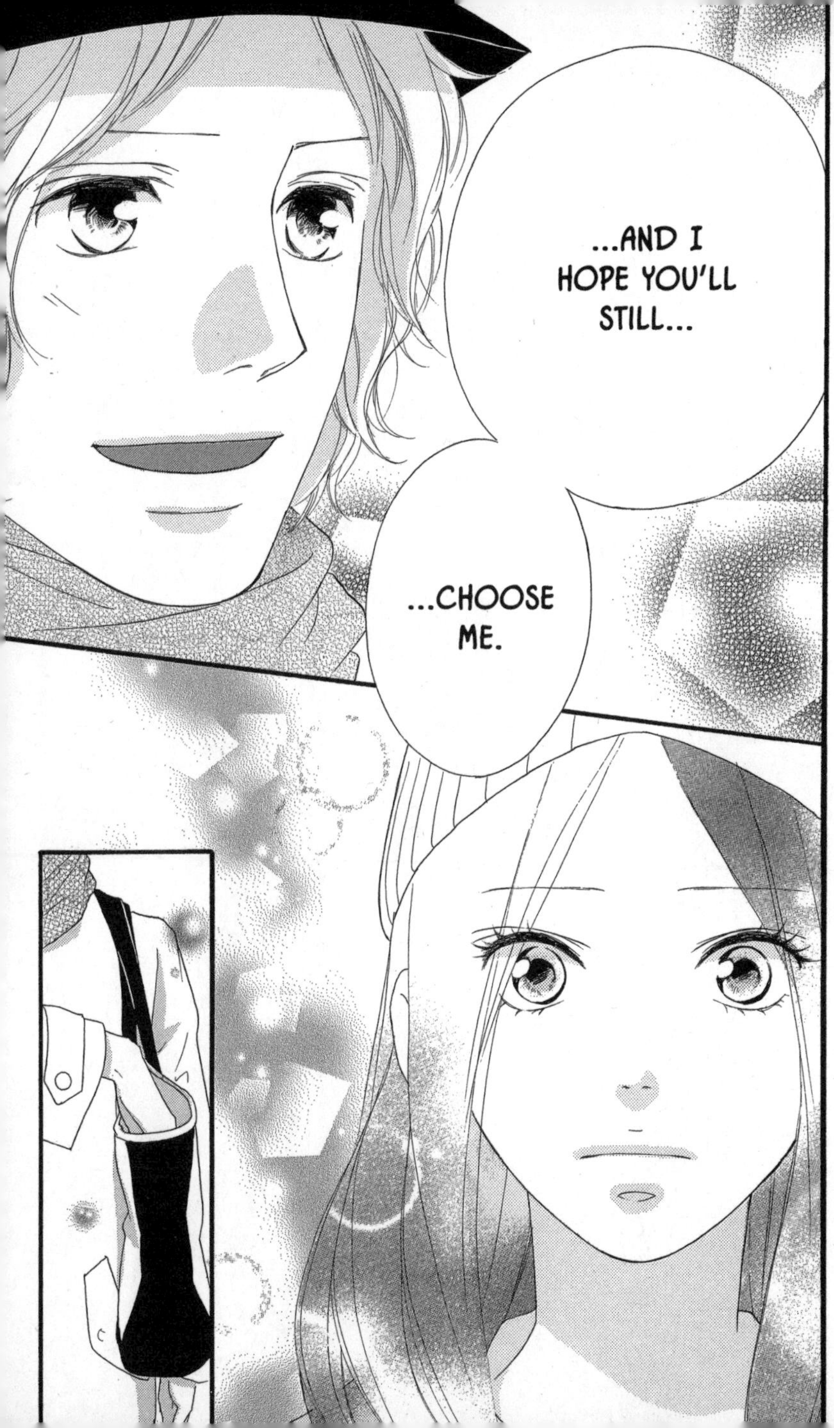
...AND I HOPE YOU'LL STILL...
...CHOOSE ME.

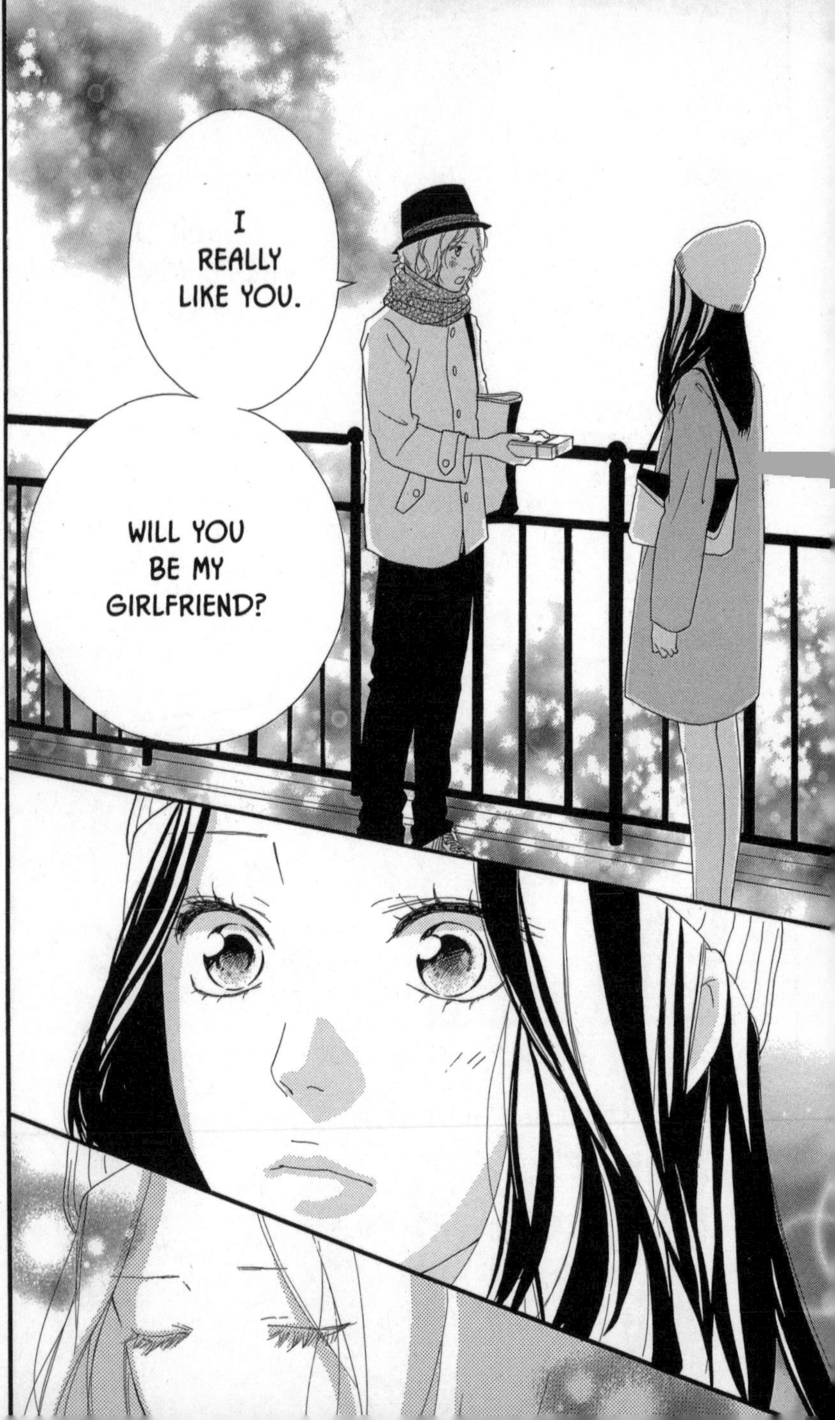
I REALLY LIKE YOU.
WILL YOU BE MY GIRLFRIEND?

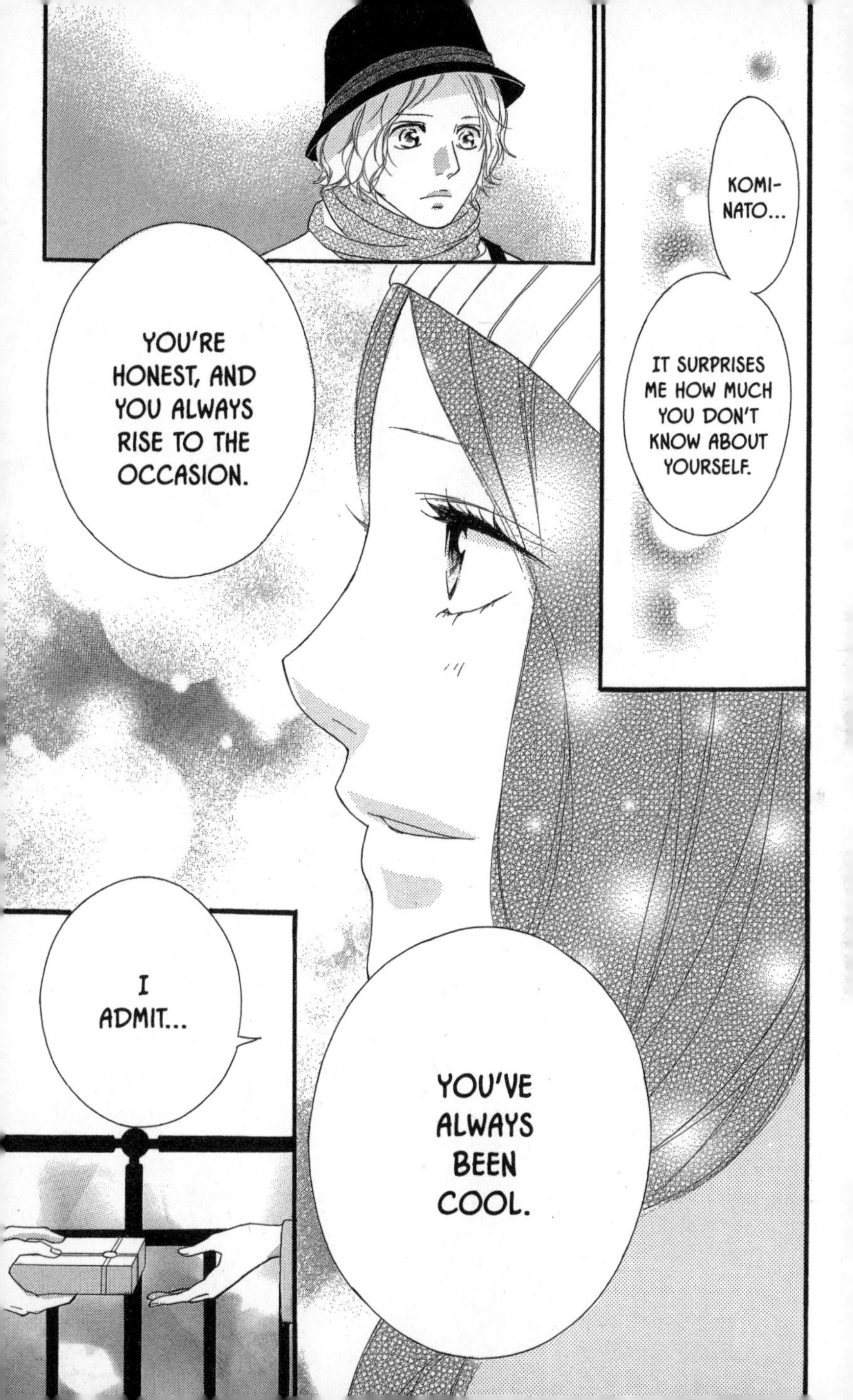
KOMI-NATO...
IT SURPRISES ME HOW MUCH YOU DON'T KNOW ABOUT YOURSELF.
YOU'RE HONEST, AND YOU ALWAYS RISE TO THE OCCASION.
I ADMIT...
YOU'VE ALWAYS BEEN COOL.

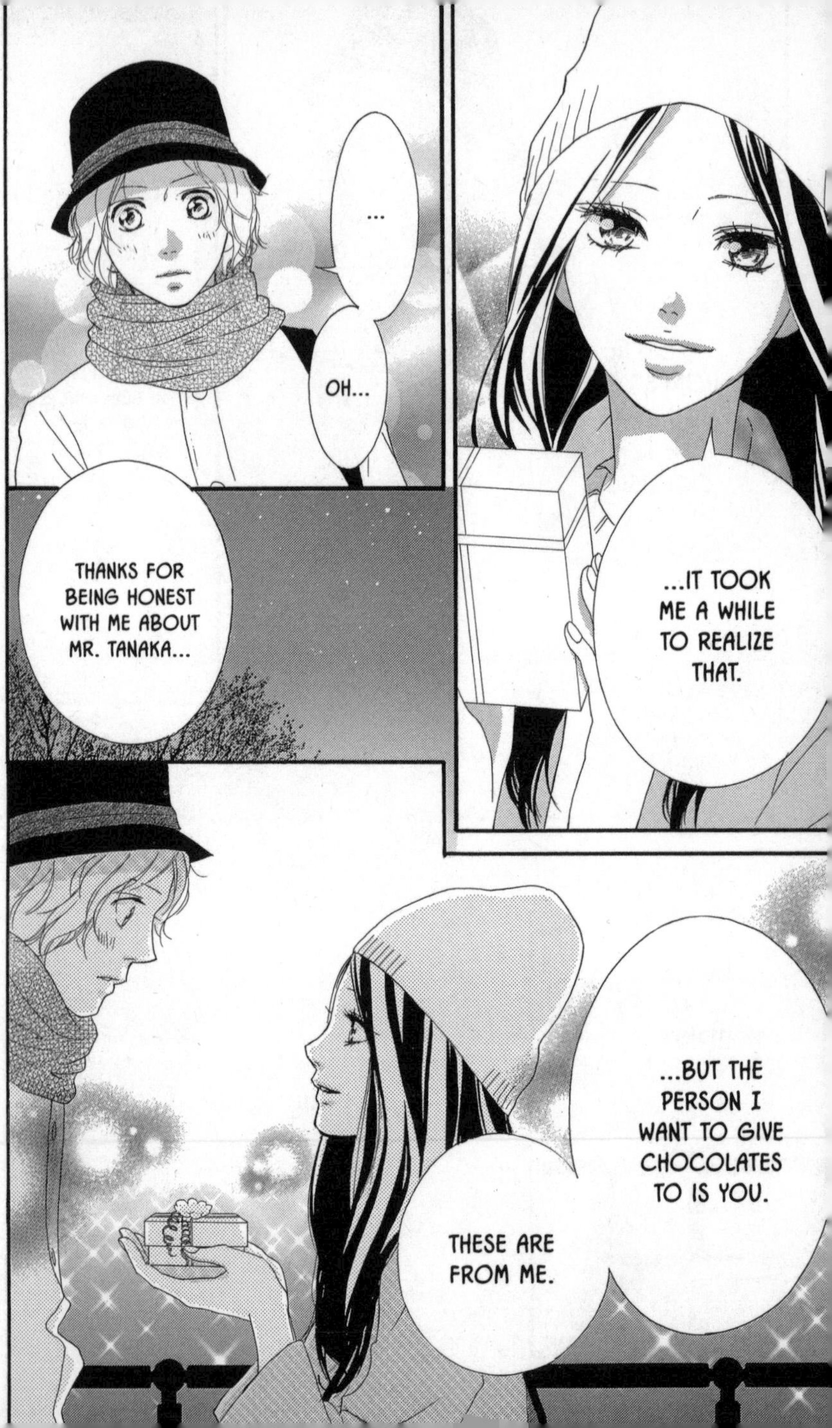
...IT TOOK ME A WHILE TO REALIZE THAT.
...
OH...
THANKS FOR BEING HONEST WITH ME ABOUT MR. TANAKA...
...BUT THE PERSON I WANT TO GIVE CHOCOLATES TO IS YOU.
THESE ARE FROM ME.

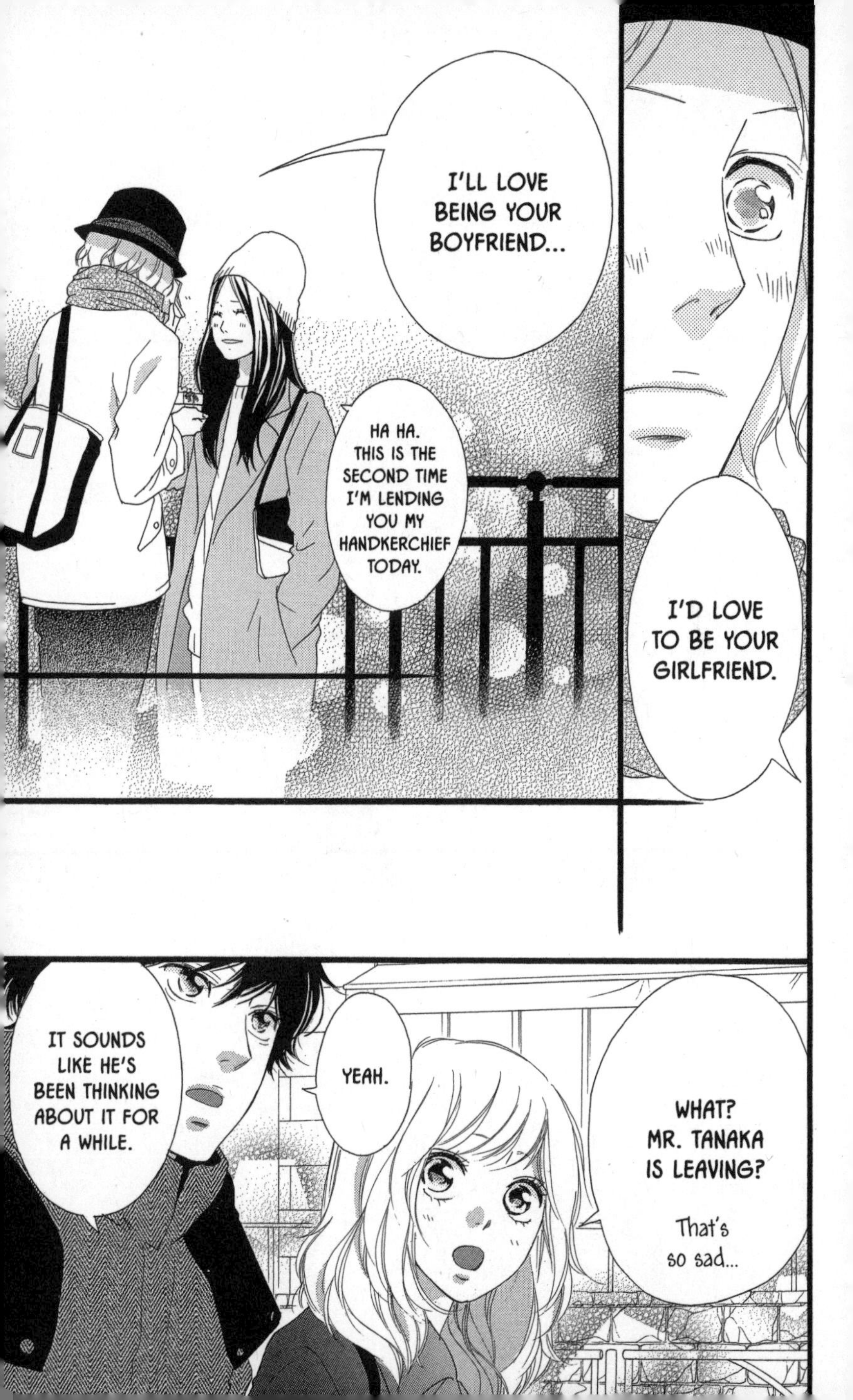
I'D LOVE TO BE YOUR GIRLFRIEND.
I'LL LOVE BEING YOUR BOYFRIEND...
HA HA. THIS IS THE SECOND TIME I'M LENDING YOU MY HANDKERCHIEF TODAY.
WHAT? MR. TANAKA IS LEAVING?
That's so sad...
YEAH.
IT SOUNDS LIKE HE'S BEEN THINKING ABOUT IT FOR A WHILE.

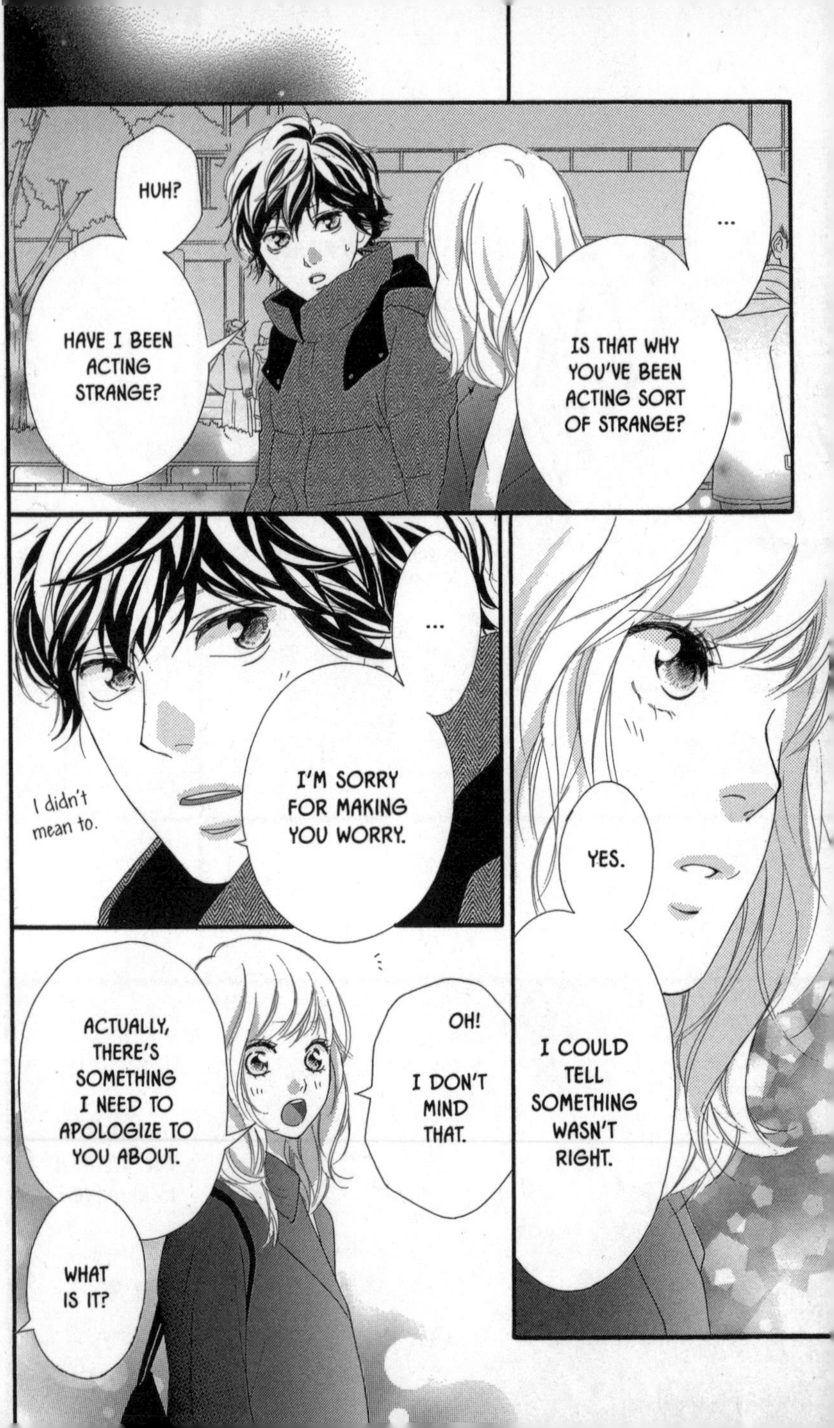
...
IS THAT WHY YOU'VE BEEN ACTING SORT OF STRANGE?
HUH?
HAVE I BEEN ACTING STRANGE?
YES.
I COULD TELL SOMETHING WASN'T RIGHT.
...
I'M SORRY FOR MAKING YOU WORRY.
I didn't mean to.
OH!
I DON'T MIND THAT.
ACTUALLY, THERE'S SOMETHING I NEED TO APOLOGIZE TO YOU ABOUT.
WHAT IS IT?

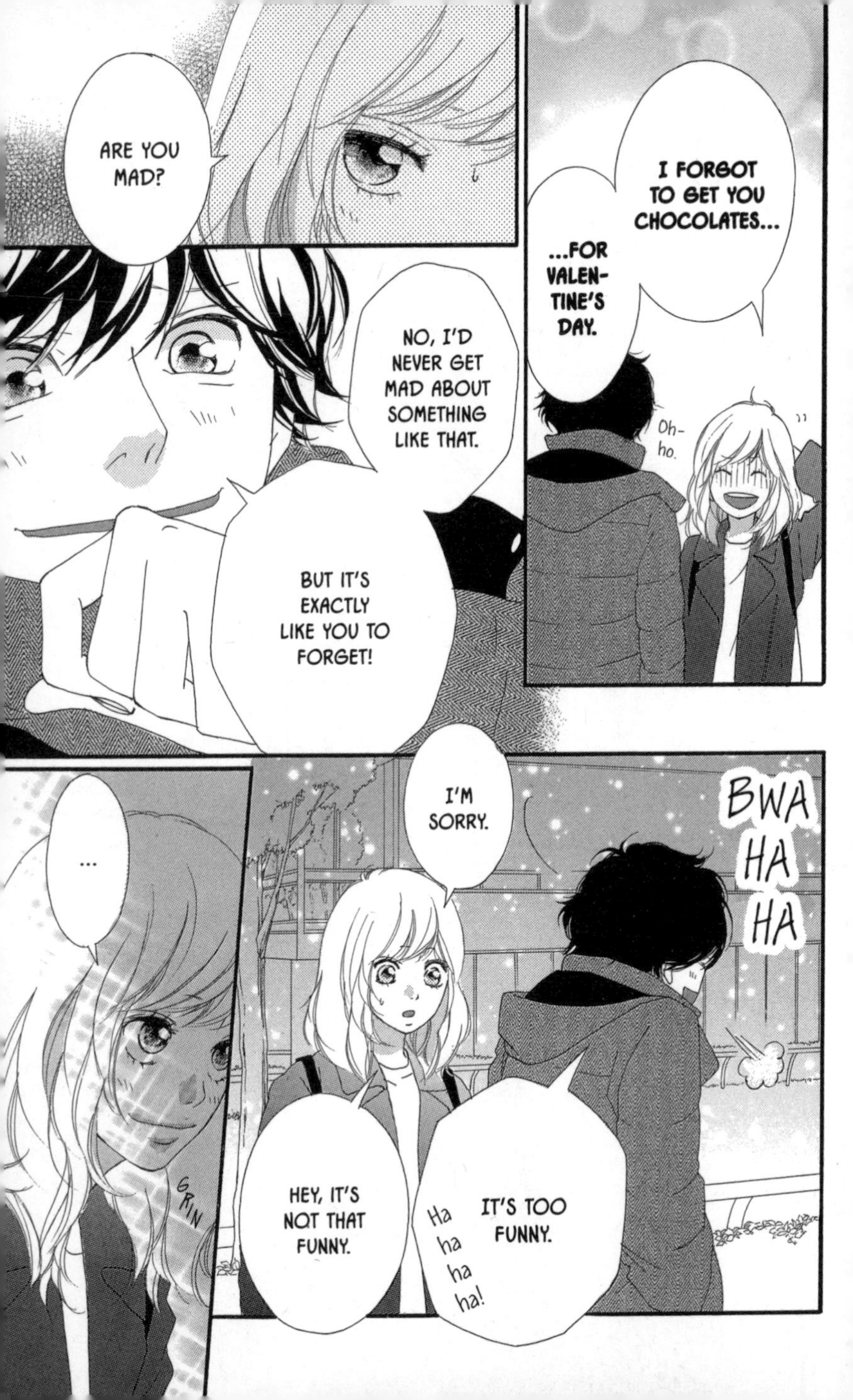
I FORGOT TO GET YOU CHOCOLATES...
...FOR VALENTINE'S DAY.
Oh-ho.
ARE YOU MAD?
NO, I'D NEVER GET MAD ABOUT SOMETHING LIKE THAT.
BUT IT'S EXACTLY LIKE YOU TO FORGET!
BWA HA HA
I'M SORRY.
IT'S TOO FUNNY.
Ha ha ha ha!
HEY, IT'S NOT THAT FUNNY.
...
GRIN

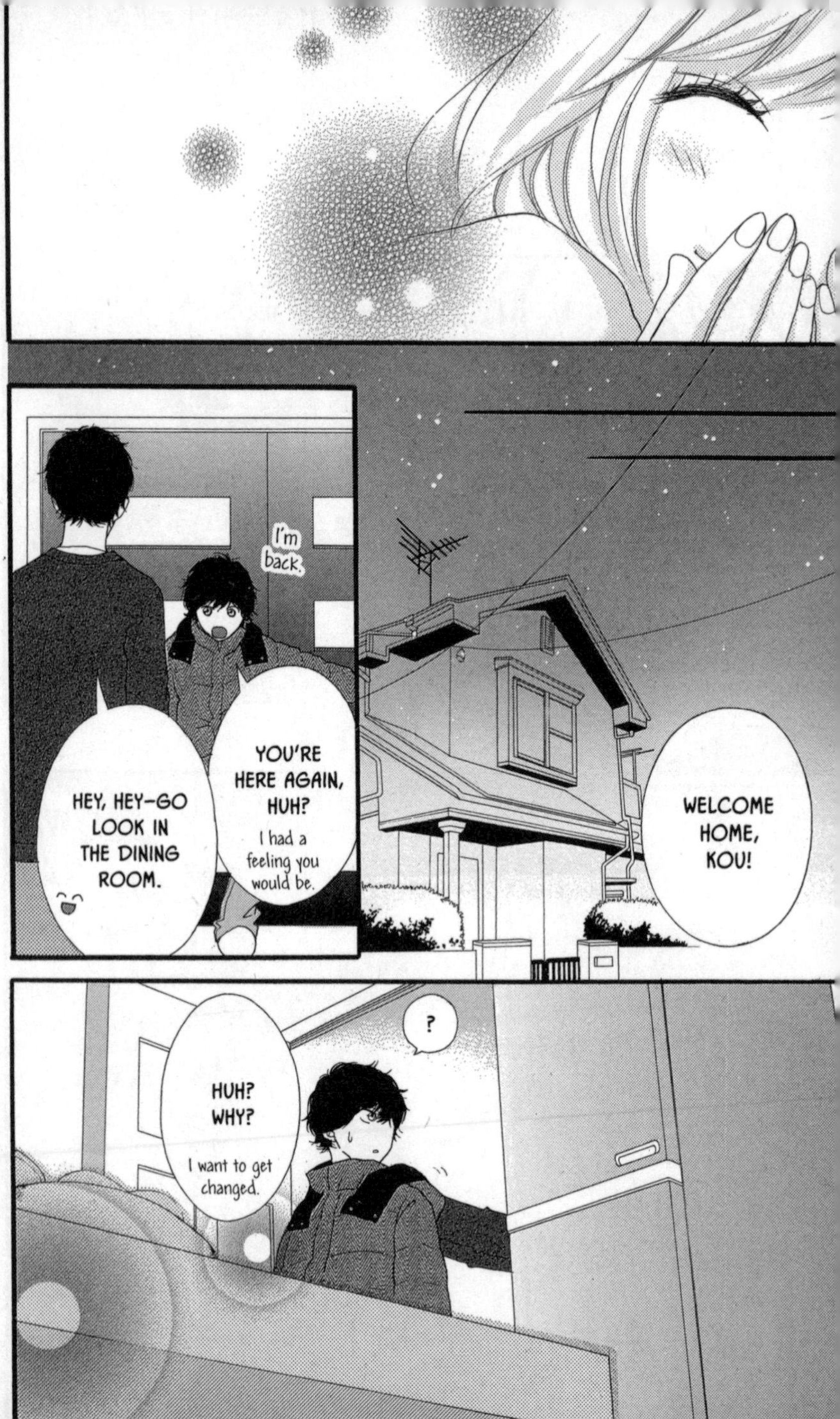
WELCOME HOME, KOU!
I'm back.
YOU'RE HERE AGAIN, HUH?
I had a feeling you would be.
HEY, HEY—GO LOOK IN THE DINING ROOM.
?
HUH? WHY?
I want to get changed.

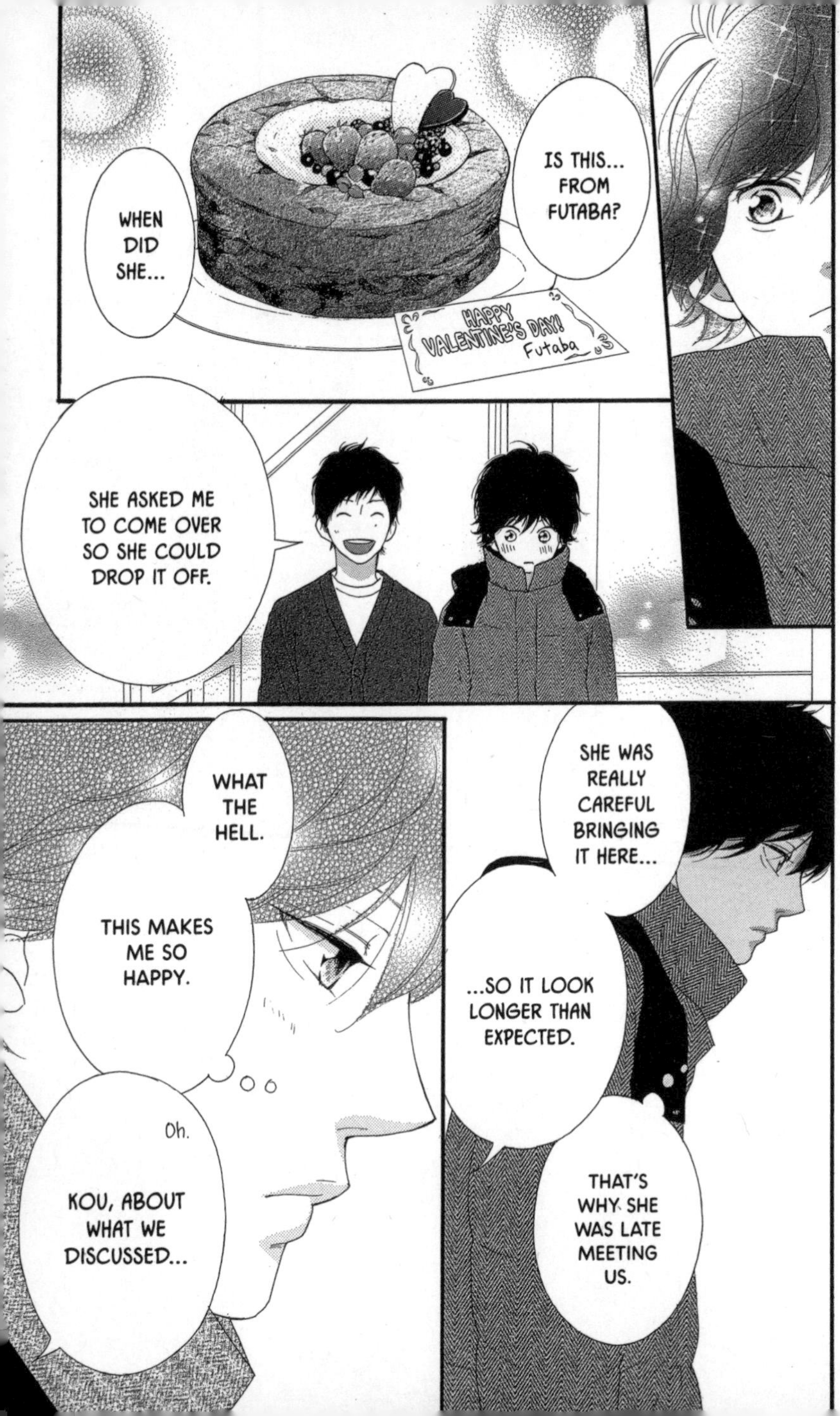
IS THIS... FROM FUTABA?
WHEN DID SHE...
HAPPY VALENTINE'S DAY! Futaba
SHE ASKED ME TO COME OVER SO SHE COULD DROP IT OFF.
SHE WAS REALLY CAREFUL BRINGING IT HERE...
...SO IT LOOK LONGER THAN EXPECTED.
THAT'S WHY SHE WAS LATE MEETING US.
WHAT THE HELL.
THIS MAKES ME SO HAPPY.
Oh.
KOU, ABOUT WHAT WE DISCUSSED...

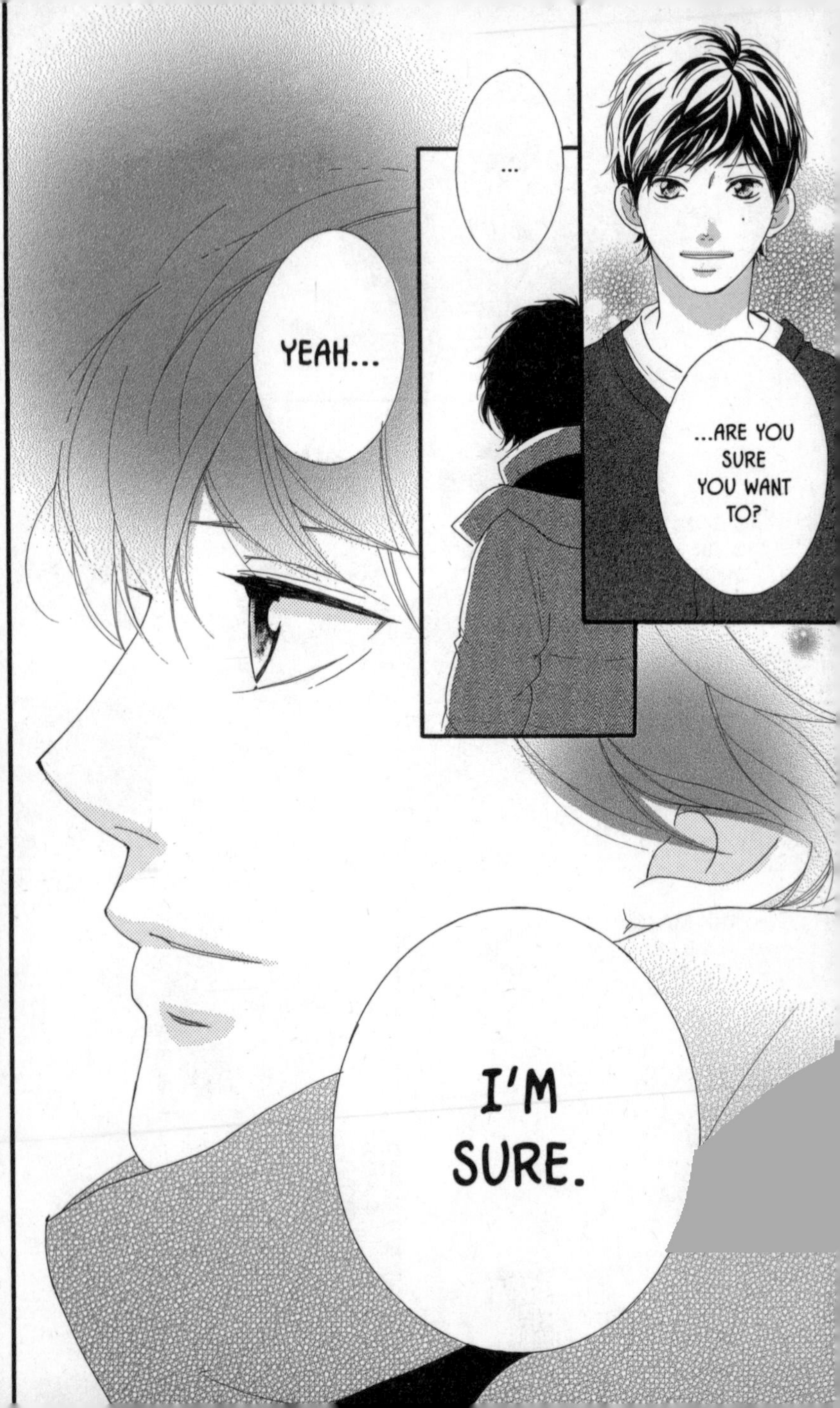
...ARE YOU SURE YOU WANT TO?
...
YEAH...
I'M SURE.

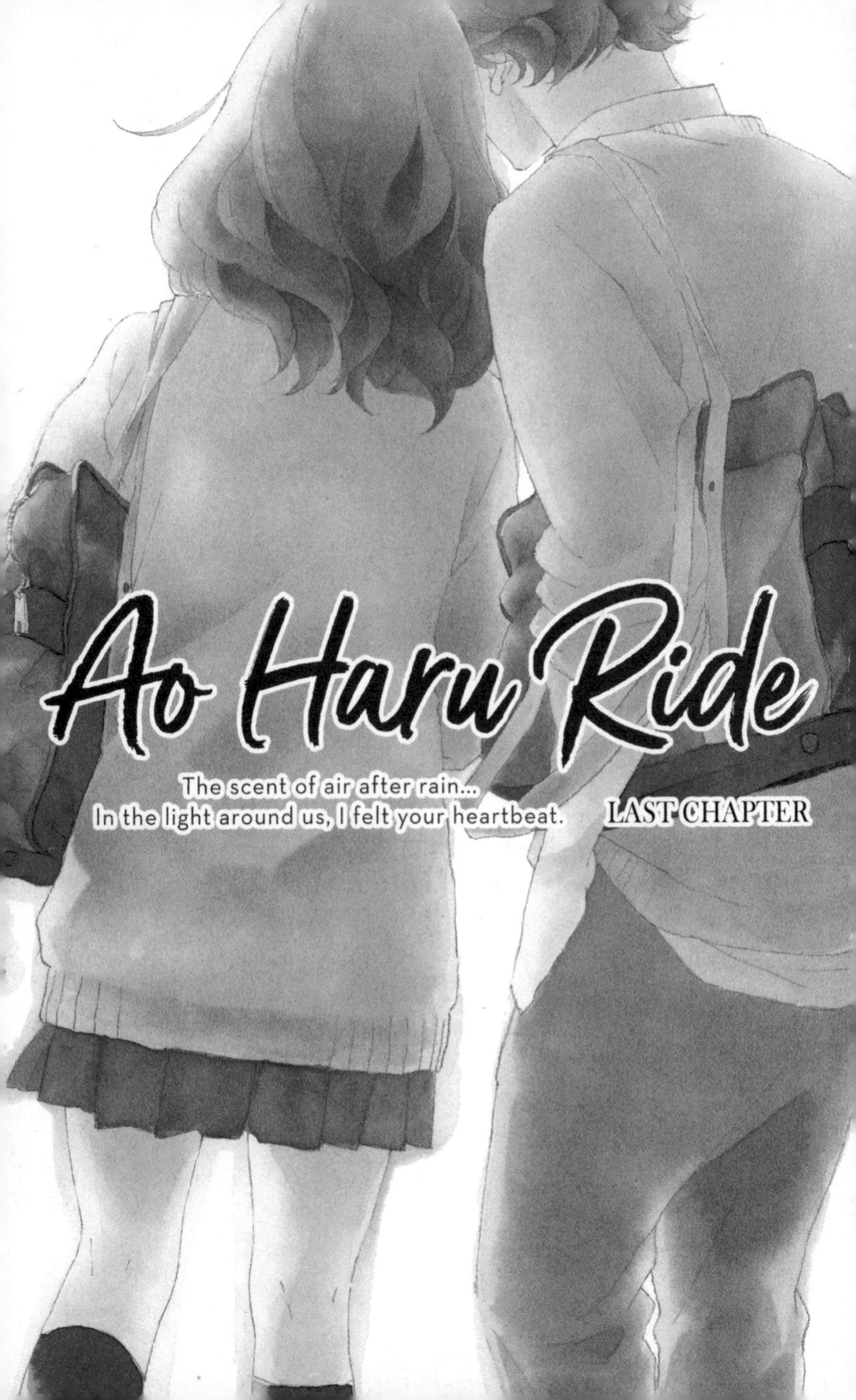
Ao Haru Ride
The scent of air after rain...
In the light around us, I felt your heartbeat.
LAST CHAPTER

I got to reveal the name of Kou's black cat in the final volume.

Its name may seem surprising given how grown-up Kou was early on, but Kou didn't realize (only I knew at the time) that it really was all an act. He said he named his cat "Yoshioka" because the cat ate a lot, but that was nothing more than Kou trying to cover up his own embarrassment. This is the kind of guy Kou really is. He just tries really hard to come off as cool. (I love guys like that!) From the moment Kou brought the cat home, I decided its name would be Yoshioka. I pictured him constantly tending to it and calling out its name. Which is why, in *Ao Haru Ride* volume 5, when Aya goes over to Kou's house, the cat meows every time Aya says "Yoshioka." Now that you know this, I invite you to go back and re-read that scene for a deeper enjoyment of that chapter. Even though it doesn't come up in the story, I think you'll be able to imagine how Kou plays with his cat. I wanted the cat to be the trigger for Kou to start calling Futaba by her first name, and I'm extremely satisfied that I was able to work it into the story. I'm sure Futaba is also grateful to Little Yoshioka for that.

(Personally, I liked it better when Kou called Futaba by her last name. But this was for Futaba... Ha!)

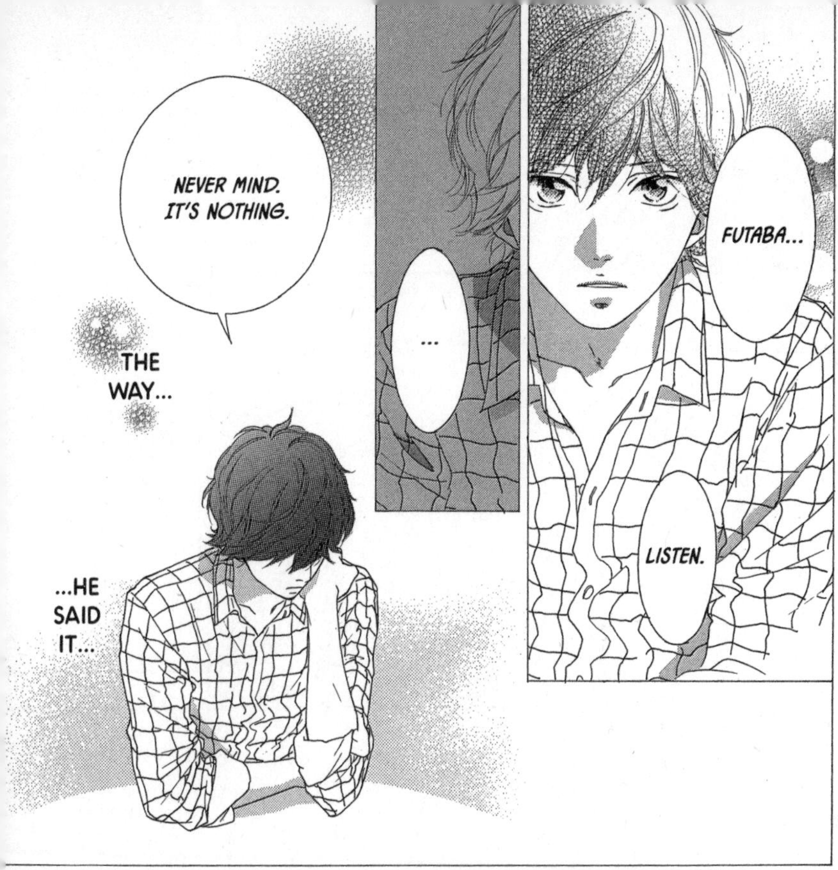
FUTABA...
LISTEN.
...
NEVER MIND. IT'S NOTHING.
THE WAY...
...HE SAID IT...

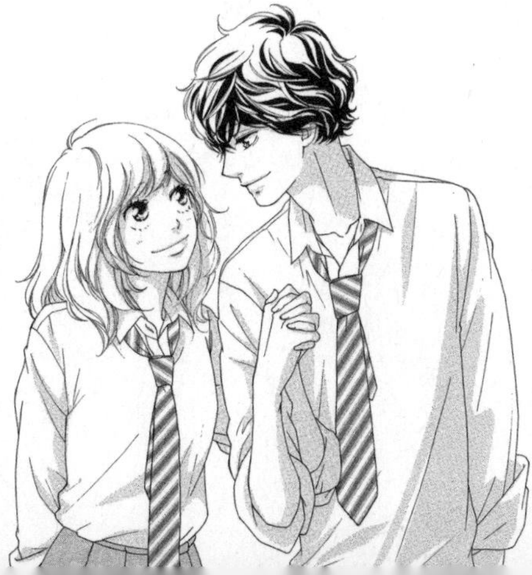

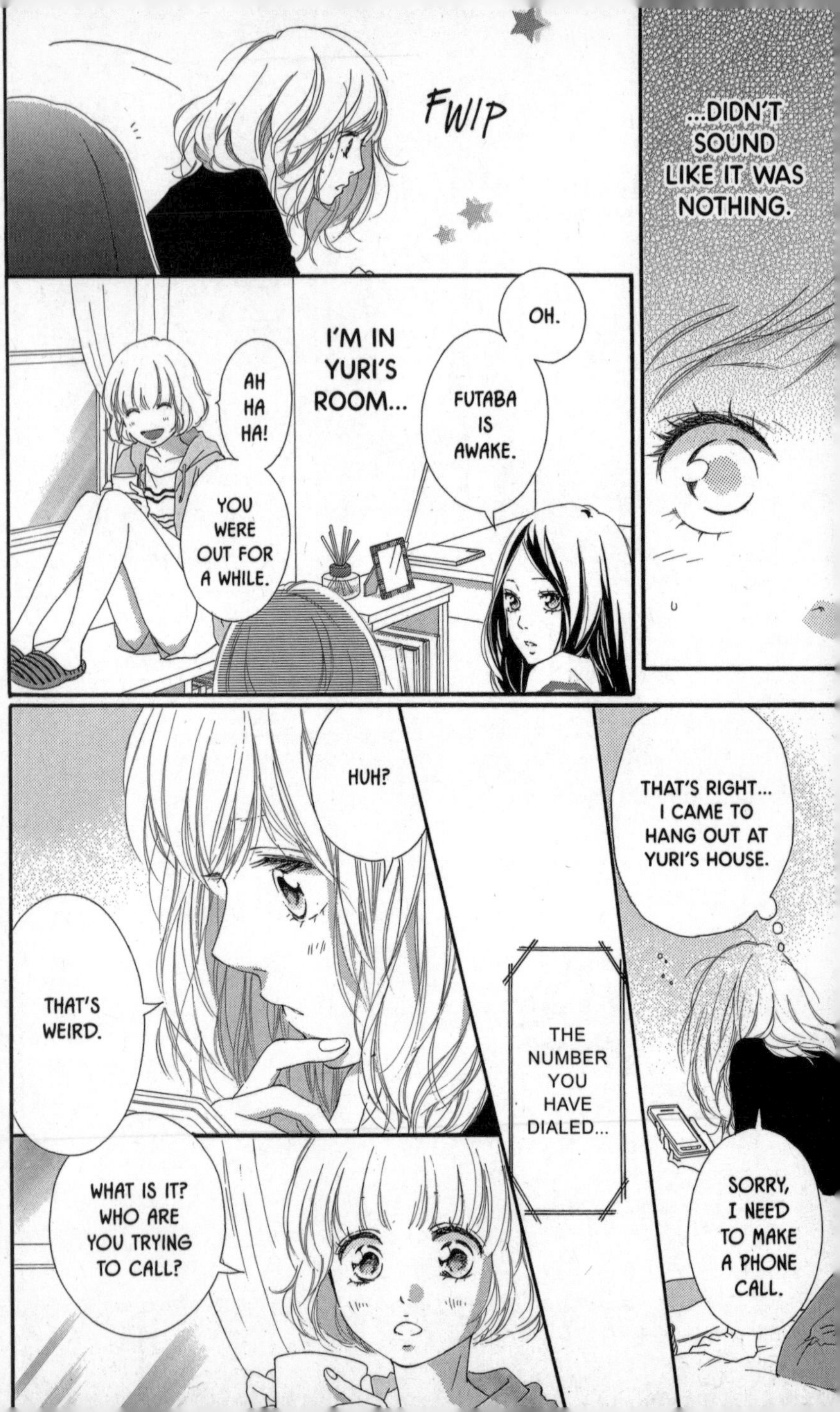
...DIDN'T SOUND LIKE IT WAS NOTHING.
FWIP
OH.
FUTABA IS AWAKE.
I'M IN YURI'S ROOM...
AH HA HA!
YOU WERE OUT FOR A WHILE.
THAT'S RIGHT... I CAME TO HANG OUT AT YURI'S HOUSE.
SORRY, I NEED TO MAKE A PHONE CALL.
THE NUMBER YOU HAVE DIALED...
HUH?
THAT'S WEIRD.
WHAT IS IT? WHO ARE YOU TRYING TO CALL?

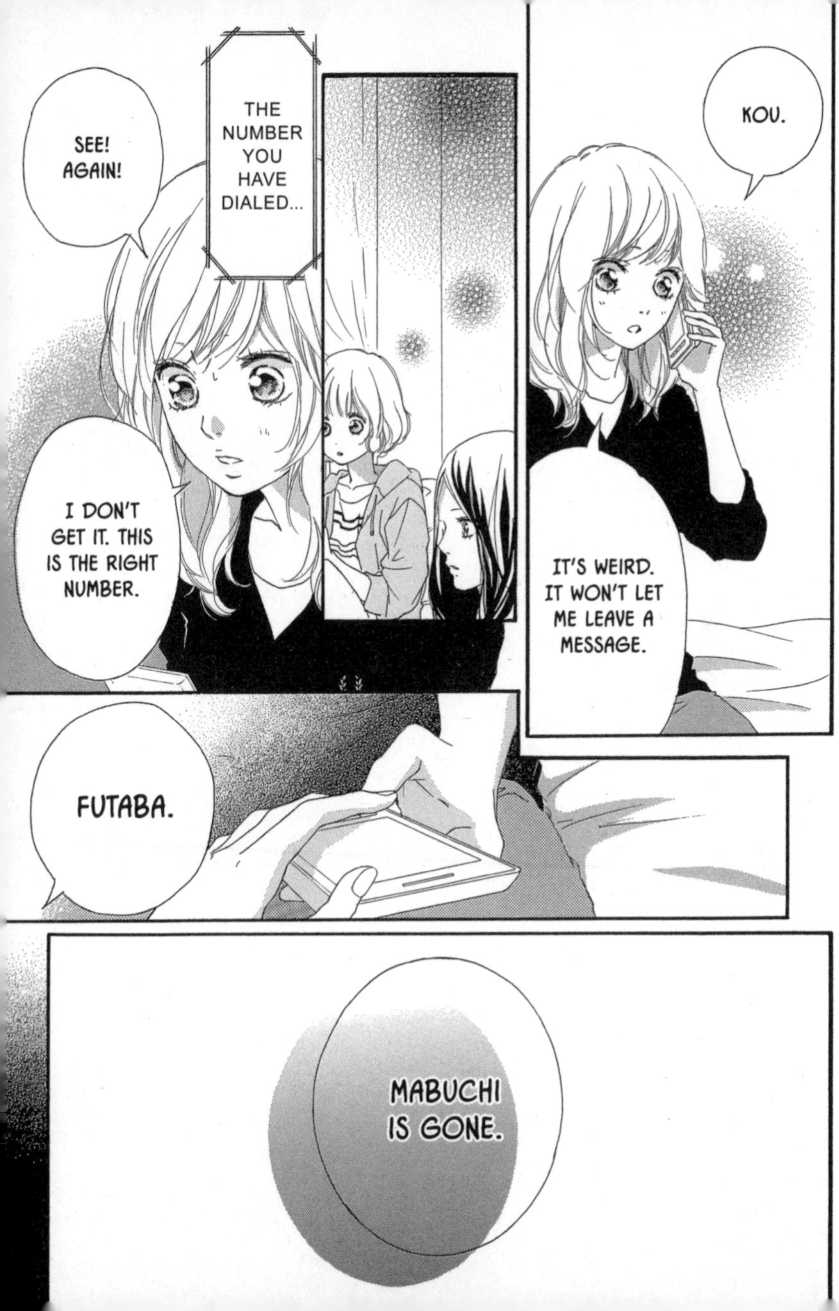
KOU.
IT'S WEIRD. IT WON'T LET ME LEAVE A MESSAGE.
THE NUMBER YOU HAVE DIALED...
SEE! AGAIN!
I DON'T GET IT. THIS IS THE RIGHT NUMBER.
FUTABA.
MABUCHI IS GONE.

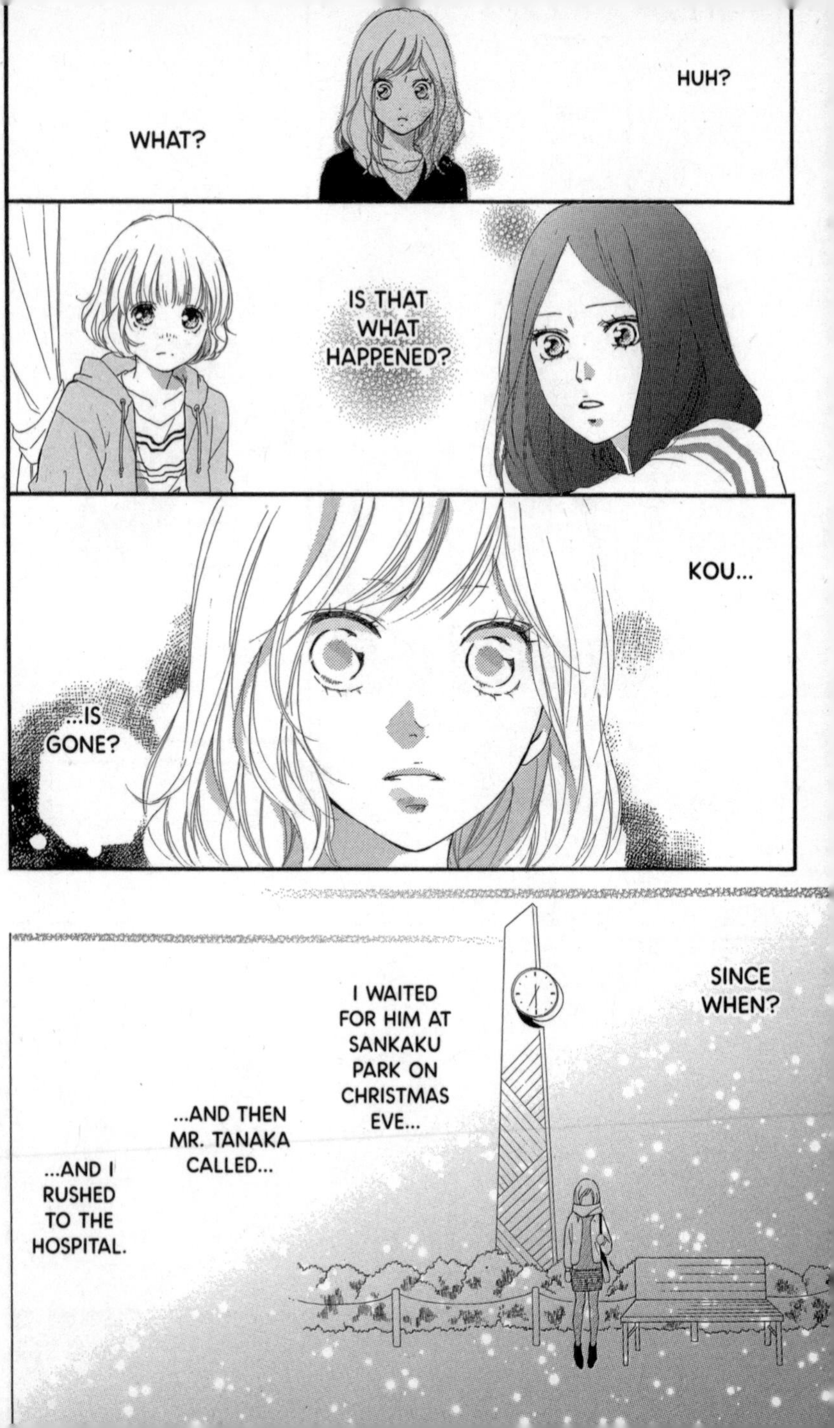
HUH?
WHAT?
IS THAT WHAT HAPPENED?
KOU...
...IS GONE?
SINCE WHEN?
I WAITED FOR HIM AT SANKAKU PARK ON CHRISTMAS EVE...
...AND THEN MR. TANAKA CALLED...
...AND I RUSHED TO THE HOSPITAL.

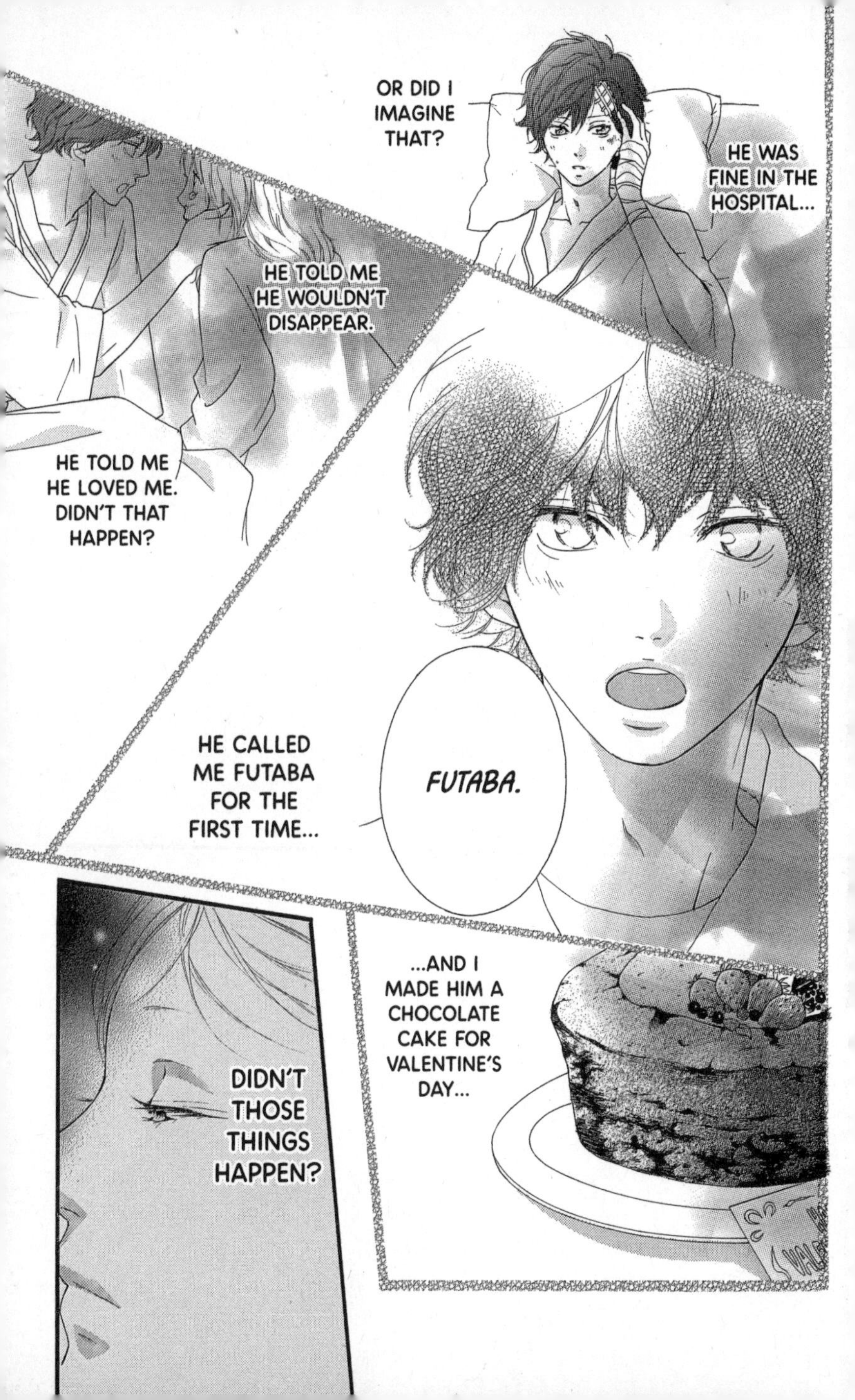
HE WAS FINE IN THE HOSPITAL...
OR DID I IMAGINE THAT?
HE TOLD ME HE WOULDN'T DISAPPEAR.
HE TOLD ME HE LOVED ME. DIDN'T THAT HAPPEN?
FUTABA.
HE CALLED ME FUTABA FOR THE FIRST TIME...
...AND I MADE HIM A CHOCOLATE CAKE FOR VALENTINE'S DAY...
DIDN'T THOSE THINGS HAPPEN?

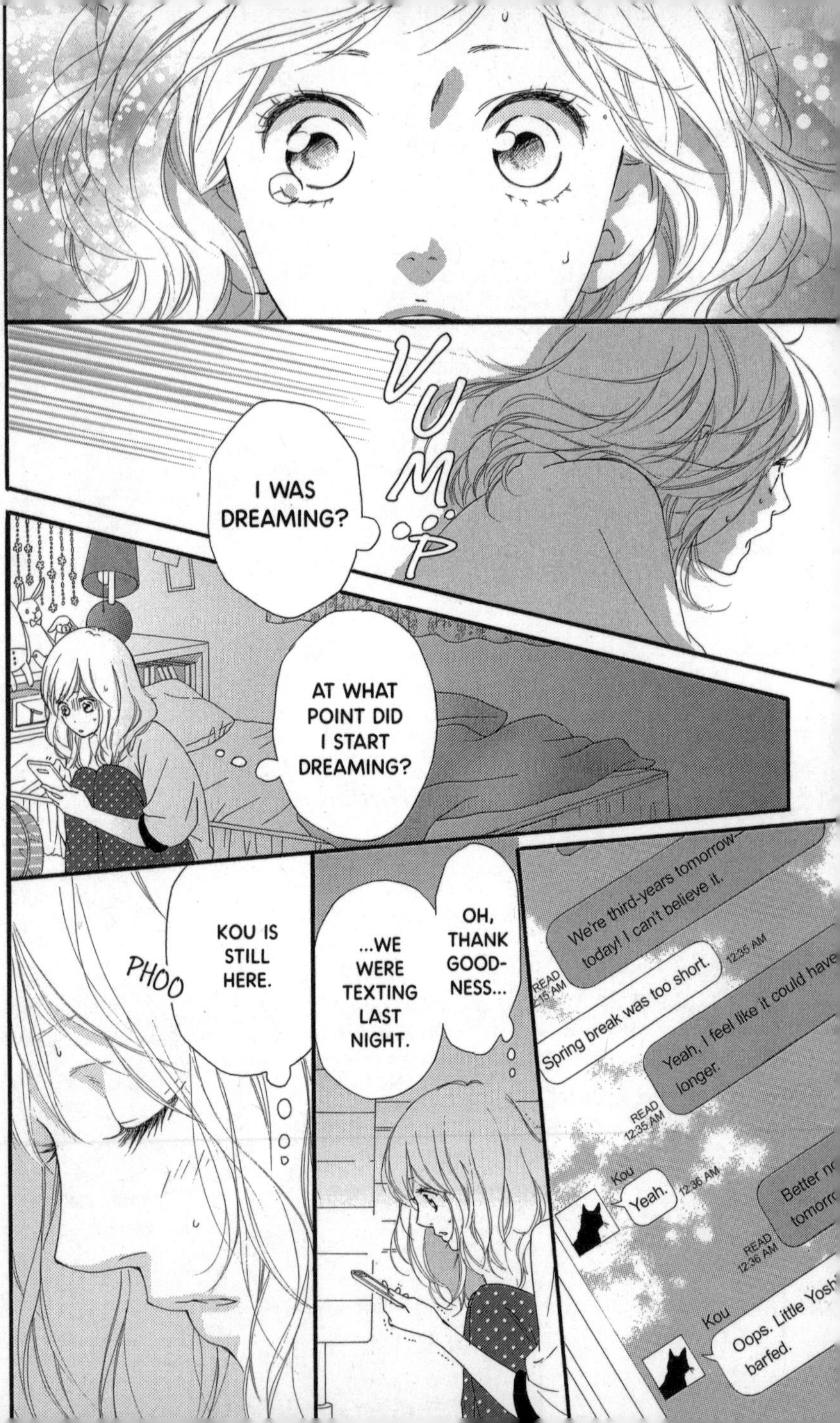
VUMP
I WAS DREAMING?
AT WHAT POINT DID I START DREAMING?
We're third-years tomorrow— today! I can't believe it.
READ
Spring break was too short.
12:35 AM
Yeah, I feel like it could have longer.
READ 12:35 AM
Kou
Yeah.
12:36 AM
READ 12:36 AM
Kou
Oops. Little barfed.
OH, THANK GOODNESS...
...WE WERE TEXTING LAST NIGHT.
KOU IS STILL HERE.
PHOO

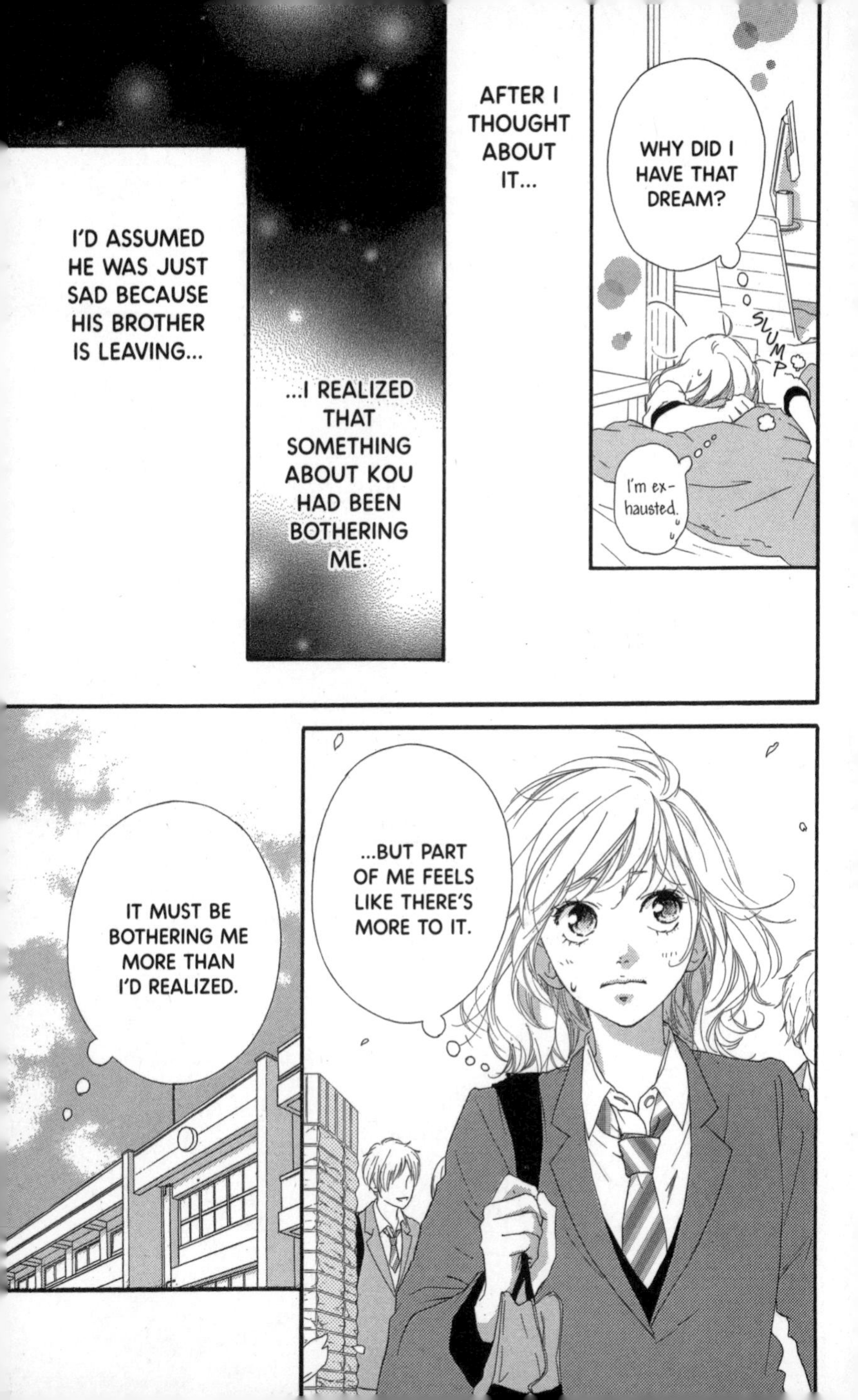
WHY DID I HAVE THAT DREAM?
SLUMP
I'm ex-hausted.
AFTER I THOUGHT ABOUT IT...
...I REALIZED THAT SOMETHING ABOUT KOU HAD BEEN BOTHERING ME.
I'D ASSUMED HE WAS JUST SAD BECAUSE HIS BROTHER IS LEAVING...
...BUT PART OF ME FEELS LIKE THERE'S MORE TO IT.
IT MUST BE BOTHERING ME MORE THAN I'D REALIZED.

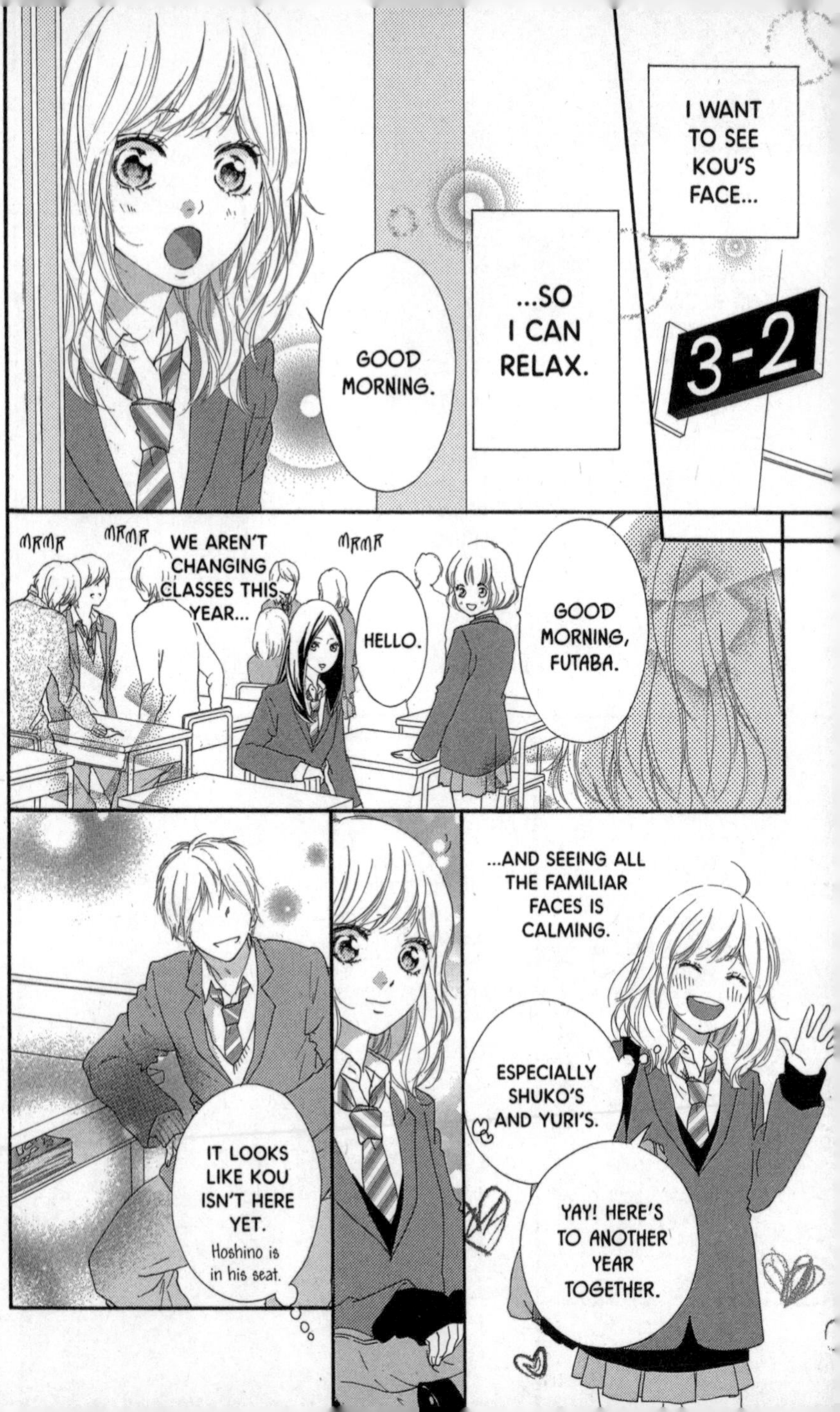
I WANT TO SEE KOU'S FACE...
...SO I CAN RELAX.
3-2
GOOD MORNING.
GOOD MORNING, FUTABA.
HELLO.
MRMR
WE AREN'T CHANGING CLASSES THIS YEAR...
MRMR
MRMR
...AND SEEING ALL THE FAMILIAR FACES IS CALMING.
ESPECIALLY SHUKO'S AND YURI'S.
YAY! HERE'S TO ANOTHER YEAR TOGETHER.
IT LOOKS LIKE KOU ISN'T HERE YET.
Hoshino is in his seat.

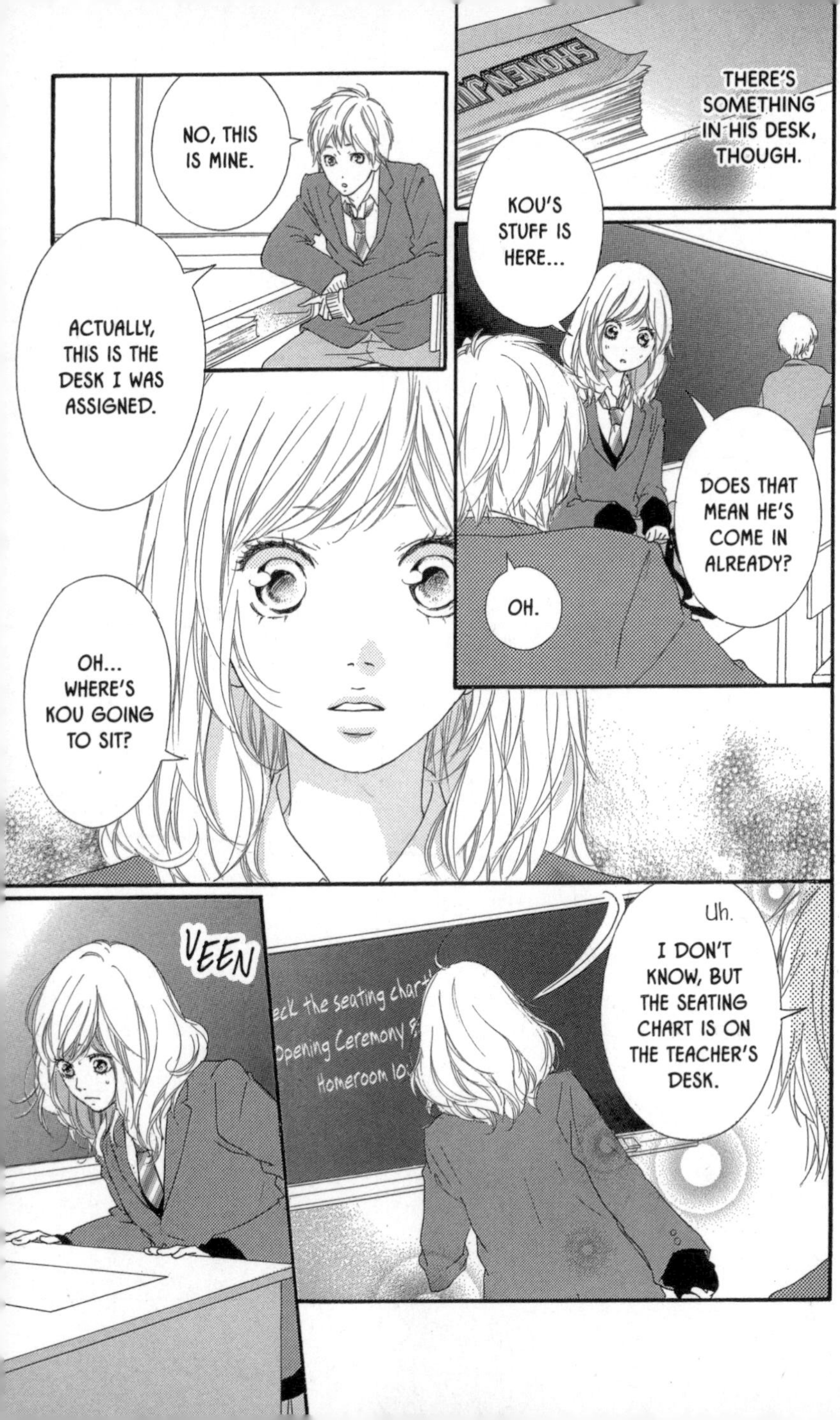
SHONEN JU
THERE'S SOMETHING IN HIS DESK, THOUGH.
KOU'S STUFF IS HERE...
DOES THAT MEAN HE'S COME IN ALREADY?
OH.
NO, THIS IS MINE.
ACTUALLY, THIS IS THE DESK I WAS ASSIGNED.
OH... WHERE'S KOU GOING TO SIT?
Uh.
I DON'T KNOW, BUT THE SEATING CHART IS ON THE TEACHER'S DESK.
eck the seating chart
Opening Ceremony
Homeroom 10
VEEN

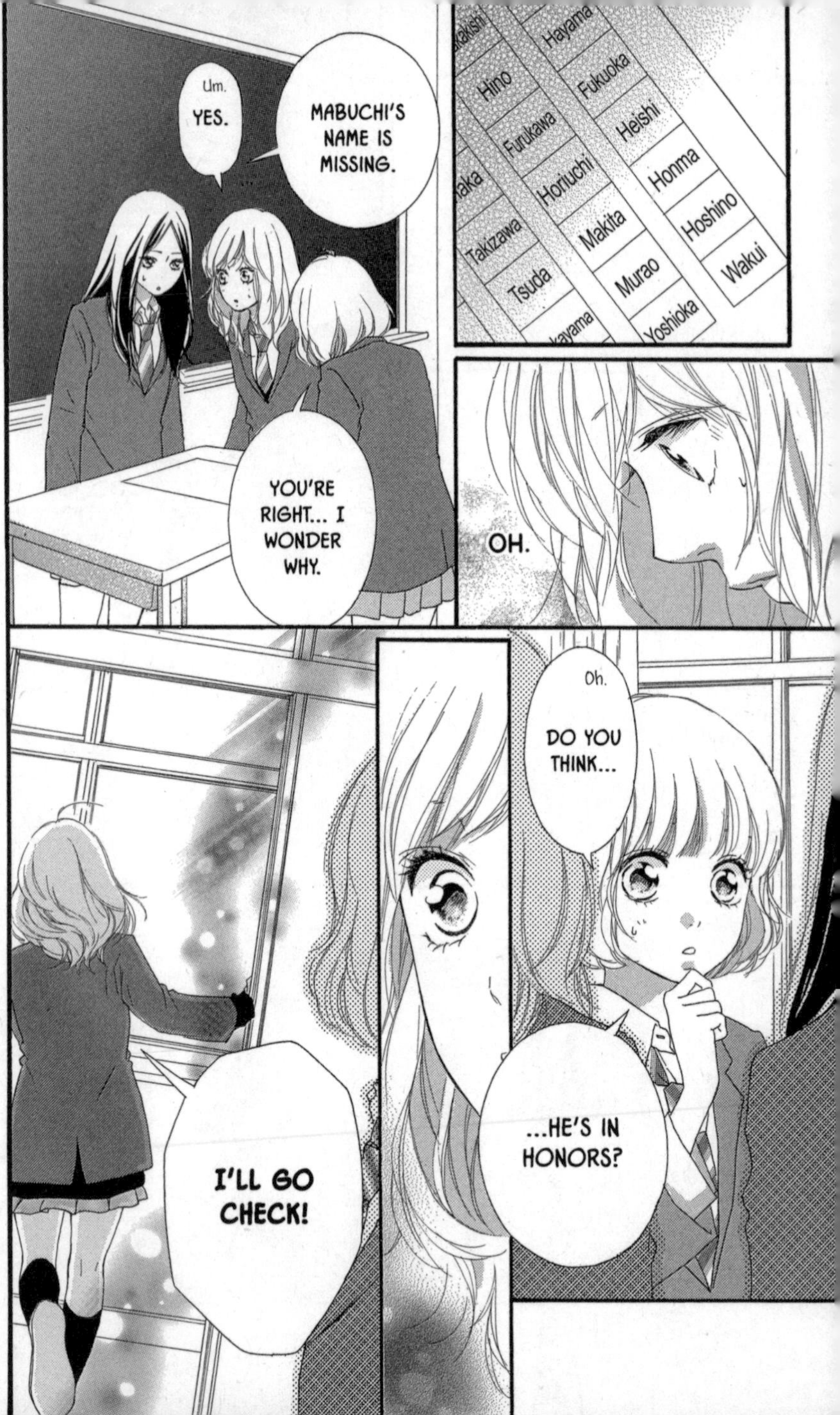
Hayama
Fukuoka
Heishi
Honma
Hoshino
Wakui
Hino
Furukawa
Horiuchi
Makita
Murao
Yoshioka
Takizawa
Tsuda
OH.
MABUCHI'S NAME IS MISSING.
Um. YES.
YOU'RE RIGHT... I WONDER WHY.
Oh. DO YOU THINK...
...HE'S IN HONORS?
I'LL GO CHECK!

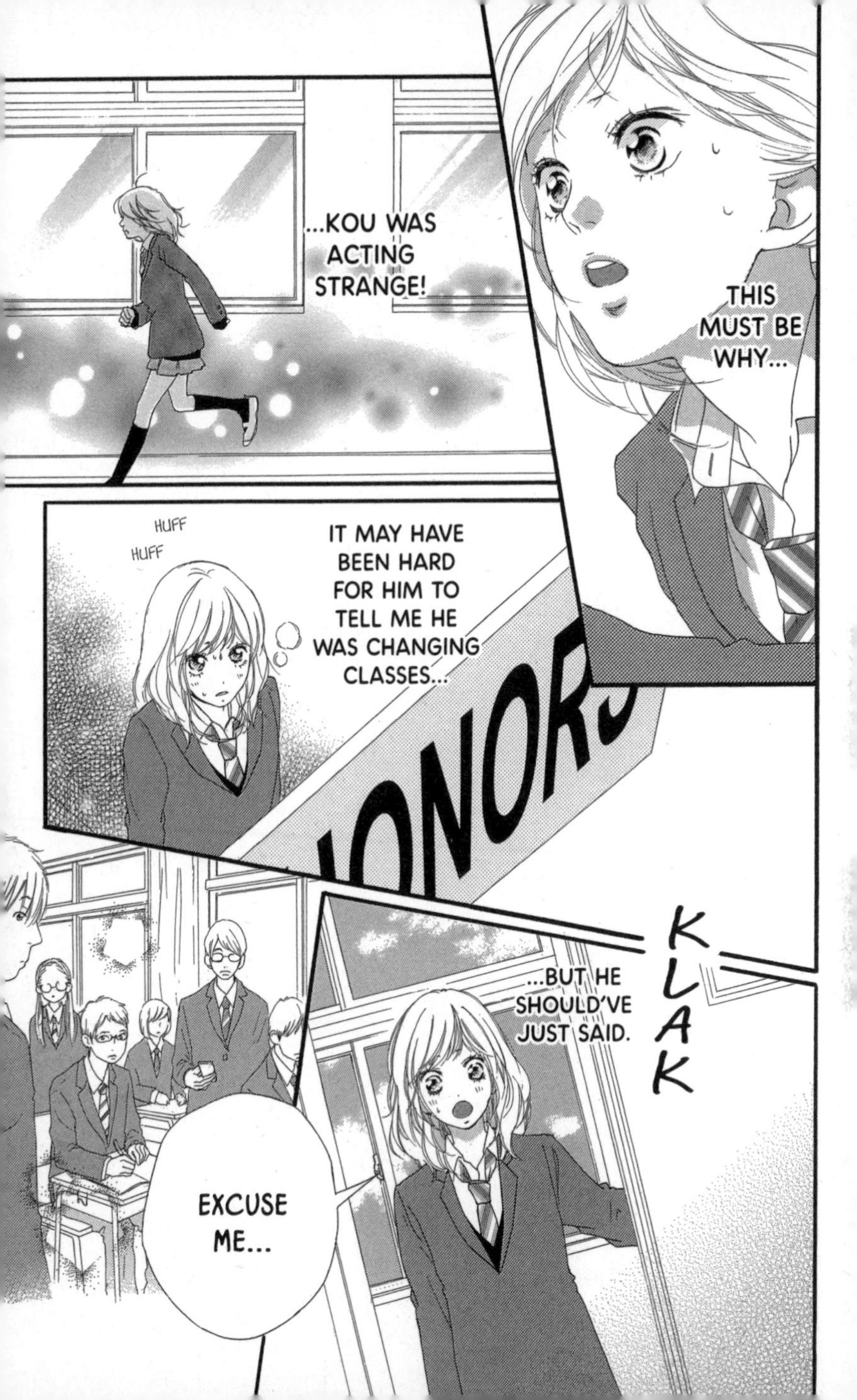
THIS MUST BE WHY...
...KOU WAS ACTING STRANGE!
HUFF
HUFF
IT MAY HAVE BEEN HARD FOR HIM TO TELL ME HE WAS CHANGING CLASSES...
KLAK
...BUT HE SHOULD'VE JUST SAID.
EXCUSE ME...

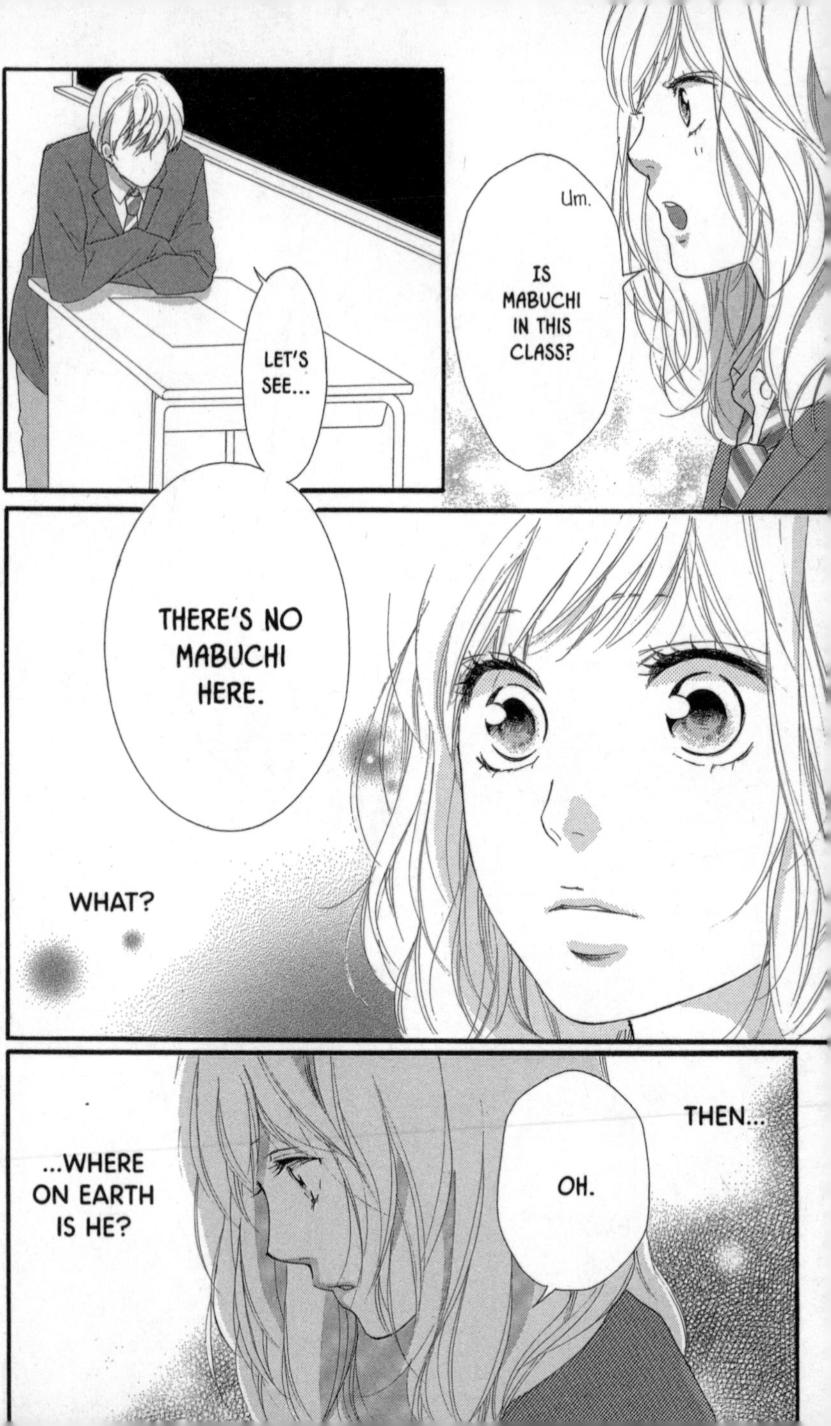
Um.
IS MABUCHI IN THIS CLASS?
LET'S SEE...
THERE'S NO MABUCHI HERE.
WHAT?
THEN...
OH.
...WHERE ON EARTH IS HE?

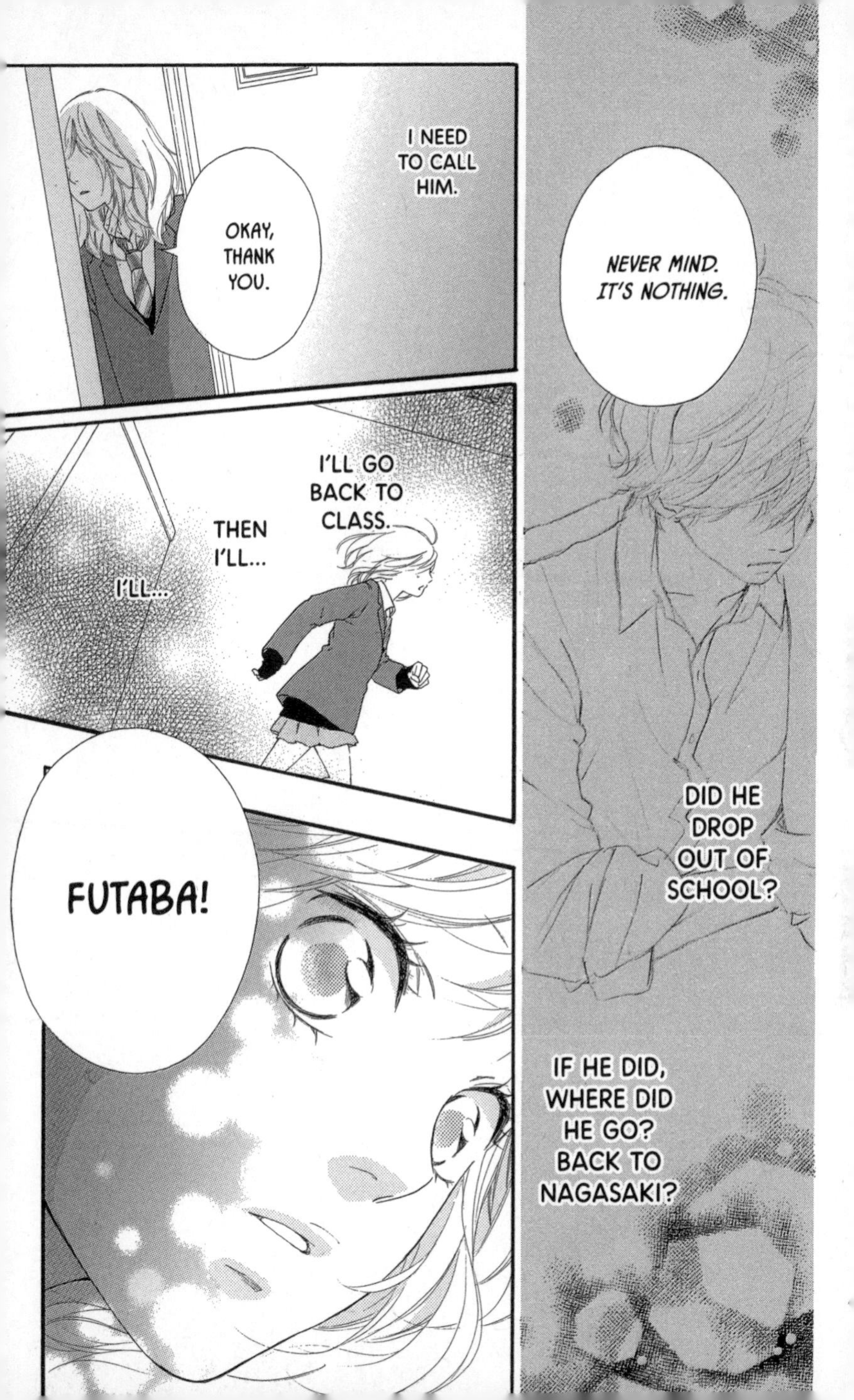
NEVER MIND. IT'S NOTHING.
DID HE DROP OUT OF SCHOOL?
IF HE DID, WHERE DID HE GO? BACK TO NAGASAKI?
I NEED TO CALL HIM.
OKAY, THANK YOU.
I'LL GO BACK TO CLASS.
THEN I'LL...
I'LL...
FUTABA!

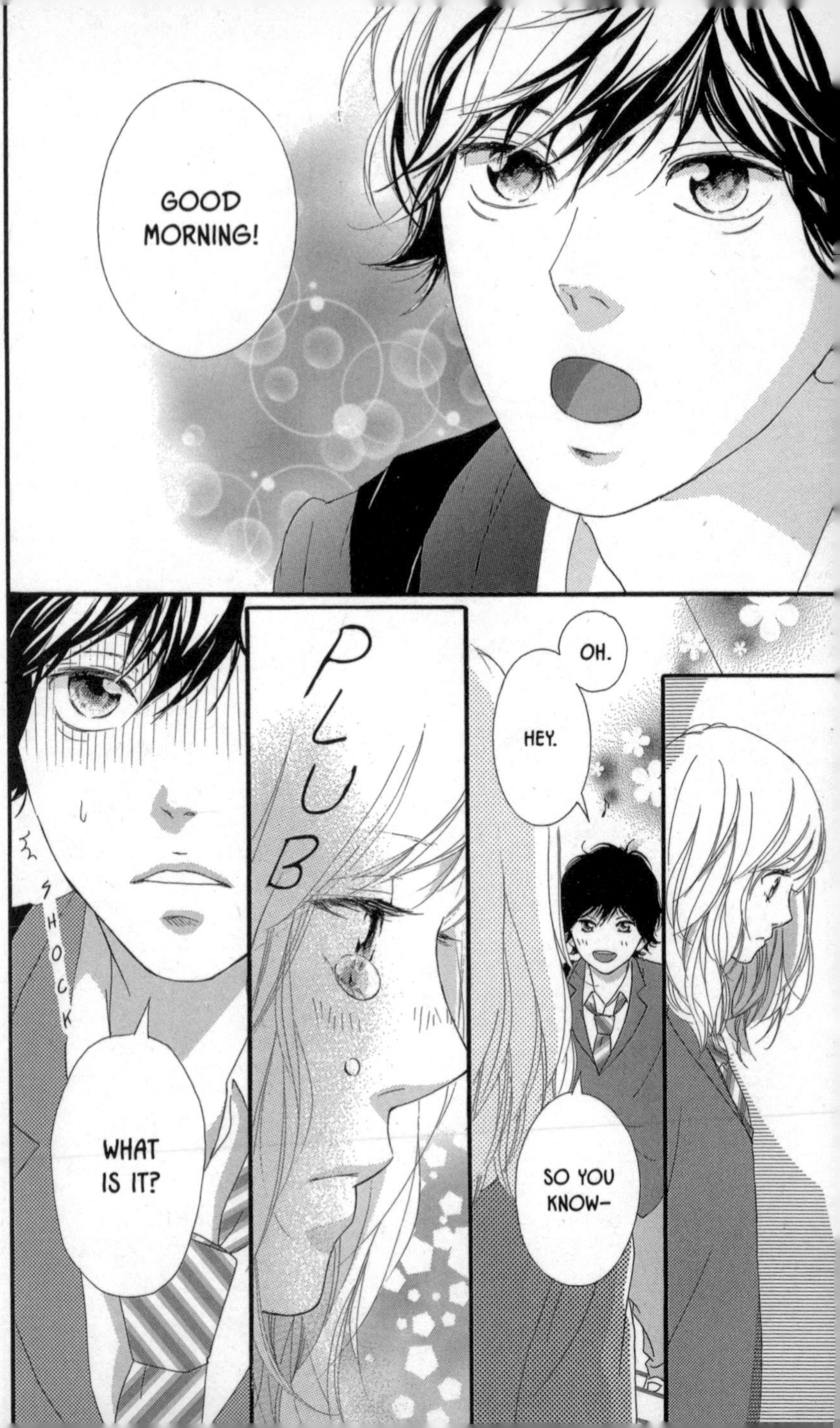
GOOD MORNING!
OH.
HEY.
SO YOU KNOW-
PLUB
SHOCK
WHAT IS IT?

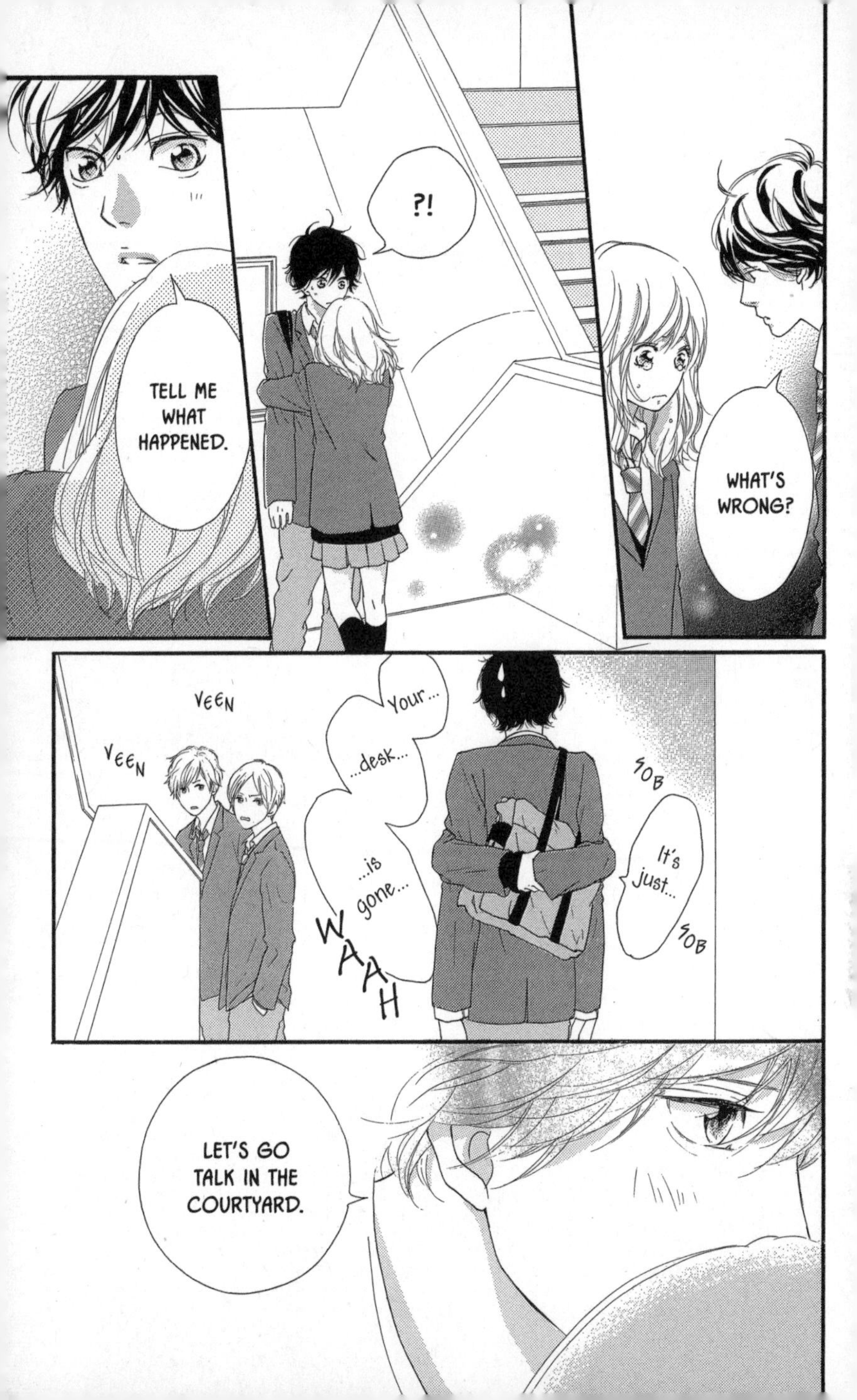
WHAT'S WRONG?
?!
TELL ME WHAT HAPPENED.
SOB
It's just...
SOB
Your...
...desk...
...is gone...
WAAH
VEEN
VEEN
LET'S GO TALK IN THE COURTYARD.

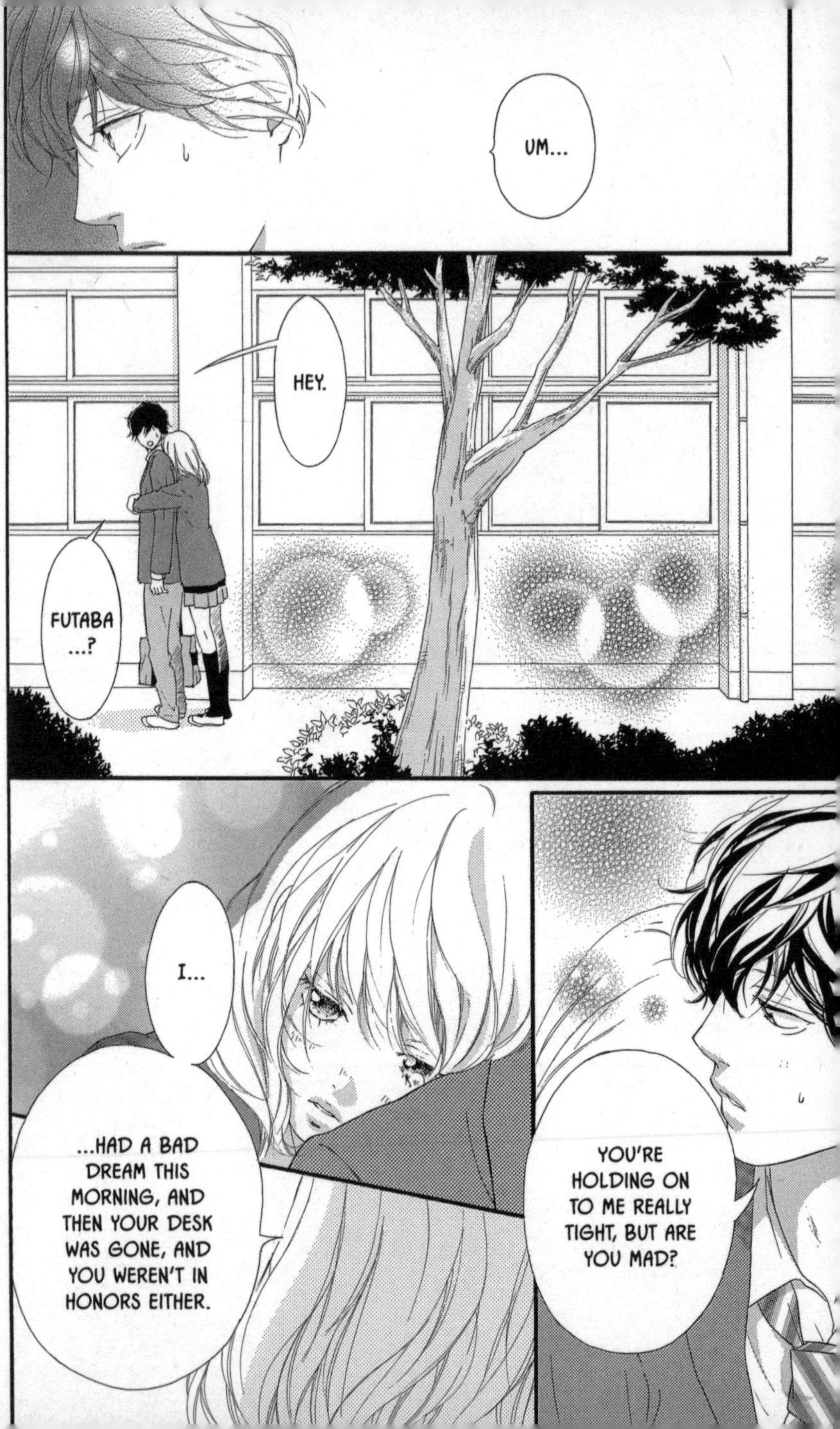
UM...
HEY.
FUTABA ...?
YOU'RE HOLDING ON TO ME REALLY TIGHT, BUT ARE YOU MAD?
I...
...HAD A BAD DREAM THIS MORNING, AND THEN YOUR DESK WAS GONE, AND YOU WEREN'T IN HONORS EITHER.

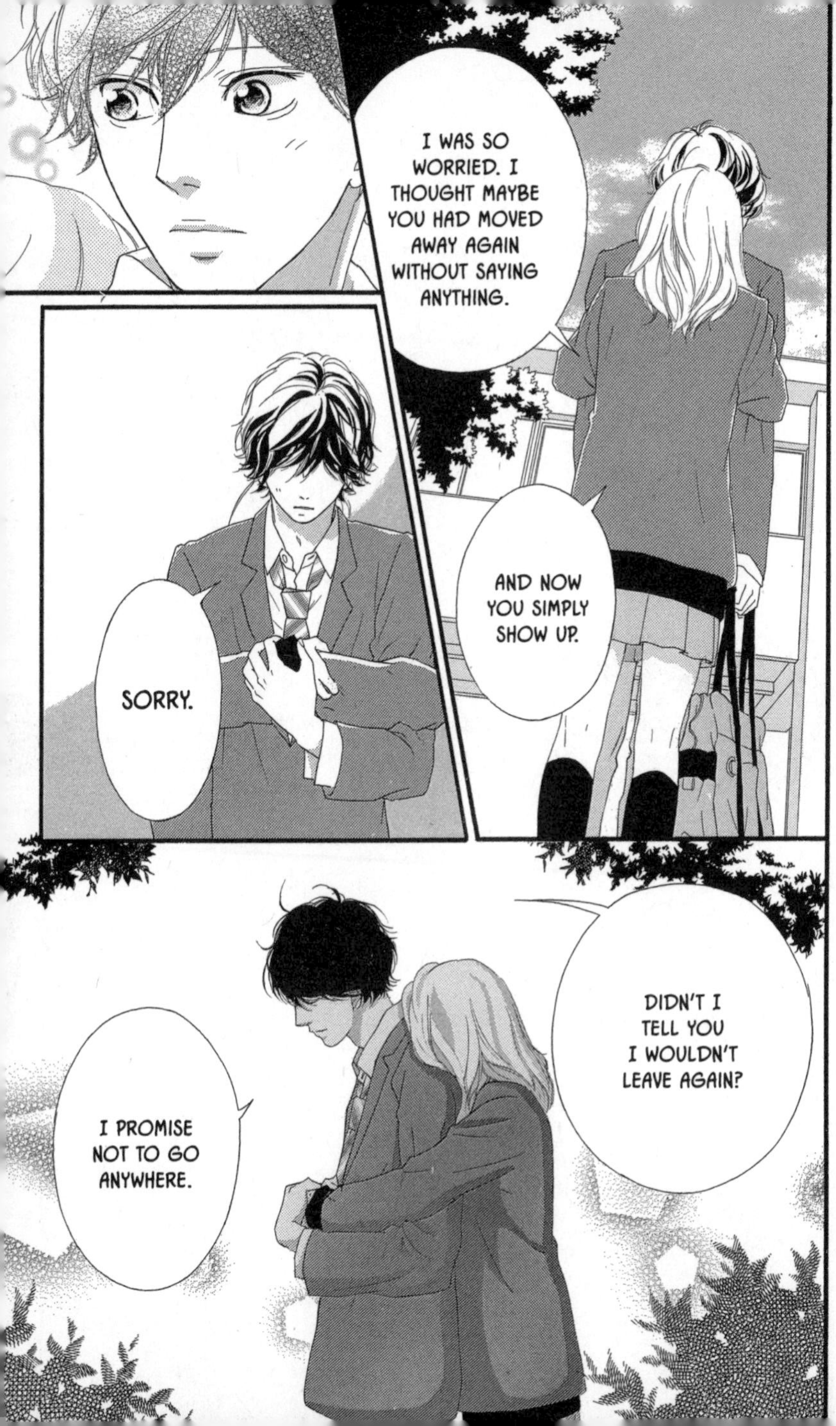
I WAS SO WORRIED. I THOUGHT MAYBE YOU HAD MOVED AWAY AGAIN WITHOUT SAYING ANYTHING.
AND NOW YOU SIMPLY SHOW UP.
SORRY.
DIDN'T I TELL YOU I WOULDN'T LEAVE AGAIN?
I PROMISE NOT TO GO ANYWHERE.

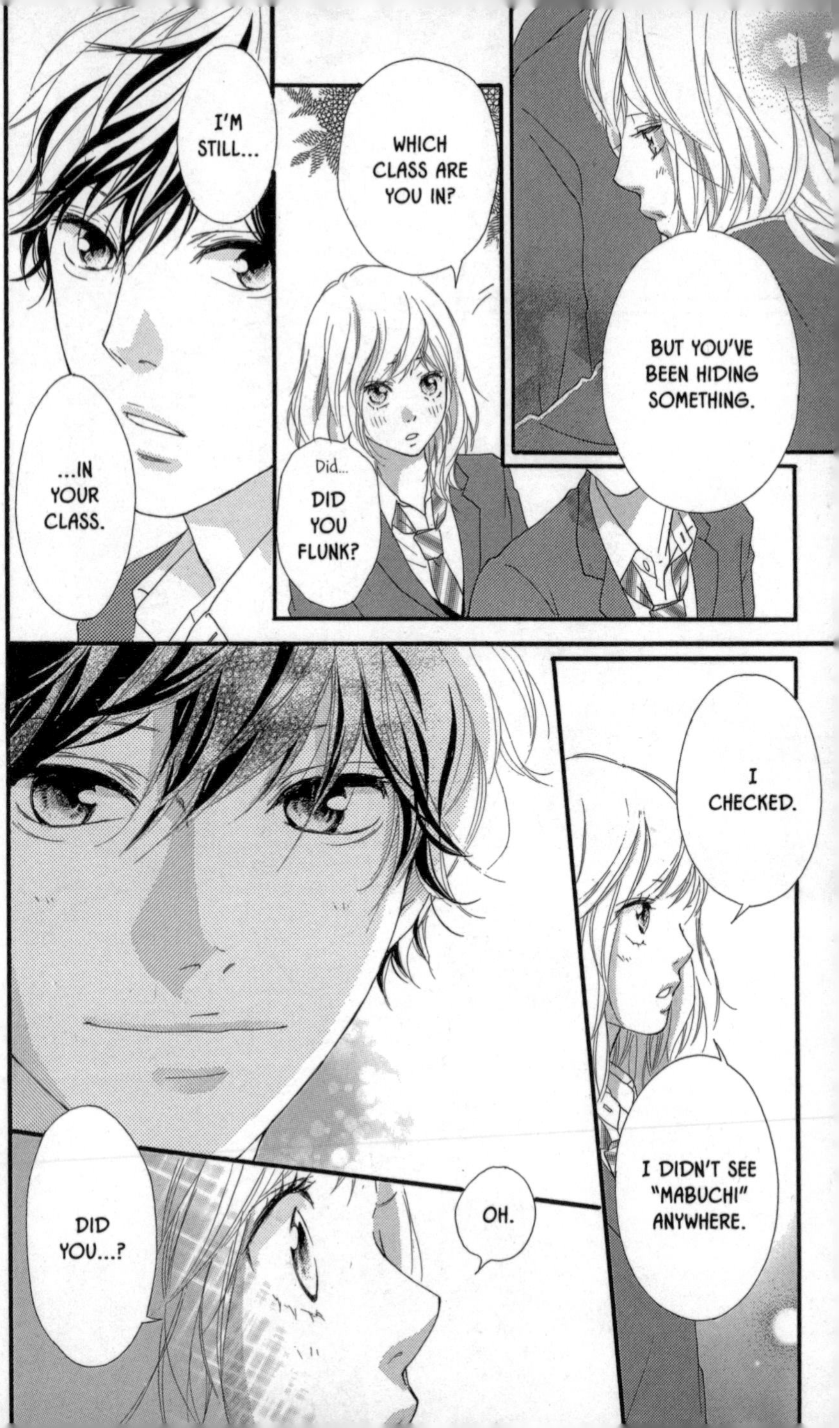
BUT YOU'VE BEEN HIDING SOMETHING.
WHICH CLASS ARE YOU IN?
Did... DID YOU FLUNK?
I'M STILL...
...IN YOUR CLASS.
I CHECKED.
I DIDN'T SEE "MABUCHI" ANYWHERE.
OH.
DID YOU...?

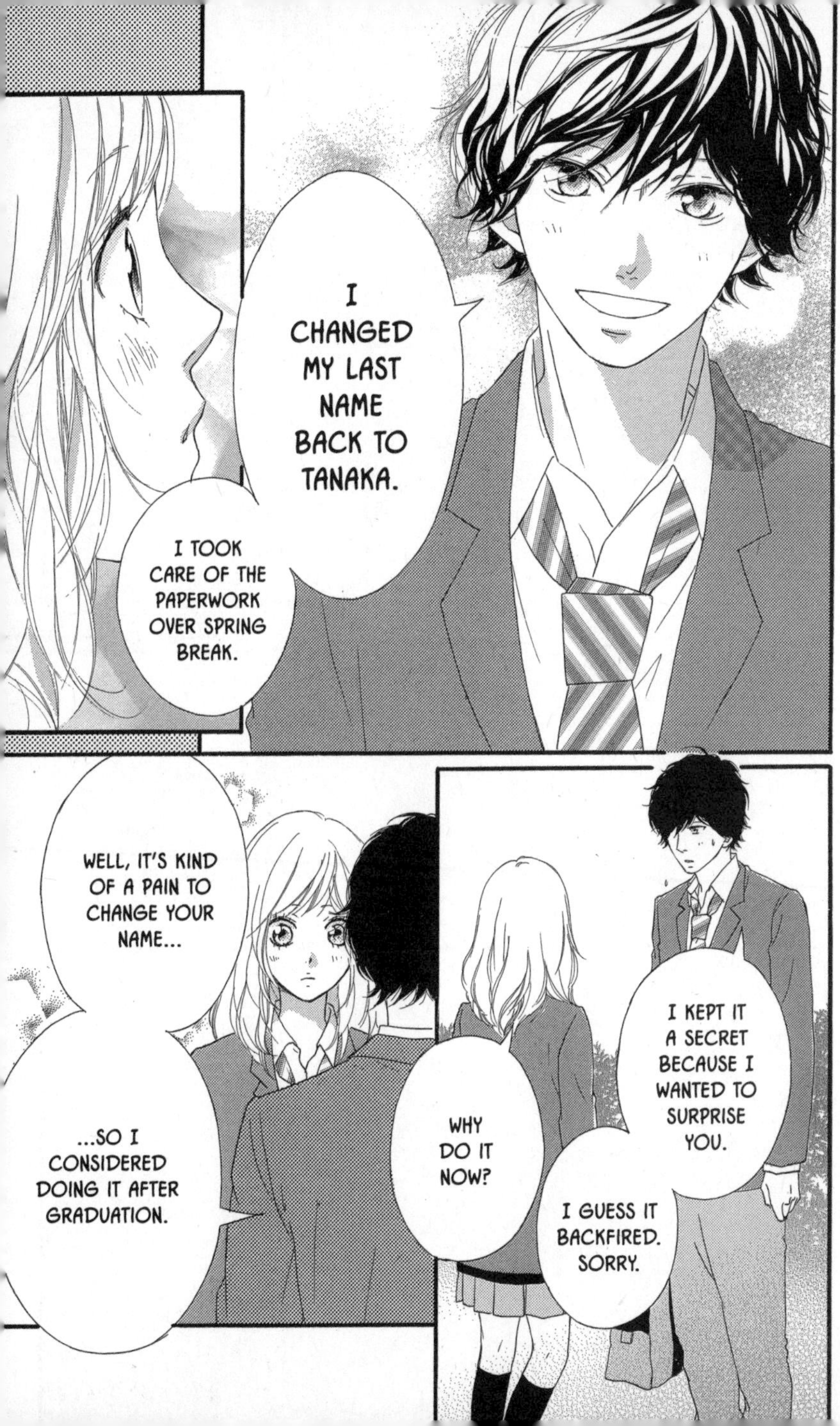
I CHANGED MY LAST NAME BACK TO TANAKA.
I TOOK CARE OF THE PAPERWORK OVER SPRING BREAK.
I KEPT IT A SECRET BECAUSE I WANTED TO SURPRISE YOU.
WHY DO IT NOW?
I GUESS IT BACKFIRED. SORRY.
WELL, IT'S KIND OF A PAIN TO CHANGE YOUR NAME...
...SO I CONSIDERED DOING IT AFTER GRADUATION.

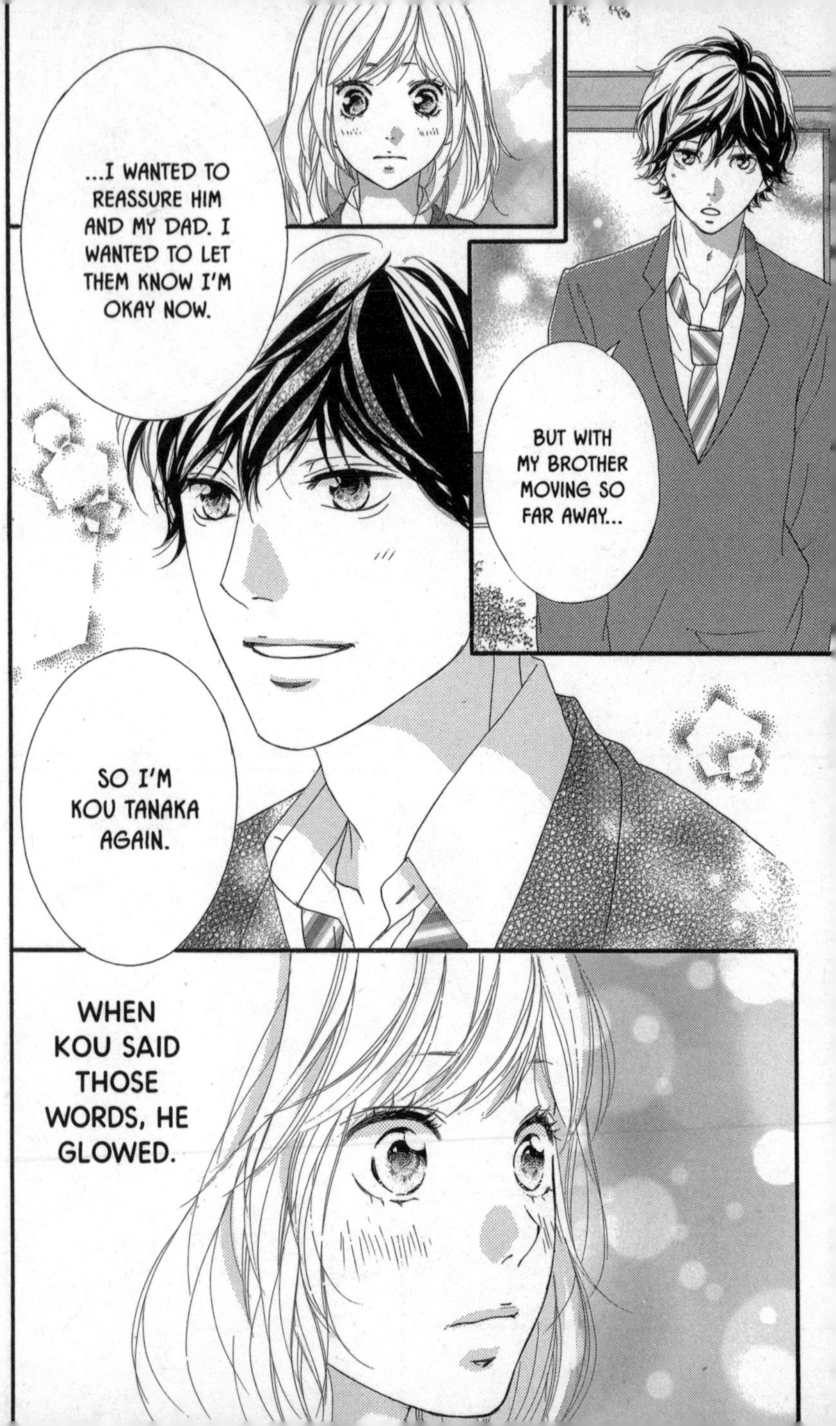
BUT WITH MY BROTHER MOVING SO FAR AWAY...
...I WANTED TO REASSURE HIM AND MY DAD. I WANTED TO LET THEM KNOW I'M OKAY NOW.
SO I'M KOU TANAKA AGAIN.
WHEN KOU SAID THOSE WORDS, HE GLOWED.

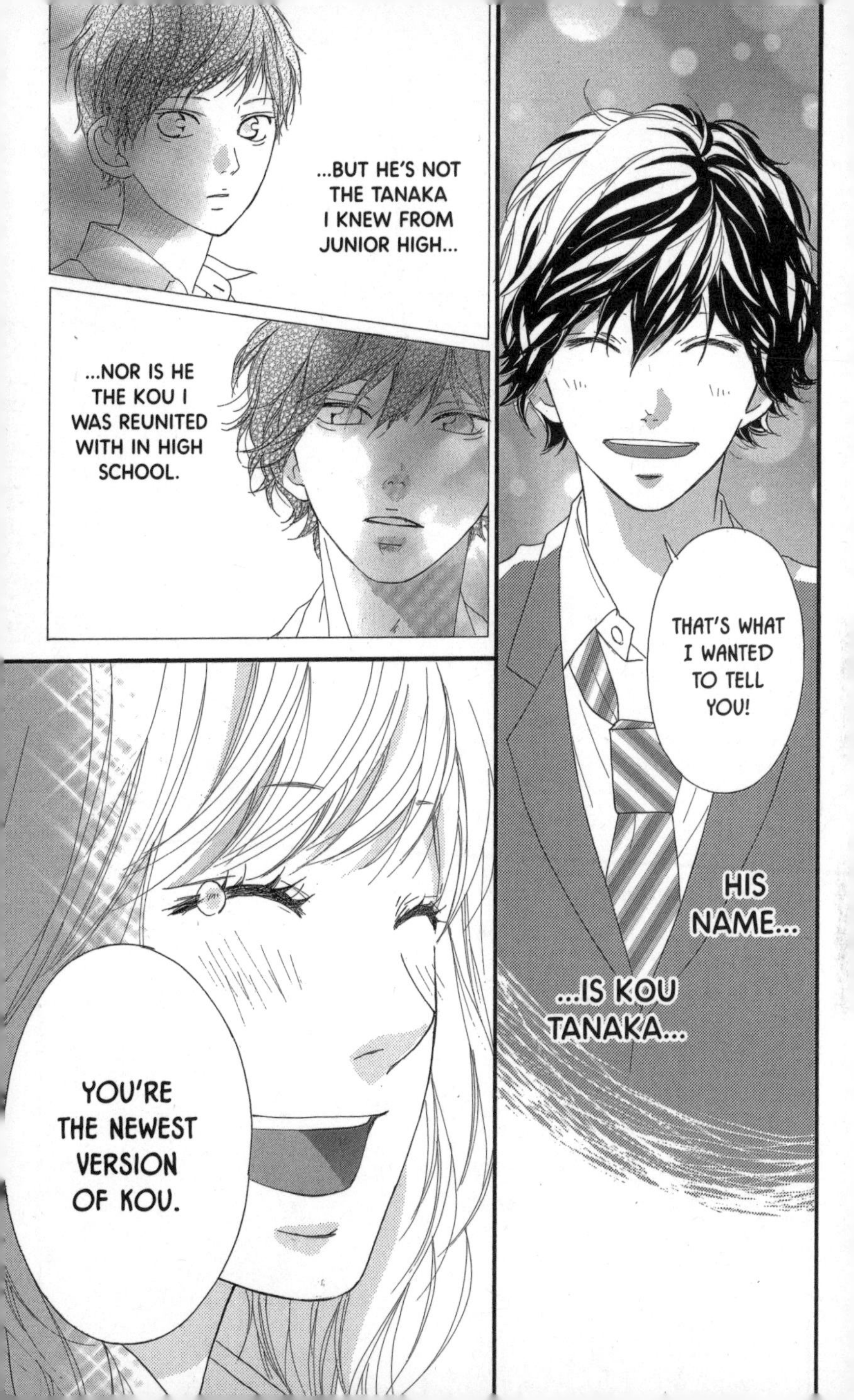
THAT'S WHAT I WANTED TO TELL YOU!
HIS NAME...
...IS KOU TANAKA...
...BUT HE'S NOT THE TANAKA I KNEW FROM JUNIOR HIGH...
...NOR IS HE THE KOU I WAS REUNITED WITH IN HIGH SCHOOL.
YOU'RE THE NEWEST VERSION OF KOU.

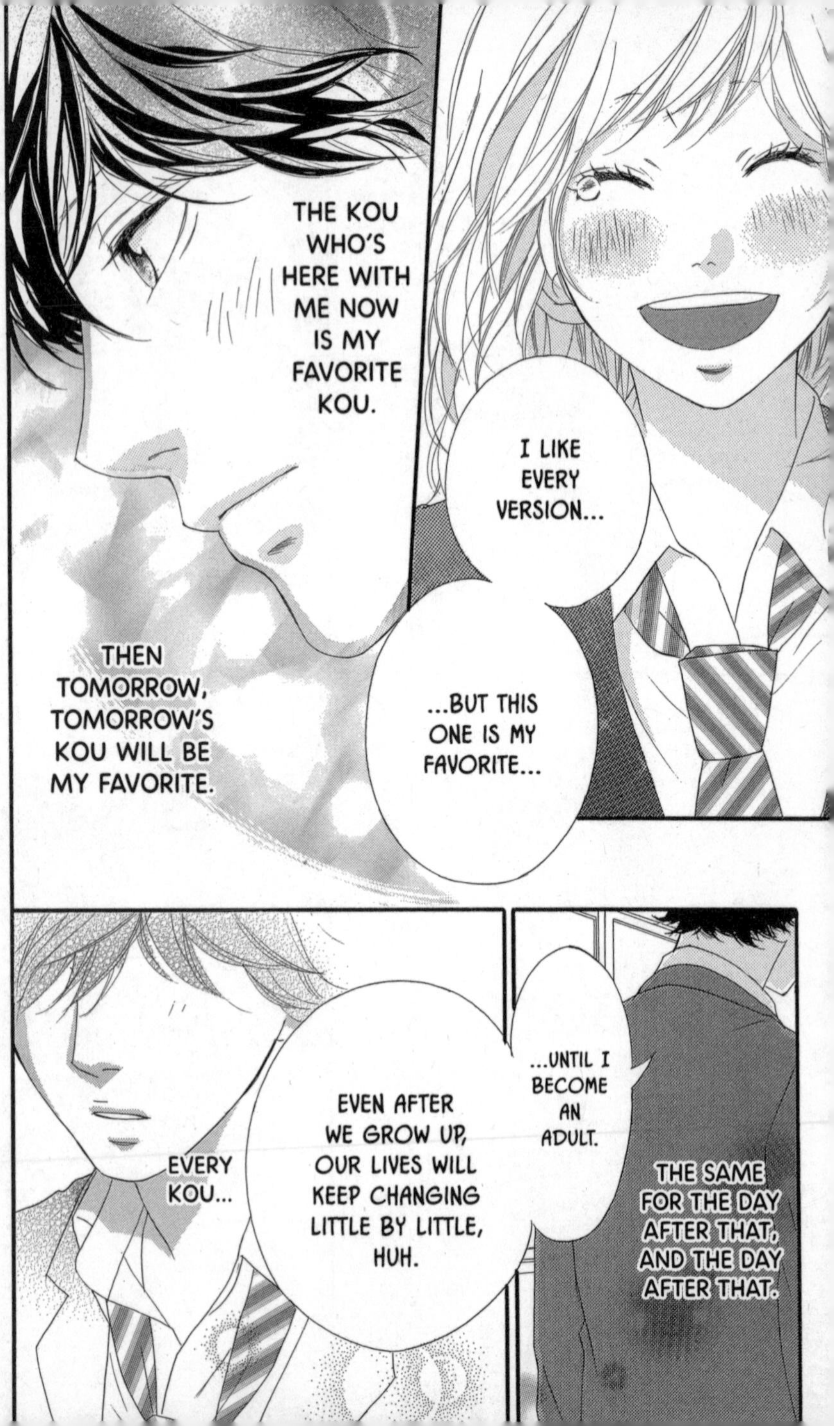
I LIKE EVERY VERSION...
...BUT THIS ONE IS MY FAVORITE...
THE KOU WHO'S HERE WITH ME NOW IS MY FAVORITE KOU.
THEN TOMORROW, TOMORROW'S KOU WILL BE MY FAVORITE.
THE SAME FOR THE DAY AFTER THAT, AND THE DAY AFTER THAT.
...UNTIL I BECOME AN ADULT.
EVEN AFTER WE GROW UP, OUR LIVES WILL KEEP CHANGING LITTLE BY LITTLE, HUH.
EVERY KOU...

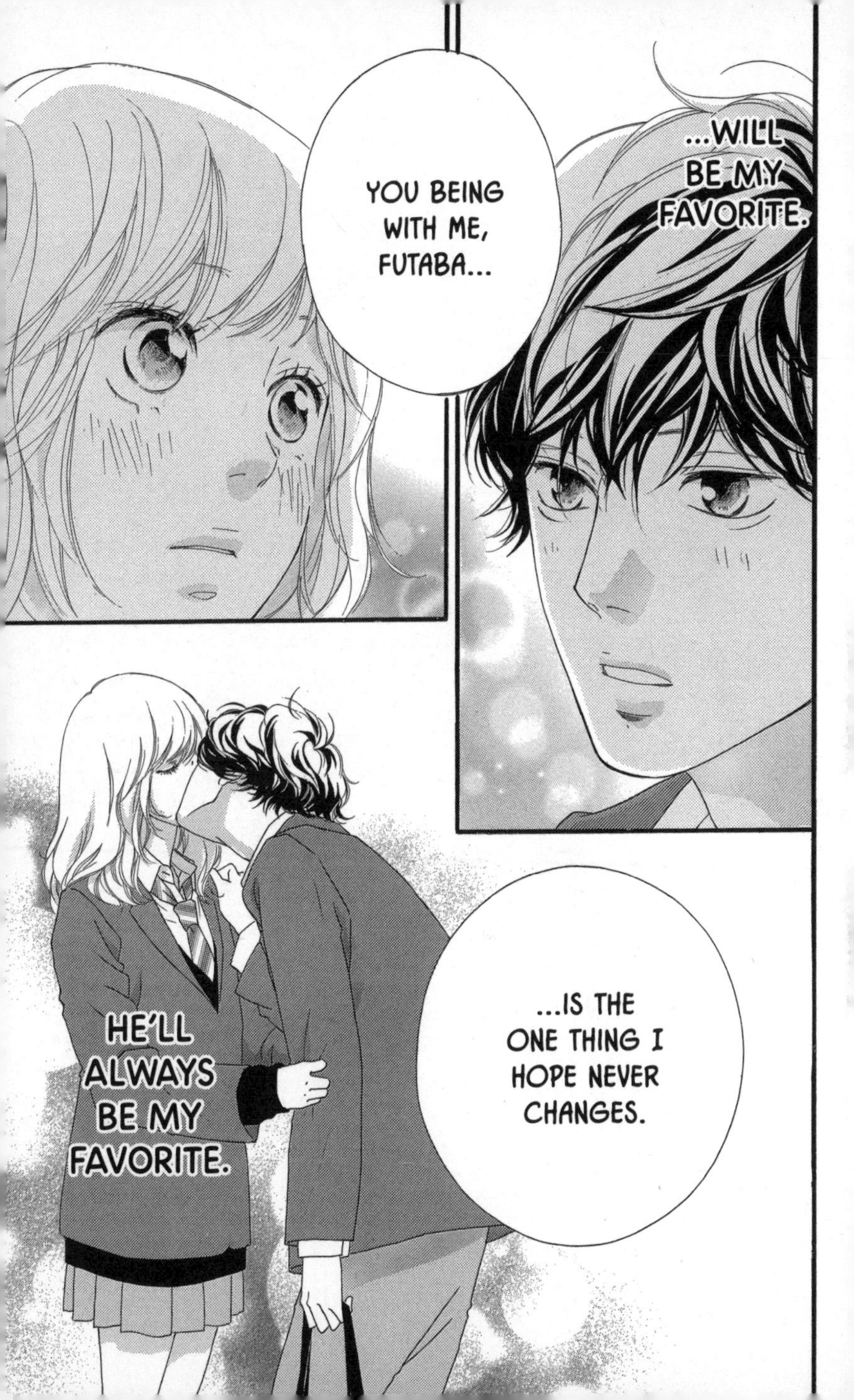
YOU BEING WITH ME, FUTABA...
...WILL BE MY FAVORITE.
...IS THE ONE THING I HOPE NEVER CHANGES.
HE'LL ALWAYS BE MY FAVORITE.

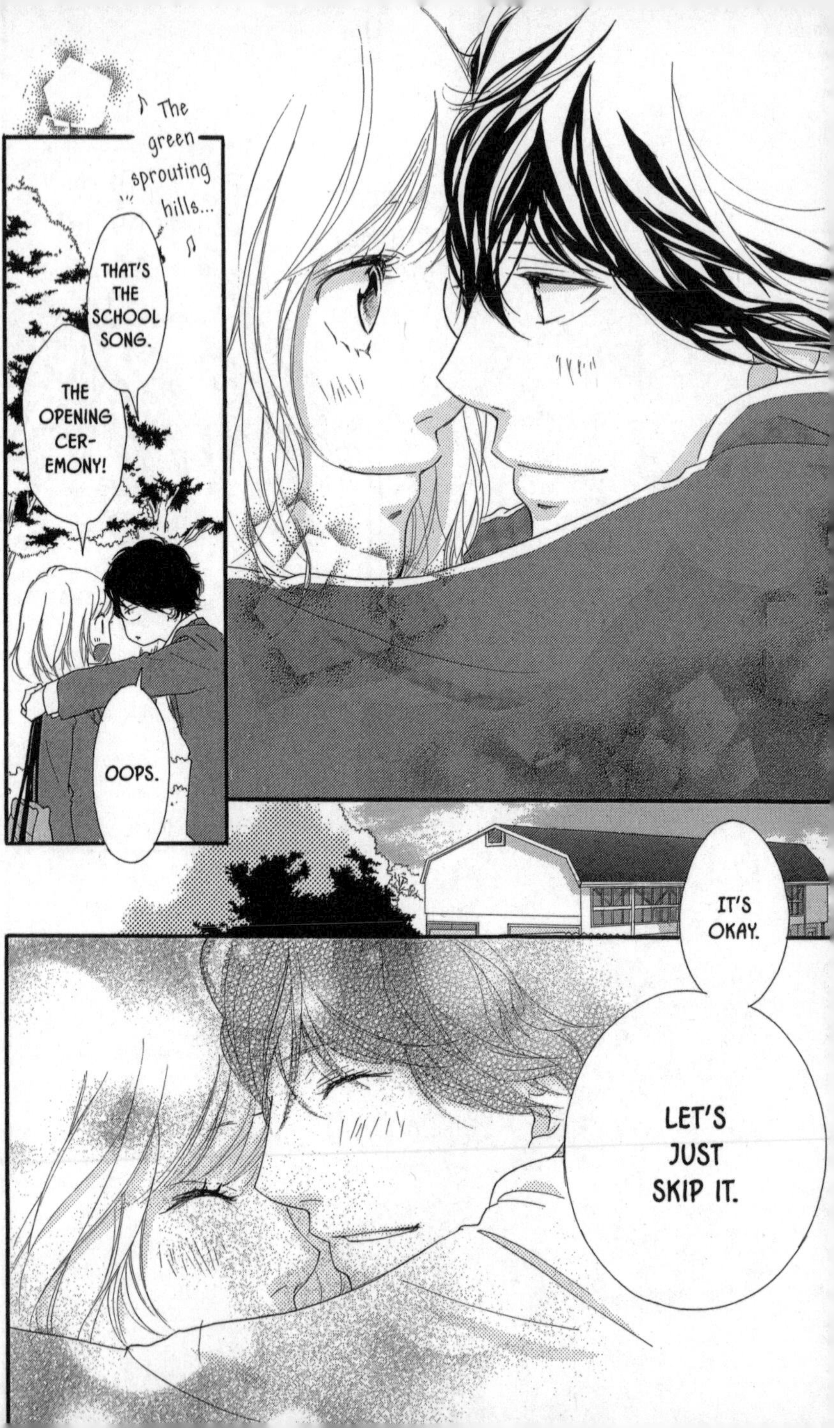
The green sprouting hills...
THAT'S THE SCHOOL SONG.
THE OPENING CER-EMONY!
OOPS.
IT'S OKAY.
LET'S JUST SKIP IT.

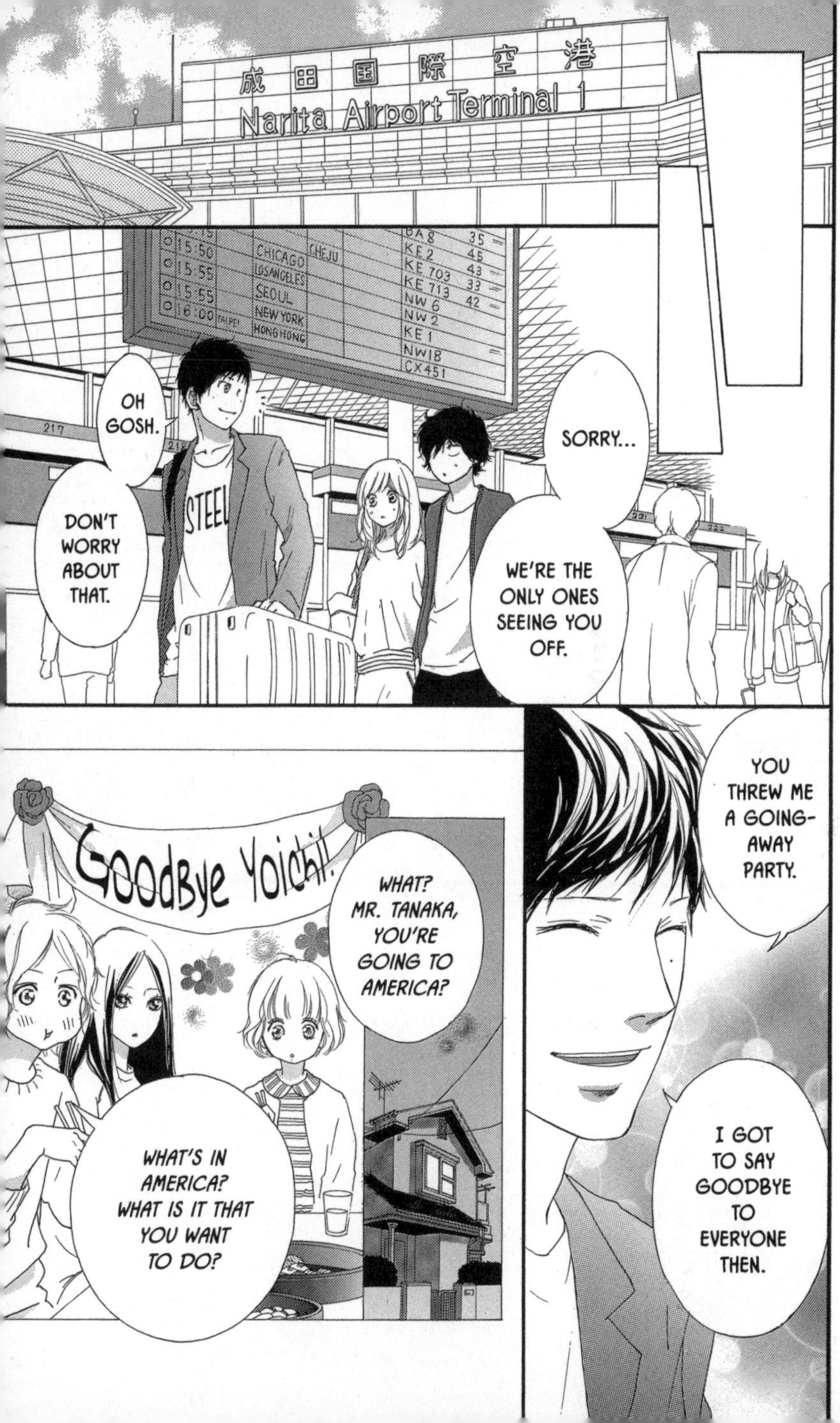
成田国際空港
Narita Airport Terminal 1
SORRY...
WE'RE THE ONLY ONES SEEING YOU OFF.
OH GOSH.
DON'T WORRY ABOUT THAT.
YOU THREW ME A GOING-AWAY PARTY.
I GOT TO SAY GOODBYE TO EVERYONE THEN.
GoodBye Yoichi!!
WHAT? MR. TANAKA, YOU'RE GOING TO AMERICA?
WHAT'S IN AMERICA? WHAT IS IT THAT YOU WANT TO DO?

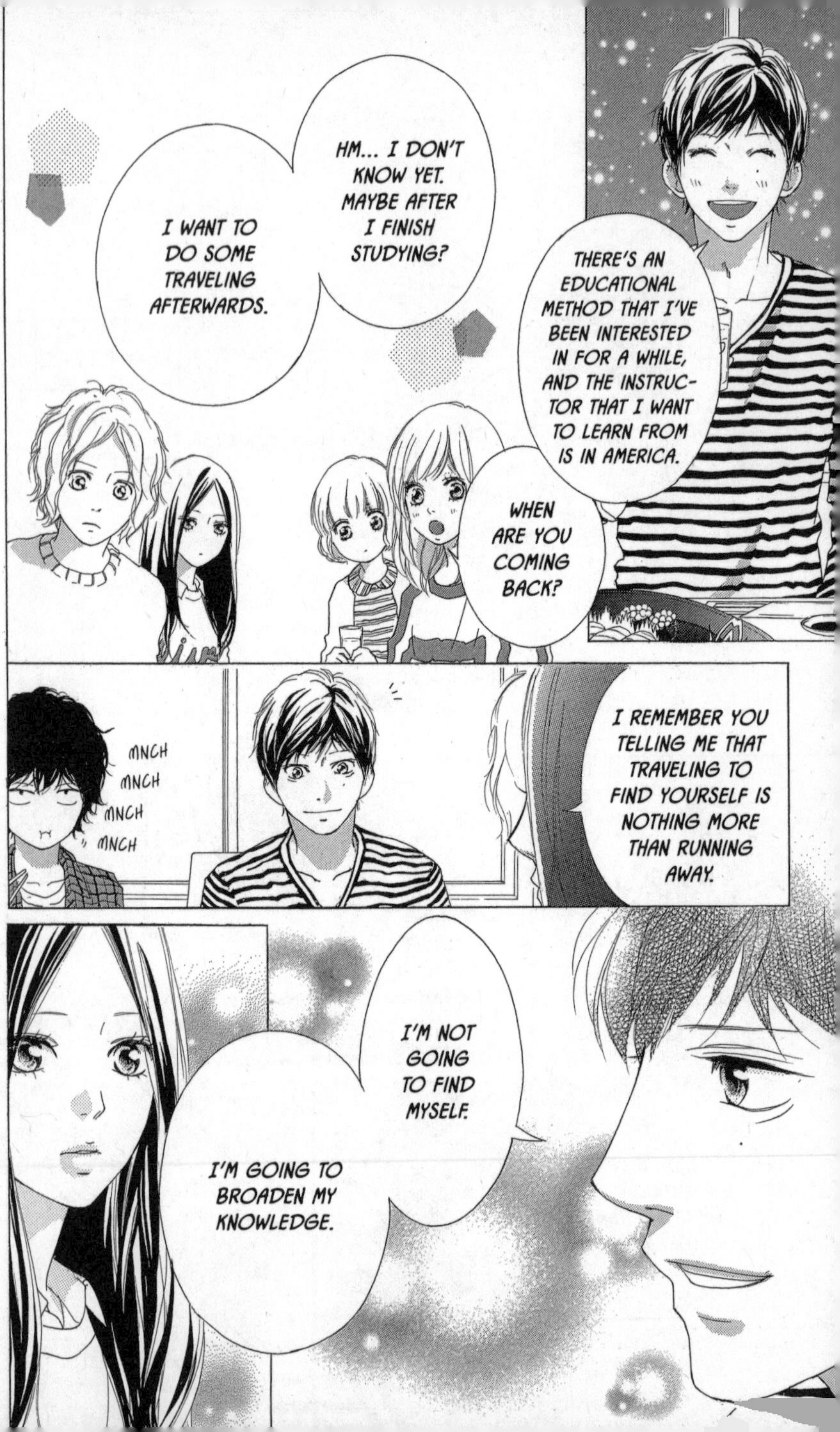
THERE'S AN EDUCATIONAL METHOD THAT I'VE BEEN INTERESTED IN FOR A WHILE, AND THE INSTRUCTOR THAT I WANT TO LEARN FROM IS IN AMERICA.
WHEN ARE YOU COMING BACK?
HM... I DON'T KNOW YET. MAYBE AFTER I FINISH STUDYING?
I WANT TO DO SOME TRAVELING AFTERWARDS.
I REMEMBER YOU TELLING ME THAT TRAVELING TO FIND YOURSELF IS NOTHING MORE THAN RUNNING AWAY.
MNCH
MNCH
MNCH
MNCH
I'M NOT GOING TO FIND MYSELF.
I'M GOING TO BROADEN MY KNOWLEDGE.

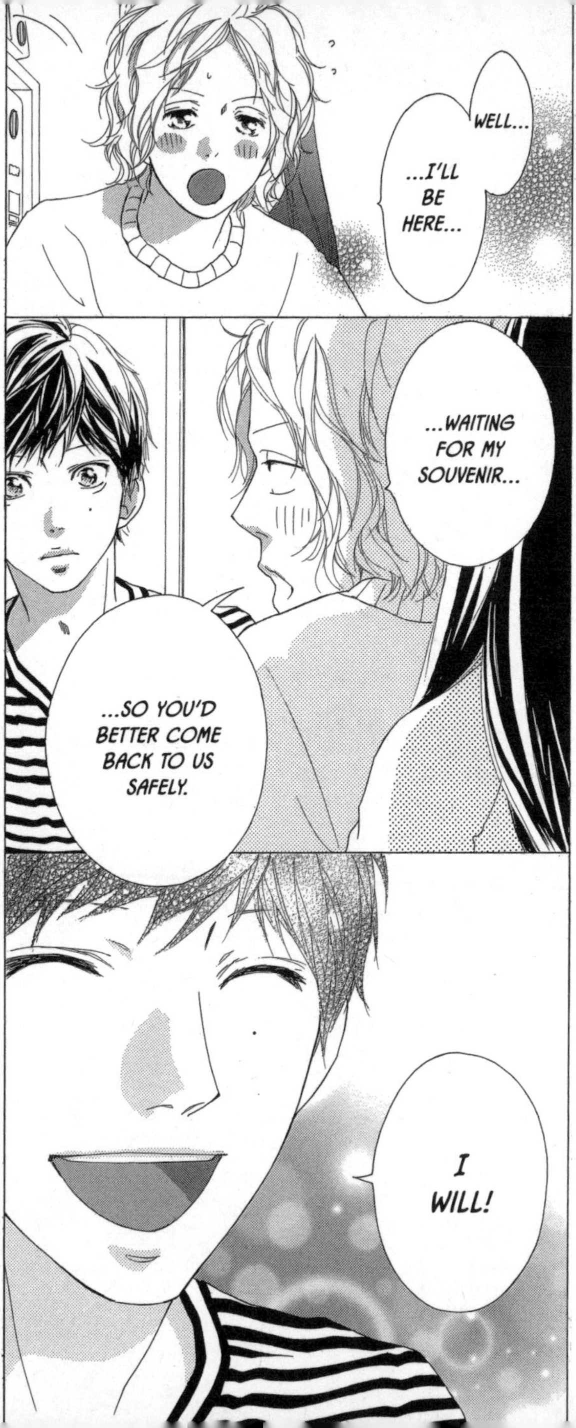
WELL...
...I'LL BE HERE...
...WAITING FOR MY SOUVENIR...
...SO YOU'D BETTER COME BACK TO US SAFELY.
I WILL!

Occasionally I incorporate my own personal experiences into the story and then add in a bit of drama. Kou's accident is an example of this. When I was in high school, I had plans to meet my boyfriend much like Futaba and Kou were supposed to meet. I waited and waited, but he didn't show up, and I couldn't get ahold of him either. I figured something must have happened, but I didn't know what to do, so I waited for about an hour. When he still didn't show up, I suspected something pretty bad had happened... That's when I heard someone calling my name loudly from far away. The loud voice kept getting closer. Uh-oh... But it was a voice I didn't recognize, so I figured that person must be calling someone else with the same name... And as I stood there flustered, I looked in the direction where the voice was coming from. I saw a man emerge from the crowd. When I saw his silhouette, I knew... (Continues on p. 141)

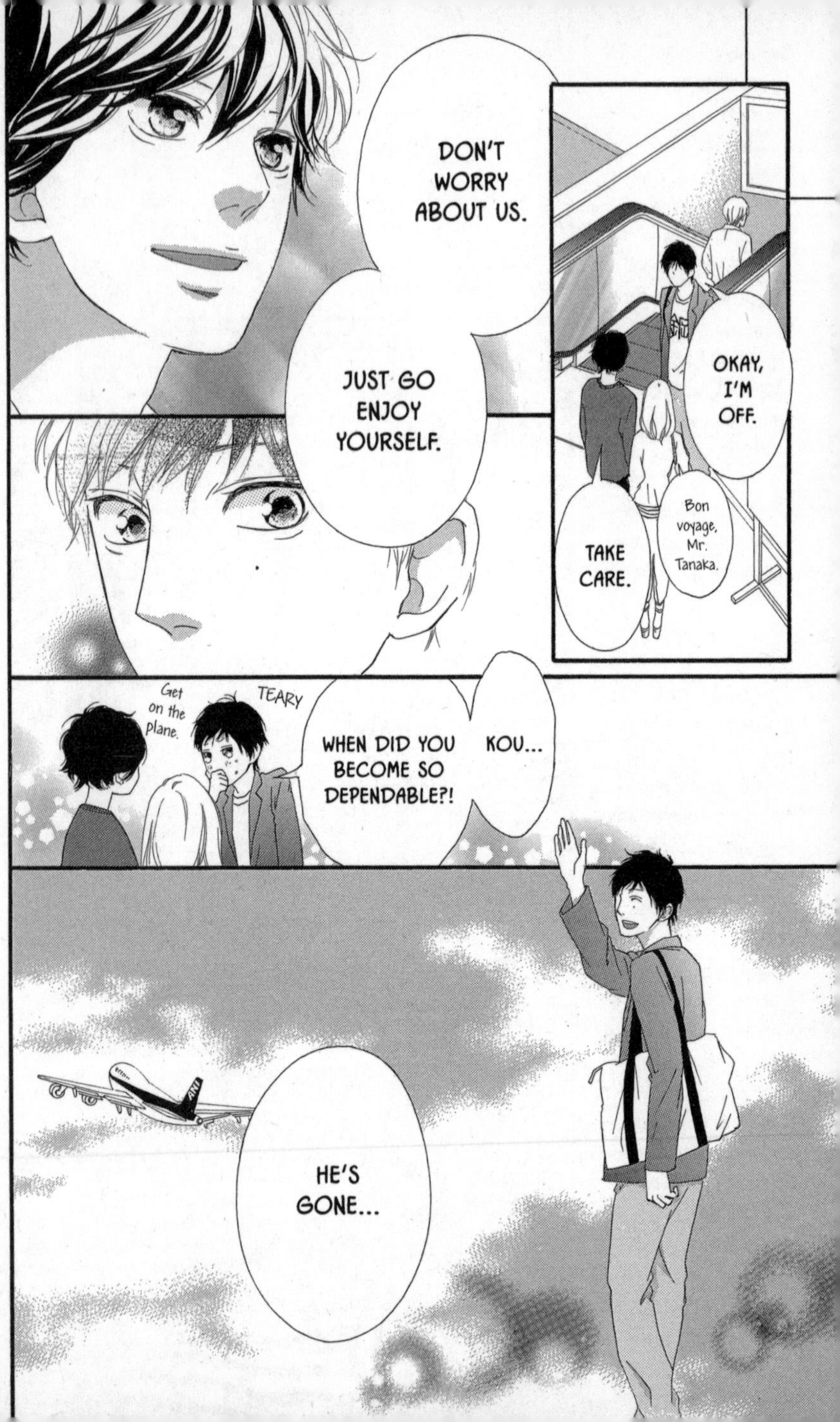
DON'T WORRY ABOUT US.
JUST GO ENJOY YOURSELF.
OKAY, I'M OFF.
Bon voyage, Mr. Tanaka.
TAKE CARE.
KOU...
WHEN DID YOU BECOME SO DEPENDABLE?!
TEARY
Get on the plane.
HE'S GONE...

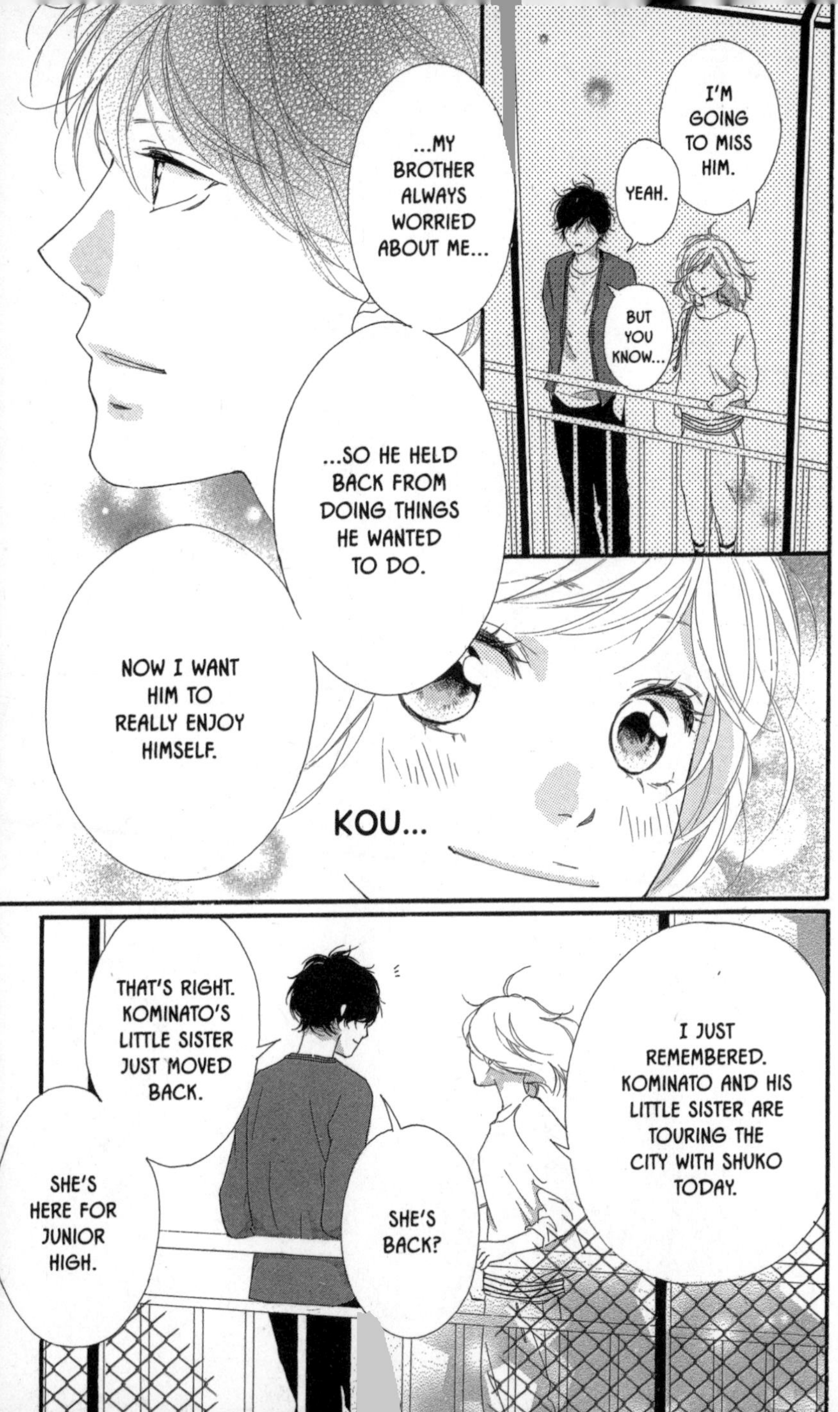
I'M GOING TO MISS HIM.
YEAH.
BUT YOU KNOW...
...MY BROTHER ALWAYS WORRIED ABOUT ME...
...SO HE HELD BACK FROM DOING THINGS HE WANTED TO DO.
NOW I WANT HIM TO REALLY ENJOY HIMSELF.
KOU...
I JUST REMEMBERED. KOMINATO AND HIS LITTLE SISTER ARE TOURING THE CITY WITH SHUKO TODAY.
SHE'S BACK?
THAT'S RIGHT. KOMINATO'S LITTLE SISTER JUST MOVED BACK.
SHE'S HERE FOR JUNIOR HIGH.

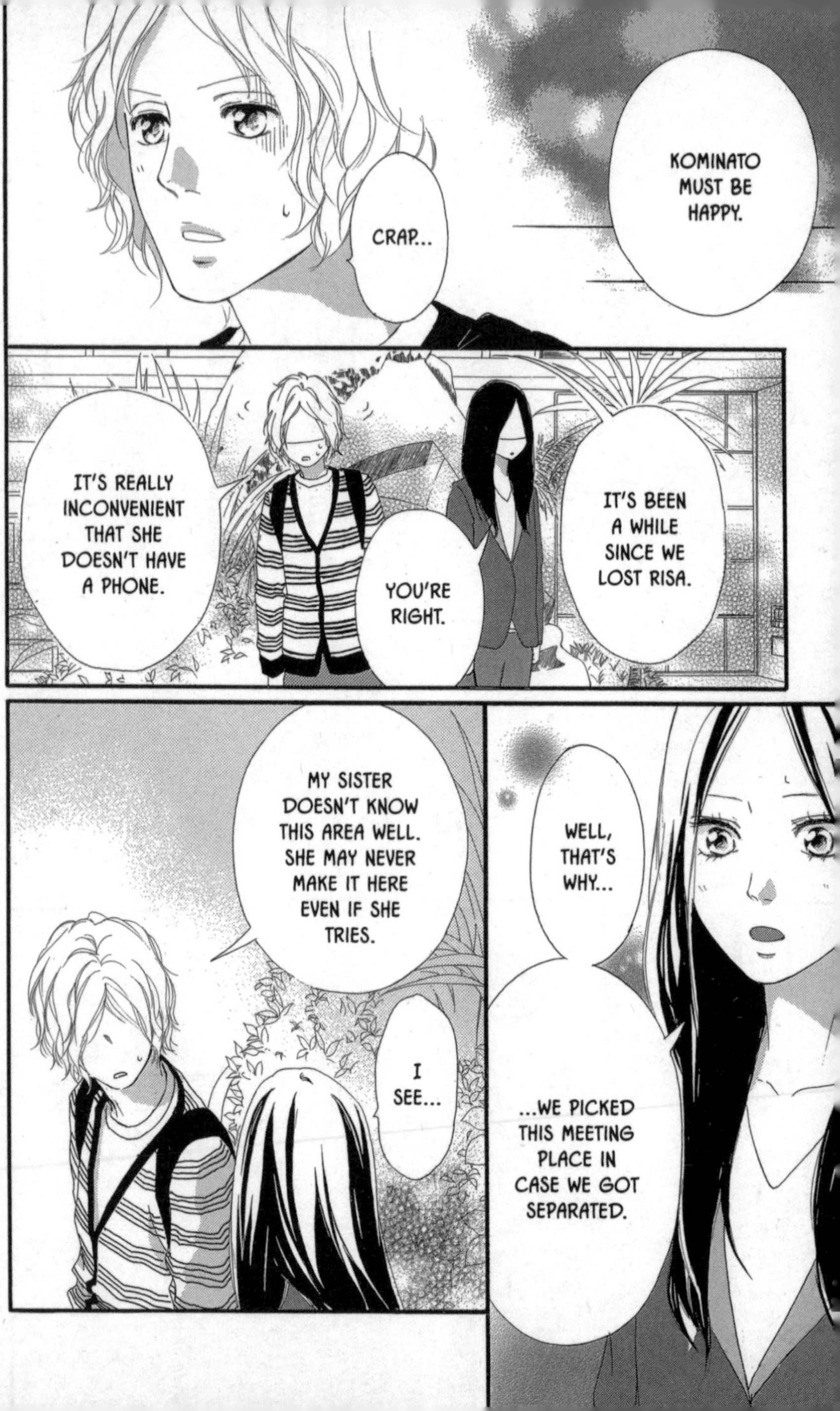
KOMINATO MUST BE HAPPY.
CRAP...
IT'S BEEN A WHILE SINCE WE LOST RISA.
YOU'RE RIGHT.
IT'S REALLY INCONVENIENT THAT SHE DOESN'T HAVE A PHONE.
WELL, THAT'S WHY...
...WE PICKED THIS MEETING PLACE IN CASE WE GOT SEPARATED.
MY SISTER DOESN'T KNOW THIS AREA WELL. SHE MAY NEVER MAKE IT HERE EVEN IF SHE TRIES.
I SEE...

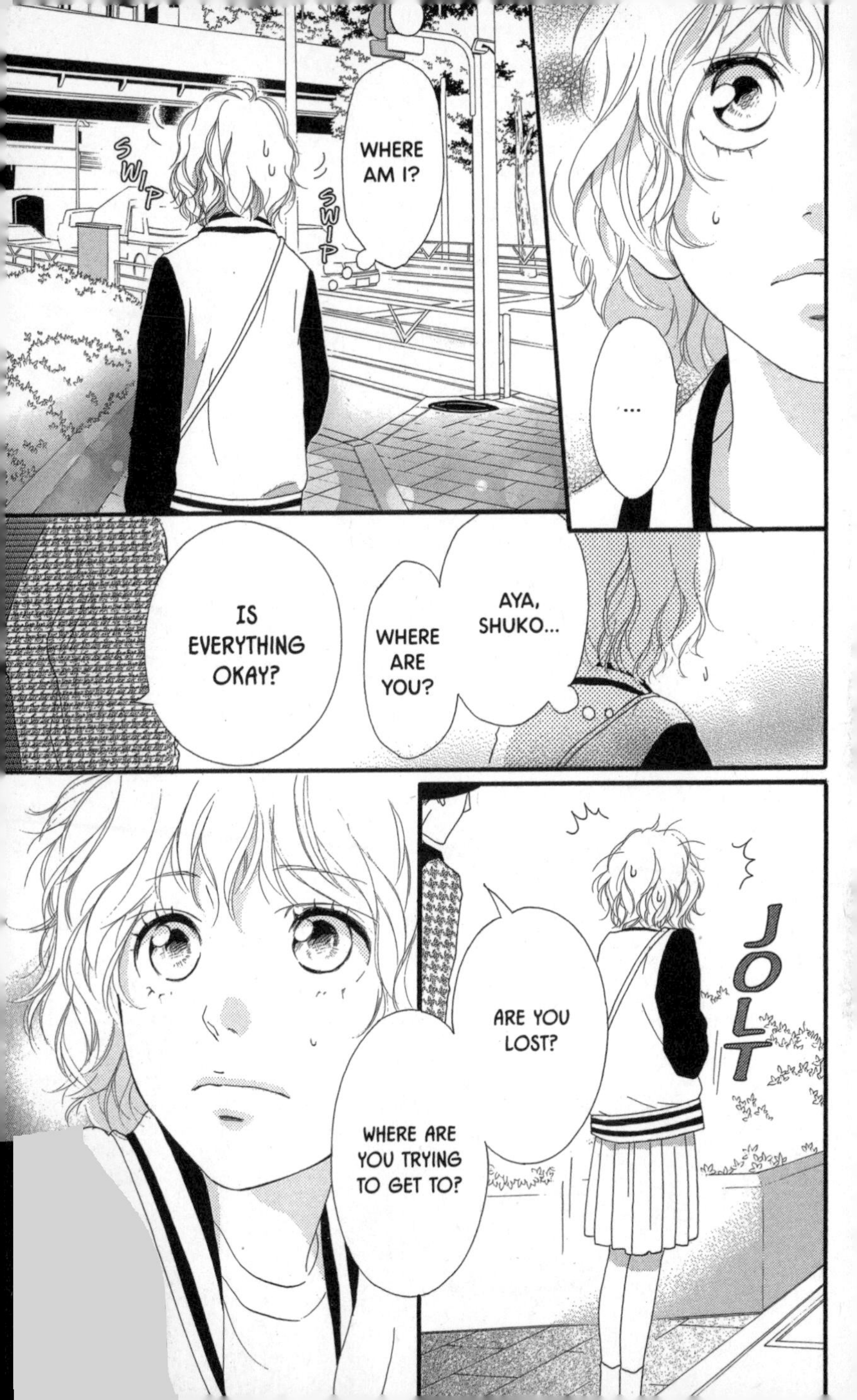
...
WHERE AM I?
SWIP
SWIP
AYA, SHUKO... WHERE ARE YOU?
IS EVERYTHING OKAY?
JOLT
ARE YOU LOST?
WHERE ARE YOU TRYING TO GET TO?

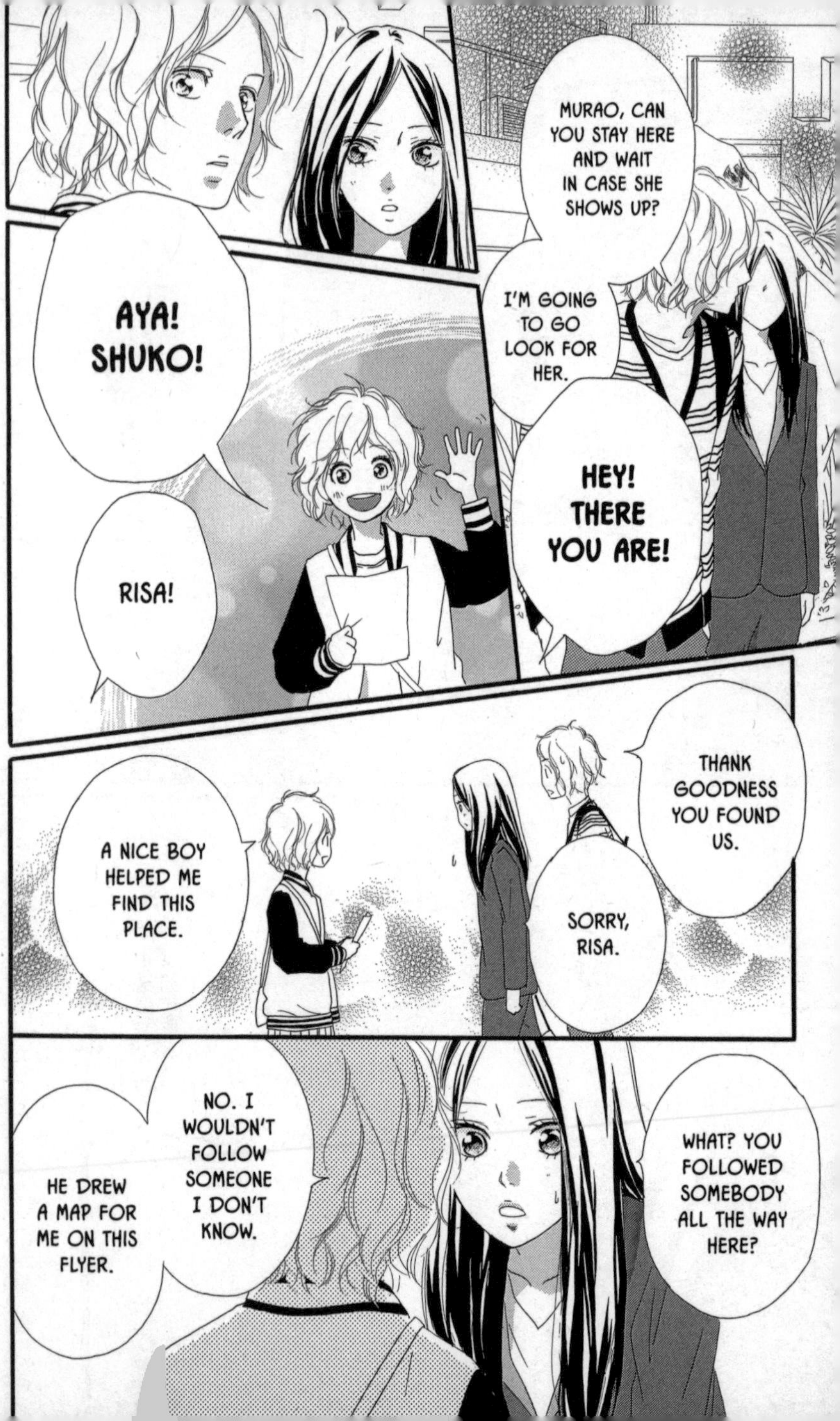
MURAO, CAN YOU STAY HERE AND WAIT IN CASE SHE SHOWS UP?
I'M GOING TO GO LOOK FOR HER.
HEY! THERE YOU ARE!
AYA! SHUKO!
RISA!
THANK GOODNESS YOU FOUND US.
SORRY, RISA.
A NICE BOY HELPED ME FIND THIS PLACE.
WHAT? YOU FOLLOWED SOMEBODY ALL THE WAY HERE?
NO. I WOULDN'T FOLLOW SOMEONE I DON'T KNOW.
HE DREW A MAP FOR ME ON THIS FLYER.

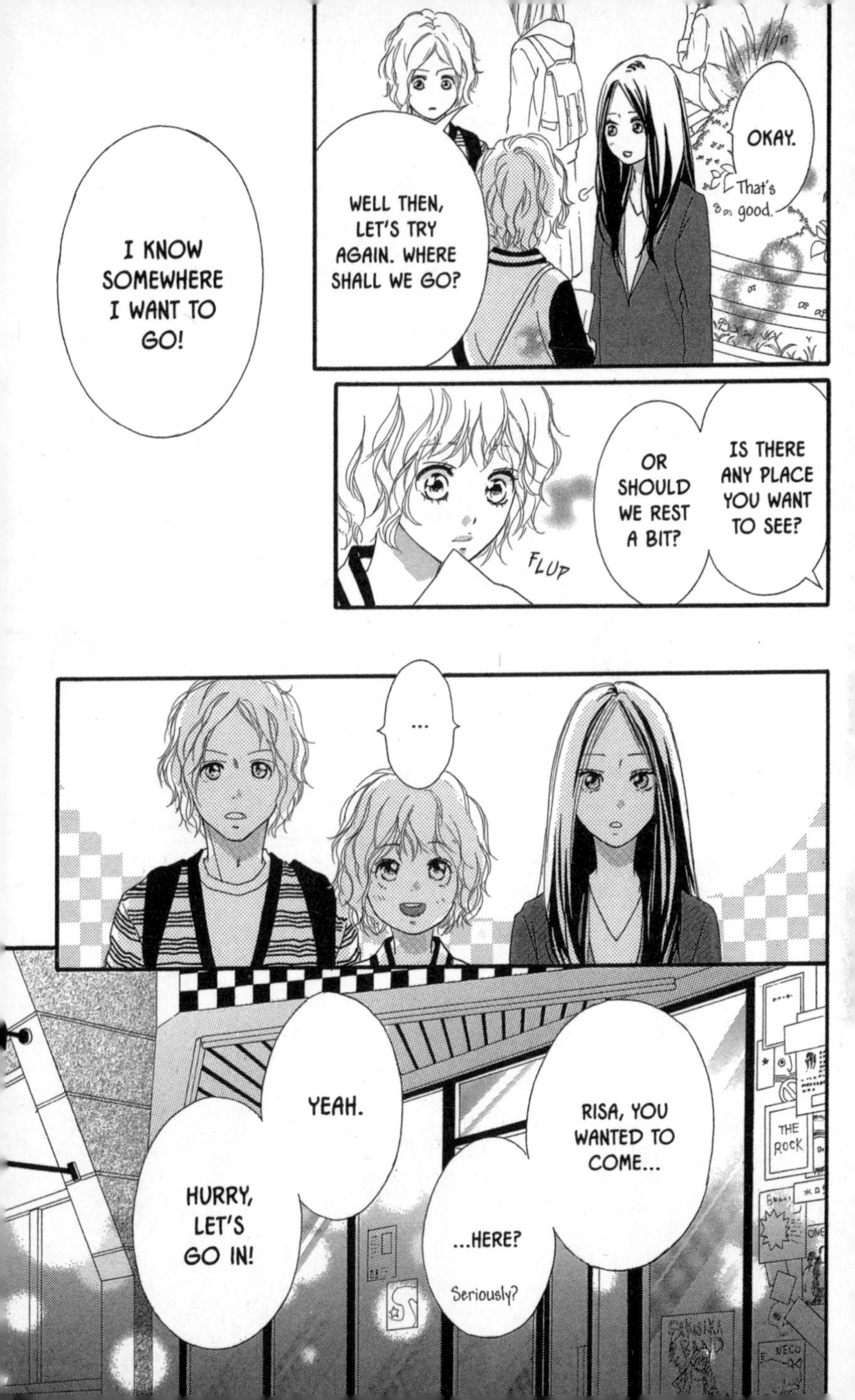
OKAY.
That's good.
WELL THEN, LET'S TRY AGAIN. WHERE SHALL WE GO?
IS THERE ANY PLACE YOU WANT TO SEE?
OR SHOULD WE REST A BIT?
FLUP
I KNOW SOMEWHERE I WANT TO GO!
...
RISA, YOU WANTED TO COME...
...HERE?
Seriously?
YEAH.
HURRY, LET'S GO IN!
THE ROCK

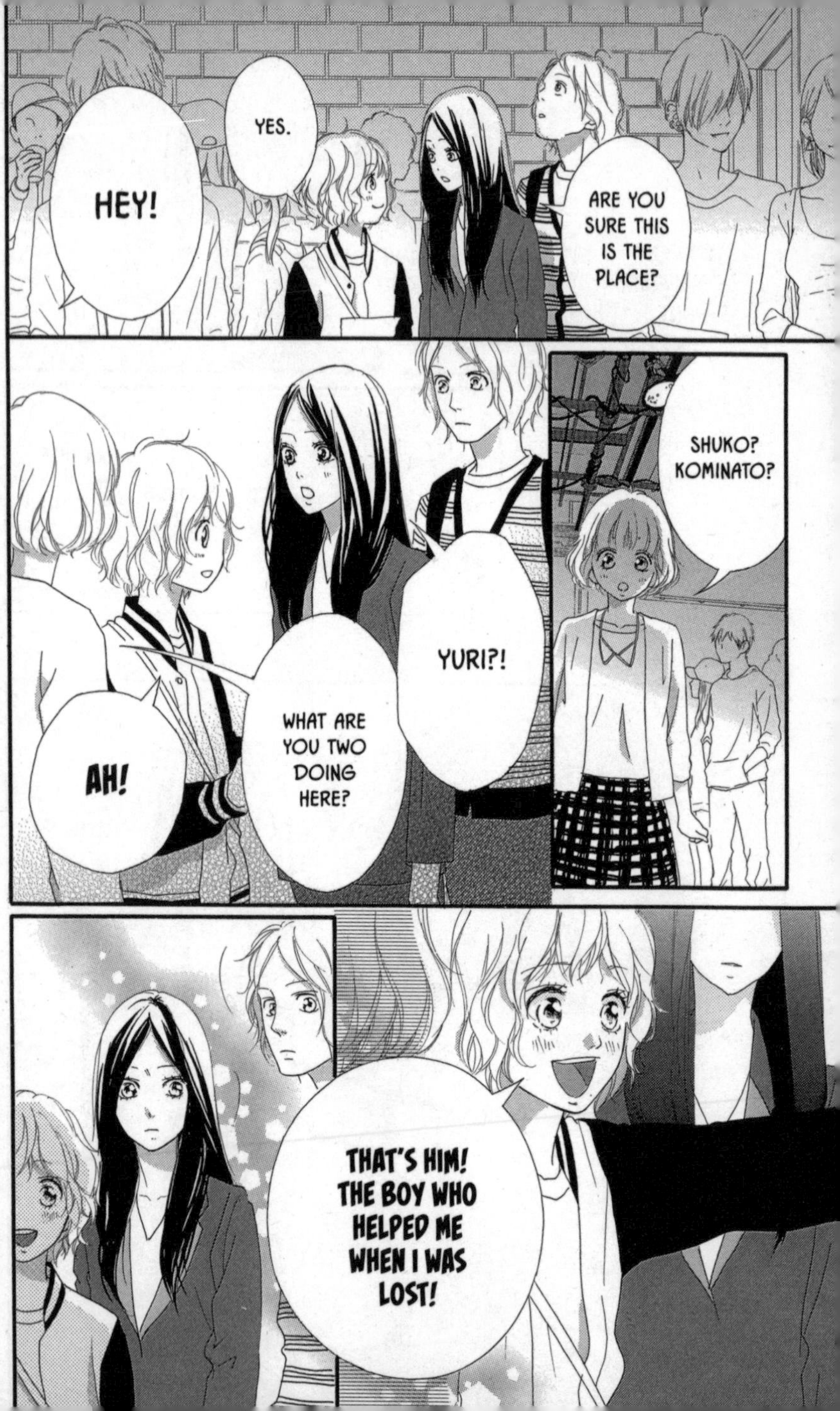
ARE YOU SURE THIS IS THE PLACE?
YES.
HEY!
SHUKO? KOMINATO?
YURI?!
WHAT ARE YOU TWO DOING HERE?
AH!
THAT'S HIM! THE BOY WHO HELPED ME WHEN I WAS LOST!

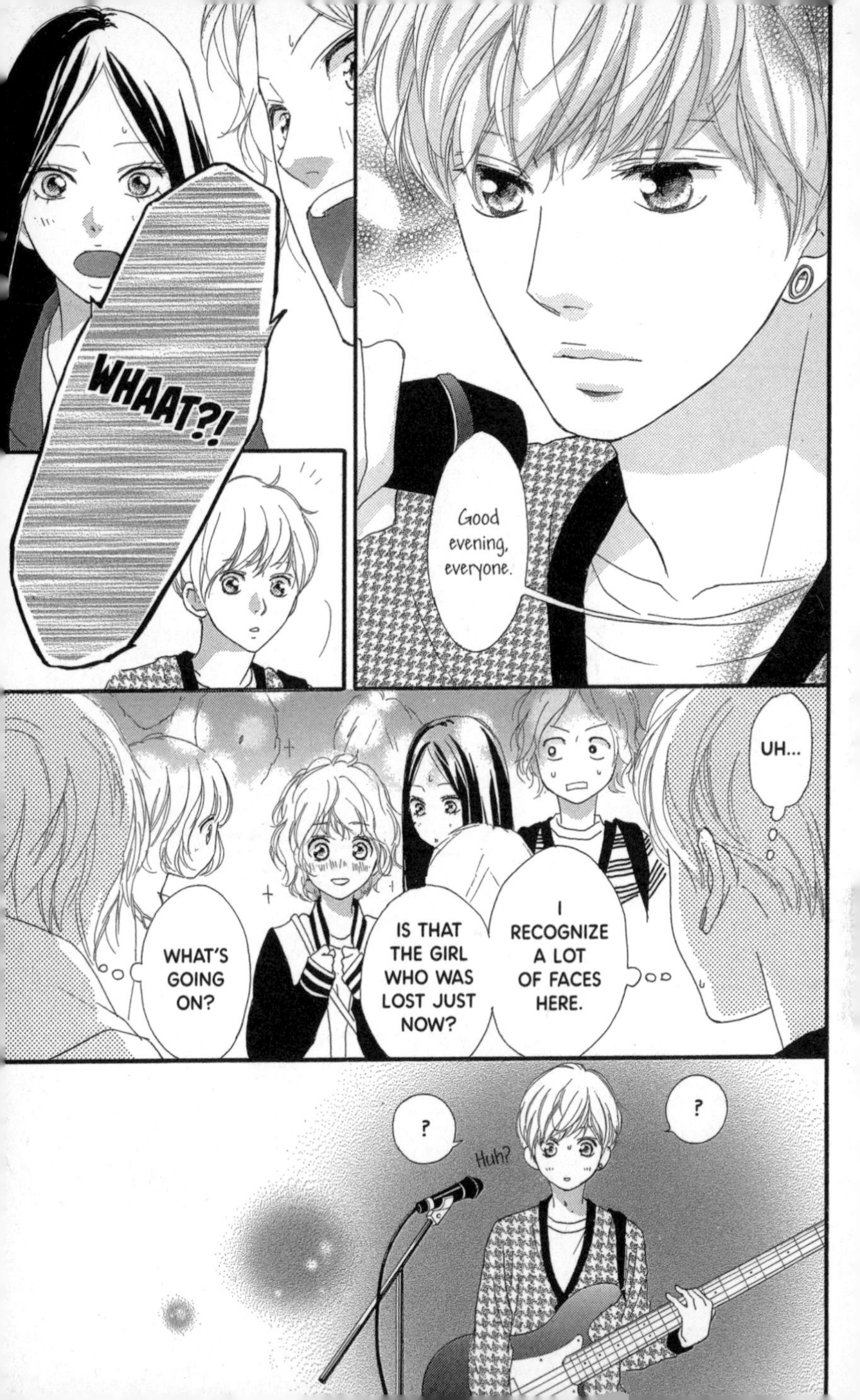
Good evening, everyone.
WHAAT?!
UH...
I RECOGNIZE A LOT OF FACES HERE.
IS THAT THE GIRL WHO WAS LOST JUST NOW?
WHAT'S GOING ON?
?
Huh?
?

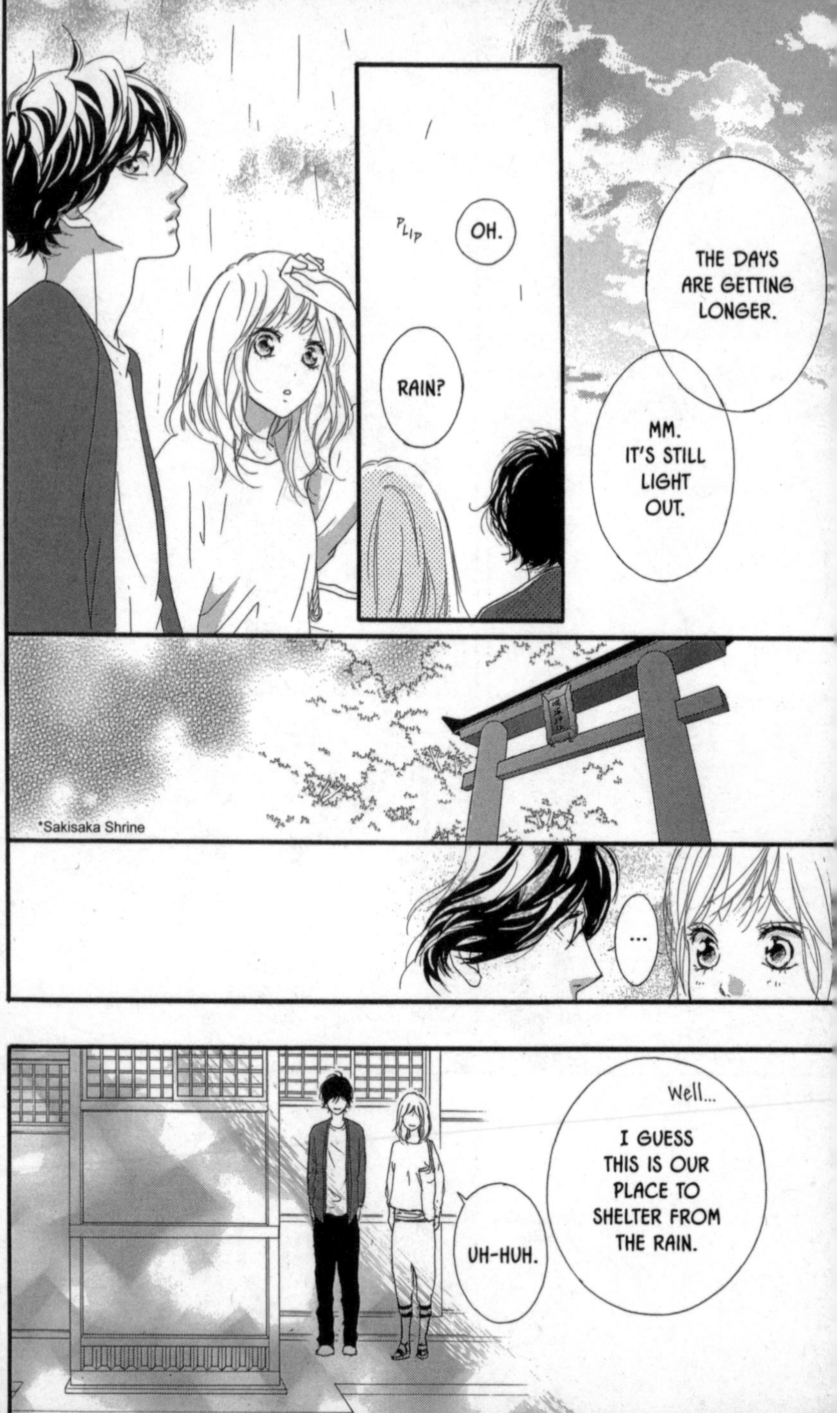
THE DAYS ARE GETTING LONGER.
MM. IT'S STILL LIGHT OUT.
PLIP
OH.
RAIN?
*Sakisaka Shrine
...
Well...
I GUESS THIS IS OUR PLACE TO SHELTER FROM THE RAIN.
UH-HUH.

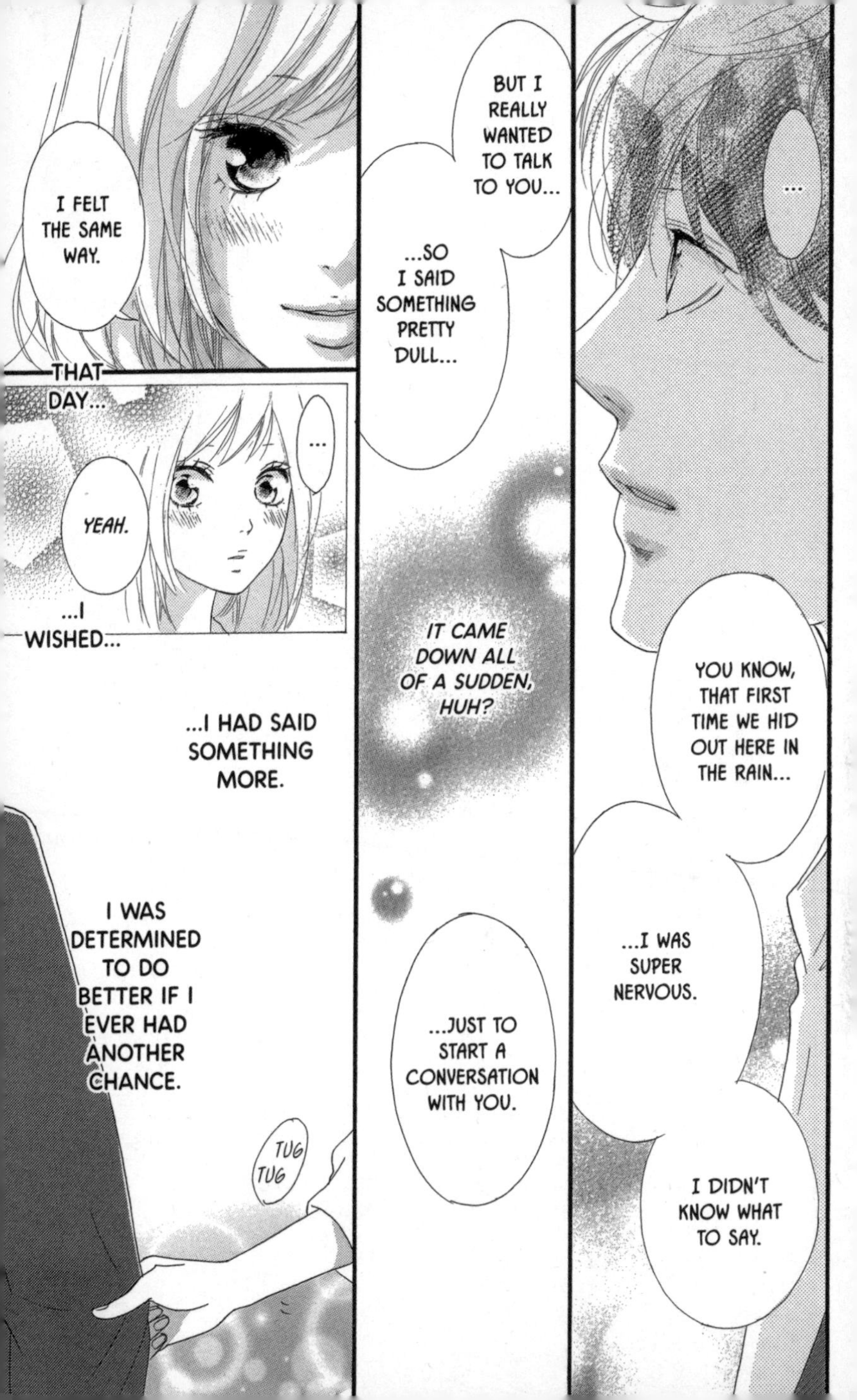
...
YOU KNOW, THAT FIRST TIME WE HID OUT HERE IN THE RAIN...
...I WAS SUPER NERVOUS.
I DIDN'T KNOW WHAT TO SAY.
BUT I REALLY WANTED TO TALK TO YOU...
...SO I SAID SOMETHING PRETTY DULL...
IT CAME DOWN ALL OF A SUDDEN, HUH?
...JUST TO START A CONVERSATION WITH YOU.
I FELT THE SAME WAY.
THAT DAY...
...
YEAH.
...I WISHED...
...I HAD SAID SOMETHING MORE.
I WAS DETERMINED TO DO BETTER IF I EVER HAD ANOTHER CHANCE.
TUG TUG

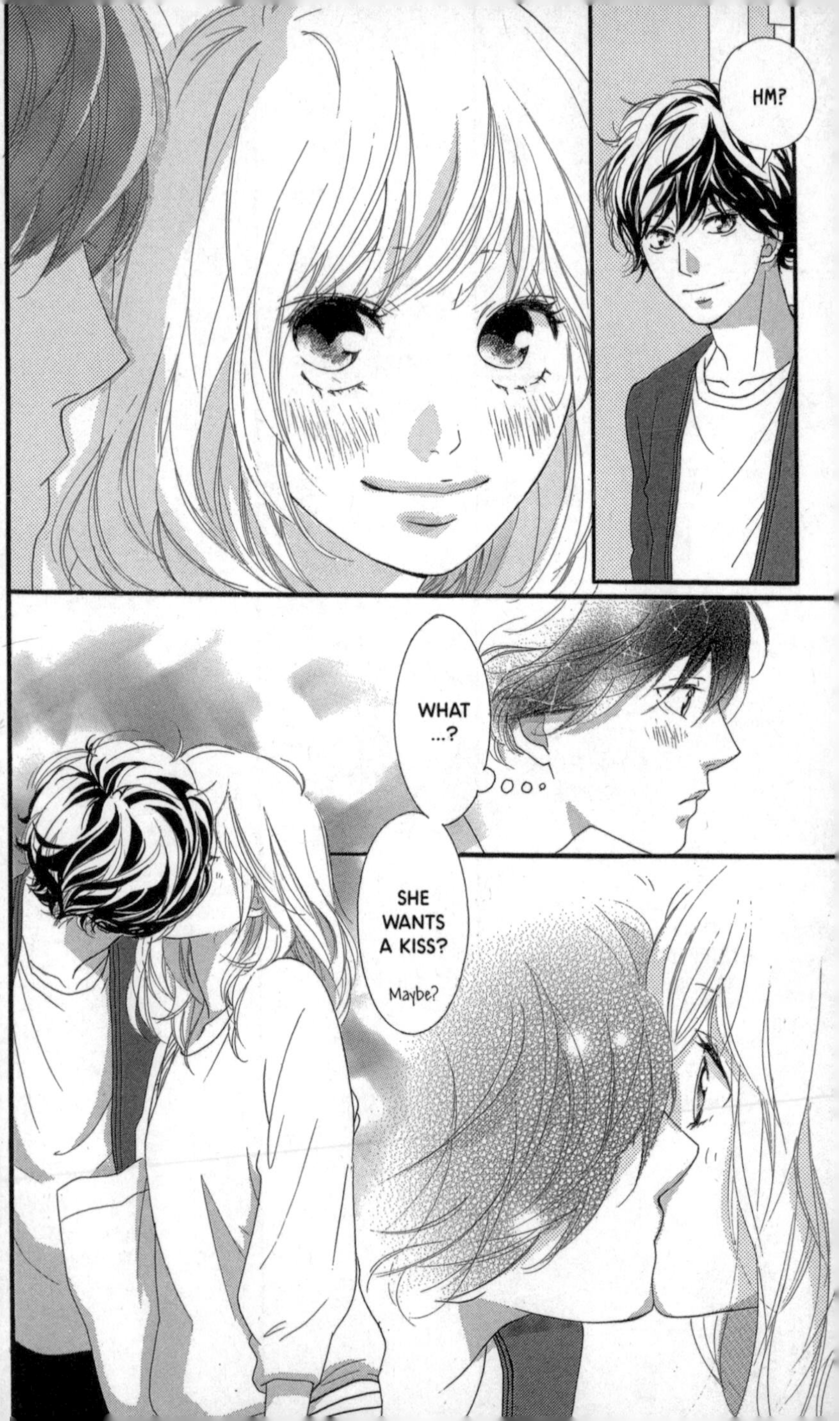
HM?
WHAT ...?
SHE WANTS A KISS?
Maybe?

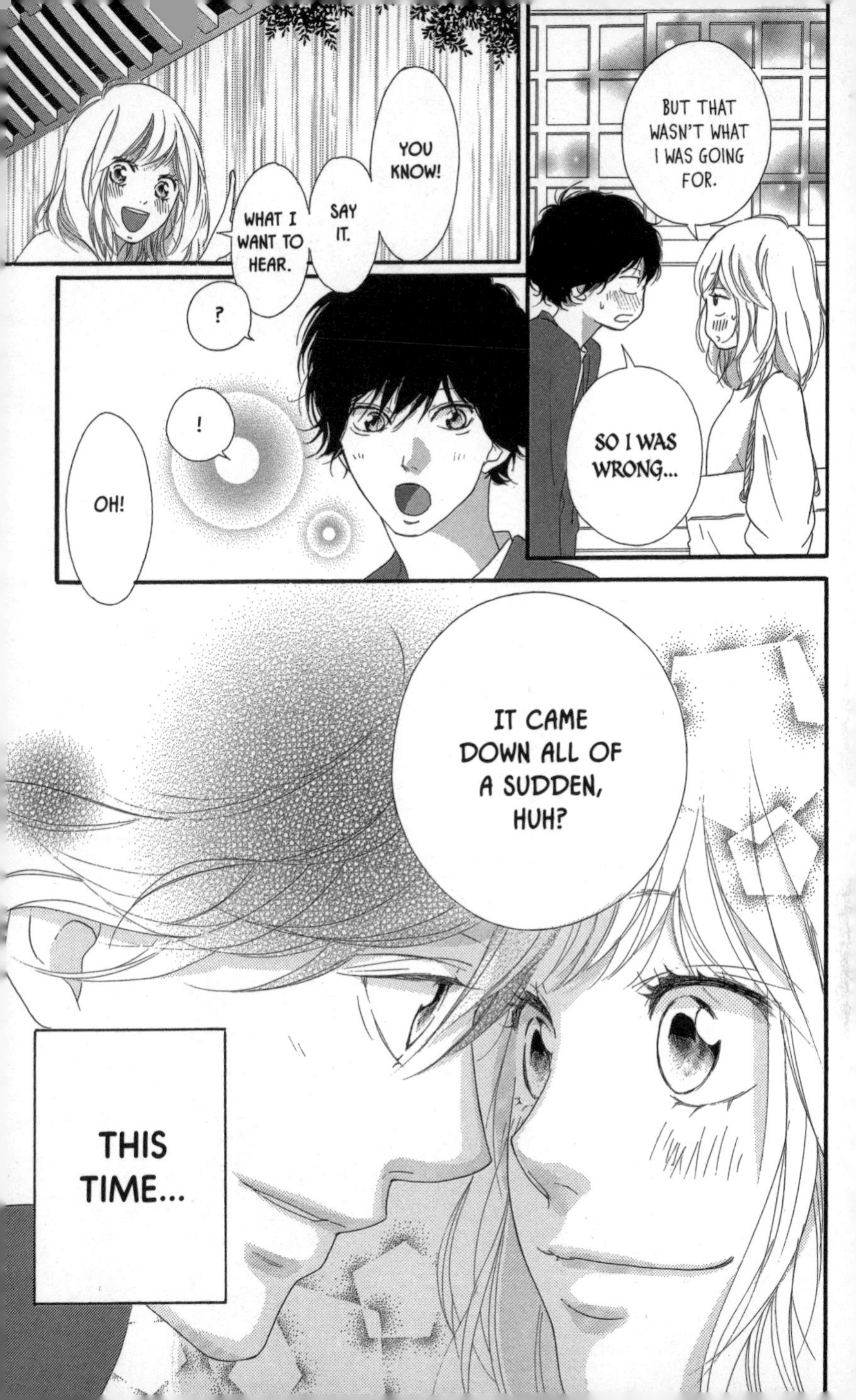
BUT THAT WASN'T WHAT I WAS GOING FOR.
SO I WAS WRONG...
YOU KNOW!
SAY IT.
WHAT I WANT TO HEAR.
?
!
OH!
IT CAME DOWN ALL OF A SUDDEN, HUH?
THIS TIME...

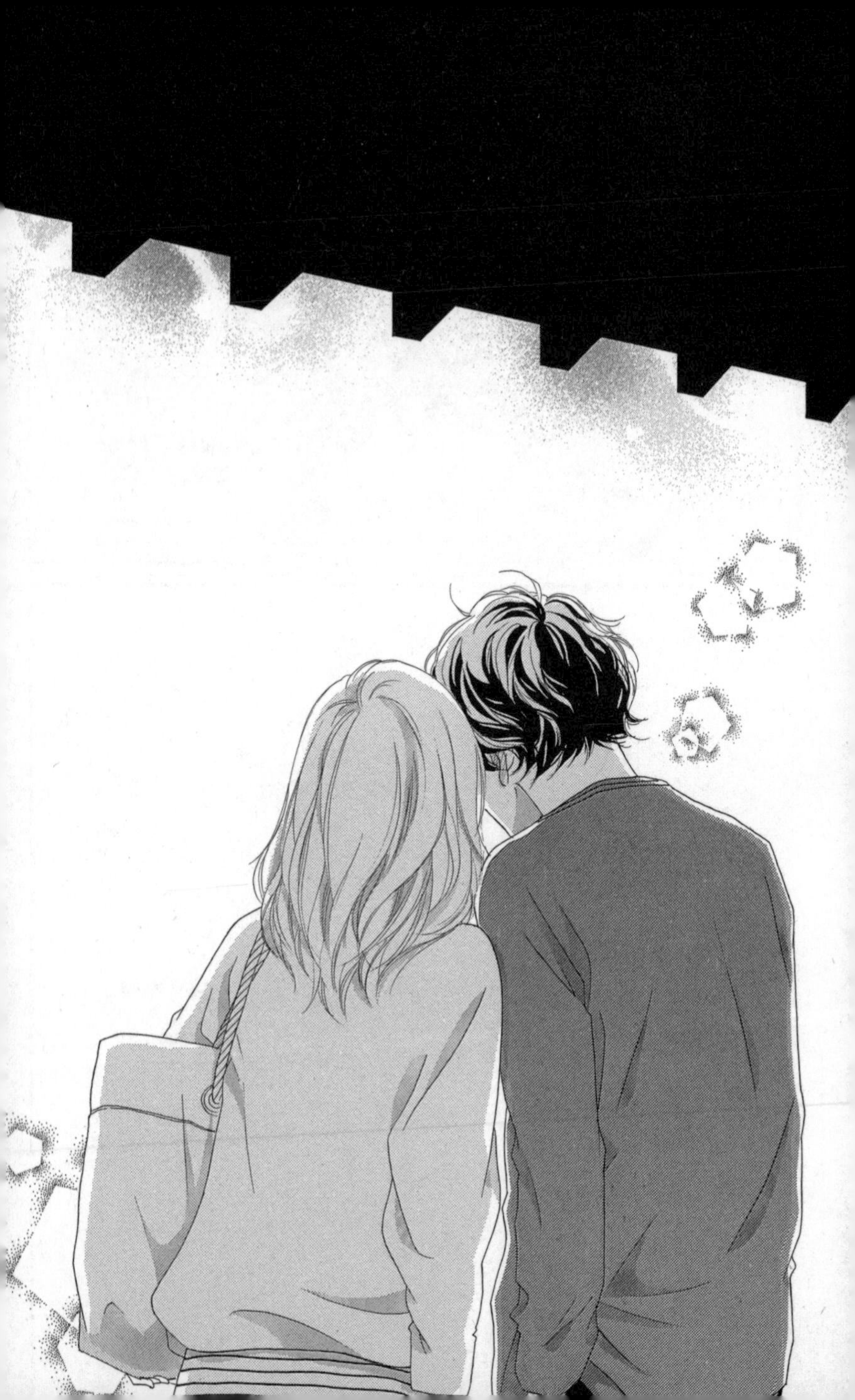

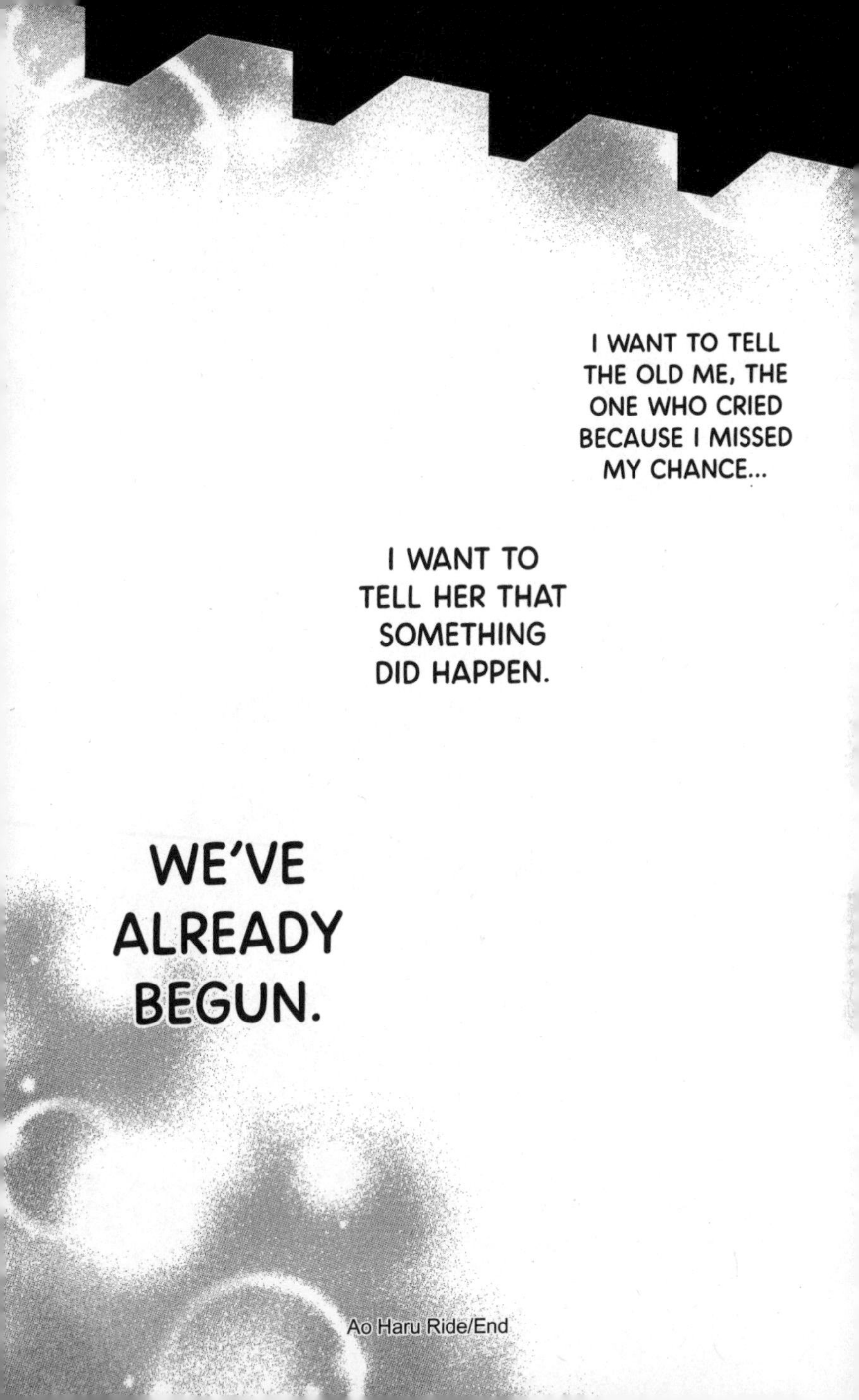
I WANT TO TELL THE OLD ME, THE ONE WHO CRIED BECAUSE I MISSED MY CHANCE...
I WANT TO TELL HER THAT SOMETHING DID HAPPEN.
WE'VE ALREADY BEGUN.
Ao Haru Ride/End

The scent of air after rain...
In the light around us,
I felt your heartbeat.

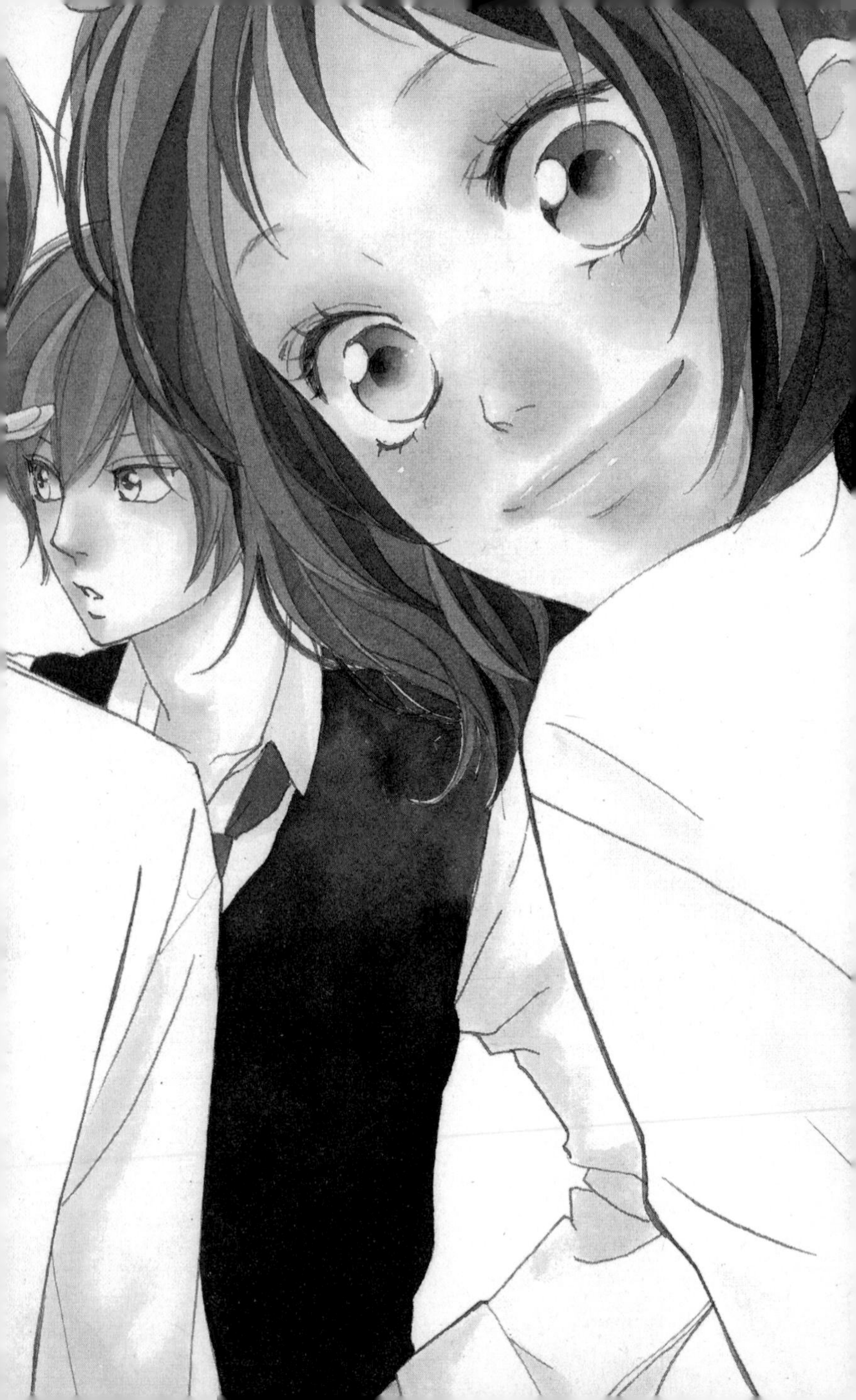

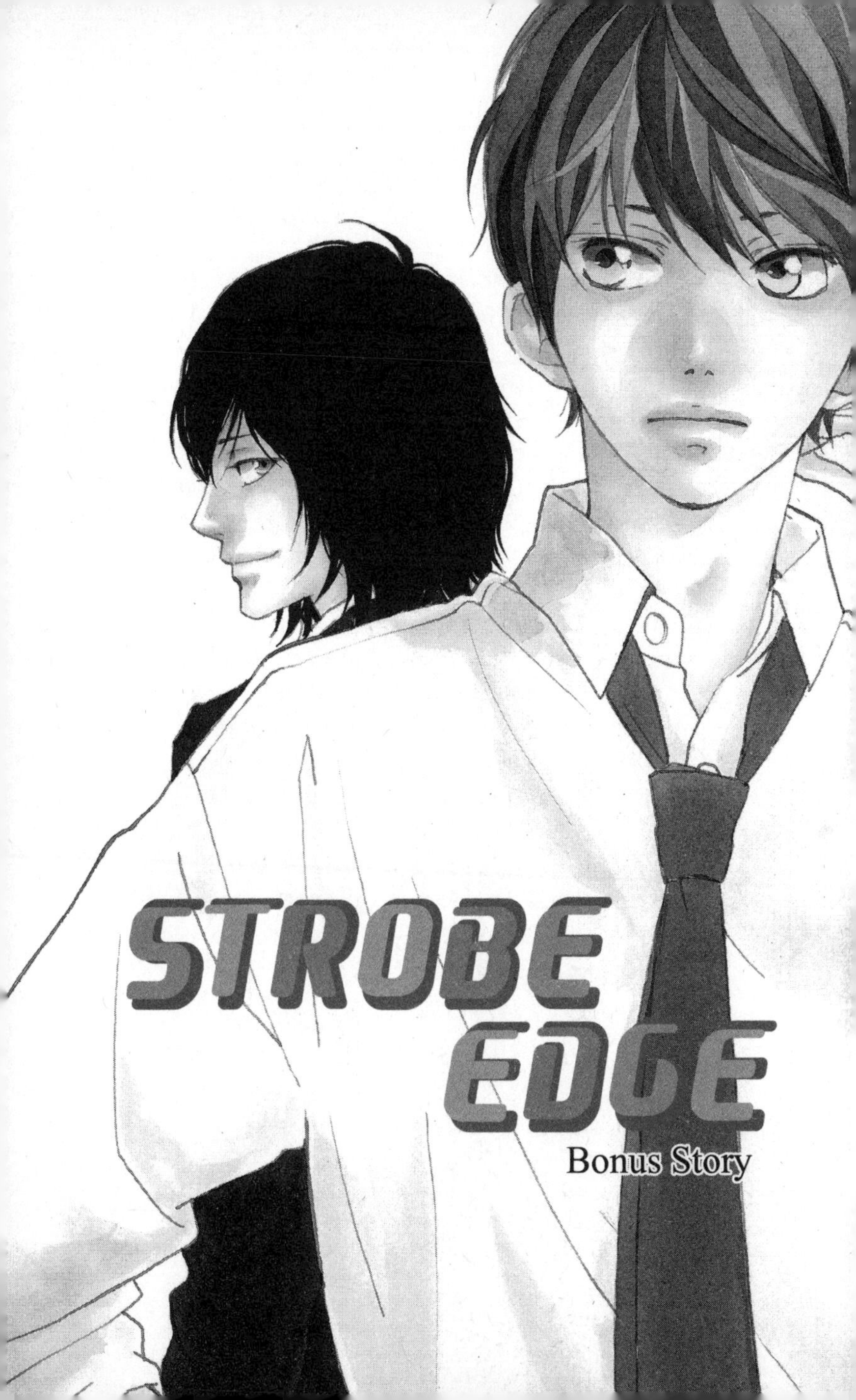
STROBE EDGE
Bonus Story

Welcome Back ♥ STROBE EDGE (Bonus Story)

The following pages contain a bonus story for *Strobe Edge* (the series I wrote before *Ao Haru Ride*). It was crazy fun to draw *Strobe* again for the first time in several years! It was nostalgic, and I felt at ease as I was reminded of just how much I like Ninako and her friends. I say I felt at ease because when I first started working on *Ao Haru Ride*, all I felt towards *Strobe* was anxiety! I took great care in making *Strobe*, so I was very, very happy that so many people enjoyed it, but because of its success, I also saw it as *Ao Haru Ride*'s rival. I was haunted by that. The truth is that just after *Ao Haru Ride* began serialization, I rather resented *Strobe*. But, little by little, as *AoHa* gained followers and I felt that the series had found its path, the ice I had in my heart towards *Strobe* finally began to melt... Ah, spring. It was wonderful. The reason I was able to enjoy working on this bonus story was because so many people liked *AoHa*. Thank you, thank you. To top it off, there's a certain character whose story I've been secretly wanting to tell since the time *Strobe* was in serialization. I'm so happy I've finally gotten to do so! With that, I hope you enjoy seeing what my favorite character is up to.

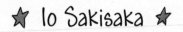

★ Io Sakisaka ★

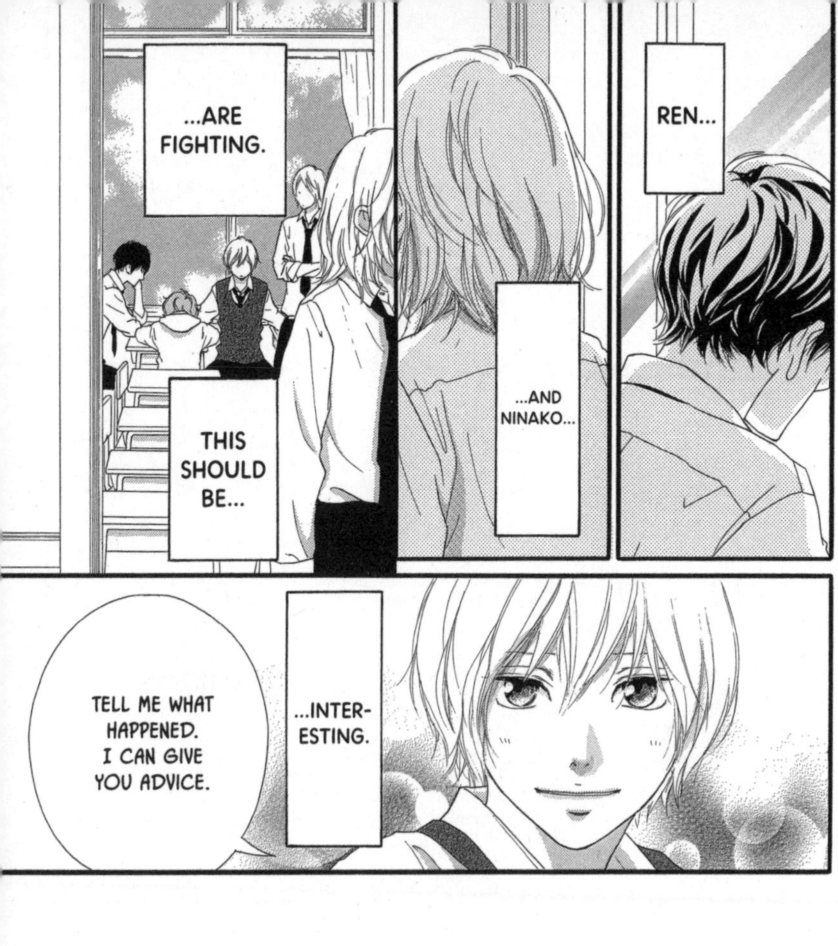
REN...
...AND NINAKO...
...ARE FIGHTING.
THIS SHOULD BE...
...INTER-ESTING.
TELL ME WHAT HAPPENED. I CAN GIVE YOU ADVICE.

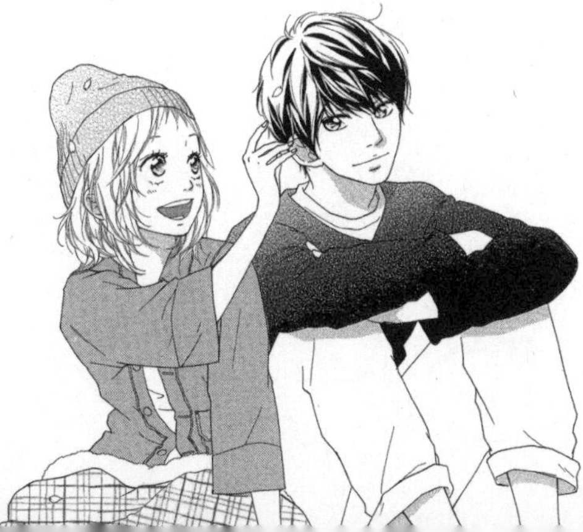

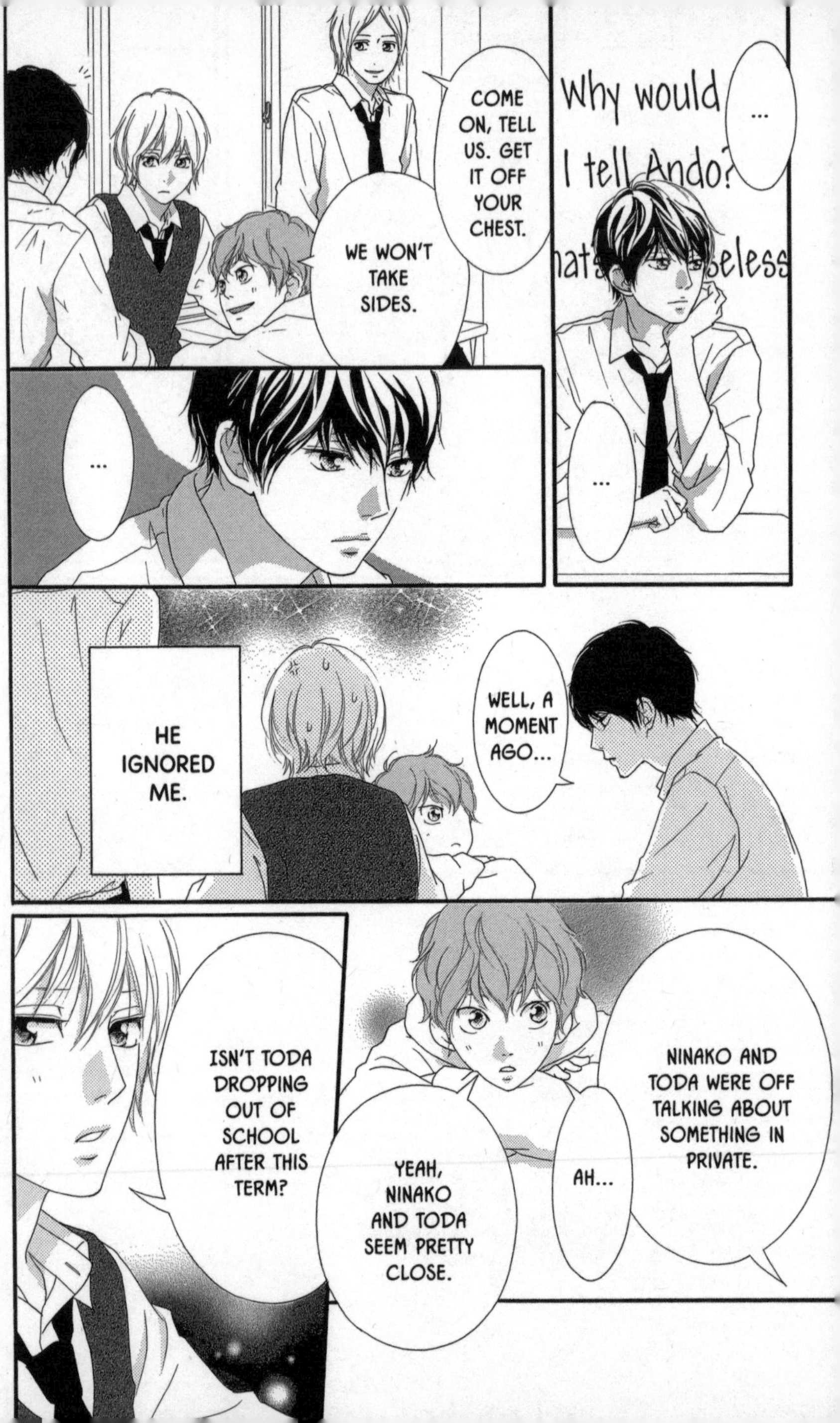
Why would I tell Ando?
...
COME ON, TELL US. GET IT OFF YOUR CHEST.
WE WON'T TAKE SIDES.
...
...
WELL, A MOMENT AGO...
HE IGNORED ME.
NINAKO AND TODA WERE OFF TALKING ABOUT SOMETHING IN PRIVATE.
AH...
YEAH, NINAKO AND TODA SEEM PRETTY CLOSE.
ISN'T TODA DROPPING OUT OF SCHOOL AFTER THIS TERM?

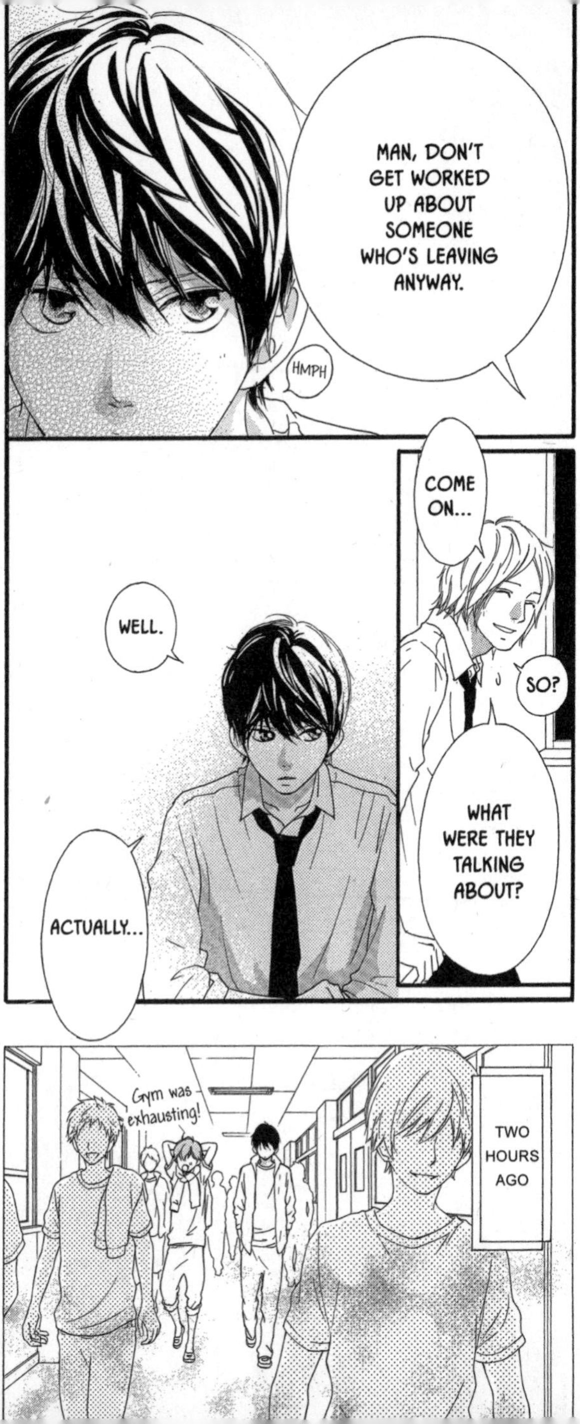
MAN, DON'T GET WORKED UP ABOUT SOMEONE WHO'S LEAVING ANYWAY.
HMPH
COME ON...
SO?
WHAT WERE THEY TALKING ABOUT?
WELL.
ACTUALLY...
TWO HOURS AGO
Gym was exhausting!

(Continued from page 119)
...that man had to be my boyfriend's father. (He looked like an identical copy.) I was embarrassed that he kept bellowing my name over and over, but it was clear that something serious had happened. I told him who I was. (By the way, we were meeting at a train station.) Indeed, my boyfriend had gotten into an accident on his way over, and the moment I heard that I grew pale, until I was informed a moment later that "he didn't even break a bone." I was so relieved. If that was the case, I wondered why this man had been bellowing as if there had been an emergency. Well, it turns out that his dad's normal voice is just very loud. His dad had happened to be at a bowling alley near the station, so he came to notify me. Meanwhile, my boyfriend had been hit by a car that went through a stop sign. His mother and sister happened to be on a bus passing by at that moment, and they wondered if they had seen him in the accident, which was hilarious. At least that's what he thought.

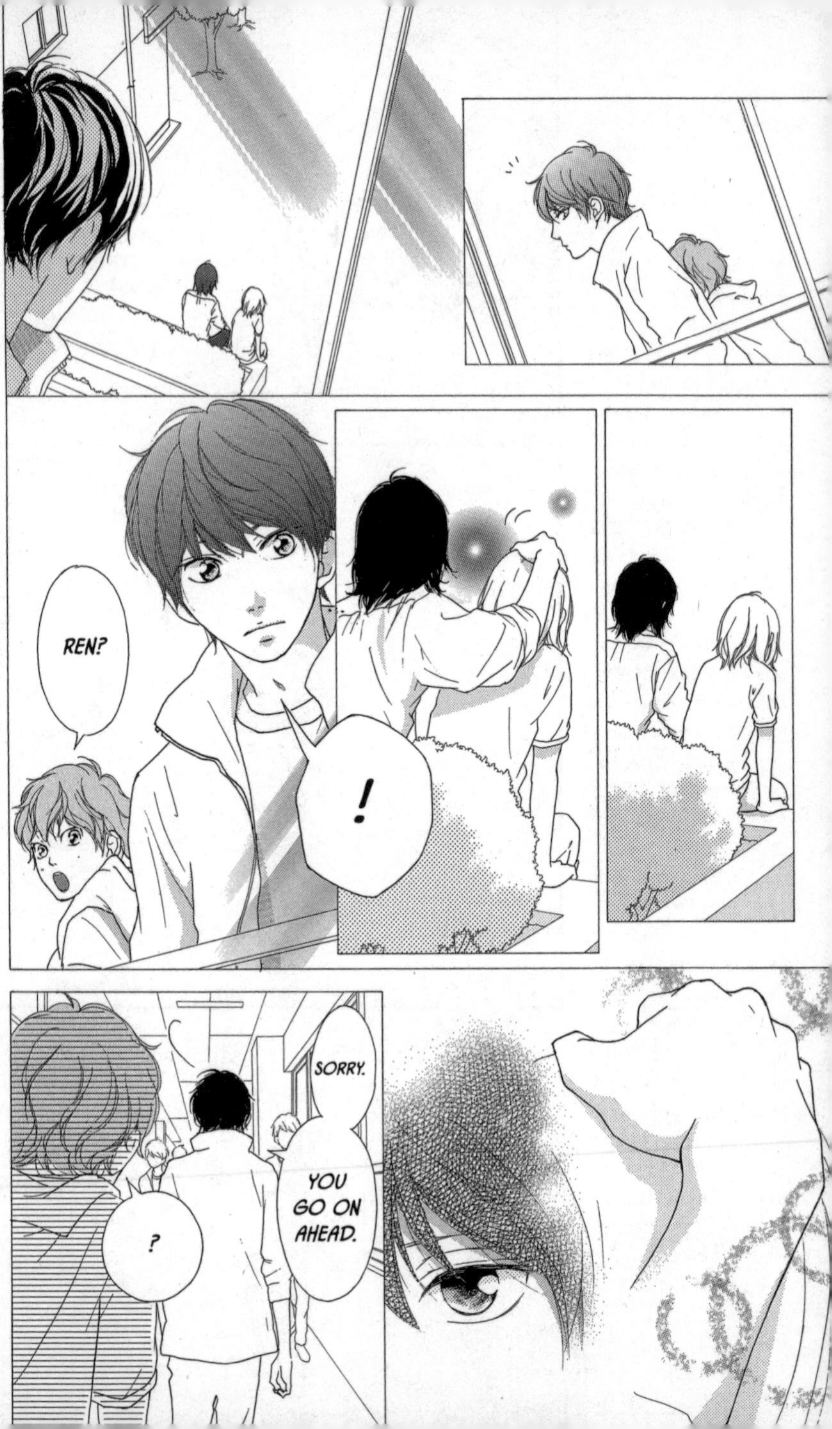
!
REN?
SORRY.
YOU GO ON AHEAD.
?

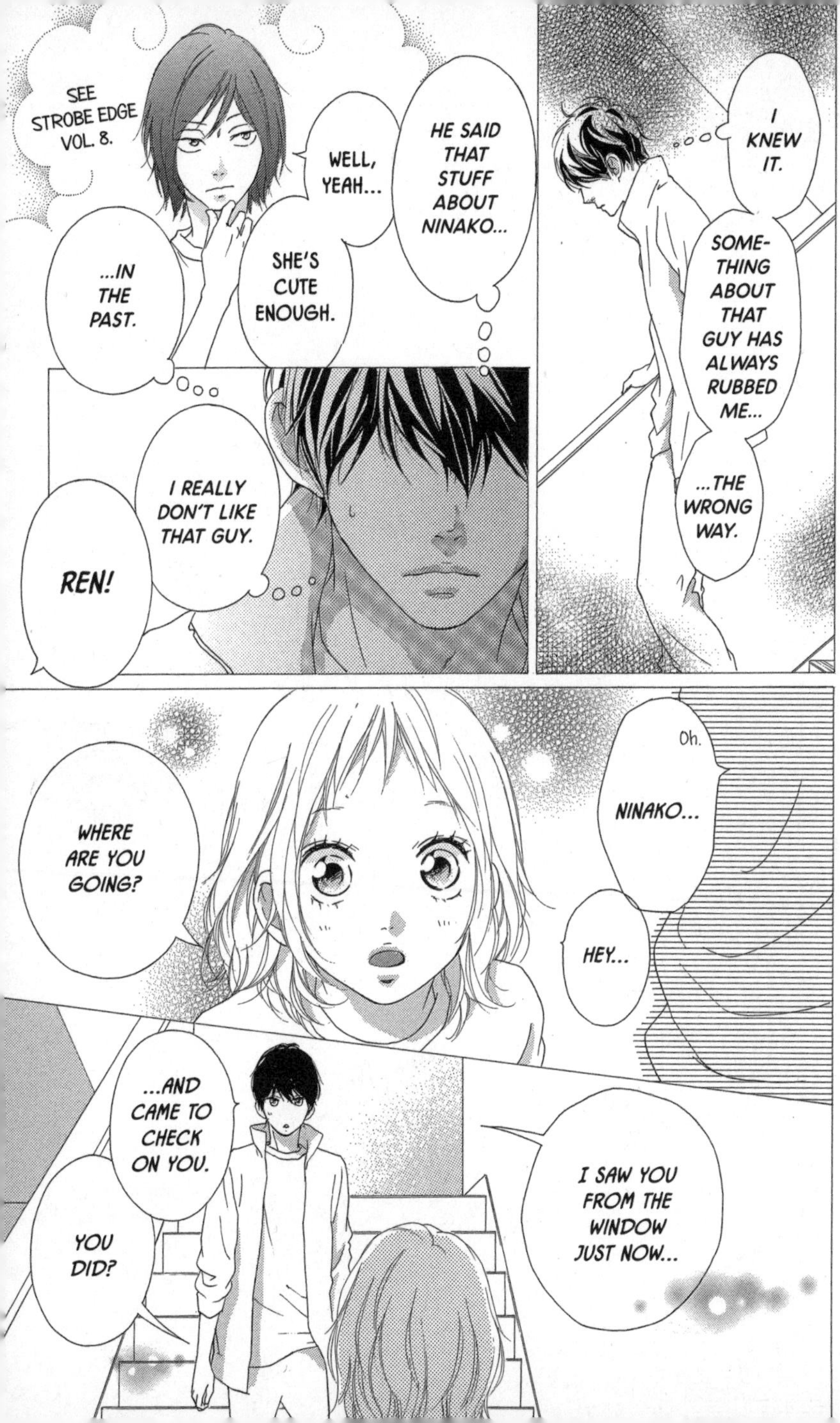
I KNEW IT.
SOMETHING ABOUT THAT GUY HAS ALWAYS RUBBED ME...
...THE WRONG WAY.
HE SAID THAT STUFF ABOUT NINAKO...
WELL, YEAH...
SHE'S CUTE ENOUGH.
...IN THE PAST.
SEE STROBE EDGE VOL. 8.
I REALLY DON'T LIKE THAT GUY.
REN!
Oh.
NINAKO...
HEY...
WHERE ARE YOU GOING?
I SAW YOU FROM THE WINDOW JUST NOW...
...AND CAME TO CHECK ON YOU.
YOU DID?

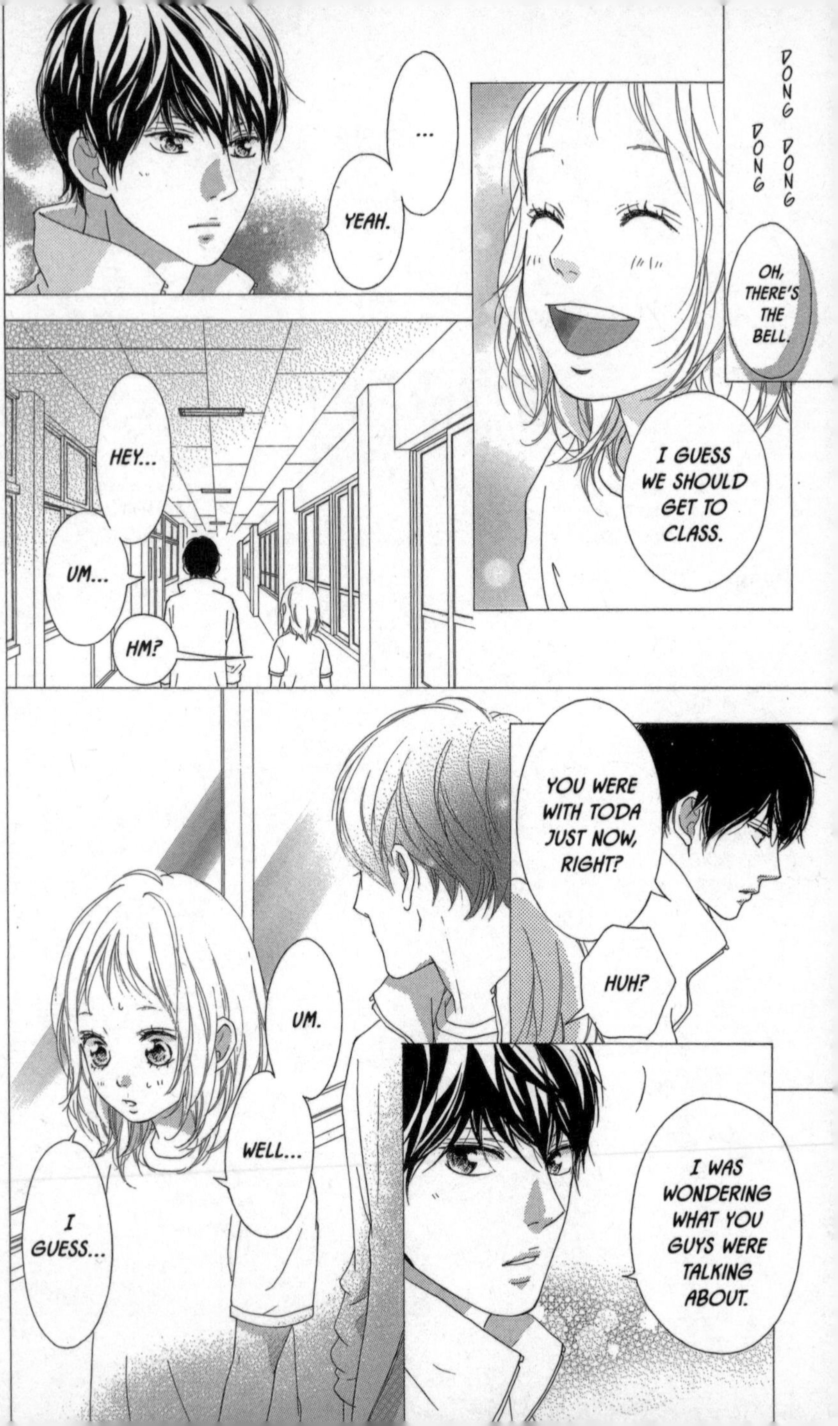
DONG DONG
DONG
OH, THERE'S THE BELL.
I GUESS WE SHOULD GET TO CLASS.
...
YEAH.
HEY...
UM...
HM?
YOU WERE WITH TODA JUST NOW, RIGHT?
HUH?
I WAS WONDERING WHAT YOU GUYS WERE TALKING ABOUT.
UM.
WELL...
I GUESS...

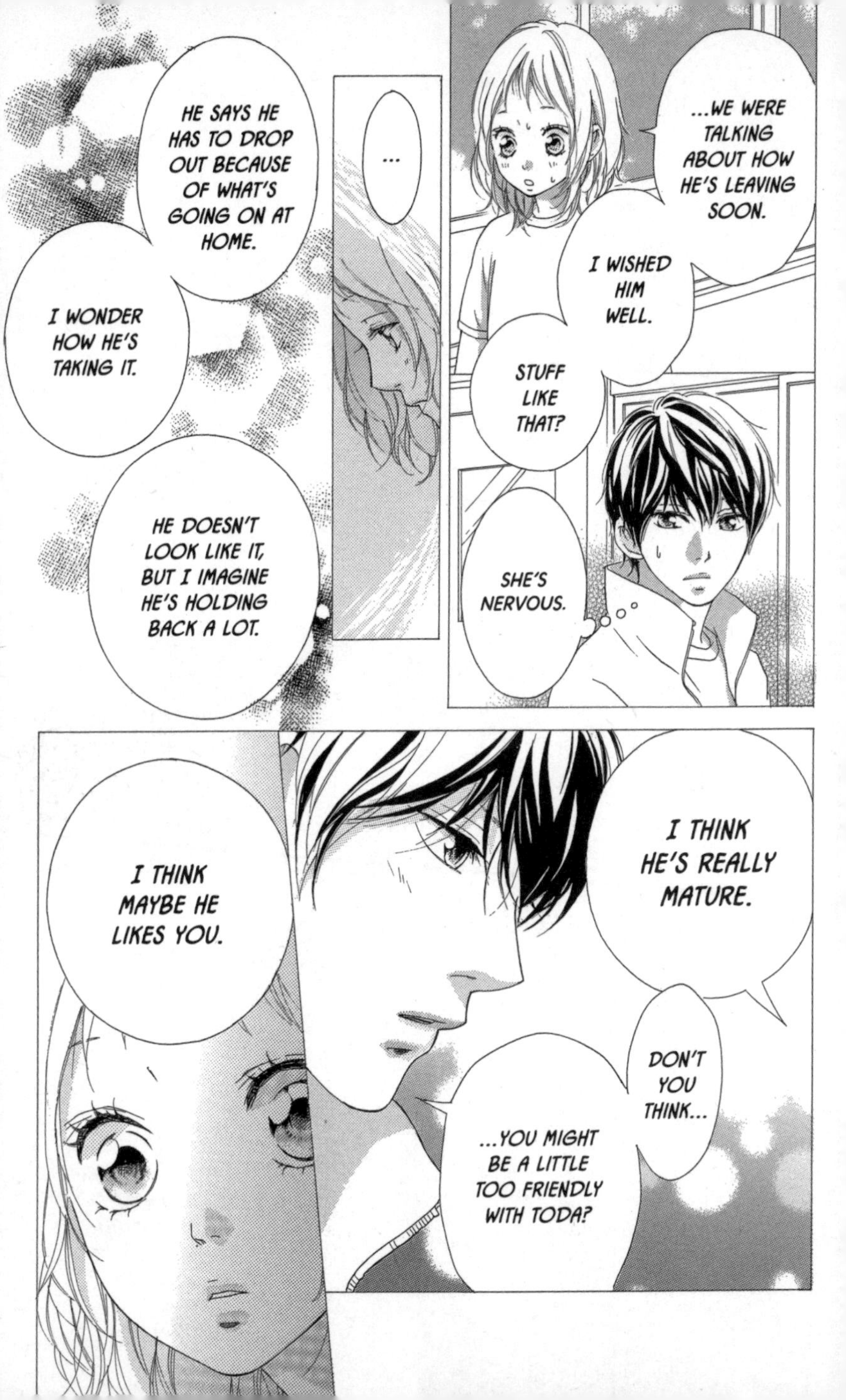
...WE WERE TALKING ABOUT HOW HE'S LEAVING SOON.
I WISHED HIM WELL.
STUFF LIKE THAT?
SHE'S NERVOUS.
...
HE SAYS HE HAS TO DROP OUT BECAUSE OF WHAT'S GOING ON AT HOME.
I WONDER HOW HE'S TAKING IT.
HE DOESN'T LOOK LIKE IT, BUT I IMAGINE HE'S HOLDING BACK A LOT.
I THINK HE'S REALLY MATURE.
I THINK MAYBE HE LIKES YOU.
DON'T YOU THINK...
...YOU MIGHT BE A LITTLE TOO FRIENDLY WITH TODA?

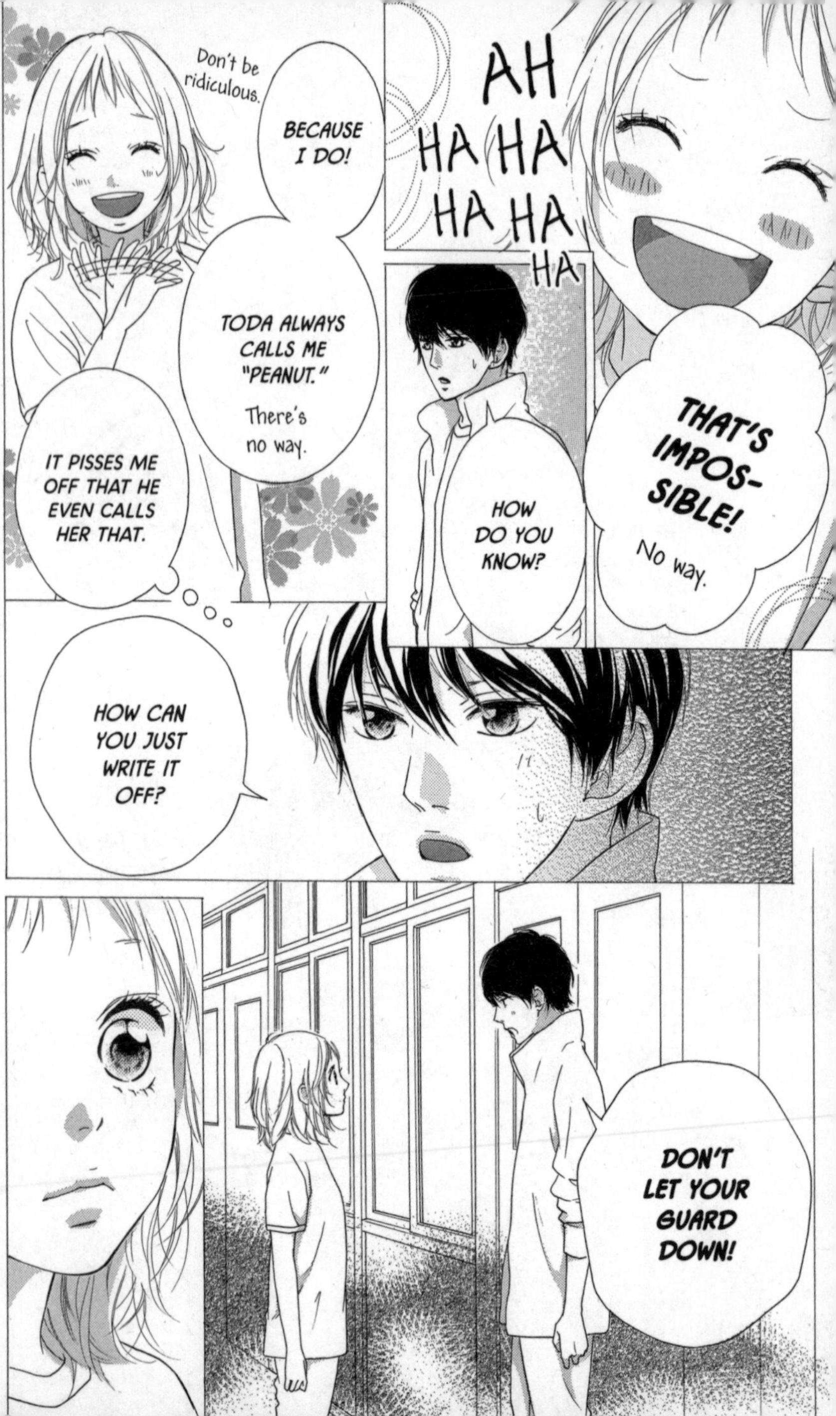
AH HA HA HA HA HA
THAT'S IMPOS-SIBLE!
No way.
HOW DO YOU KNOW?
BECAUSE I DO!
Don't be ridiculous.
TODA ALWAYS CALLS ME "PEANUT."
There's no way.
IT PISSES ME OFF THAT HE EVEN CALLS HER THAT.
HOW CAN YOU JUST WRITE IT OFF?
DON'T LET YOUR GUARD DOWN!

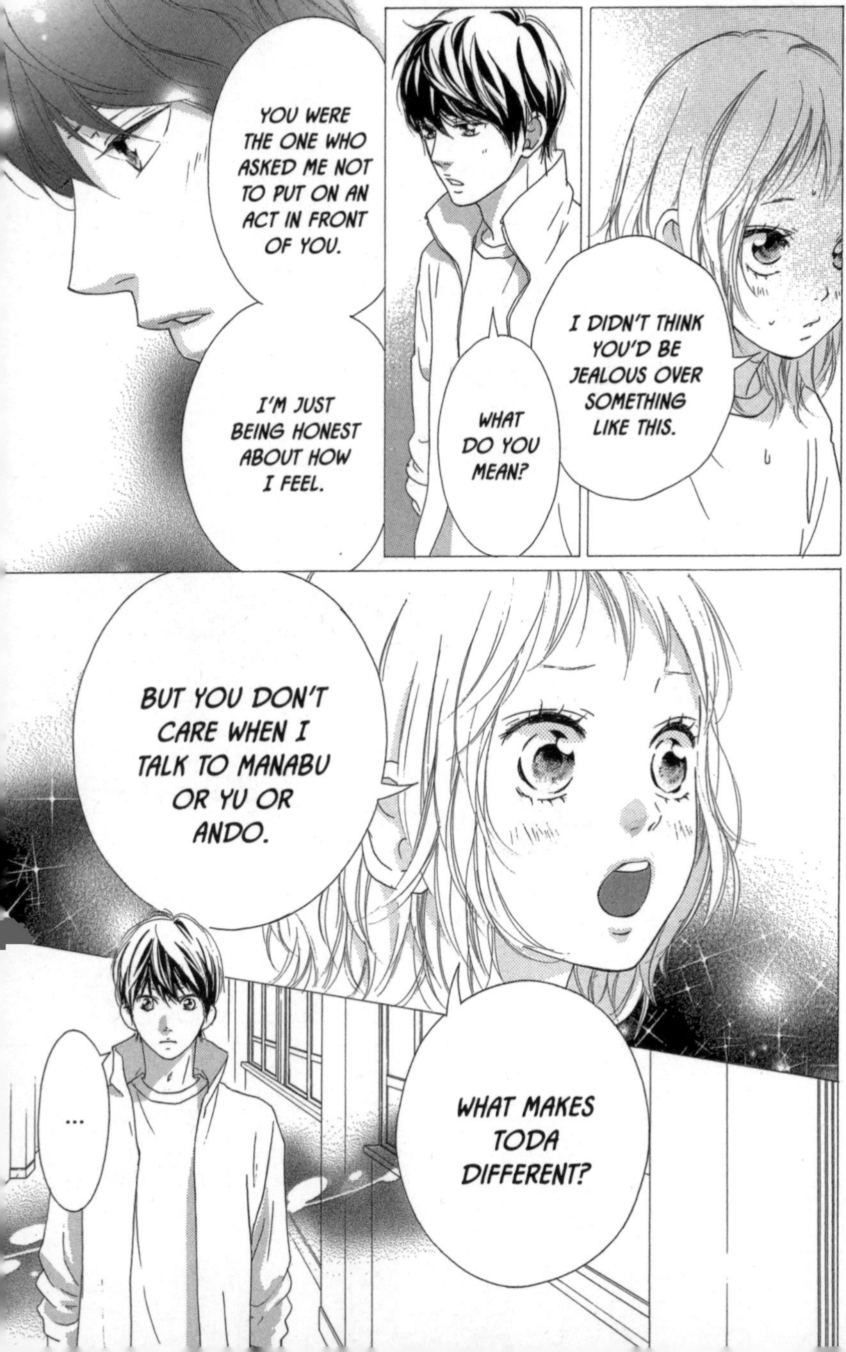
I DIDN'T THINK YOU'D BE JEALOUS OVER SOMETHING LIKE THIS.
WHAT DO YOU MEAN?
YOU WERE THE ONE WHO ASKED ME NOT TO PUT ON AN ACT IN FRONT OF YOU.
I'M JUST BEING HONEST ABOUT HOW I FEEL.
BUT YOU DON'T CARE WHEN I TALK TO MANABU OR YU OR ANDO.
WHAT MAKES TODA DIFFERENT?
...

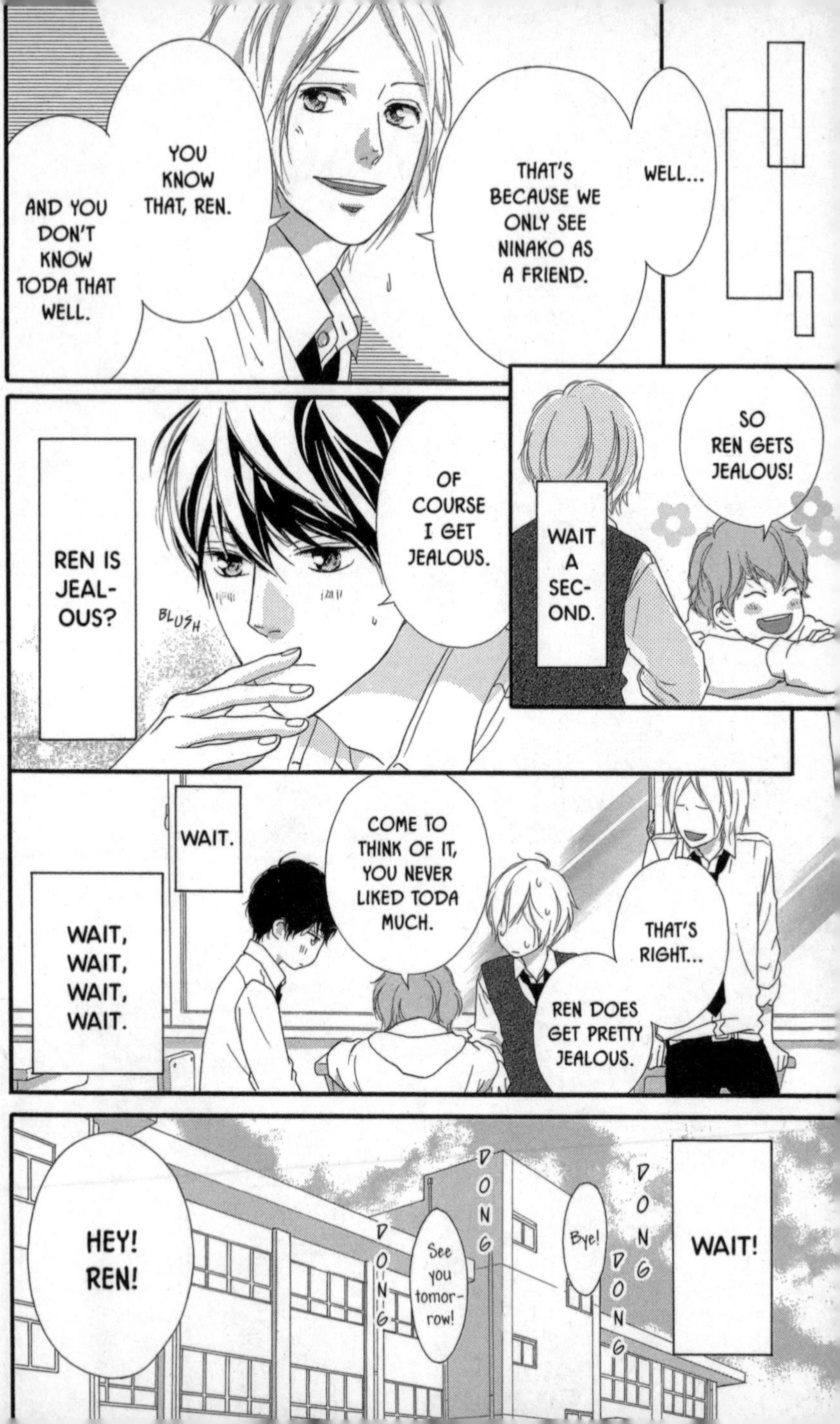

WELL...
THAT'S BECAUSE WE ONLY SEE NINAKO AS A FRIEND.
YOU KNOW THAT, REN.
AND YOU DON'T KNOW TODA THAT WELL.
SO REN GETS JEALOUS!
WAIT A SEC-OND.
OF COURSE I GET JEALOUS.
BLUSH
REN IS JEAL-OUS?
THAT'S RIGHT...
REN DOES GET PRETTY JEALOUS.
COME TO THINK OF IT, YOU NEVER LIKED TODA MUCH.
WAIT.
WAIT, WAIT, WAIT, WAIT.
WAIT!
DONG
DONG
Bye!
DONG
See you tomor-row!
DONG
HEY! REN!

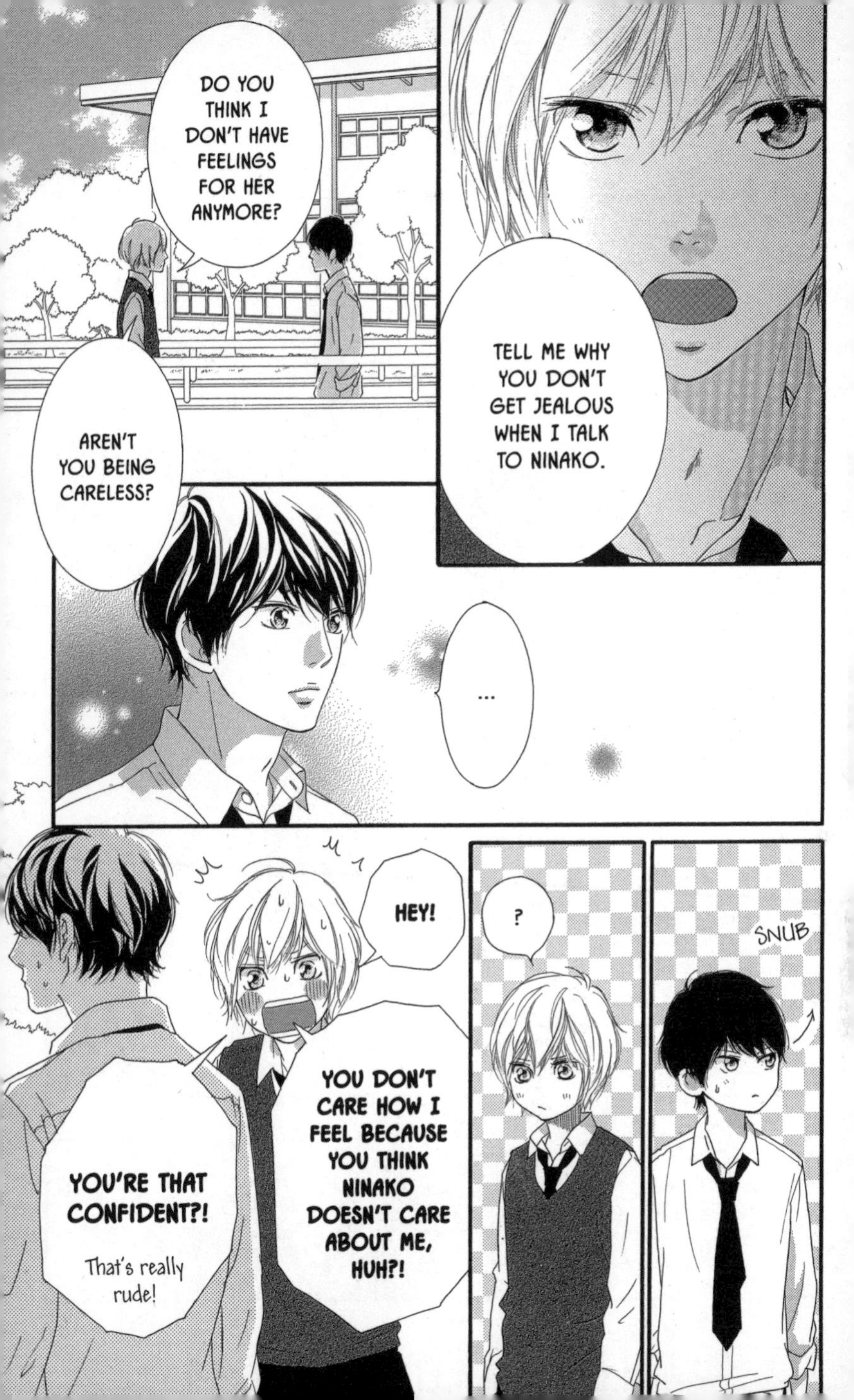
TELL ME WHY YOU DON'T GET JEALOUS WHEN I TALK TO NINAKO.
DO YOU THINK I DON'T HAVE FEELINGS FOR HER ANYMORE?
AREN'T YOU BEING CARELESS?
...
SNUB
?
HEY!
YOU DON'T CARE HOW I FEEL BECAUSE YOU THINK NINAKO DOESN'T CARE ABOUT ME, HUH?!
YOU'RE THAT CONFIDENT?!
That's really rude!

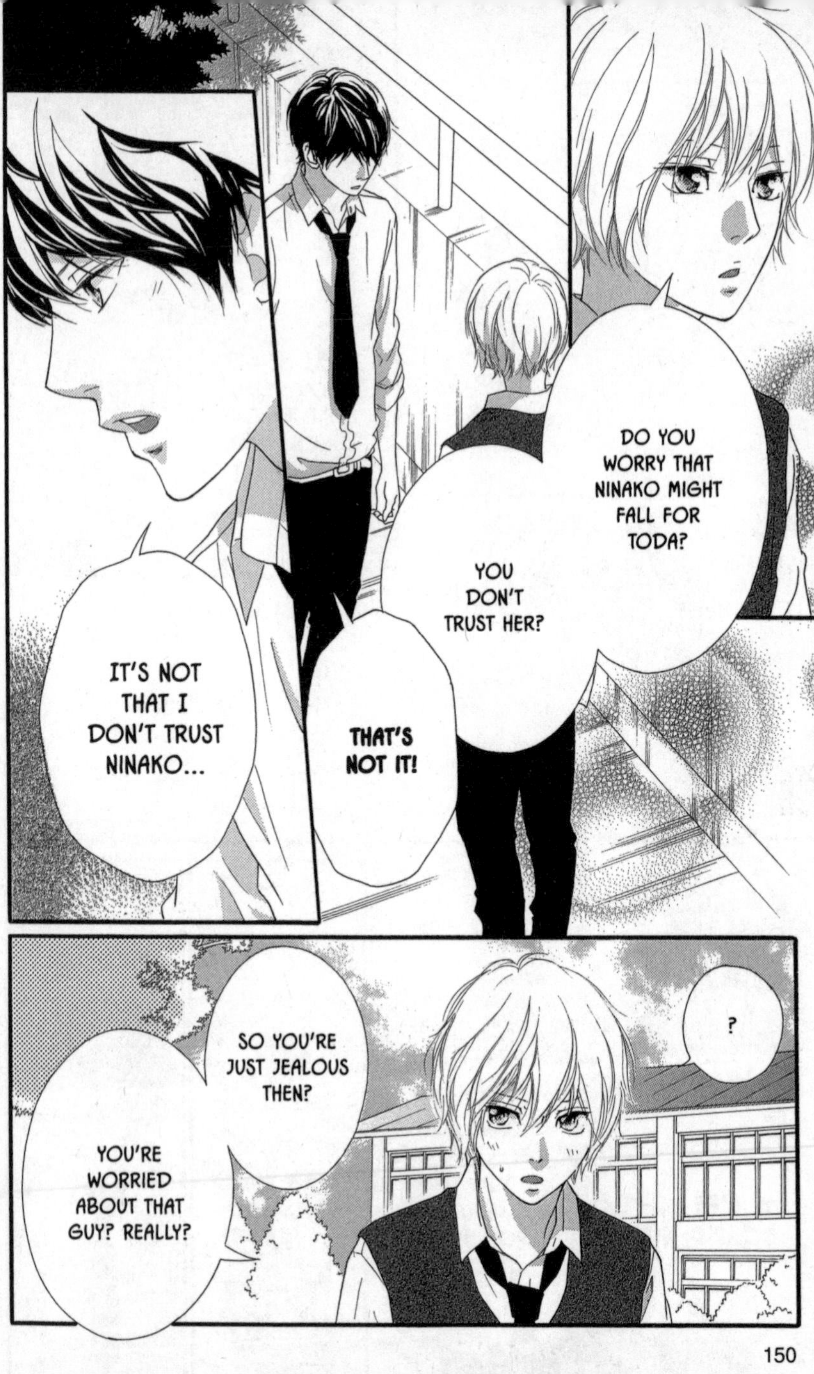
DO YOU WORRY THAT NINAKO MIGHT FALL FOR TODA?
YOU DON'T TRUST HER?
THAT'S NOT IT!
IT'S NOT THAT I DON'T TRUST NINAKO...
?
SO YOU'RE JUST JEALOUS THEN?
YOU'RE WORRIED ABOUT THAT GUY? REALLY?

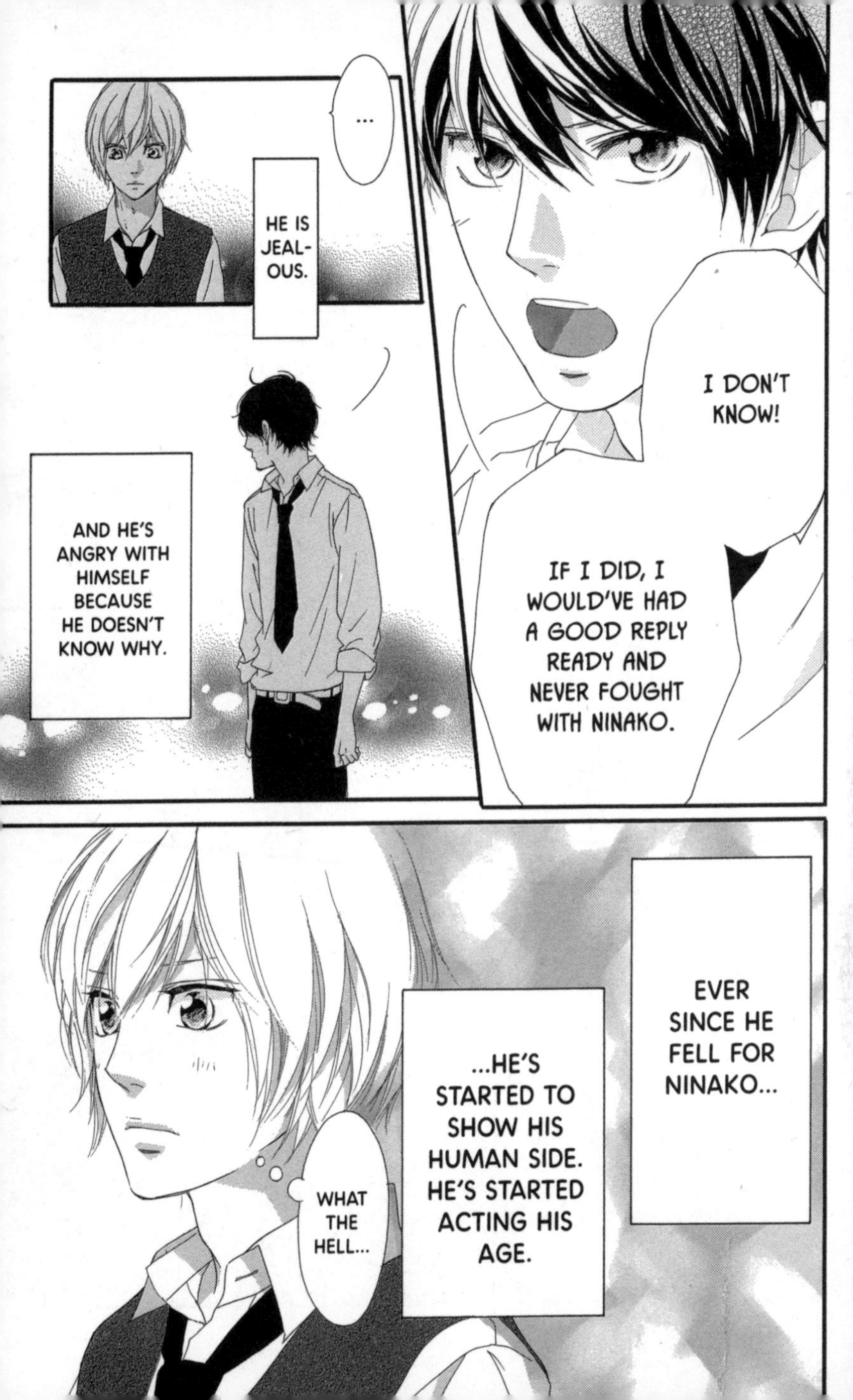
I DON'T KNOW!
IF I DID, I WOULD'VE HAD A GOOD REPLY READY AND NEVER FOUGHT WITH NINAKO.
...
HE IS JEAL-OUS.
AND HE'S ANGRY WITH HIMSELF BECAUSE HE DOESN'T KNOW WHY.
EVER SINCE HE FELL FOR NINAKO...
...HE'S STARTED TO SHOW HIS HUMAN SIDE. HE'S STARTED ACTING HIS AGE.
WHAT THE HELL...

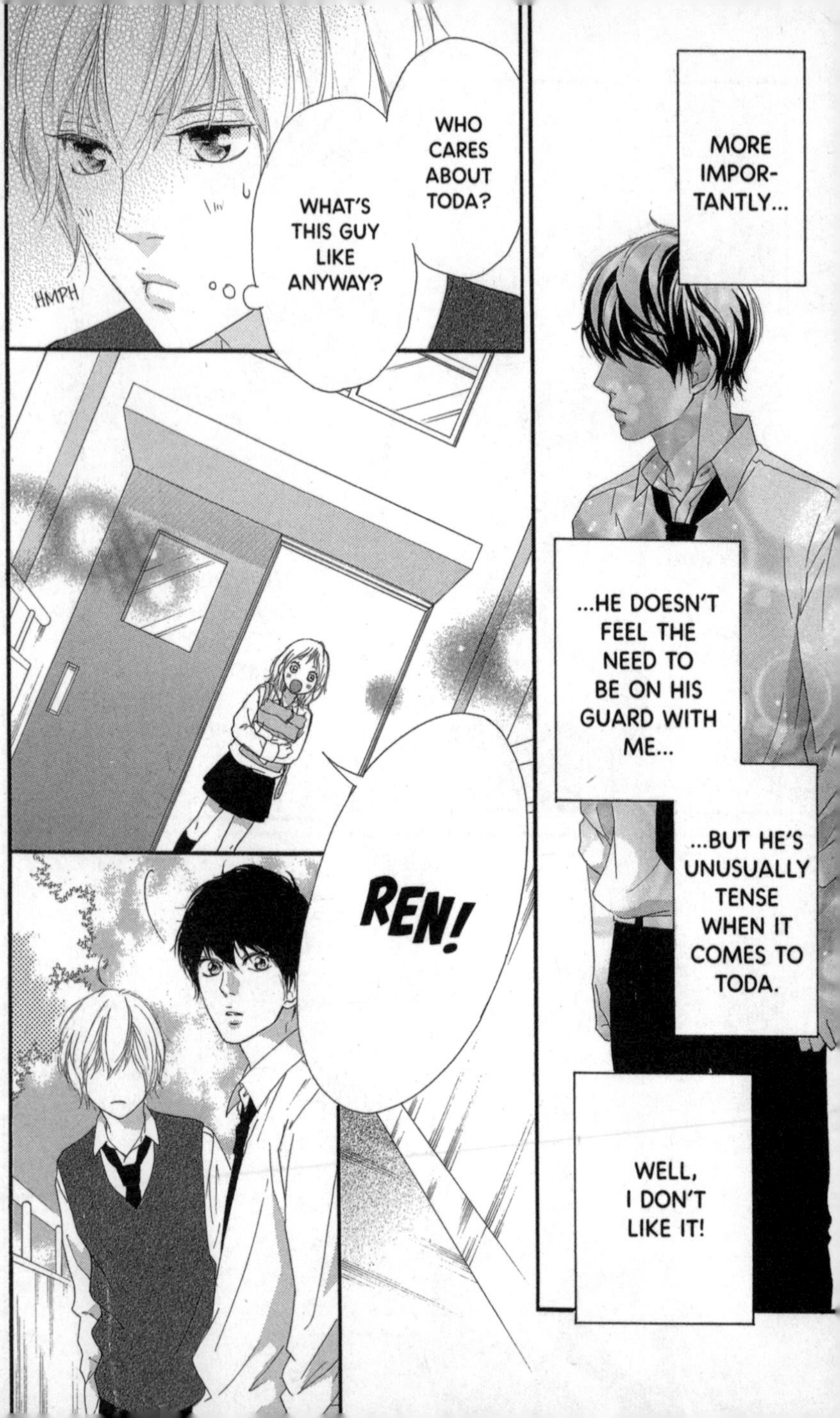

MORE IMPORTANTLY...
...HE DOESN'T FEEL THE NEED TO BE ON HIS GUARD WITH ME...
...BUT HE'S UNUSUALLY TENSE WHEN IT COMES TO TODA.
WELL, I DON'T LIKE IT!
WHO CARES ABOUT TODA?
WHAT'S THIS GUY LIKE ANYWAY?
HMPH
REN!

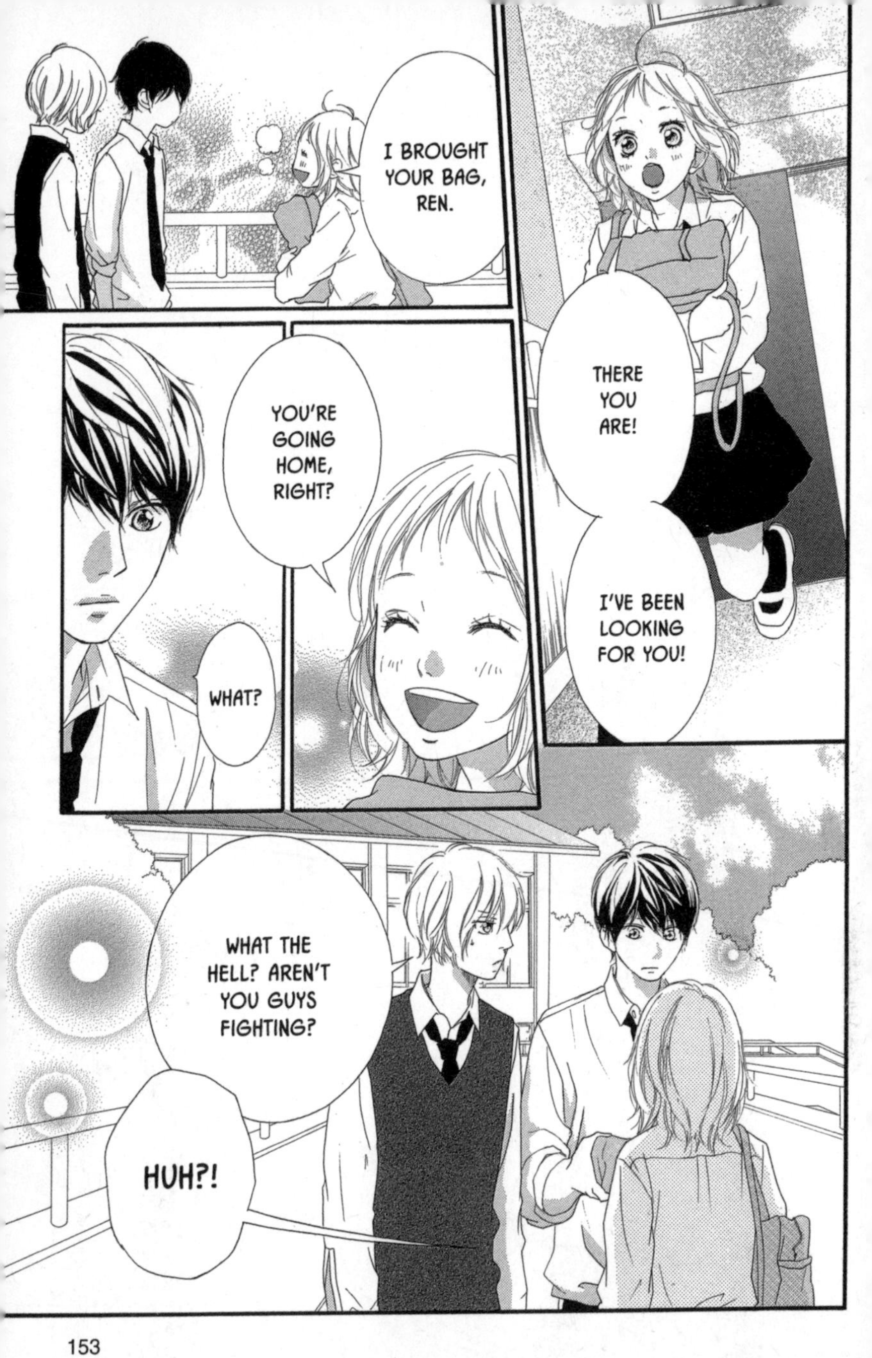
THERE YOU ARE!
I'VE BEEN LOOKING FOR YOU!
I BROUGHT YOUR BAG, REN.
YOU'RE GOING HOME, RIGHT?
WHAT?
WHAT THE HELL? AREN'T YOU GUYS FIGHTING?
HUH?!

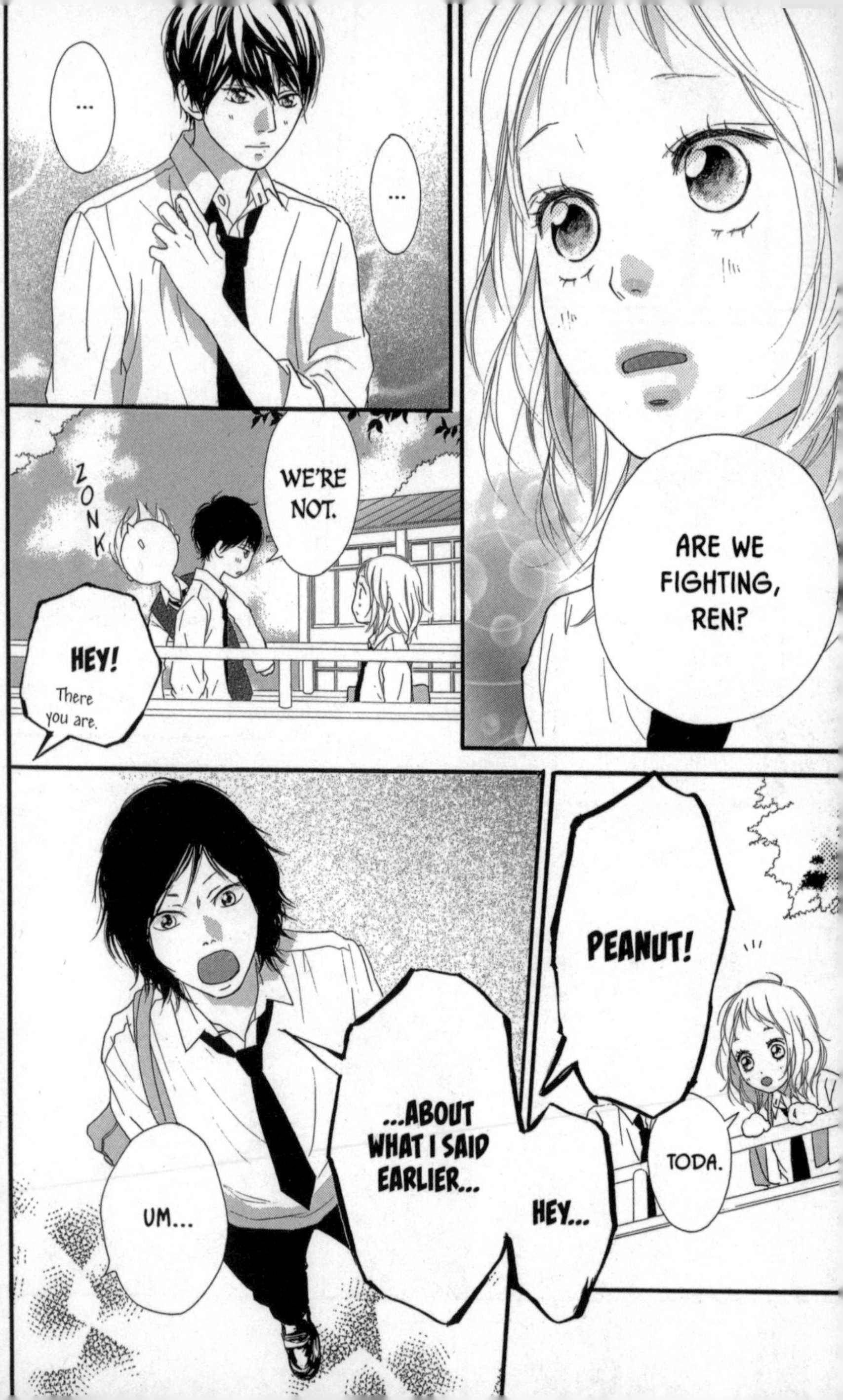
ARE WE FIGHTING, REN?
...
...
WE'RE NOT.
ZONK
HEY!
There you are.
PEANUT!
TODA.
HEY...
...ABOUT WHAT I SAID EARLIER...
UM...

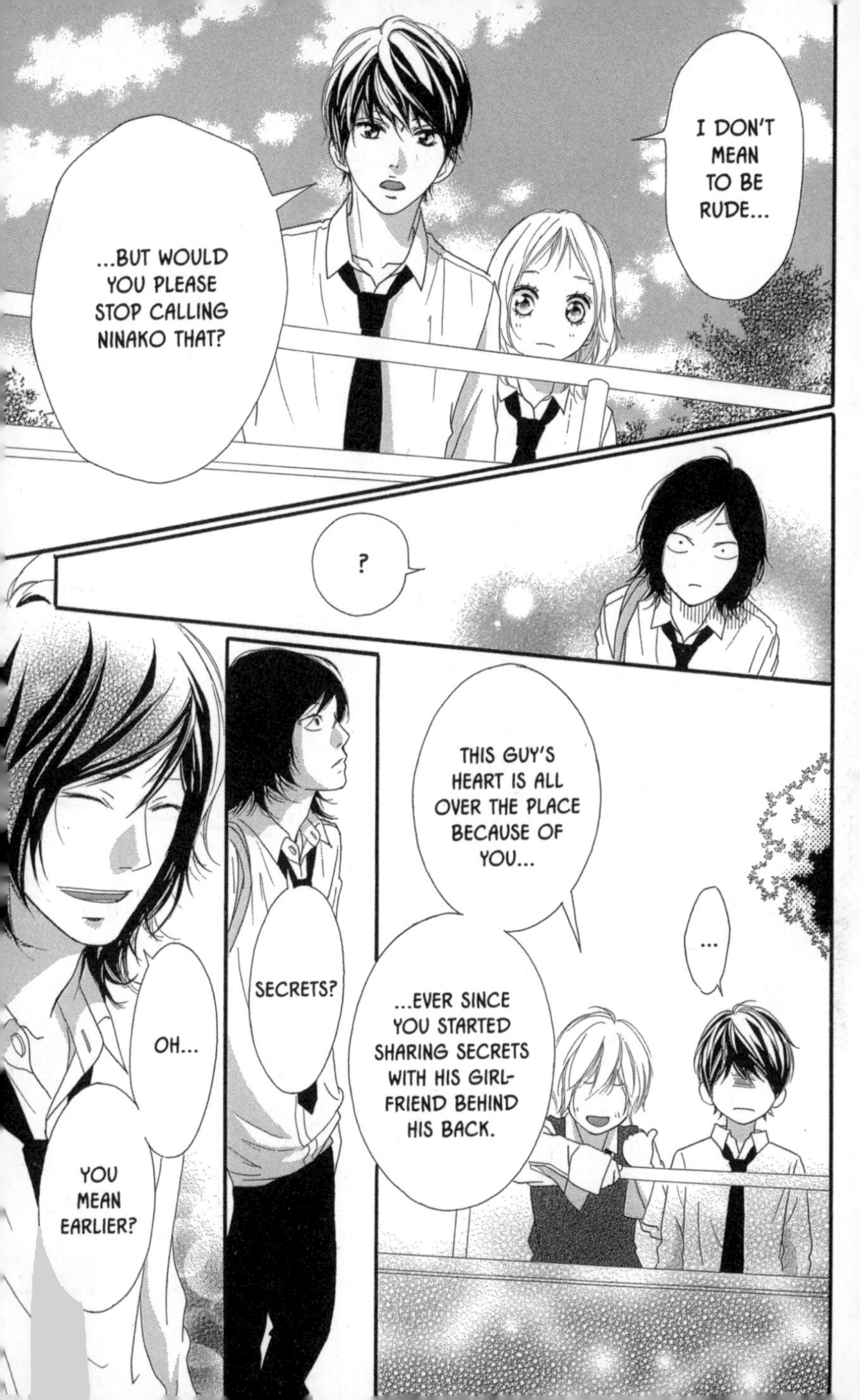

I DON'T MEAN TO BE RUDE...
...BUT WOULD YOU PLEASE STOP CALLING NINAKO THAT?
?
THIS GUY'S HEART IS ALL OVER THE PLACE BECAUSE OF YOU...
...EVER SINCE YOU STARTED SHARING SECRETS WITH HIS GIRL-FRIEND BEHIND HIS BACK.
...
SECRETS?
OH...
YOU MEAN EARLIER?

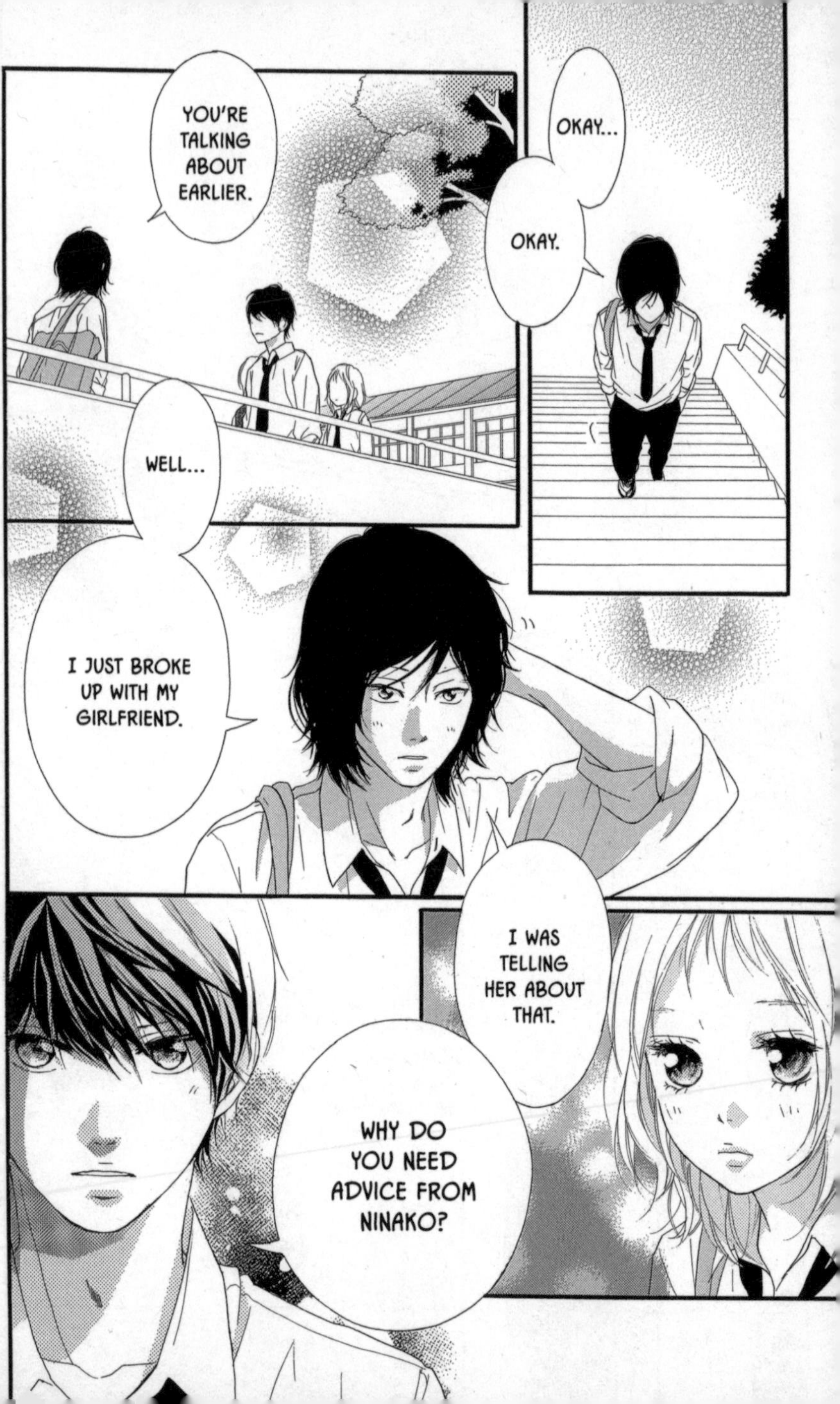
OKAY...
OKAY.
YOU'RE TALKING ABOUT EARLIER.
WELL...
I JUST BROKE UP WITH MY GIRLFRIEND.
I WAS TELLING HER ABOUT THAT.
WHY DO YOU NEED ADVICE FROM NINAKO?

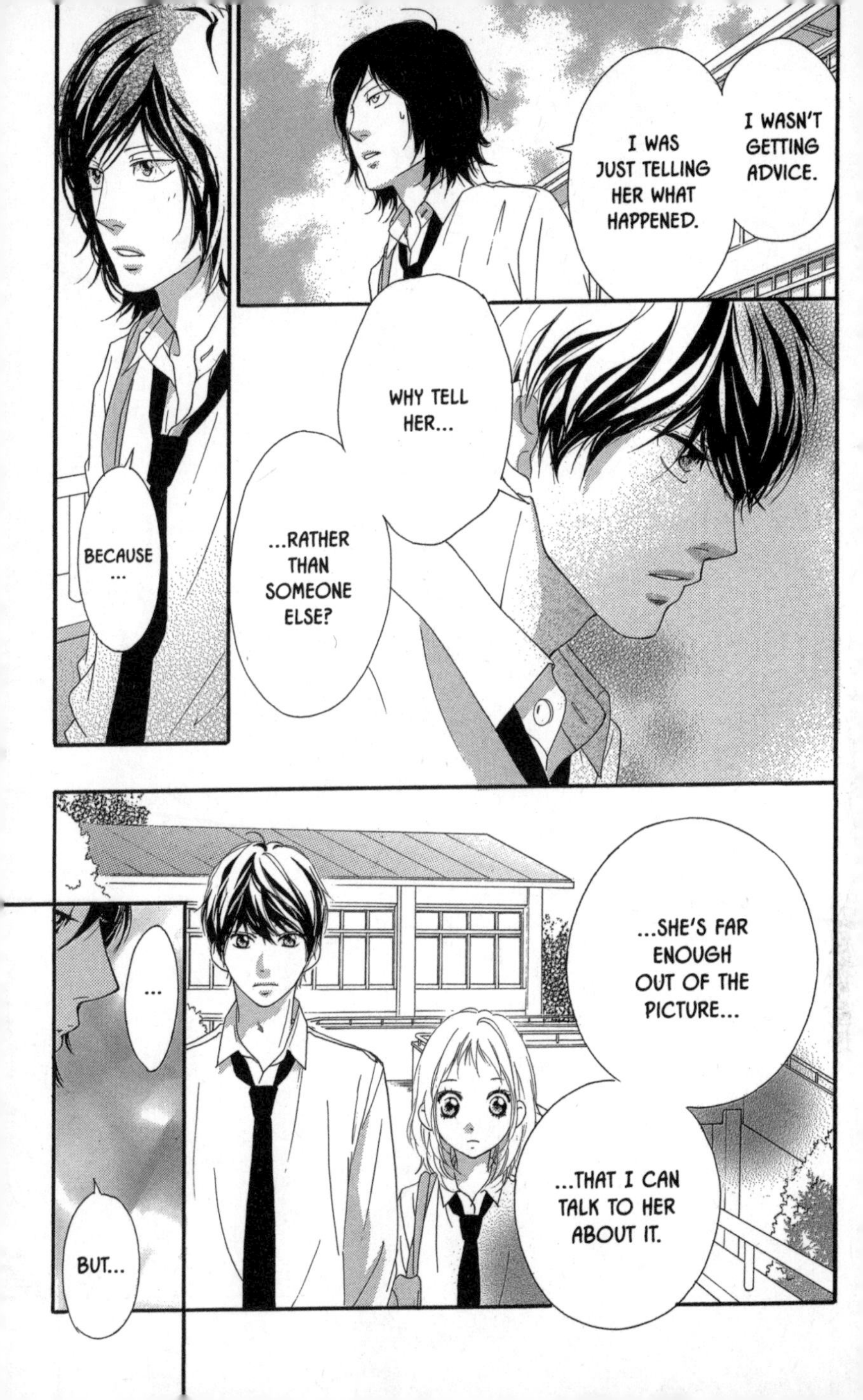
I WASN'T GETTING ADVICE.
I WAS JUST TELLING HER WHAT HAPPENED.
WHY TELL HER...
...RATHER THAN SOMEONE ELSE?
BECAUSE...
...SHE'S FAR ENOUGH OUT OF THE PICTURE...
...THAT I CAN TALK TO HER ABOUT IT.
...
BUT...

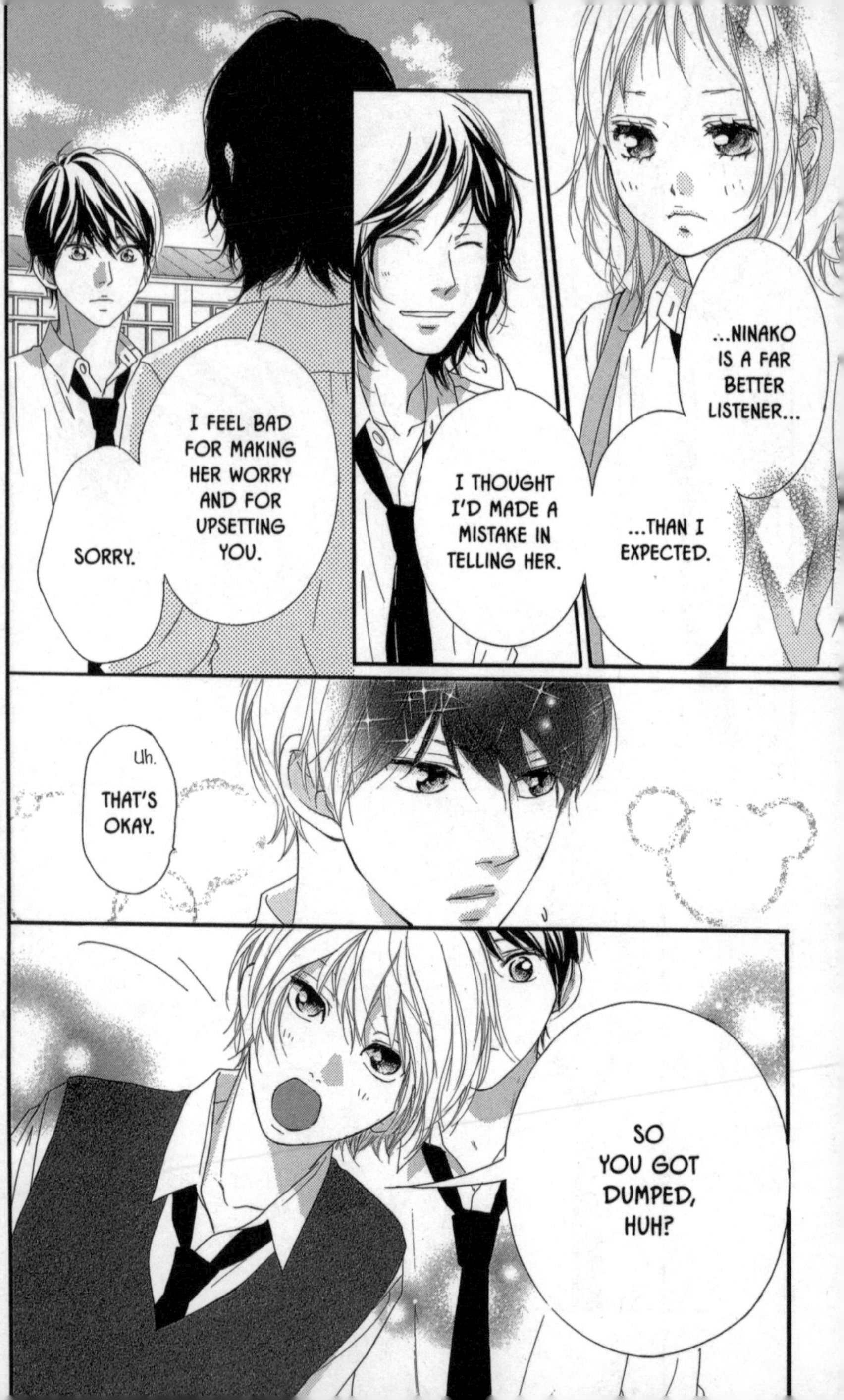
...NINAKO IS A FAR BETTER LISTENER...
...THAN I EXPECTED.
I THOUGHT I'D MADE A MISTAKE IN TELLING HER.
I FEEL BAD FOR MAKING HER WORRY AND FOR UPSETTING YOU.
SORRY.
Uh.
THAT'S OKAY.
SO YOU GOT DUMPED, HUH?

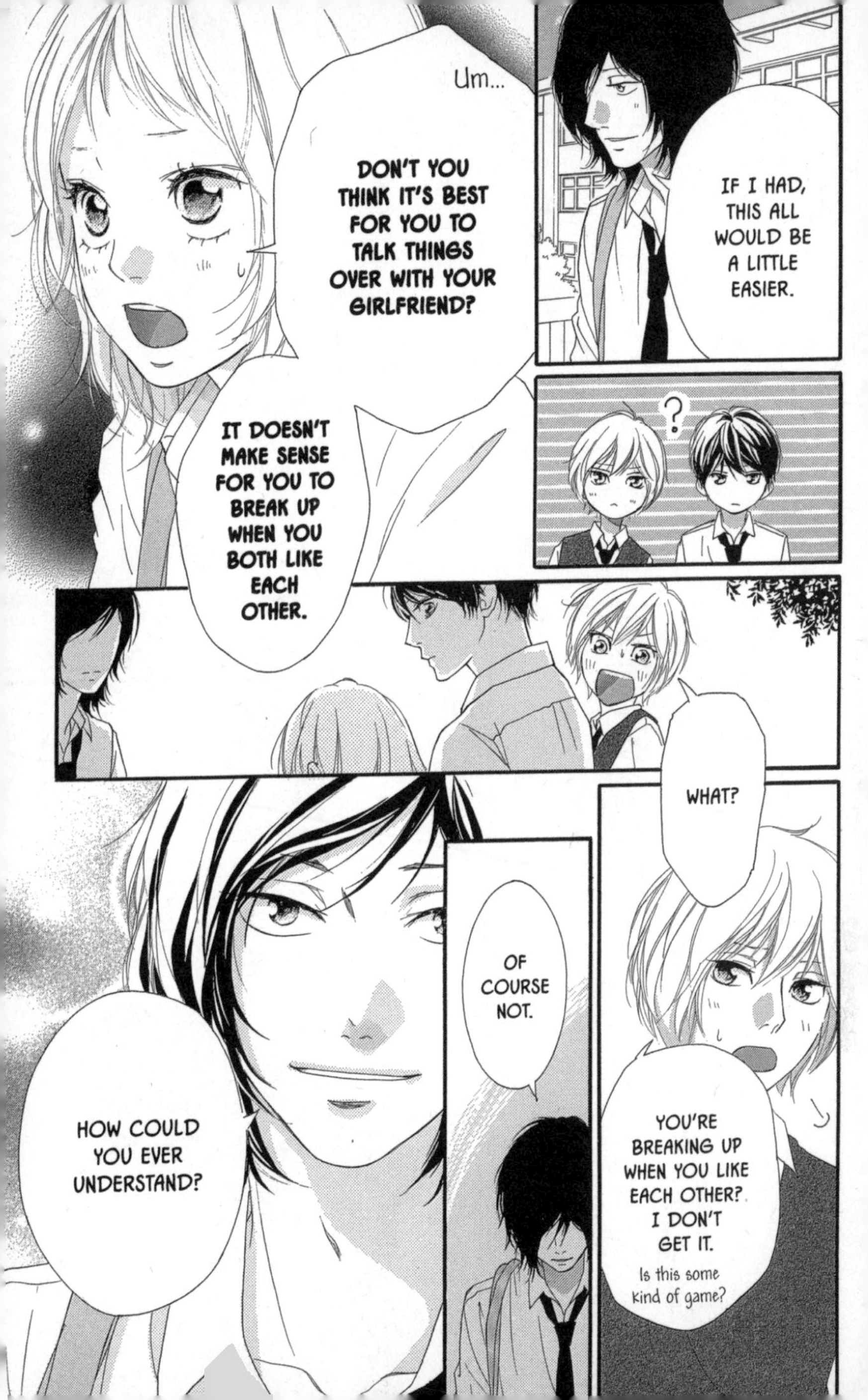
IF I HAD, THIS ALL WOULD BE A LITTLE EASIER.
?
Um...
DON'T YOU THINK IT'S BEST FOR YOU TO TALK THINGS OVER WITH YOUR GIRLFRIEND?
IT DOESN'T MAKE SENSE FOR YOU TO BREAK UP WHEN YOU BOTH LIKE EACH OTHER.
WHAT?
YOU'RE BREAKING UP WHEN YOU LIKE EACH OTHER? I DON'T GET IT.
Is this some kind of game?
OF COURSE NOT.
HOW COULD YOU EVER UNDERSTAND?

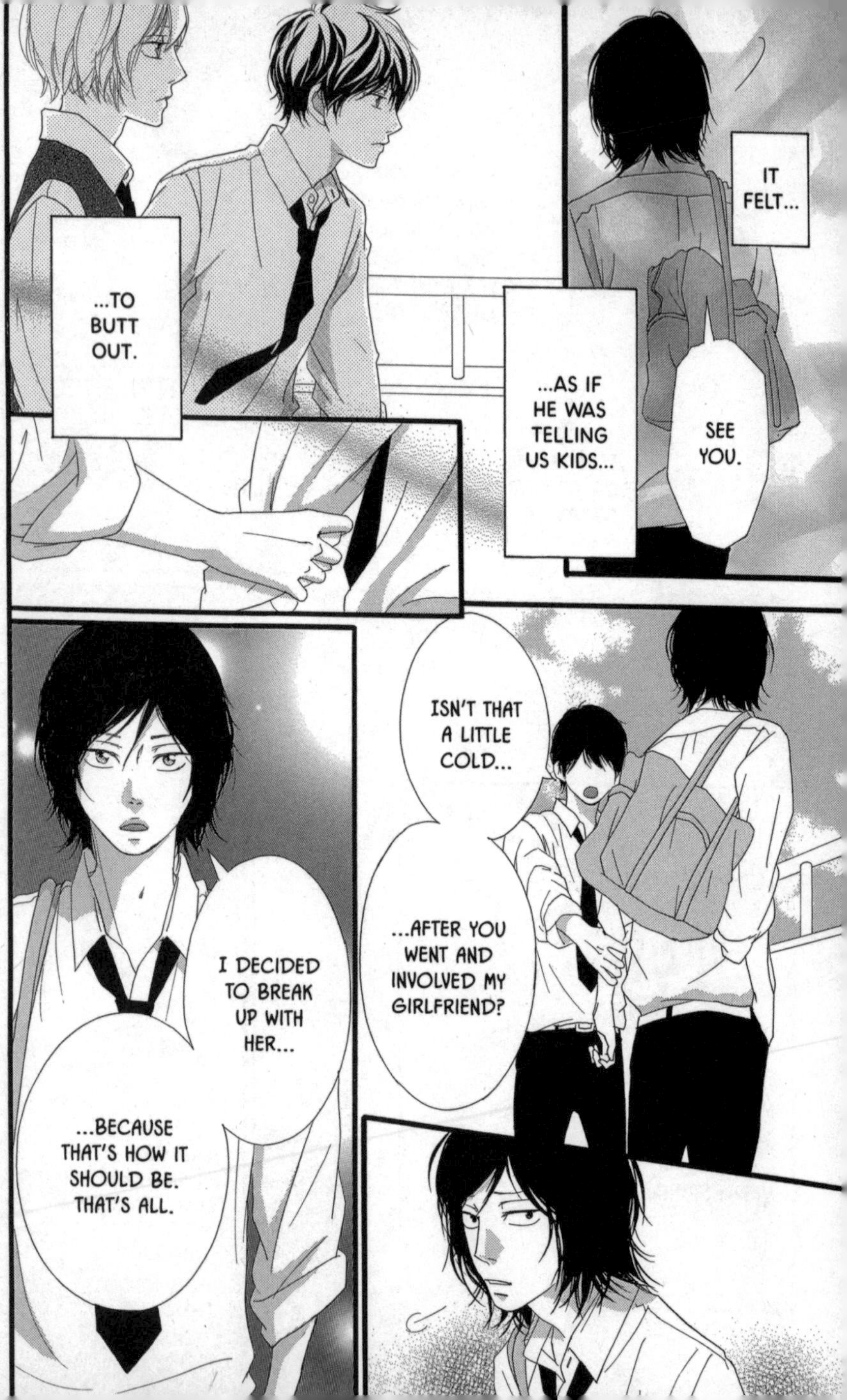
IT FELT...
SEE YOU.
...AS IF HE WAS TELLING US KIDS...
...TO BUTT OUT.
ISN'T THAT A LITTLE COLD...
...AFTER YOU WENT AND INVOLVED MY GIRLFRIEND?
I DECIDED TO BREAK UP WITH HER...
...BECAUSE THAT'S HOW IT SHOULD BE. THAT'S ALL.

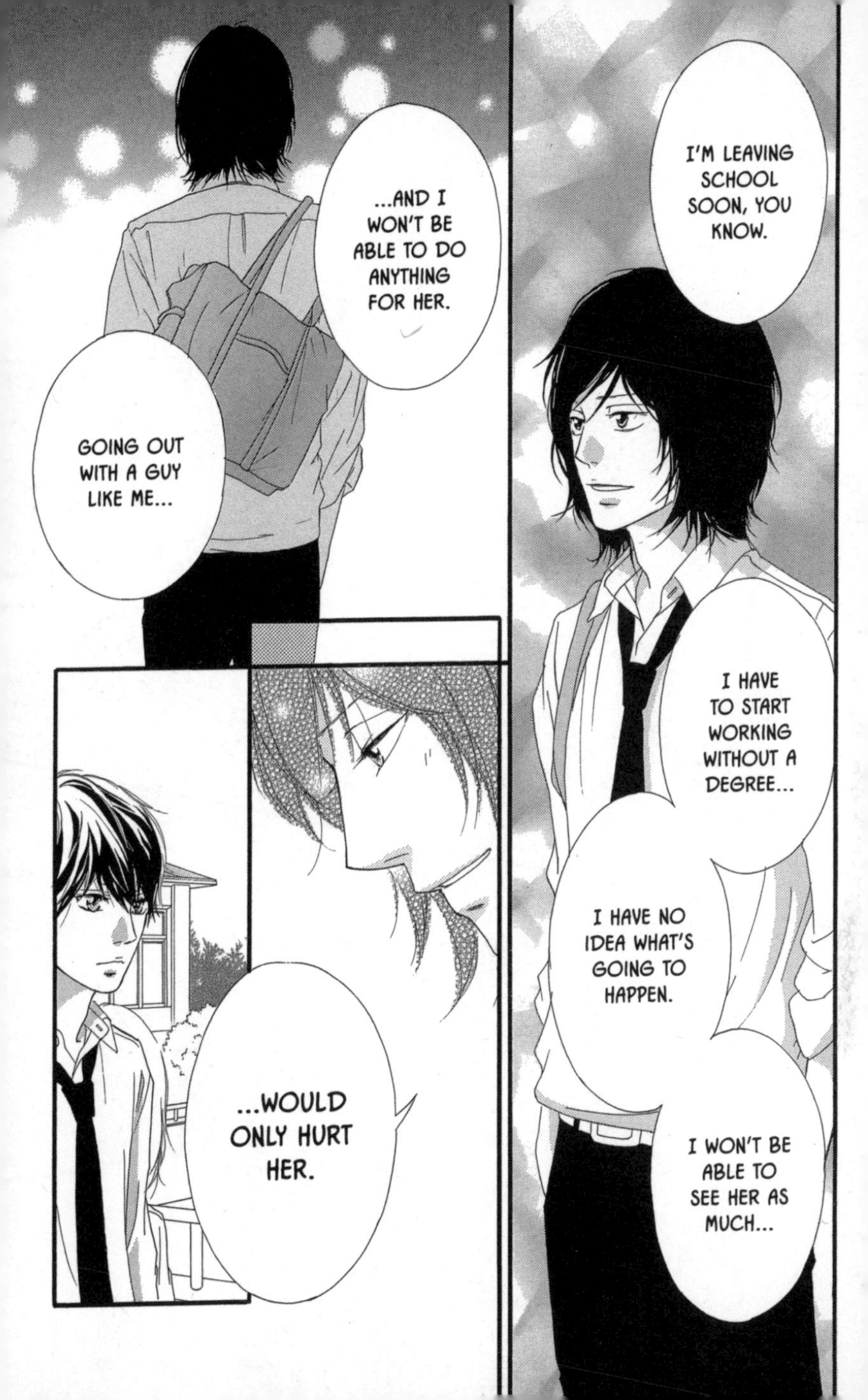
I'M LEAVING SCHOOL SOON, YOU KNOW.
I HAVE TO START WORKING WITHOUT A DEGREE...
I HAVE NO IDEA WHAT'S GOING TO HAPPEN.
I WON'T BE ABLE TO SEE HER AS MUCH...
...AND I WON'T BE ABLE TO DO ANYTHING FOR HER.
GOING OUT WITH A GUY LIKE ME...
...WOULD ONLY HURT HER.

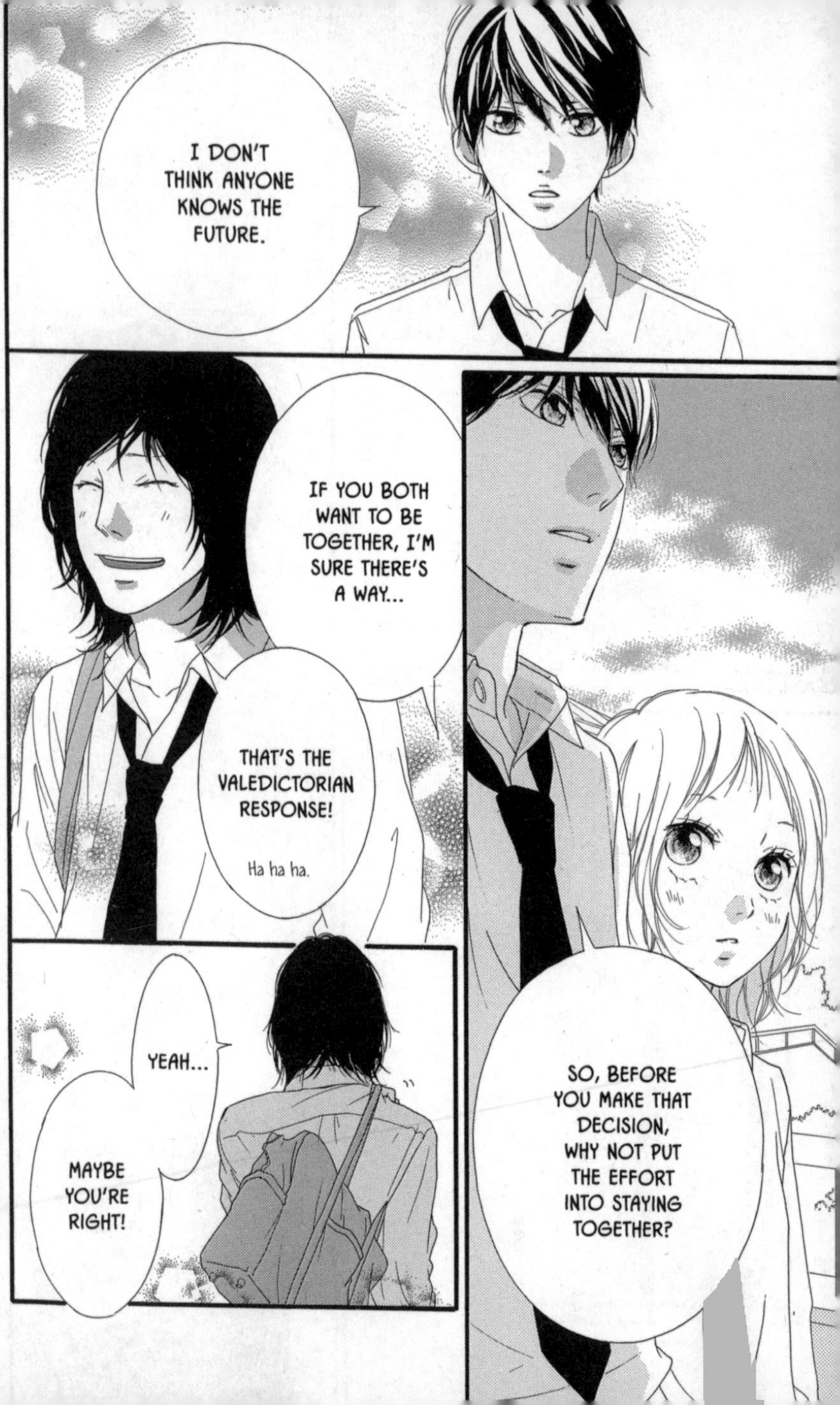
I DON'T THINK ANYONE KNOWS THE FUTURE.
SO, BEFORE YOU MAKE THAT DECISION, WHY NOT PUT THE EFFORT INTO STAYING TOGETHER?
IF YOU BOTH WANT TO BE TOGETHER, I'M SURE THERE'S A WAY...
THAT'S THE VALEDICTORIAN RESPONSE!
Ha ha ha.
YEAH...
MAYBE YOU'RE RIGHT!

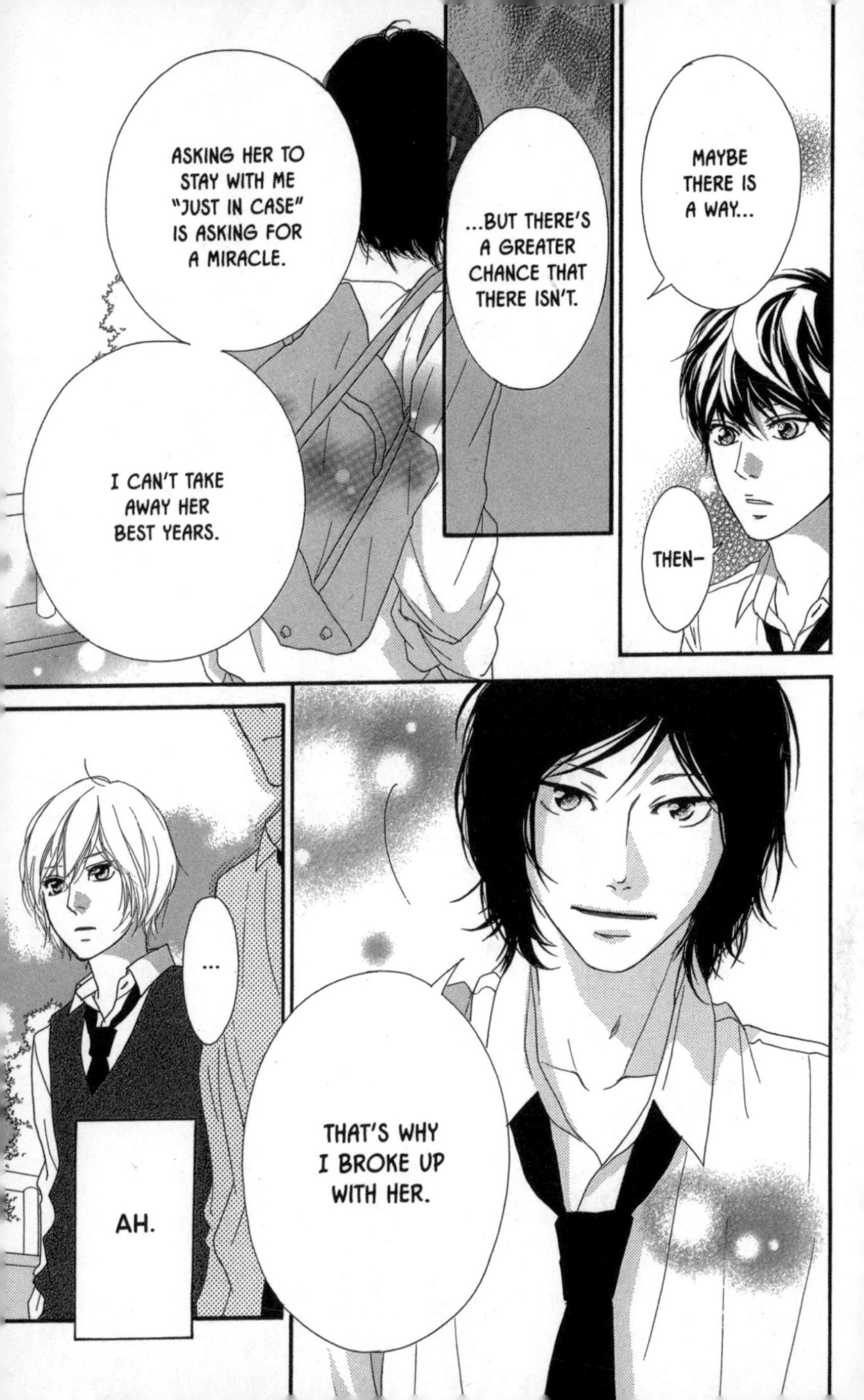
MAYBE THERE IS A WAY...
THEN—
...BUT THERE'S A GREATER CHANCE THAT THERE ISN'T.
ASKING HER TO STAY WITH ME "JUST IN CASE" IS ASKING FOR A MIRACLE.
I CAN'T TAKE AWAY HER BEST YEARS.
THAT'S WHY I BROKE UP WITH HER.
...
AH.

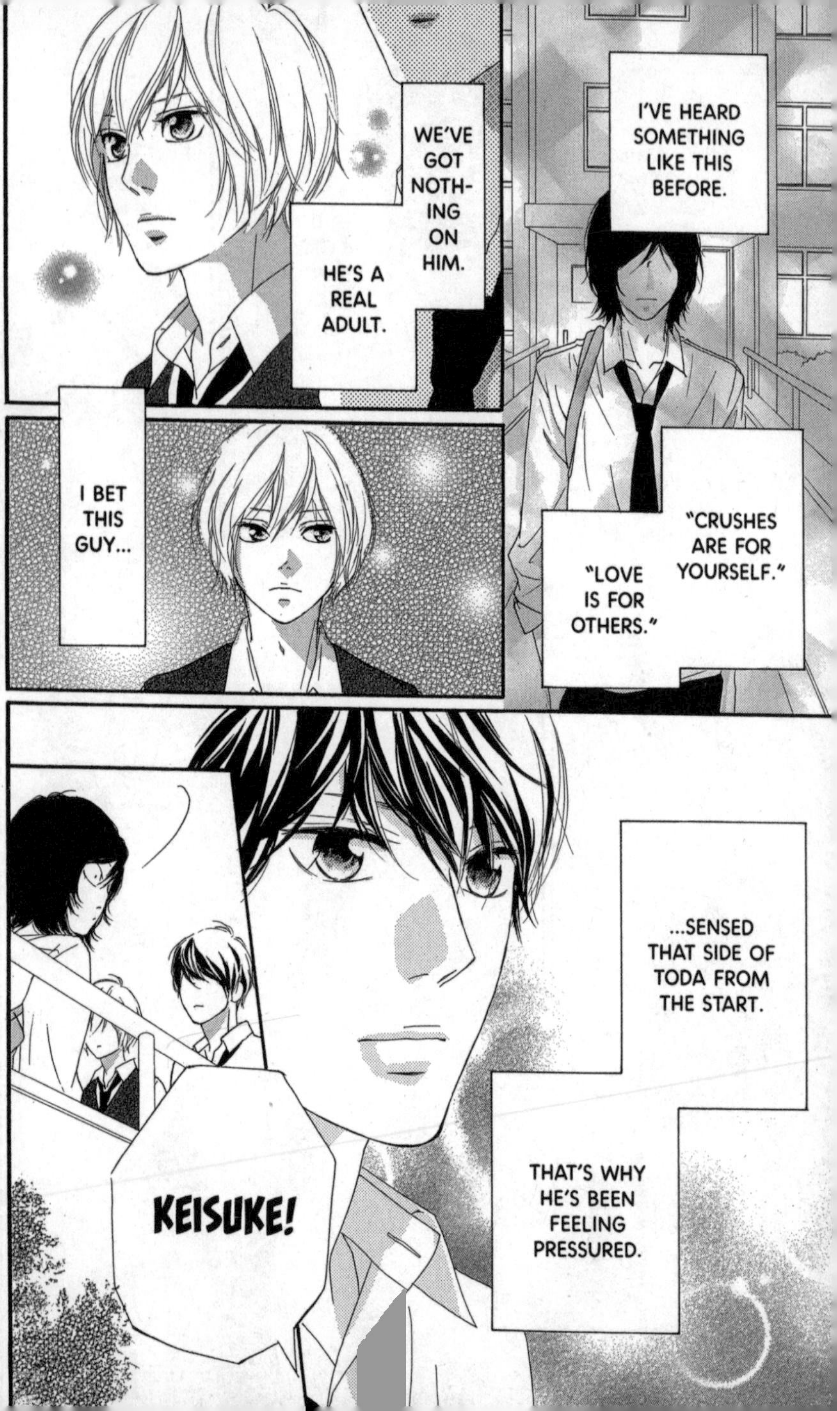
I'VE HEARD SOMETHING LIKE THIS BEFORE.
"CRUSHES ARE FOR YOURSELF."
"LOVE IS FOR OTHERS."
WE'VE GOT NOTH-ING ON HIM.
HE'S A REAL ADULT.
I BET THIS GUY...
...SENSED THAT SIDE OF TODA FROM THE START.
THAT'S WHY HE'S BEEN FEELING PRESSURED.
KEISUKE!

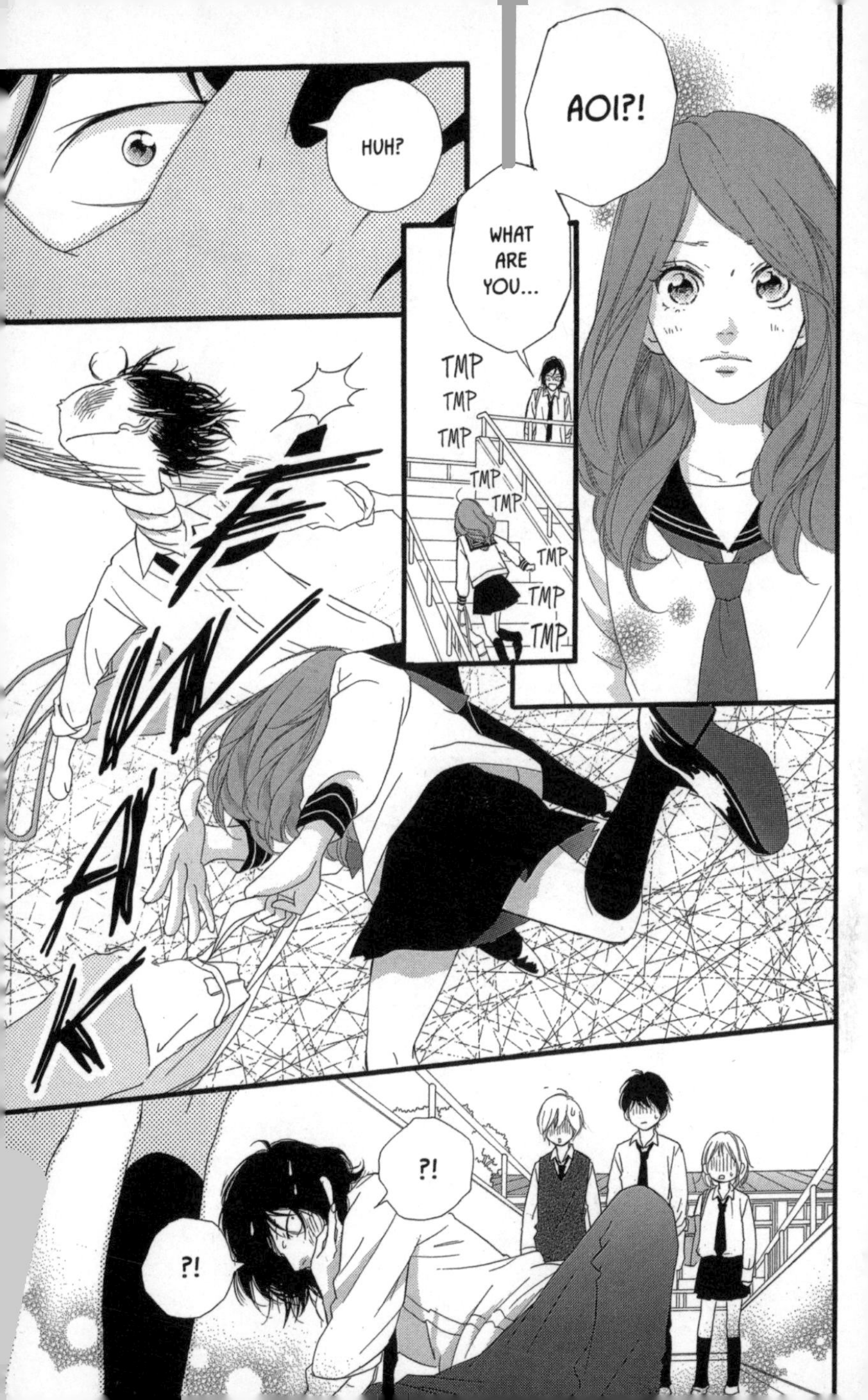
AOI?!
WHAT ARE YOU...
TMP TMP TMP
TMP TMP
TMP TMP TMP
HUH?
FWAK
?!
?!

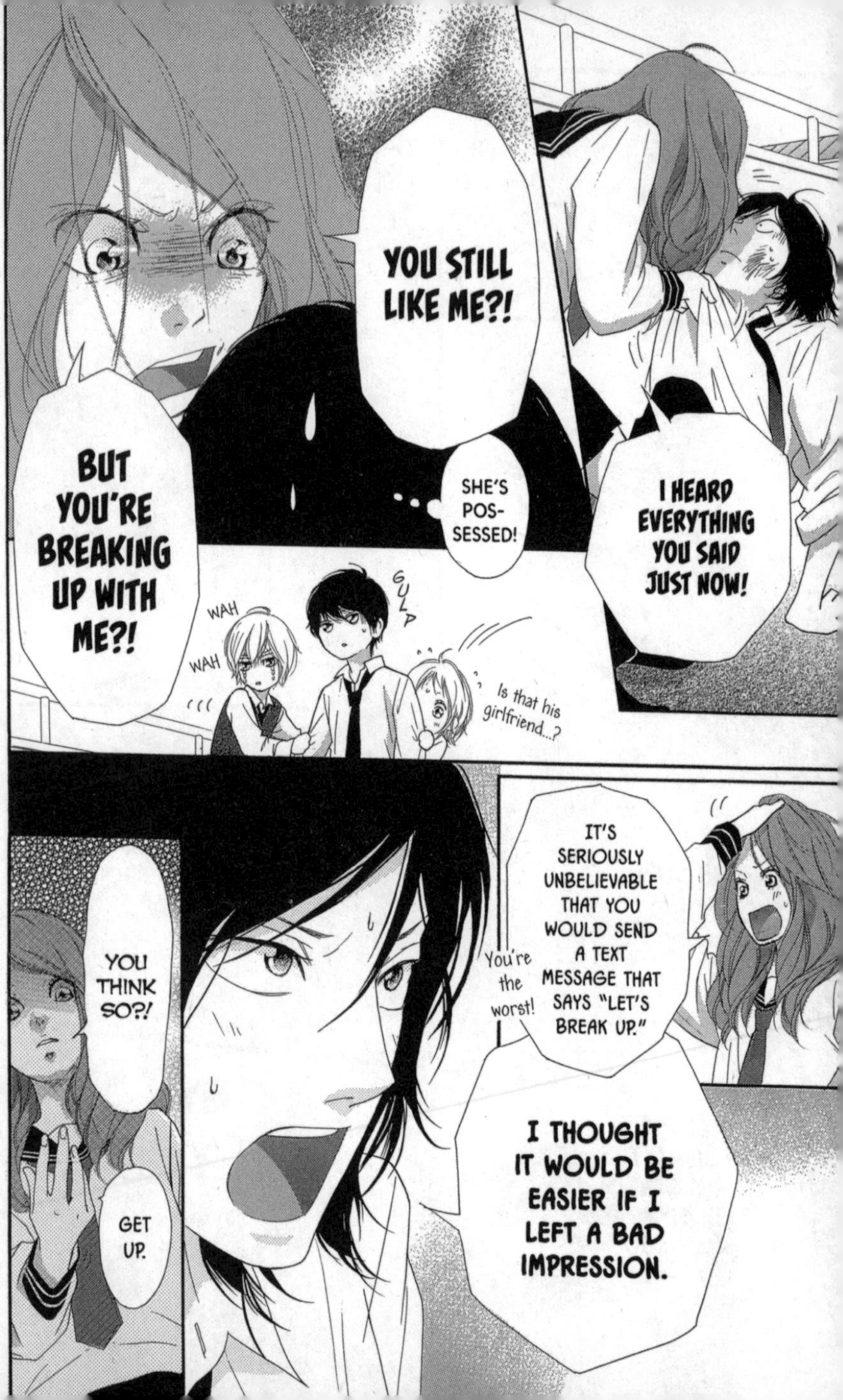
I HEARD EVERYTHING YOU SAID JUST NOW!
YOU STILL LIKE ME?!
BUT YOU'RE BREAKING UP WITH ME?!
...SHE'S POSSESSED!
GULP
WAH
WAH
Is that his girlfriend...?
IT'S SERIOUSLY UNBELIEVABLE THAT YOU WOULD SEND A TEXT MESSAGE THAT SAYS "LET'S BREAK UP."
You're the worst!
I THOUGHT IT WOULD BE EASIER IF I LEFT A BAD IMPRESSION.
YOU THINK SO?!
GET UP.

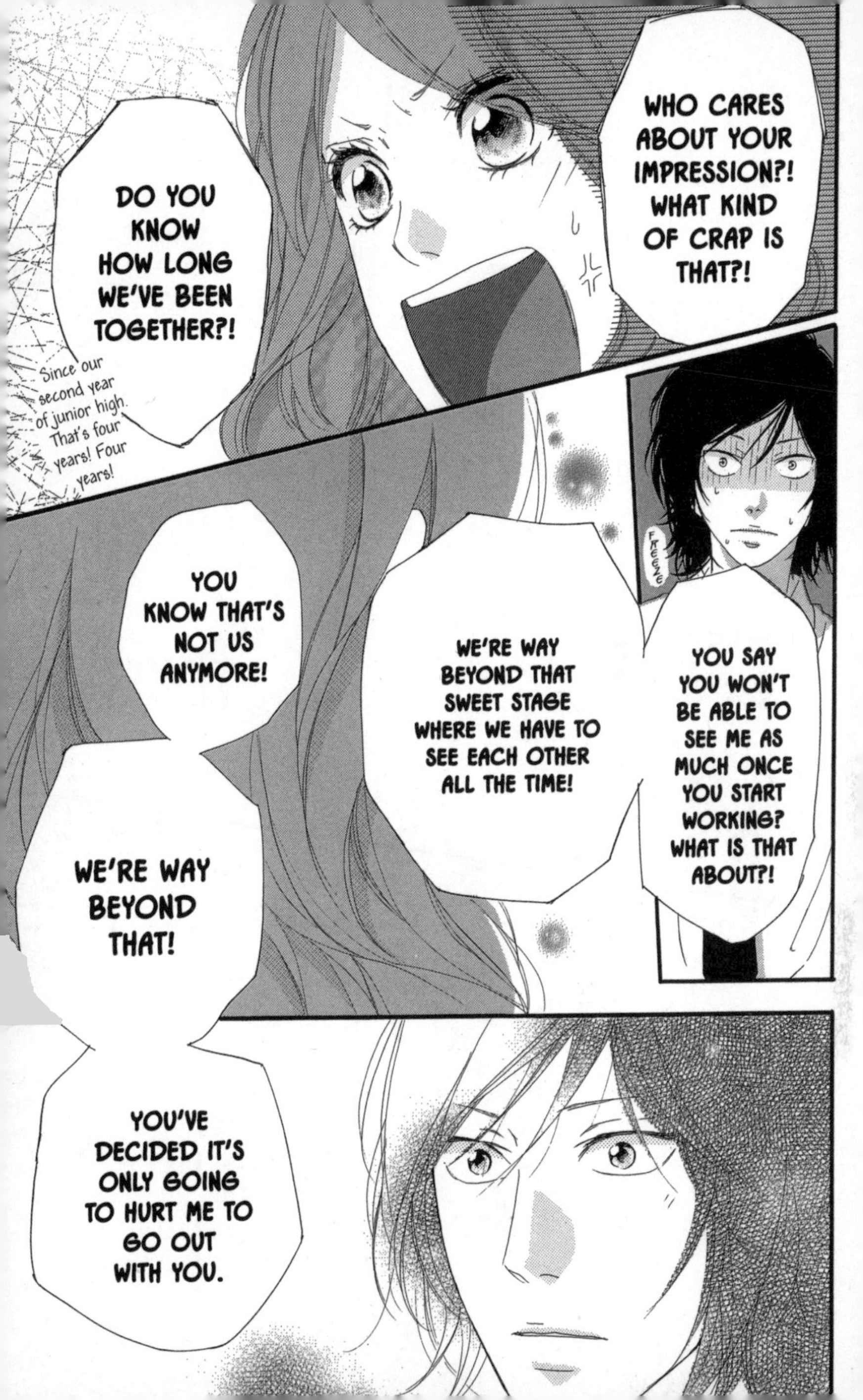
WHO CARES ABOUT YOUR IMPRESSION?! WHAT KIND OF CRAP IS THAT?!
DO YOU KNOW HOW LONG WE'VE BEEN TOGETHER?!
Since our second year of junior high. That's four years! Four years!
FREEZE
YOU SAY YOU WON'T BE ABLE TO SEE ME AS MUCH ONCE YOU START WORKING? WHAT IS THAT ABOUT?!
WE'RE WAY BEYOND THAT SWEET STAGE WHERE WE HAVE TO SEE EACH OTHER ALL THE TIME!
YOU KNOW THAT'S NOT US ANYMORE!
WE'RE WAY BEYOND THAT!
YOU'VE DECIDED IT'S ONLY GOING TO HURT ME TO GO OUT WITH YOU.

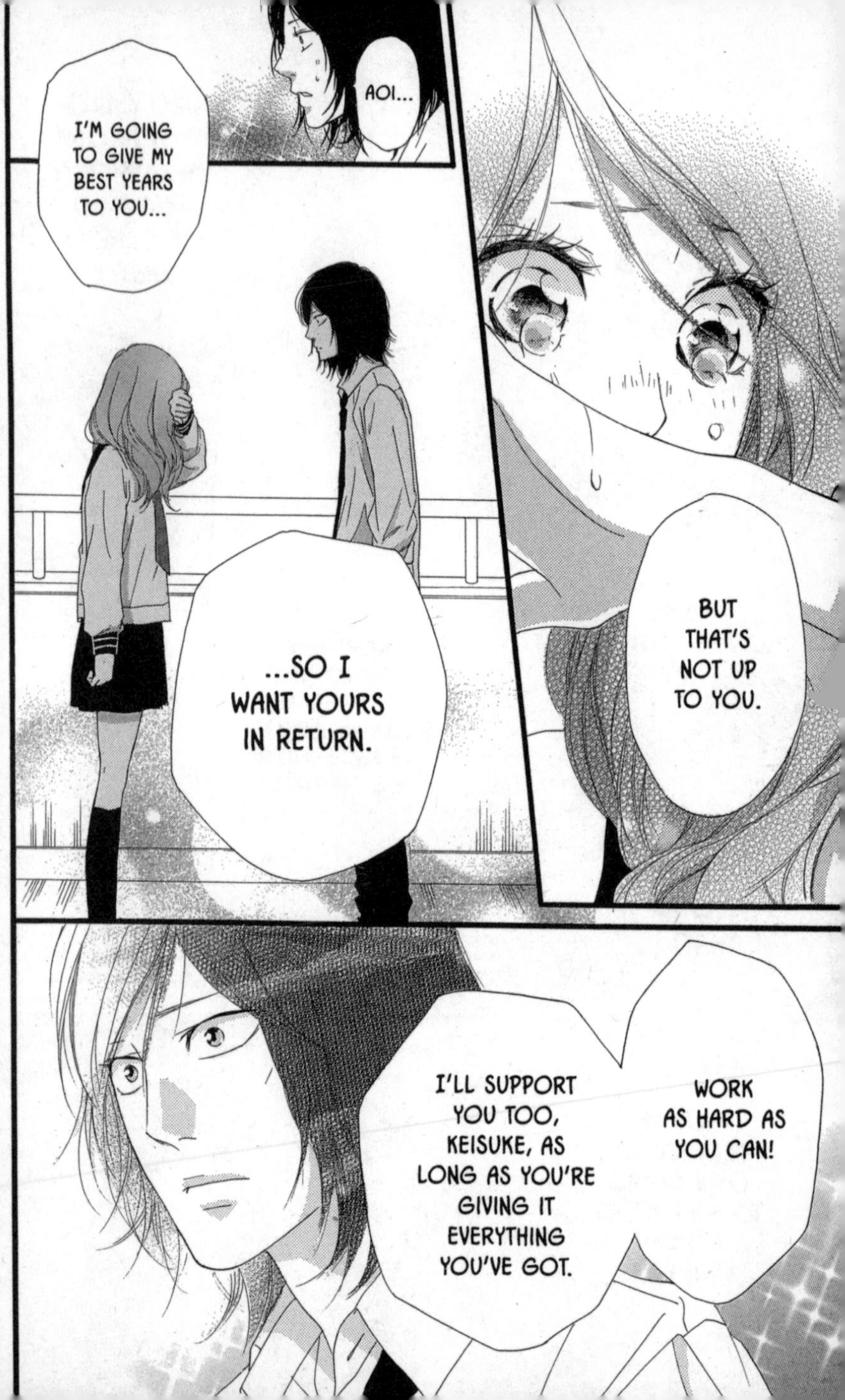
BUT THAT'S NOT UP TO YOU.
AOI...
I'M GOING TO GIVE MY BEST YEARS TO YOU...
...SO I WANT YOURS IN RETURN.
WORK AS HARD AS YOU CAN!
I'LL SUPPORT YOU TOO, KEISUKE, AS LONG AS YOU'RE GIVING IT EVERYTHING YOU'VE GOT.

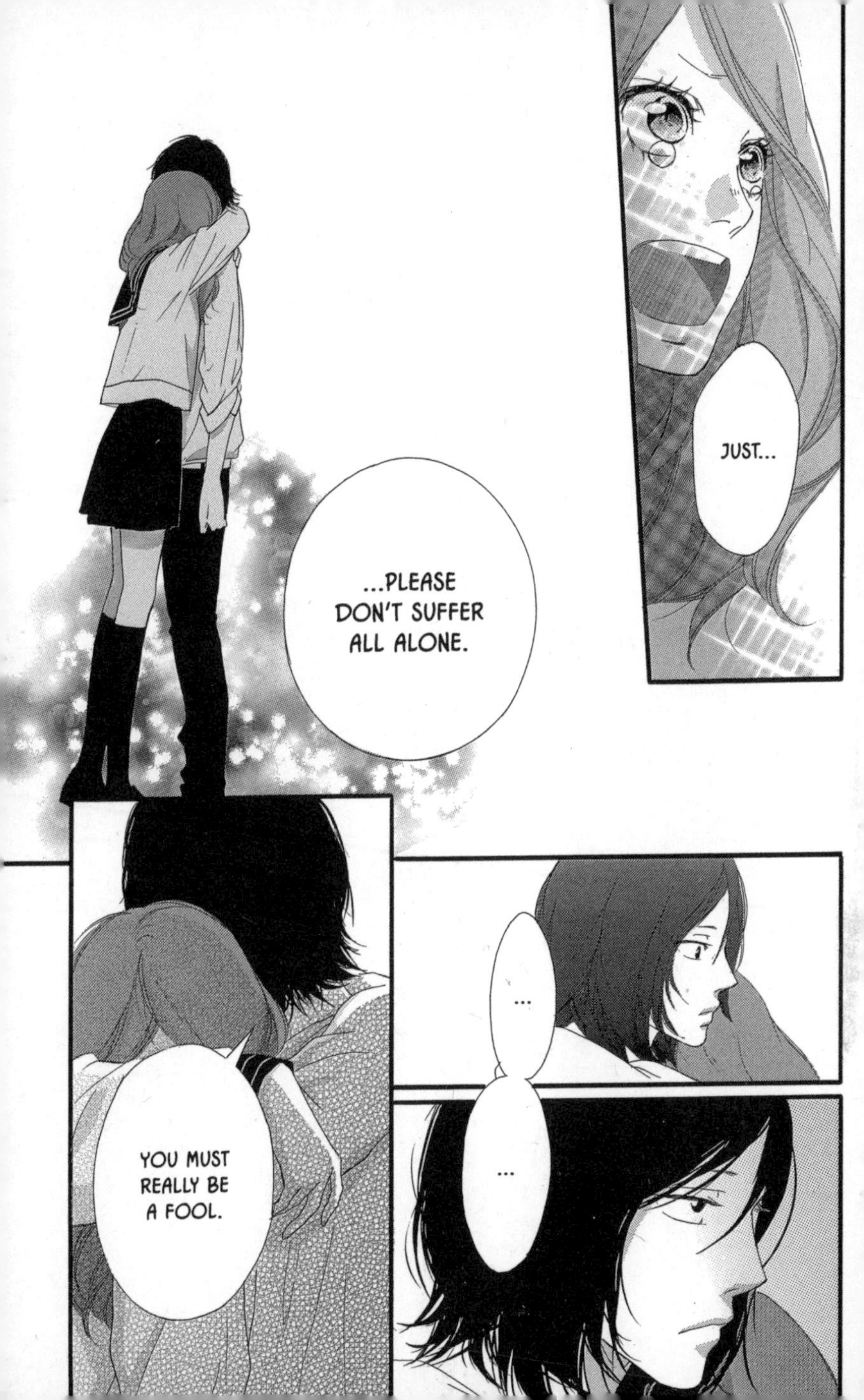
JUST...
...PLEASE DON'T SUFFER ALL ALONE.
...
...
YOU MUST REALLY BE A FOOL.

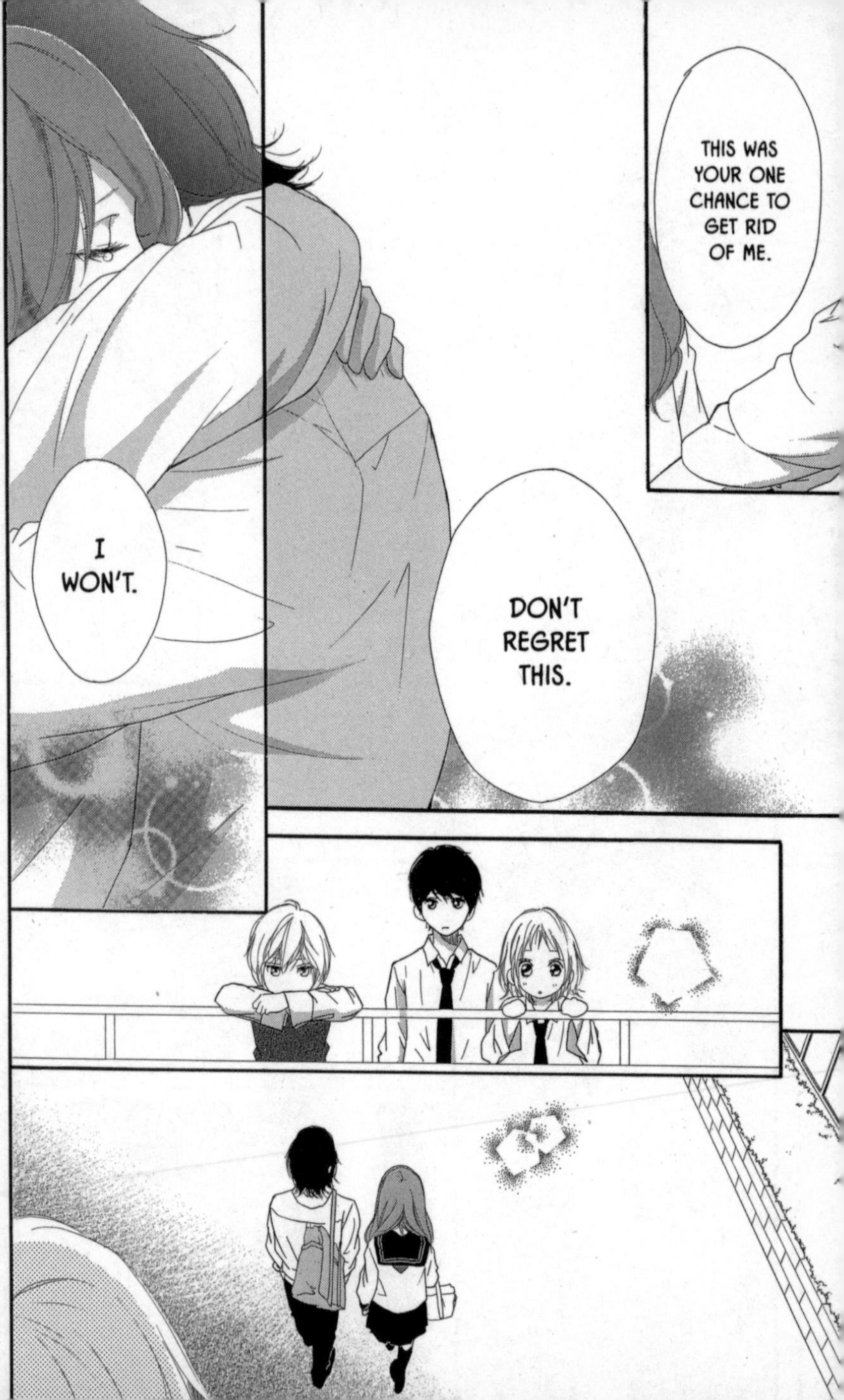
THIS WAS YOUR ONE CHANCE TO GET RID OF ME.
DON'T REGRET THIS.
I WON'T.

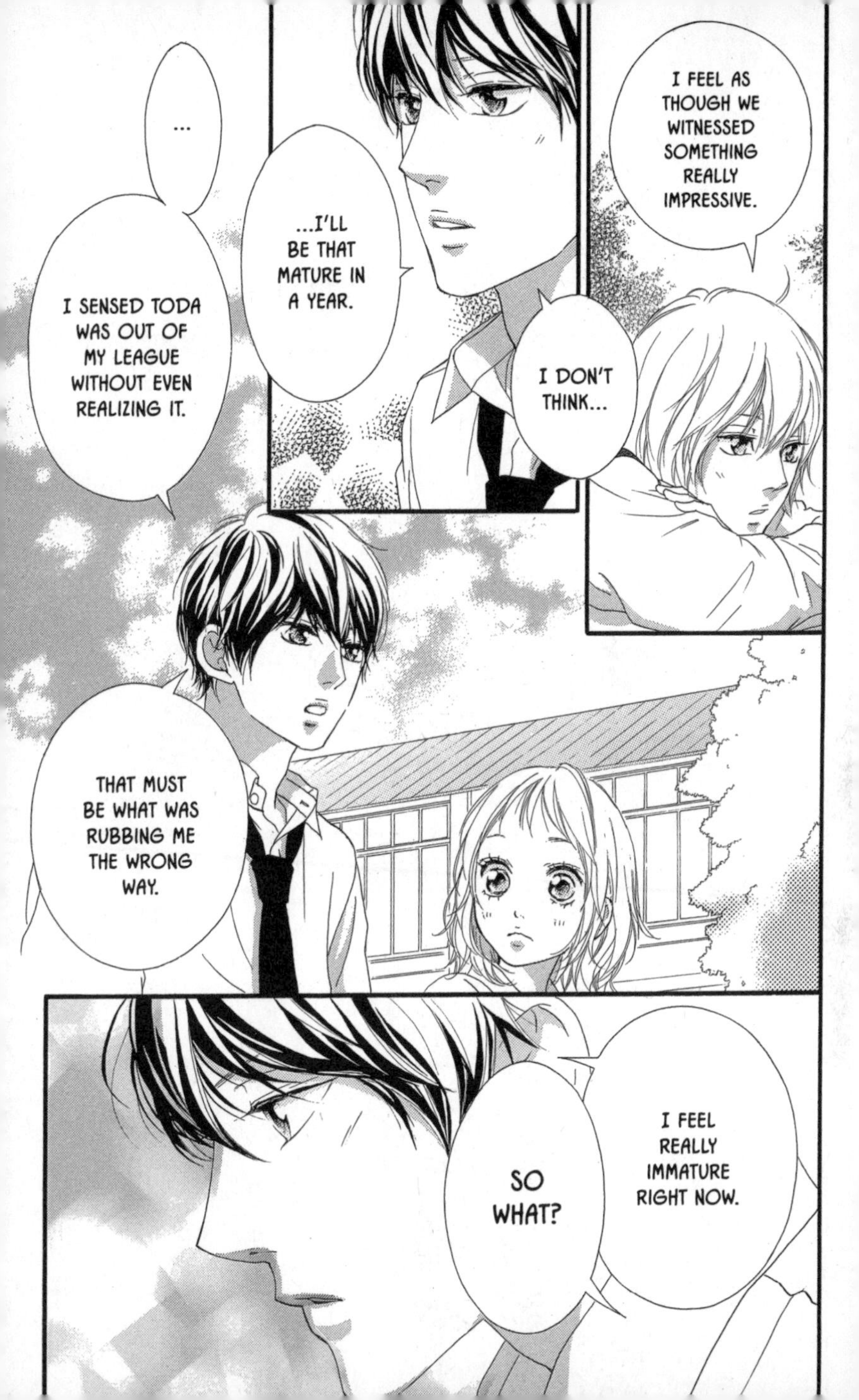
I FEEL AS THOUGH WE WITNESSED SOMETHING REALLY IMPRESSIVE.
I DON'T THINK...
...I'LL BE THAT MATURE IN A YEAR.
...
I SENSED TODA WAS OUT OF MY LEAGUE WITHOUT EVEN REALIZING IT.
THAT MUST BE WHAT WAS RUBBING ME THE WRONG WAY.
I FEEL REALLY IMMATURE RIGHT NOW.
SO WHAT?

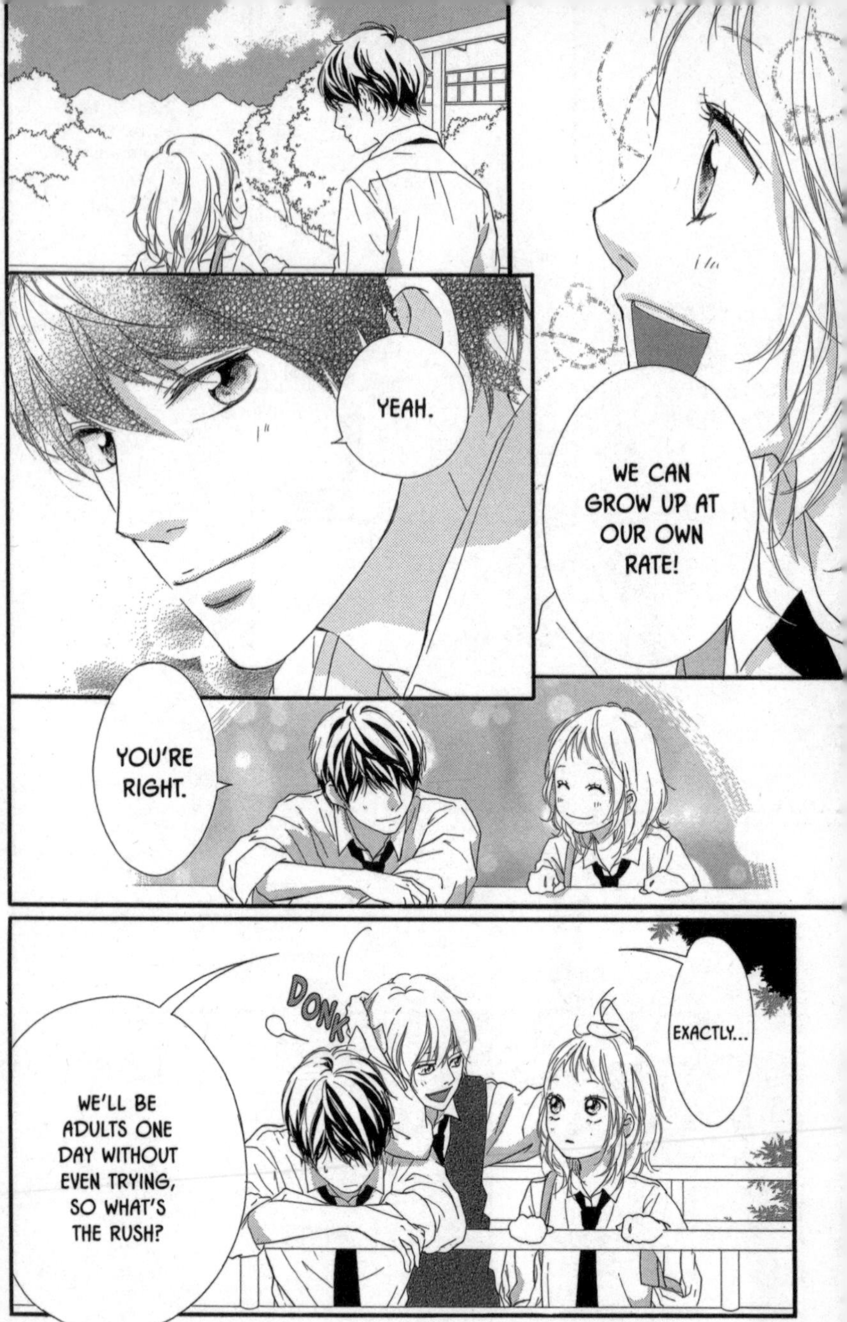
WE CAN GROW UP AT OUR OWN RATE!
YEAH.
YOU'RE RIGHT.
EXACTLY...
DONK
WE'LL BE ADULTS ONE DAY WITHOUT EVEN TRYING, SO WHAT'S THE RUSH?

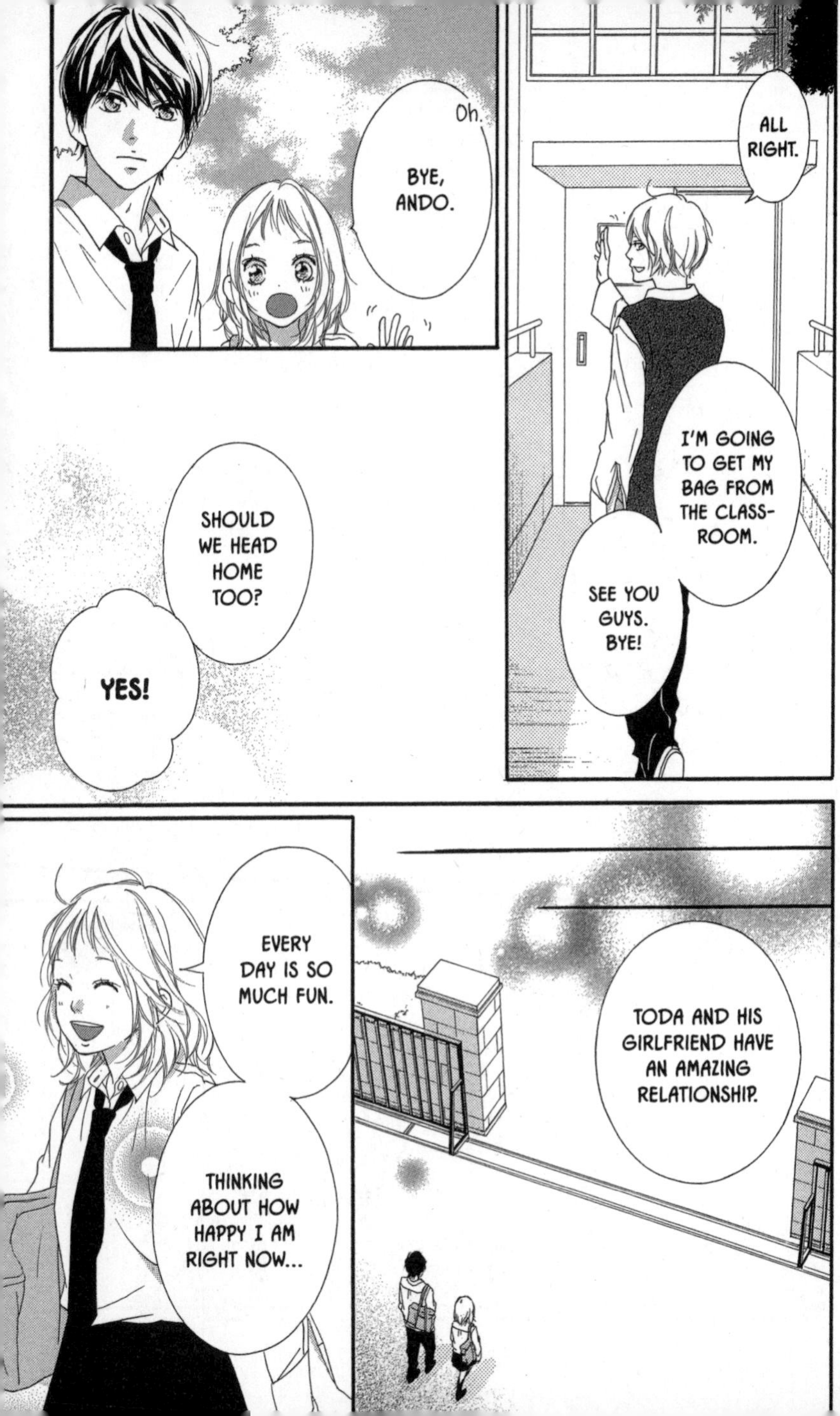
ALL RIGHT.
I'M GOING TO GET MY BAG FROM THE CLASS-ROOM.
SEE YOU GUYS. BYE!
Oh.
BYE, ANDO.
SHOULD WE HEAD HOME TOO?
YES!
TODA AND HIS GIRLFRIEND HAVE AN AMAZING RELATIONSHIP.
EVERY DAY IS SO MUCH FUN.
THINKING ABOUT HOW HAPPY I AM RIGHT NOW...

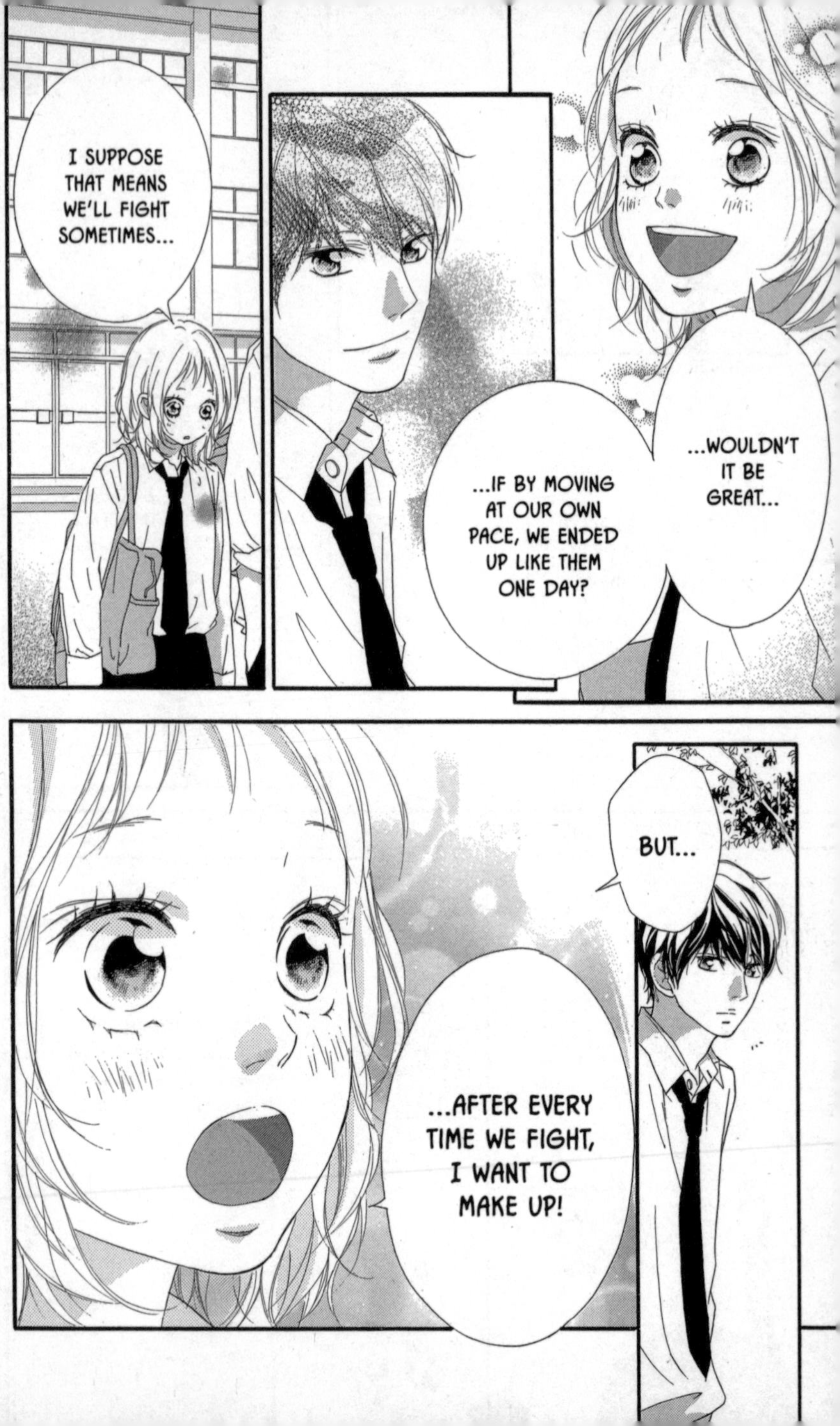
...WOULDN'T IT BE GREAT...
...IF BY MOVING AT OUR OWN PACE, WE ENDED UP LIKE THEM ONE DAY?
I SUPPOSE THAT MEANS WE'LL FIGHT SOMETIMES...
BUT...
...AFTER EVERY TIME WE FIGHT, I WANT TO MAKE UP!

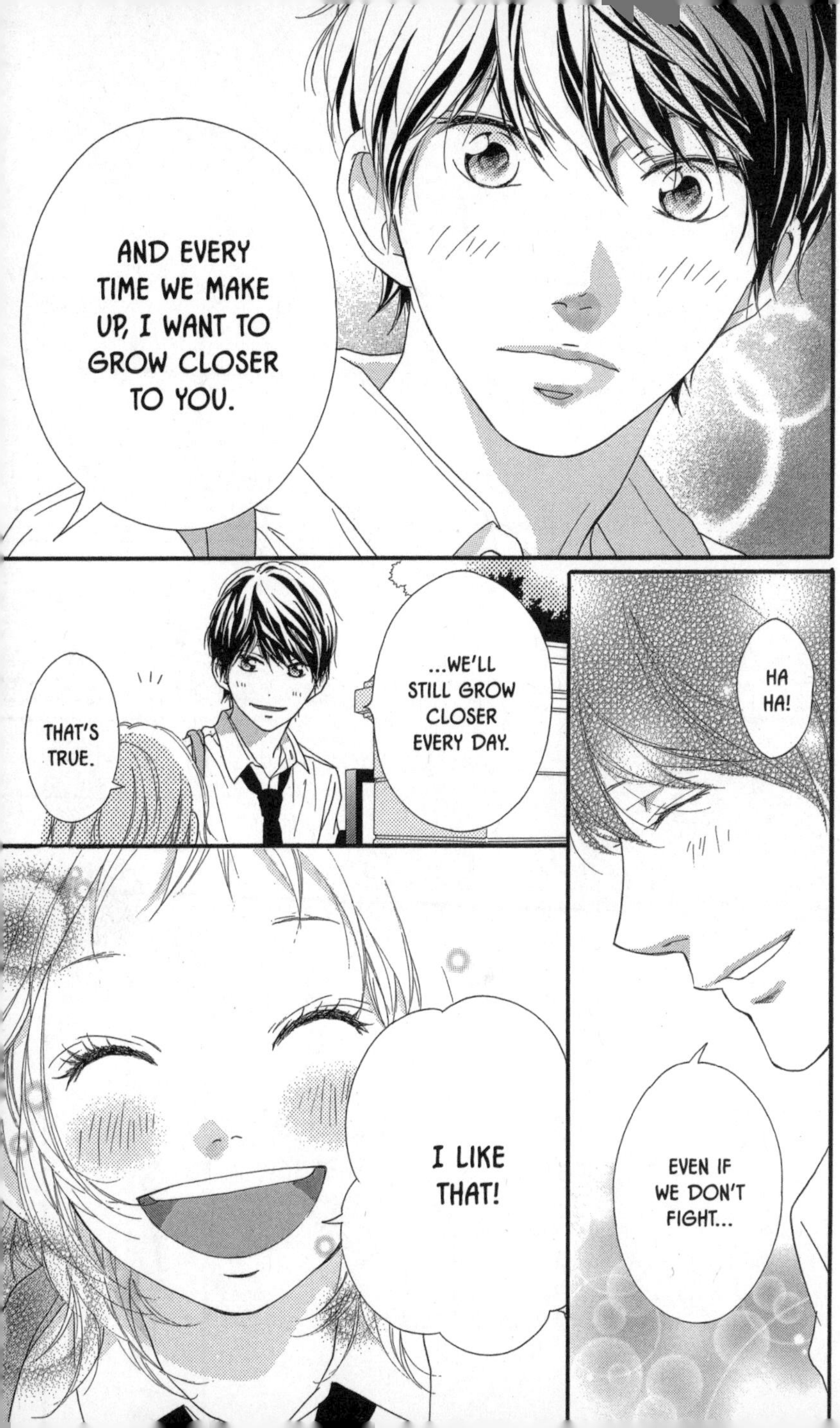
AND EVERY TIME WE MAKE UP, I WANT TO GROW CLOSER TO YOU.
HA HA!
EVEN IF WE DON'T FIGHT...
...WE'LL STILL GROW CLOSER EVERY DAY.
THAT'S TRUE.
I LIKE THAT!

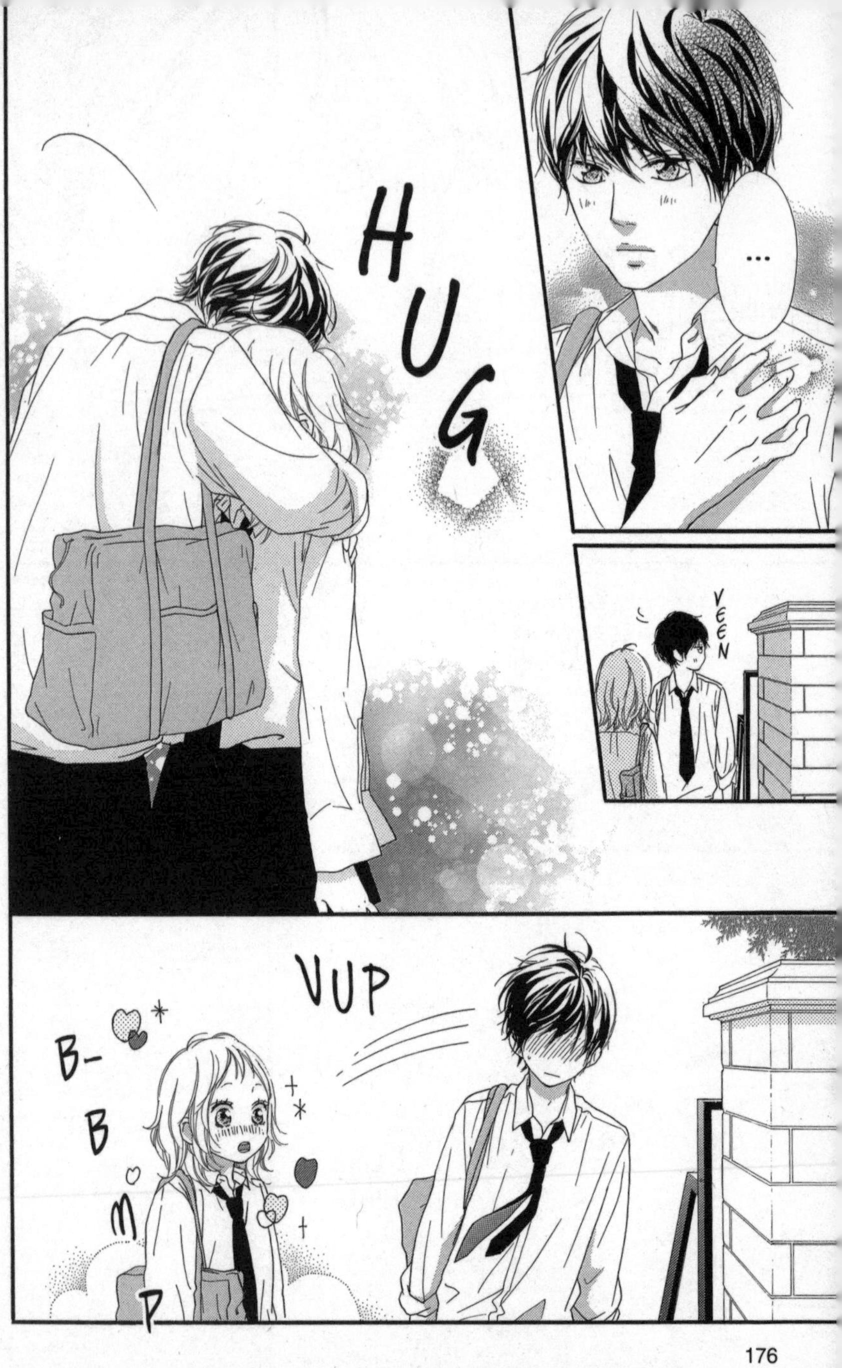
...
VEEN
HUG
VUP
B- B M P

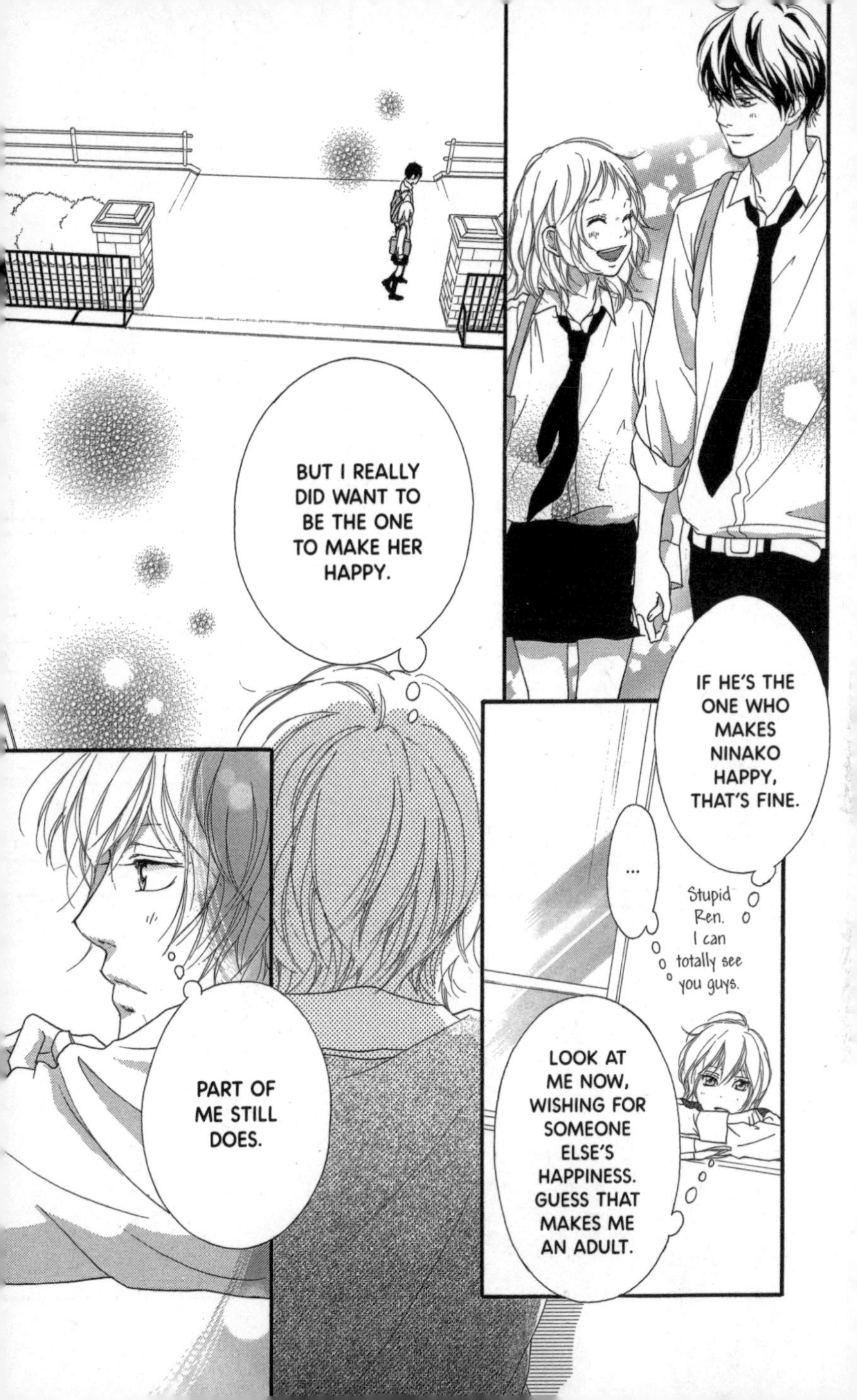
BUT I REALLY DID WANT TO BE THE ONE TO MAKE HER HAPPY.
IF HE'S THE ONE WHO MAKES NINAKO HAPPY, THAT'S FINE.
...
Stupid Ren. I can totally see you guys.
LOOK AT ME NOW, WISHING FOR SOMEONE ELSE'S HAPPINESS. GUESS THAT MAKES ME AN ADULT.
PART OF ME STILL DOES.

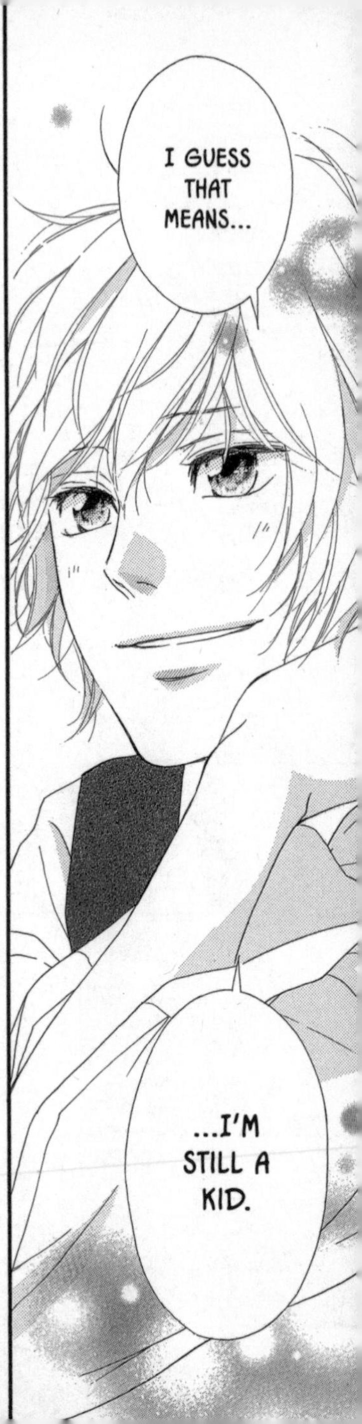
I GUESS THAT MEANS...
...I'M STILL A KID.
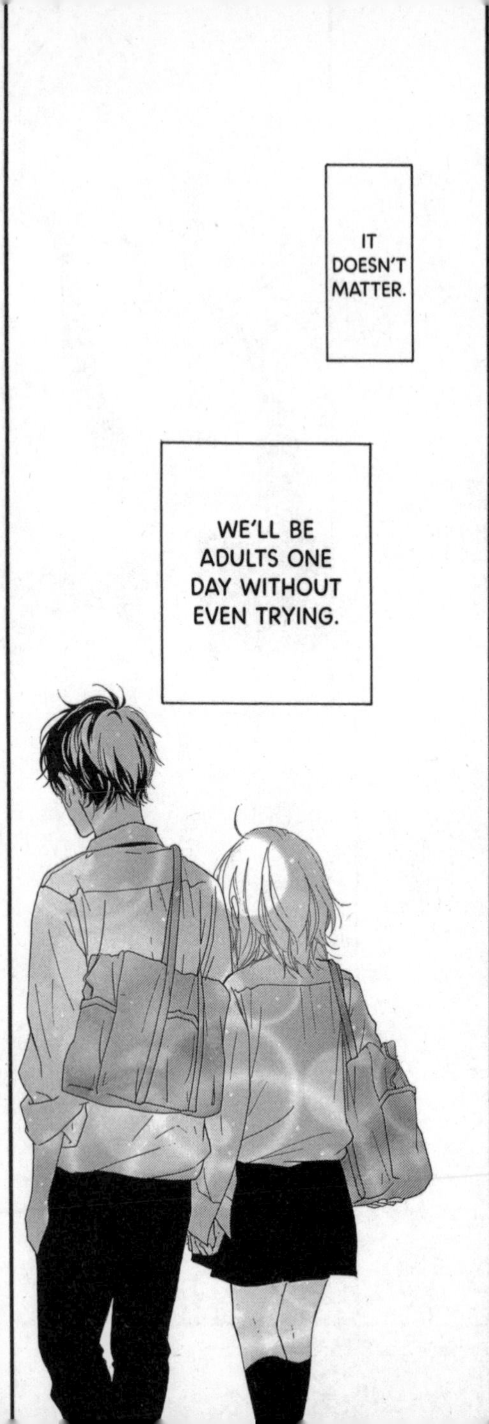
IT DOESN'T MATTER.
WE'LL BE ADULTS ONE DAY WITHOUT EVEN TRYING.

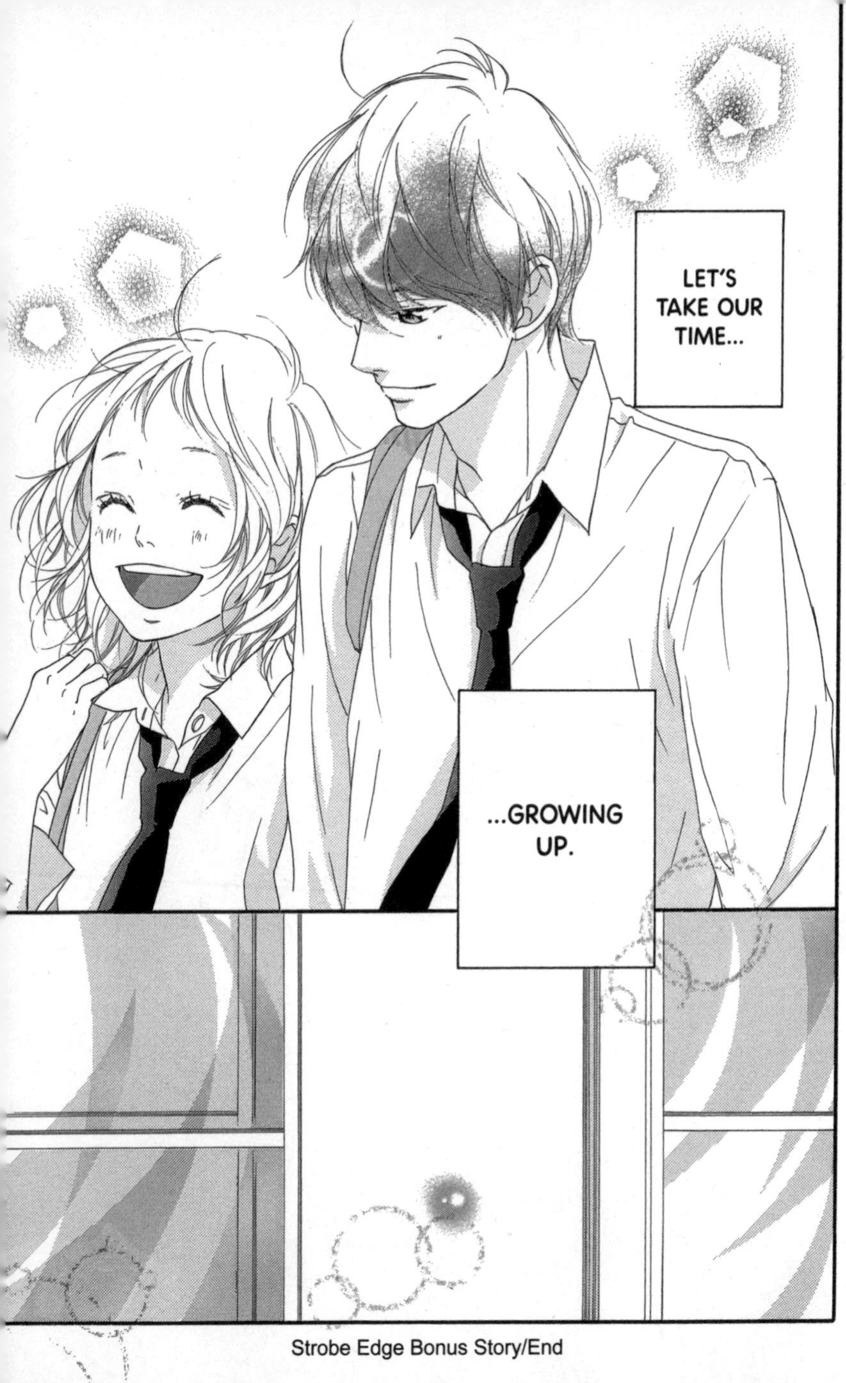
LET'S TAKE OUR TIME...
...GROWING UP.

Strobe Edge Bonus Story/End

Afterword

Thank you for reading through to the end.

When I began planning *Ao Haru Ride,* I decided I wanted to draw a girl who was like a hero and a boy who was imperfect. Rather than a heroine who is always saved by her hero, I wanted her to sometimes be a hero for the boy she likes. And using that, I thought and thought, and finally ended up with Futaba and Kou's relationship. In the beginning, Kou seemed like he could handle anything. At first he saves an indecisive Futaba, but the next time, Futaba saves Kou. This was exactly what I wanted. In the end, Kou matured, grew stronger and became someone to lean on thanks to Futaba. I wanted them to make mistakes and experience pain so that they would value each other even more. That meant some people would have to get hurt, but I'm fine with that. I really do like illustrating the sadness that comes during the period when innocence ends. I hope to continue to tell those kind of stories.

Working on *Ao Haru Ride* was truly a lot of fun! Thank you all for reading this far. I hope that we meet again somewhere else. Until then!

 ☆ Io Sakisaka ☆

Thank you for reading *Ao Haru Ride*.
During its serialization, I was grateful for
many opportunities, including *Ao Haru Ride*
being adapted into an anime and then a live-
action movie. I received so much inspiration
throughout this process, and I hope to
incorporate it into my future work.

IO SAKISAKA

Born on June 8, Io Sakisaka made her debut
as a manga creator with *Sakura, Chiru*. Her
works include *Call My Name*, *Gate of Planet*
and *Blue*. *Strobe Edge*, her previous work, is
also published by VIZ Media's Shojo Beat
imprint. *Ao Haru Ride* was adapted into an
anime series in 2014. In her spare time,
Sakisaka likes to paint things and sleep.

Ao Haru Ride

VOLUME 13
SHOJO BEAT EDITION

STORY AND ART BY **IO SAKISAKA**

TRANSLATION **Emi Louie-Nishikawa**
TOUCH-UP ART + LETTERING **Inori Fukuda Trant**
DESIGN **Joy Zhang**
EDITOR **Nancy Thistlethwaite**

AOHA RIDE © 2011 by Io Sakisaka
All rights reserved.
First published in Japan in 2011 by SHUEISHA Inc., Tokyo.
English translation rights arranged by SHUEISHA Inc.

Printed in the U.S.A.

Published by VIZ Media, LLC
P.O. Box 77010
San Francisco, CA 94107

10 9 8 7 6 5 4 3 2 1
First printing, October 2020

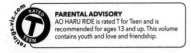

 **MEDIA**
viz.com

shojobeat.com

YA

Ao Haru Ride 13
09/30/2020

**READING THE
WRONG WAY.**

...riginal
...at, this
...t to left—so action, sound effects and word balloons are completely reversed to preserve the orientation of the original artwork.